The Princeton Review

Cracking the GMAT
with DVD

GEOFF MARTZ AND ADAM ROBINSON

2007 EDITION

RANDOM HOUSE, INC.
NEW YORK

www.PrincetonReview.com

The Princeton Review, Inc.
2315 Broadway
New York, NY 10024
E-mail: booksupport@review.com

ISBN: 0-375-76553–0
ISSN: 1549-7933

Editor: Amy Perry
Production Editor: Patricia Dublin
Production Coordinator: Ryan Tozzi
Illustrations by: The Production Department of The Princeton Review

Manufactured in the United States of America on partially recycled paper.

10 9 8 7 6 5 4 3 2 1

2007 Edition

ACKNOWLEDGMENTS

Our GMAT course is much more than clever techniques and powerful computer score reports; the reason our results are great is that our teachers care so much about their students. Thanks to all the teachers who have made the GMAT course so successful, but in particular the core group of teachers and development people who helped get it off the ground: Alicia Ernst, Tom Meltzer, Paul Foglino, John Sheehan, Mark Sawula, Nell Goddin, Teresa Connelly, and Phillip Yee. Thanks also to Editorial Director Ellen Mendlow, Editor Amy Perry, Production Editor Patricia Dublin, and Production Coordinator Ryan Tozzi.

Special thanks also go to Jeff Rubenstein, Tricia McCloskey, Will Hsu, Allegra Viner, Maria Dente, Wendy Voelkle, Scott Thompson, and Cathryn Still for lending their expertise to this book, and to Akil Bello for his expert eyes.

And special thanks to Adam Robinson, who conceived of and perfected the Joe Bloggs approach to standarized tests, and many other techniques in this book.

CONTENTS

Foreword

In 1981, I founded The Princeton Review in order to help prepare high-school students for the SAT. My first course had 19 students, and it was held in my parents' apartment. Within five years, The Princeton Review had become the largest SAT course in the country.

The Princeton Review's SAT techniques are based in part on what we feel to be essential flaws in the design of the test—flaws that could cause students to score well below their true potentials. When we looked at the GMAT (Graduate Management Admission Test), we realized that it contains many of the same flaws as the SAT. We felt that our techniques for tackling the SAT could be equally useful in tackling the GMAT. So, along with Geoff Martz, one of our veteran teachers and development experts, we designed a course specifically geared for the GMAT. For the past 20 years, this course has been taught across the country. It has helped GMAT students attain the same phenomenal score improvements as our SAT students.

How do we do it?

First, unlike many coaches, we don't insist that the student learn dozens of math theorems or memorize all the rules of written grammar. Our extensive examination of the GMAT has shown that the information needed to do well on this test is surprisingly limited. For this reason, we concentrate on a small number of crucial concepts.

Those who have struggled through the GMAT and who've felt that their scores did not reflect their college grades or business acumen probably suspect that there's more to mastering a standardized test than just honing rusty math and verbal skills. So we take our preparation a step further and teach techniques specifically designed to master multiple-choice standardized tests.

Finally, The Princeton Review offers even more than a thorough review and great techniques. Our classes are small (no more than eight students per class) and grouped according to ability. For students who require extra help, we provide smaller group work sessions and even one-on-one tutoring. In addition, students get to take several diagnostic GMATs and receive detailed analysis of their results.

Unfortunately, many students can't get to our courses. So for you we have written this book. Although the book explains our strongest techniques, it cannot substitute for small classes and great teaching. Still, careful study and practice of the techniques will provide you with the means to boost your score significantly.

If you have any questions about our course, or about academic matters in general, give us a call at 800-2REVIEW.

And finally, in the words of physicist Richard Feynman, *"Disregard!"*

Good luck on your GMAT!

John Katzman
President

More Review, More Strategy, More Ways to Learn

There's more to this book than just this book. Our new edition of *Cracking the GMAT with DVD* includes exclusive access to the following online tools designed to enhance your studies:

- 4 online practice tests with detailed performance analysis available on completion

- Interactive lessons and drills from our award-winning online courses

- In-depth information on schools and assistance for your admissions process

- Optional essay scoring with our exclusive LiveGrader℠ service

To access your online tools, go to: **PrincetonReview.com/Cracking**.

Now Playing: The Princeton Review

You can learn directly from our dynamic, rigorously-trained GMAT instructors — just pop the enclosed disk into a DVD drive on your computer or entertainment system to get started! Our DVD includes:

- Engaging video instruction from Princeton Review instructors

- Expert guidance on the B-school admissions process and tips for creating an outstanding application

- Detailed strategic advice on some of the most important aspects of your GMAT preparation

Using Your Resources

The DVD and online tools that accompany *Cracking the GMAT with DVD* are specifically designed to enhance your book preparation. Here's how you can make the most of these resources.

DVD: Start Out Strong

A great way to begin your preparation for the GMAT is to watch the enclosed DVD. Our expert instructors will give you an overview of what's on the test and will identify some of the most critical issues to look out for as you prepare. Armed with this information, you'll be in great shape to begin your studies.

You can return to the DVD at any point during your preparation to refresh your memory or review topics that trip you up. Look for the DVD icon in the book, which indicates the topics that are also covered in your DVD.

Online Tools: Just a Few Clicks Away

To get the maximum benefit out of your online tools, simply register your book at **PrincetonReview.com/Cracking** and be sure to do the following:

- **Access Your Study Plan** — Will you be ready when test day comes? Visit our website to access a customized study plan that will help you stay on track with your studies. We'll guide you through every step of your preparation based on how much time you have to study, so you'll be in top form on test day.

- **Take Full-Length Practice Tests** — By working through a full-length test early on, you'll be able to identify your strengths and weaknesses and better focus your studies. As you get closer to test day, taking simulated tests will help you practice techniques, build your stamina and confidence, and gain familiarity with the kinds of questions you're going to see.

- **Target Your Preparation** — If you come across a particular GMAT concept or question type that gives you trouble, don't worry. Our online drills and lessons will allow you to quickly gain mastery over even the trickiest topics.

- **Research Schools** — Visit our B-Schools and Careers website, where you'll find a wealth of information about schools that match your specific criteria. You can also use the site to manage your applications process and even submit applications directly to schools!

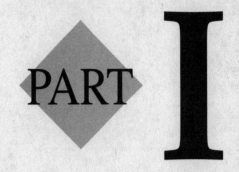

PART I

Orientation

1 Introduction

HOW TO USE THIS BOOK: A STRATEGIC PLAN FOR ACING THE GMAT

1. LEARN THE FAMED PRINCETON REVIEW TEST-TAKING STRATEGIES

In the next few chapters, you'll find the strategies that have given our GMAT students the edge for the past 20 years.

2. LEARN THE SPECIFIC MATH AND VERBAL SKILLS YOU'LL NEED

Our courses include an extremely thorough review of the math and verbal skills our students need to ace the GMAT, and this book will give you that same review.

Important Phone Numbers:

To register for the GMAT: 800-717-GMAT

To reach The Princeton Review: 800-2REVIEW

3. PRACTICE EACH TYPE OF QUESTION — AT THE DIFFICULTY LEVEL YOU NEED TO MASTER

The GMAT is an interactive test, administered on computer. It quickly hones in on your level of ability and then proceeds to give you questions at or just above that level. It makes sense for you to practice on the level of problem you will actually see during the test. *Cracking the GMAT* is the only book out there with practice questions grouped by difficulty. Page after page of practice questions are arranged at the back of this book in difficulty "bins"—just like the questions on the real GMAT—so that you can concentrate on the question level you will have to answer on the actual test in order to get the score you need.

4. PERIODICALLY TAKE SIMULATED GMATs TO MEASURE YOUR PROGRESS

As you work through the book, you'll want to take our online practice tests to see how you're doing. These interactive tests closely mimic the GMAT so you can become familiar with both the test's content and its format. Our practice tests can be found at **www.PrincetonReview.com/Cracking**. In addition, we actively encourage students to use *The Official Guide for GMAT Review*, which is published by the Graduate Management Admission Council (GMAC). It contains actual test questions from previous administrations of the GMAT. You should also take at least one of the real practice tests available through the GMAT website, www.mba.com.

5. HONE YOUR SKILLS

Using the detailed score reports from your practice exams, you'll be able to zero in on problem areas and quickly achieve mastery through additional practice. And as your score rises, this book is ready with more difficult bins to keep you on track for the score you need.

6. KEEP TRACK OF THE APPLICATION PROCESS

Throughout the book, you will find informative sidebars explaining how and when to register for the test, how and when to apply to business school, and the advantages and disadvantages of applying early. Plus, at **www.PrincetonReview.com**, you'll be able to take advantage of our powerful web-based tools to match yourself with schools that meet your needs and preferences.

WHAT IS THE GRADUATE MANAGEMENT ADMISSION TEST?

The Graduate Management Admission Test (GMAT) is a standardized test used by business schools as a tool to decide whom they are going to let into their M.B.A. programs.

WHAT DOES THE TEST LOOK LIKE?

The GMAT is only offered on computer. The four-hour test is administered at a secure computer terminal at an approved testing center. You enter your multiple-choice answers on the screen with a mouse; you must compose your essays for the Writing Assessment section on the computer as well.

Here's what you'll find on the GMAT:

1. two 30-minute essays to be written on the computer using a generic word-processing program

    (optional break)

2. a 75-minute, 37-question multiple-choice Math section

    (optional break)

3. a 75-minute, 41-question multiple-choice Verbal section

On average, this gives you two minutes for each math question, and a little less than two minutes for each verbal question. You must answer a question in order to get to the next question—which means that you can't skip a question and come back to it. And while you are not required to finish any of the sections, your score will be adjusted downward to reflect questions you did not get to.

There are two optional short breaks: one after you finish the two essays, and the other after you finish the Math section.

On each of the Math and Verbal sections, one quarter of the questions you encounter will be experimental and will not count toward your score. These 20 questions, which will be mixed in among the regular questions, are there so the test company can try out new questions for future tests. We'll have much more to say about the experimental questions later.

WHAT INFORMATION IS TESTED ON THE GMAT?

You will find several different types of multiple-choice questions on the GMAT.

Math

- problem solving (the type of math problem you remember from your SAT, no doubt)

- data sufficiency (a strange type of problem that exists on no other test in the world)

Verbal

- reading comprehension (tests your ability to answer questions about a passage)

- sentence correction (a grammar-related question type)

- critical reasoning (a logic-based question type recycled from the LSAT)

WHERE DOES THE GMAT COME FROM?

The GMAT is published by ACT, a test development company, under the sponsorship of the Graduate Management Admission Council (GMAC). Both ACT and GMAC are private companies. We'll tell you more about them later on in this book.

HOW IS THE GMAT SCORED?

As soon as you've finished taking the GMAT, your computer will calculate and display your unofficial results, not including your Writing Assessment score. You can print out a copy of your unofficial results to take with you. Within 20 days, you will receive your score report online; a written report will be available by request only.

Most people think of the GMAT score as a single number, but in fact there are four separate numbers:

1. Math score (reported on a scale that runs from 0 to 60)

2. Verbal score (reported on a scale that runs from 0 to 60)

3. Total score (reported on a scale that runs from 200 to 800)

4. Writing Assessment score (reported on a scale of 0 to 6, in half-point increments; 6 is the highest score)

The report will look something like this:

Math	%	Verbal	%	Total	%	AWA	%
36	48	30	59	550	54	4.5	57

Business schools tend to focus on the total score, which means that you may make up for weakness in one area by being strong in another. For example, if your quantitative skills are better than your verbal skills, they'll help pull up your total score—although some of the more selective schools say they prefer to see math and verbal sub-scores that are balanced. Total scores go up or down in ten-point increments. In other words, you might receive 490 or 500 on the GMAT, but never 494 or 495.

You will also see a percentile ranking next to each score. For example, if you see a percentile of 72 next to your Verbal score, it means that 72 percent of the people who took this test scored lower than you did on the Verbal section.

ARE GMAT SCORES EQUIVALENT TO SAT SCORES?

No. Even though they both use the same 200 to 800 scale, GMAT scores are not the same as SAT scores. For one thing, the pool of applicants to business schools is much more select than the pool of applicants to colleges. People who take the GMAT have usually already graduated from college. In addition, most have several years of business experience.

The GMAT itself is more complex than the SAT. GMAT questions cover a broader range of topics and have a greater degree of difficulty.

Most people find that their GMAT scores are somewhat lower than the scores they received on the Writing, Critical Reading, or Math SAT. According to figures from GMAC, two-thirds of the people who take the GMAT score between 380 and 590.

WHAT IS THE PRINCETON REVIEW?

The Princeton Review is a test-preparation company based in New York City. It has branches in more than 50 cities across the country, as well as abroad. The Princeton Review's techniques are unique and powerful, and they were developed after a study of dozens of real GMAT exams. They work because they are based on the same principles that are used in writing the actual test. The Princeton Review's techniques for beating the GMAT will help you improve your scores by teaching you to:

1. Think like the test writers.

2. Take full advantage of the computer-adaptive algorithms upon which the GMAT is based.

3. Find the answers to questions you don't understand by using Process of Elimination.

4. Avoid the traps that test writers have set for you (and use those traps to your advantage).

A WARNING

Many of our techniques for beating the GMAT are counterintuitive. Some of them seem to violate common sense. To get the full benefit of our techniques, you must trust them. The only way to develop this trust is to practice the techniques and persuade yourself that they work.

But you have to practice them *properly*. If you try our techniques on the practice problems in most popular GMAT coaching books, you will probably decide that they don't work.

Why?

Because the practice questions in those books are very different from the questions on real GMATs. Other books may have data sufficiency questions, sentence correction questions, and reading comprehension questions, but if you compare them with the questions on the real GMAT, you'll find that the resemblance is only superficial. In fact, studying the practice questions and techniques in some of the other books could actually hurt your GMAT score.

PRACTICE WITH REAL QUESTIONS

One reason coaching books do not use real GMAT questions is that the GMAC won't let them. So far, the council has refused to let anyone (including us) license actual questions from old tests. As we mentioned above, the council has its own review book called *The Official Guide for GMAT Review*, which we heartily recommend that you purchase. GMAC also puts out preparation software called *GMATPrep*, which can be downloaded for free from **www.mba.com**. This software includes two computer-adaptive tests, plus additional practice sets, all of which feature real GMAT questions. By practicing our techniques on real GMAT items, you will be able to prove to yourself that the techniques work and increase your confidence when you actually take the test.

And, remember, by using The Princeton Review's practice questions grouped by level of difficulty at the back of this book, you'll be able to concentrate on types of questions you are actually likely to see.

THERE'S MORE TO THIS BOOK THAN THIS BOOK

When preparing for the GMAT, don't forget to take advantage of the many resources that accompany this book. Pop in the DVD and let some of our talented Princeton Review instructors help you master the trickiest aspects of studying for and taking the GMAT. Plus, by registering your book at **www.PrincetonReview. com/Cracking**, you'll gain access to our computer-adaptive practice tests, drills, lessons, and more. All of these tools will help you reinforce what you've learned in this book and take it to the next level.

2

How to Think About the GMAT

What Does the GMAT Measure?

The GMAT is not a test of how smart you are. Nor is it a test of your business acumen. It's simply a test of how good you are at taking the GMAT. In fact, you will learn that by studying the very specific knowledge outlined in this book, you can substantially improve your score.

The GMAT As a Job Interview

The first axiom of any how-to book on job interviewing is that you must always tell your interviewer what he or she wants to hear. Whether or not this is good job-hunting advice, it happens to be a very useful strategy on the GMAT. The test writers think in predictable ways. You can improve your score by learning to think the way they do and anticipating the kinds of answers that they think are correct.

Is the GMAT Just Like the SAT?

There are substantial differences between the two tests. The GMAT is a much tougher test, and it contains question types not found on the SAT. Many of the techniques developed by The Princeton Review for the SAT are useful on some sections of the GMAT, but we have also developed new techniques and expanded on some of the old ones.

How Closely Does The Princeton Review Monitor the GMAT?

Very closely. Each year, we publish a new edition of this book to reflect the subtle shifts that happen over time, as well as any changes in question types. These changes show up as experimental questions several years before they ever actually make it to the real exam. For the latest information on the GMAT, please visit our website at www.PrincetonReview.com.

Did the GMAT Change Last Year?

On January 1, 2006, GMAC switched vendors. The GMAT had been written by your old nemesis, ETS (the maker of the SAT), and administered by Thompson Prometric Centers. Now, the GMAT is written by ACT and administered by Pearson VUE. Aside from all the different acronyms and a few procedural changes, the test has remained exactly the same.

Is This Book Just Like The Princeton Review Course?

No. You won't have the benefit of taking five computer-adaptive GMATs that are scored and analyzed by our computers. You won't get to sit in small classes with seven other highly motivated students who will spur you on. You won't get to work with our expert instructors who can assess your strengths and pinpoint your weaknesses. There is no way to put these things in a book.

What you will find in this book are some of the techniques and methods that have enabled our students to crack the system—plus a review of the essentials that you cannot afford not to know.

If at all possible, you should take our course. If that is not possible, then use this book.

How to Crack the System

In the following chapters we're going to teach you our method for cracking the GMAT. Read each chapter carefully. Some of our ideas may seem strange at first. For example, when we tell you that it is sometimes easier to answer GMAT questions without actually working out the entire problem, you may think, "This isn't the way I conduct business."

But the GMAT Isn't About Business

We're not going to teach you business skills. We're not going to teach you math and English. We're going to teach you the GMAT.

3

Cracking the System:
Basic Principles

HOW THE COMPUTER-ADAPTIVE GMAT WORKS

To understand how to beat the computer-adaptive GMAT, you have to understand how it works.

Unlike paper-and-pencil standardized tests that begin with an easy question and then get progressively tougher, the computer-adaptive test always begins by giving you a medium question. If you get it right, the computer gives you a slightly harder question. If you get it wrong, the computer gives you a slightly easier question, and so on. The idea is that the computer will zero in on your exact level of ability very quickly, which allows you to answer fewer questions overall, and allows the computer to make a more finely honed assessment of your abilities.

WHAT YOU WILL SEE ON YOUR SCREEN

During the test itself, your screen will display the question you're currently working on, with little circles in front of the five answer choices. To answer the question, you use your mouse to click on the circle next to the answer choice you think is correct. Then you press a button at the bottom of the screen to verify that this is the answer you want to pick.

WHAT YOU WILL NEVER SEE ON YOUR SCREEN

What you will *never* see is the score that GMAC has assigned you even before you began the exam, nor the process by which the computer keeps track of your progress. As you go through the test, the computer will keep revising its assessment of you based on your responses.

Let's watch the process in action. In the left-hand column below, you'll see what a hypothetical test taker—let's call her Jane—sees on her screen as she takes the test. In the right column, we'll show you how GMAC keeps track of how she's doing. (We've simplified this example a bit in the interest of clarity.)

WHAT JANE SEES:

To regard the overwhelming beauty of the Mojave Desert is <u>understanding the great forces of</u> nature that shape our planet.

- understanding the great forces of
- to understand the great forces to
- to understand the great forces of
- understanding the greatest forces in
- understanding the greater forces on

WHAT JANE *DOESN'T* SEE:

The GMAT test writers lead off Jane's Verbal section with a medium question, chosen by the computer at random from a bin of medium questions—in this case, a sentence correction question. Her score starting out: 500.

current score: 500

Jane gets the first question right (she chooses the third answer down—what we call choice C), so her current score goes up to a 540, and the computer selects a harder problem for her second question.

current score: 540

What Jane Sees:

Hawks in a certain region depend heavily for their diet on a particular variety of field mouse. The killing of field mice by farmers will seriously endanger the survival of hawks in this region.

Which of the following, if true, casts the most doubt on the conclusion drawn above?

○ The number of mice killed by farmers has increased in recent years.

○ Farmers kill many other types of pests besides field mice without any adverse effect on hawks.

○ Hawks have been found in other areas besides this region.

○ Killing field mice leaves more food for the remaining mice, who have larger broods the following season.

○ Hawks are also endangered because of pollution and deforestation.

What Jane Doesn't See:

The computer happens to select a critical reasoning problem.

Oops. Jane gets the second question wrong (the correct answer is the fourth answer down—what we call choice D), so her score goes down to a 510, and the computer gives her a slightly easier problem.

current score: 510

What Jane Sees:

<u>Nuclear weapons being invented, there was wide expectation in the scientific community that</u> all war would end.

○ Nuclear weapons being invented, there was wide expectation in the scientific community that

○ When nuclear weapons were invented, expectation was that

○ As nuclear weapons were invented, there was wide expectation that

○ Insofar as nuclear weapons were invented, it was widely expected

○ With the invention of nuclear weapons, there was wide expectation that

What Jane Doesn't See:

Jane has no idea what the correct answer is on this third question, but she guesses choice E and gets it correct. Her score goes up to a 530.

current score: 530

You get the idea. At the very beginning of the test, your score moves up or down in larger increments (perhaps as much as 40 points at a time) than it does at the end, when GMAC believes it is merely refining whether you deserve, say, a 610 or a 620.

The questions come from a huge pool of items held in the computer in what the GMAT test writers call "bins." In theory, there could be as many as 60 different bins available, each with a different level of difficulty. In practice, we believe that there are far fewer difficulty bins for the sake of simplicity. Each of the various kinds of questions on the test must get equal time, and all of the basic subject areas must be covered (for example, the Math portion of the test must cover arithmetic, algebra, and geometry). GMAC also tracks what it calls "social sensitivity." Several items concerning a minority group must appear on every test. We'll talk more about this later.

THE EXPERIMENTAL QUESTIONS

Unfortunately, almost one-fourth of the questions that you answer won't actually count toward your score. Eleven of the 41 verbal questions and nine of the 37 math questions are experimental. Because the GMAT mixes real questions with experimental questions, if you are answering upper-medium problems and you suddenly get one that seems too easy, there are two possibilities: a) you are about to fall into a trap, or b) it is an experimental question that actually *is* too easy.

WHAT THE COMPUTER-ADAPTIVE GMAT USES TO CALCULATE YOUR SCORE

The GMAT keeps a running tally of your score as it goes, based on the number of questions you get correct and their levels of difficulty—but there are two other important factors that can affect your score:

- early questions, which count more than later questions

- questions you leave blank, which will lower your score

WHY EARLY QUESTIONS COUNT MORE THAN LATER QUESTIONS

At the beginning of the test, your score moves up or down in larger increments as the computer hones in on what will turn out to be your ultimate score. If you make a mistake early on, the computer will choose a much easier question, and it will take you a while to work back to where you started from. Similarly, if you get an early problem correct, the computer will then give you a much harder question, in an effort to triangulate your place in the scoring ranks.

However, later in the test, a mistake is less costly—this is because the computer will have decided your general place in the scoring ranks and is merely refining your exact score.

While it is not impossible to come back from behind, you can see that it is particularly important that you do well at the beginning of the test. Answering just a few questions correctly at the beginning will propel your interim score quite high.

Pace Yourself

Make sure that you get these early questions correct by starting slowly, checking your work on early problems, and then gradually picking up the pace so that you finish all the problems in the section. Although questions left blank at the end of a section will lower your score, it is more damaging to rush and get more questions wrong early on.

Still, if you are running out of time at the end, it makes sense to spend a few moments to guess intelligently on the remaining questions, using POE rather than random guesses or (let's hope it never comes to this) not guessing at all. You will be pleased to know that it is possible to guess on several questions at the end and still end up with a 700.

The Princeton Review Approach to the GMAT

To help you ace the computer-adaptive GMAT, this book is going to provide you with

- the test-taking techniques that have made The Princeton Review famous and that will enable you to turn the inherent weaknesses of the computer-adaptive GMAT to your advantage

- a thorough review of all the major topics covered on the GMAT

- a short practice test to help you predict your current scoring level

- practice questions to help you raise your scoring level

According to computer-adaptive theory, a test like the GMAT hones in on a test taker's general score level within three or four questions—after which she spends the rest of each section answering questions at about that level and slightly above. Each time she gets one correct, the computer gives her a slightly tougher problem, and more often than not, she gets it wrong—because, after all, this question is beyond her abilities.

Never mind (for the moment) that this is not exactly how it works. People's ability to answer questions depends to a large degree on the subjects of those questions. One person might be an algebra ace (and able to answer algebra questions of any difficulty level) but rusty in geometry (and thus unable to answer even the simplest geometry problems). Another might be terrific at reading comprehension but lousy at grammar. Sometimes a test taker will really know how to do a problem but will make a careless error; other times she will get a question right by mistake.

Know Your Bin

According to classic theory, the average test taker spends most of his or her time answering questions at his level of competency (which he gets right) and questions that are just above his level of competency (which he gets wrong). In other words, most testers will see questions from only a few difficulty "bins."

This means that to raise your score, you must learn to answer questions from the bins immediately *above* your current scoring level. At the back of this book, you will find a short diagnostic test to determine your current scoring level and then bins filled with questions at various scoring levels. When combined with a thorough review of the topics covered on the GMAT, this should put you well on your way to the score you're looking for.

But first, let's begin with some test-taking strategies.

4

Cracking the System:
Intermediate Principles

Imagine for a moment that you are a contestant on *Let's Make a Deal*. It's the final big deal of the day. Monty Hall asks you, "Do you want curtain number one, curtain number two, or curtain number three?"

As you carefully weigh your options, the members of the audience are shouting out *their* suggestions. But you can bet that there is *one* thing no one in the audience is going to shout at you: "Skip the question!"

It's just not an option. You have to make a choice—and you have to make it *now*. An all-expenses-paid trip around the world, a washer-dryer, or a lifetime supply of toilet paper—these are the prizes lurking behind the curtains. One of these choices is much better than the others, but on *Let's Make a Deal*, you have no idea which it is.

LET'S MAKE A GMAT

Normally when you don't know the correct answer on a test, you skip the question and come back to it later. But on the computer-adaptive GMAT, as in *Let's Make a Deal*, you can never skip the question.

TO GET TO THE NEXT QUESTION, YOU HAVE TO ANSWER THE ONE YOU'RE CURRENTLY ON

Because of the way the GMAT's scoring algorithm works, the question you see on your computer screen at any particular moment depends on your response to the question before. This creates an odd situation for the test designers: If they allowed you to skip a question, they wouldn't know which question to give you next.

It's clear from articles that GMAT test designers have published that they know test takers are at a real disadvantage when they can't skip a problem and come back to it later. Still, the idea of using a computer to administer tests was too tempting to give up. In the end, GMAC decided that you should generously be willing to make the sacrifice in the name of progress.

So whether you know the answer to a problem or not, you have to answer it in order to move on.

This means that, like it or not, you may have to do some guessing on the GMAT. Ah, but there's guessing, and then there's *guessing*.

IF YOU DON'T KNOW THE RIGHT ANSWER, DON'T YOU DARE JUST PICK AN ANSWER AT RANDOM

This may sound a little loony, but it turns out that you don't always have to know the correct answer to get a question right.

Try answering the following question:

What is the unit of currency in Sweden?

What? You don't know?

Unless you work for an international bank or have traveled in Scandinavia, there is no reason why you should know what the unit of currency in Sweden is. (By the way, the GMAT doesn't ask such factual questions. We're using this one to make a point.) As it stands now, because you don't know the answer, you would have to answer this question at random, right?

Not necessarily. GMAT questions are written in multiple-choice format. One of the five choices has to be the answer. You just have to find it.

LOOK FOR WRONG ANSWERS INSTEAD OF RIGHT ONES

Let's put this question into multiple-choice format—the only format you'll find on the GMAT—and see if you still want to answer at random.

What is the unit of currency in Sweden?
- ○ the dollar
- ○ the franc
- ○ the pound sterling
- ○ the yen
- ● the krona

PROCESS OF ELIMINATION

Suddenly this question isn't difficult anymore. You may not have known the right answer, but you certainly knew enough to eliminate the wrong answers. Wrong answers are often easier to spot than right answers. Sometimes they just sound weird. At other times they're logically impossible. While it is rare to be able to eliminate all four of the incorrect answer choices on the GMAT, you will almost always be able to eliminate at least one of them—and frequently two or more—by using Process of Elimination. Process of Elimination (POE for short) will enable you to answer questions that you don't have the time or the inclination to figure out exactly. We will refer to POE in every single chapter of this book. It is one of the most important and fundamental tools you will use to increase your score.

Try another example:

See your DVD for more.

Which of the following countries uses the peso as its unit of currency?
- ○ Russia
- ○ Canada
- ○ Venezuela
- ○ England
- ● Chile

This time you can probably only get rid of three of the five answer choices using POE. The answer is clearly *not* Russia, Canada, or England, but most people probably don't know for sure whether the answer is Venezuela or Chile.

You've got the question down to two possibilities. What should you do?

Heads or Tails

A Chilean might flip a peso. You have a fifty-fifty chance of getting this question right, which is much better than if you had guessed at random. And because the GMAT forces you to guess anyway, it makes sense to guess intelligently.

In the chapters that follow, we'll show you specific ways to make use of POE to increase your score. You may feel uncomfortable about using these techniques at first, but the sooner you make them your own, the sooner you'll start to improve your score.

Is It Fair to Get a Question Right When You Don't Know the Answer?

If you took any math courses in college, you probably remember that the correct answer to a problem, while important, wasn't the only thing you were graded on. Your professor was probably more interested in how you got the answer, whether you wrote an elegant equation, or if you used the right formula.

If your equation was correct but you messed up your addition at the end, did you get the entire question wrong? Most college professors give partial credit for an answer like that. After all, what's most important is the mental process that goes into getting the answer, not the answer alone.

On the GMAT, if you don't click the correct circle with your mouse, you're wrong. It doesn't matter that you knew how to do the problem, or that you clicked the wrong answer by mistake. GMAC doesn't care: You're just wrong. And a wrong answer means that the running score that GMAC is keeping on you will go down by 10 or 20 points and you'll be forced to answer several easier questions correctly before you get back to the level at which you were.

This really isn't fair. It seems only fitting that you should also be able to benefit from the flip side of this situation: If you click on the correct circle, GMAC doesn't care how you got that answer either.

Scratch Work

Process of Elimination is a powerful tool, but it's only powerful if you keep track of the answer choices you've eliminated. On a computer-adaptive test, you obviously can't cross off choices on the screen—but you can cross them off on your scratch work.

The testing center provides each tester with a blank ten-page booklet and a fine-tipped black marker for scratch work. The pages are laminated and printed with a faint grid pattern useful for drawing math diagrams. In our course, we encourage our students to divide up each page into boxes, and label each box with five answer choices as shown on the next page.

Each letter corresponds to an answer. Of course, the answers on the computer-adaptive GMAT are no longer labeled with letters, but to be able to track the answers you've crossed off, it helps to think of them as if they were. The first answer choice is equivalent to A, the second to B, and so on.

Throughout this book, you will see us using the scratch booklet to keep track of the answer choices that have already been eliminated. By making this part of the ritual of how you take the GMAT, you will be able to prevent careless errors and make your guesses count.

SUMMARY

1. Because of the way the GMAT is designed, you will be forced to answer questions whether or not you know the correct answer.

2. However, not knowing the exact answer to a question does not mean that you have to get it wrong.

3. When you don't know the right answer to a question, look for wrong answers instead. This is called POE, or Process of Elimination.

4. The best way to keep track of the answer choices that you've eliminated is to use your scratch work to cross them off as you go.

So, What Are the Appropriate Uses?

The following is a list of what GMAC considers "inappropriate uses" of GMAT scores:

1. as a requisite for awarding a degree
2. as a requirement for employment, for licensing or certification to perform a job, or for job-related rewards (raises, promotions, etc.)
3. as an achievement test

5

Cracking the System: Advanced Principles

The people who write the computer-adaptive GMAT think the test is wonderful—and not just because they wrote it, or because it makes them a lot of money. They like it because it ensures that the only problems a test taker gets to see are problems at, and slightly above and below, her level of ability. One of the things they always hated about the paper-and-pencil test was that a student scoring 300 could guess the correct answer to a 700-level question.

BUT THEY HAVE THIS LITTLE PROBLEM

The questions on the GMAT are still multiple-choice.

That may not seem like a problem to you, but consider the following situation. Suppose an average student takes the GMAT. He's answered 36 of the 37 problems on the Math section. There's one left, and as he looks at this last question, he realizes he has absolutely no idea of how to answer it. However, one of the answer choices just "seems" right. So he picks it.

And he gets it right.

The test writers get nightmares just thinking about this situation. That average student was supposed to get 500. He "deserved" 500. But by guessing the correct answer to one last problem, he may have gotten 510.

Ten points more than he "deserved."

GMAC'S SOLUTION

GMAC's tests wouldn't be worth much if students could routinely guess the correct answer to difficult questions by picking answers that seemed right.

So the test writers came up with a wonderful solution:

On difficult questions, answer choices that seem right to the average student are almost always wrong.

CHOOSING ANSWERS THAT SEEM RIGHT

When we take the GMAT, most of us don't have time to work out every problem completely, or to check and double-check our answers. We just go as far as we can on each problem and then choose the answer that seems correct based on what we've been able to figure out. Sometimes we're completely sure of our answer, and at other times we simply do as much as we can and then follow our hunch. We may pick an answer because it "just looks right," or because something about it seems to go naturally with the question.

WHICH ANSWERS SEEM RIGHT?

That all depends on how high your score is.

Suppose you took the GMAT and scored 800. That means every answer that seemed right to you actually was right.

Now suppose your friend took the GMAT and scored 200. That means every answer that seemed right to your friend actually was wrong.

Of course, most people who take the GMAT don't score 800 or 200. The average person scores somewhere in between.

WHAT HAPPENS WHEN THE AVERAGE PERSON TAKES THE GMAT?

The average person picks the answer that seems right on every problem. Sometimes these hunches are correct; sometimes they are not.

- On easy questions, the average person tends to pick the correct answer. The answers that seem right to the average person actually are right on the easy questions.

- On medium questions, the average person's hunches are right only some of the time. Sometimes the answers that seem right to the average person really are right and sometimes they're wrong.

- Finally, on difficult problems, the average person's hunches are almost always wrong. The answers that seem right to the average person on these questions are invariably wrong.

Meet Joe Bloggs

We're going to talk a lot about "the average person" from now on. For the sake of convenience, let's give him a name: Joe Bloggs. Joe Bloggs is just the average American prospective business-school student. He has average grades from college and will get an average grade on the GMAT. There's a little bit of him in everyone, and there's a little bit of everyone in him. He isn't brilliant. He isn't dumb. He's just average.

How Does Joe Bloggs Approach the GMAT?

Joe Bloggs, the average person, spends most of his time answering questions of average difficulty. But whenever he gets several questions correct in a row, the computer gives him a more difficult question.

Joe approaches the GMAT just as everybody else does. Whether the question is hard or easy, he always chooses the answer that *seems* to be correct.

Here's an example of what a more difficult problem might look like on a GMAT problem-solving section:

> The output of a factory was increased by 10% to keep up with rising demand. To handle the holiday rush, this new output was increased by 20%. By approximately what percent would the output now have to be decreased in order to restore the original output?
>
> ○   20%
> ○   24%
> ○   30%
> ○   32%
> ○   79%

This question is from an upper medium difficulty bin. Don't bother trying to work the problem out now. You will learn how to do this type of problem (percentage decrease) in the first math chapter.

How Did Joe Bloggs Do on This Question?

He got it wrong. Why? Because GMAC set a trap for him.

Which Answer Did Joe Bloggs Pick on This Question?

Joe didn't think this was a hard problem. The answer seemed perfectly obvious. Joe Bloggs picked the middle choice—what we call C. (Please note that the first answer choice is called A, the second B, etc.) Joe assumed that if you increase production first by 10% and then by 20%, you have to take away 30% to get back to where you started.

The test writers led Joe away from the correct answer by giving him an answer that seemed right. In fact, the correct answer is B. Here's the same problem with slightly different answer choices. We've changed the choices to make a point:

> The output of a factory was increased by 10% to keep up with rising demand. To handle the holiday rush, this new output was raised by 20%. By approximately what percent would the output now have to be decreased in order to restore the original output?
>
> ○   21%
> ○   24%
> ○   34.2%
> ○   37%
> ○   71.5%

If Joe had seen this version, he wouldn't have thought it was an easy question. Now none of the answers would seem right to Joe. He would have been forced to guess at random. This would have made the question fairer, but GMAC didn't want to take the chance that an average person might get this question right by mistake.

Could GMAC Have Made This an Easy Question Instead?

Sure, by writing different answer choices.

Here's the same question with choices we've substituted to make the correct answer choice obvious:

> The output of a factory was increased by 10% to keep up with rising demand. To handle the holiday rush, this new output was raised by 20%. By approximately what percent would the output now have to be decreased in order to restore the original output?
>
> ○   a million %
> ○   24%
> ○   a billion %
> ○   a trillion %
> ○   a zillion %

When the problem is written this way, Joe Bloggs can see that the answer has to be choice B. It seems right to Joe because all the other answers seem obviously wrong.

Profiting from Other People's Bankruptcy

Let's look at a textbook example of how *not* to run a company.

Suppose you started your own company, with three partners: Kenneth Lay (formerly of Enron), Julie Wainwright (formerly of Pets.com), and Martha Stewart (now back with Martha Stewart Omnimedia). You have an important business decision to make, and each of your partners gives you his or her advice. Lay says, "Take an established company with actual assets and turn it into an Internet company without assets. It always worked for me." Wainwright says, "Profits are an outdated concept; offer your product for less than it costs you to deliver it." Stewart says, "What you need is inside information."

Are you going to make use of the advice of these people? Sure, you now know three things you're not going to do.

Joe Bloggs is our textbook example of how *not* to take a test.

Your Partner on the Test: Joe Bloggs

When you take the GMAT a few weeks or months from now, you'll have to take it on your own, of course. But suppose for a moment that GMAC allowed you to take it with Joe Bloggs as your partner. Would Joe be any help to you on the GMAT?

You Probably Don't Think So

After all, Joe is wrong as often as he's right. He knows the answers to the easy questions, but so do you. You'd like to do better than average on the GMAT, and Joe earns only an average score (he's the average person, remember). All things considered, you'd probably prefer to have someone else for your partner.

But Joe might turn out to be a pretty helpful partner, after all. Because his hunches on difficult questions are always wrong, couldn't you improve your chances on those questions simply by finding out what Joe wanted to pick, and then picking something else?

If you could use what you know about Joe Bloggs to eliminate one, two, or even three obviously incorrect choices on a hard problem, wouldn't you improve your score by guessing among the remaining choices?

WHATEVER YOUR CURRENT SCORING LEVEL, THE JOE BLOGGS PRINCIPLE CAN HELP YOU

We're going to teach you how to use Joe Bloggs while taking the GMAT.

After you've taken the practice test at the back of this book, the free tests on our websites, or the practice tests available in *GMATPrep*, you will have some idea of how you are scoring at any given moment on the GMAT. This means that you'll know approximately the level of difficulty of most of the problems you'll face.

If, at the moment, you find yourself facing mostly easy questions, you'll know not to out-think the question by picking hard answers.

If, at the moment, you are facing mostly medium questions, you can concentrate on practicing medium problems and get used to the kinds of traps these types of questions have in store for you.

If, at the moment, you are facing mostly difficult questions, you can stop and ask yourself, "How would Joe Bloggs answer these questions?" And when you see what he would do, you're going to do something else. Why? Because you know that on hard questions, Joe Bloggs is always wrong.

SHOULD YOU ALWAYS JUST ELIMINATE ANY ANSWER THAT SEEMS TO BE CORRECT?

No! Remember what we said about Joe Bloggs:

1. His hunches are often correct on easy questions.

2. His hunches are sometimes correct and sometimes incorrect on medium questions.

3. His hunches are always wrong on difficult questions.

PUTTING JOE BLOGGS TO WORK FOR YOU

In the following chapters, we'll teach you many specific problem-solving techniques based on the Joe Bloggs principle. The Joe Bloggs principle will help you:

1. Use POE to eliminate incorrect answer choices.

2. Avoid careless mistakes.

BLOGGS AND YOUR BIN

Knowing your bin is key to knowing how to use Joe Bloggs. Based on your scores on practice tests, you will have a good sense of what bins the test writers will be drawing from during the real test. If those bins are from the upper medium or difficult problems, then you can expect to see Joe Bloggs answers in some of these questions—and you will know that they are almost certainly wrong. On the other hand, if you know that you are drawing questions from the easy and early medium questions, then you will also know that the Joe Bloggs answer you spot could well be correct.

A WORD OF CAUTION

If you go through our review of the math and verbal topics covered on the GMAT, do all the drills we provide, and practice our techniques on real GMAT questions, then your scores on practice tests will almost certainly start to go up.

But as your scores improve, the level of difficulty of the questions you will be seeing on the computer-adaptive GMAT will increase as well—which means that you'll have to make adjustments to your use of the Joe Bloggs principle.

SUMMARY

1. Almost everyone approaches the GMAT by choosing the answer that seems correct, all things considered.

2. Joe Bloggs is the average person. He earns an average score on the GMAT. On easy GMAT questions, the answers that seem correct to him are usually correct. On medium questions, his answers are sometimes correct and sometimes not. On hard questions, the answers that seem correct to him are always wrong.

3. By taking a practice test from time to time, you can predict your current scoring level—which, in turn, will tell you what type of questions you will generally be answering: easy, medium, or difficult.

4. Whatever your current scoring level, the Joe Bloggs principle can help you to eliminate answer choices when you don't know the correct answer.

6

Taking the GMAT

REGISTERING TO TAKE THE GMAT

The easiest way to register for the exam is by telephone or online. You will be given a list of dates, times, and testing centers that are located near you. One of the actual advantages of the CAT is that you get to schedule the time of the exam. If you are not a morning person, ask for an afternoon time slot. If you can't think after midday, ask for a morning time slot.

To register for the GMAT call 1-800-717-GMAT or visit the website at www.mba.com

Keep in mind that certain slots get filled quickly, so be sure to call ahead of time. The registration fee is $250 (worldwide) and can be paid for by credit card (Visa, Mastercard, or American Express), check, or money order. Note that checks or money orders payable in U.S. dollars must be drawn from banks located in the United States or Canada.

PRACTICING TO TAKE THE GMAT

As you prepare for the GMAT, it's important to know—in advance—what the experience of taking the test is like, so that you can mimic those conditions during practice tests. When you are taking a practice test, turn off your telephone, and try to strictly observe the time limits of the test sections, and even the time limits of the breaks in between sections. To mimic the experience of working with a scratch booklet, buy a spiral notebook filled with grid paper. If you know when you will be taking the real GMAT, try to schedule your practice tests around the same time of day.

If you are the sort of person who likes to have a mental picture of what a new experience will be like, you might even consider visiting the test center ahead of time. This serves two purposes: first, you'll know how to get there on the day of the test, and second, you'll be familiar with the ambiance in advance.

ON THE DAYS BEFORE THE TEST

Try to keep to your regular routine. Staying up late to study the last few nights before the test is counterproductive. It's important to get regular amounts of exercise and sleep. Continue the study plan you've been on from the beginning, but taper off toward the end. You'll want to take your last practice exam no later than several days before the real test, so you'll have time to go over the results carefully. The last day or so should be devoted to any topics that still give you trouble.

ON THE NIGHT BEFORE THE TEST

What to Bring to the Test Center

1. your registration ticket
2. a government-issued ID
3. a reliable watch
4. a snack
5. a bottle of water

Get together the things you will need to bring with you for the test: directions to the test center (if you haven't already been there); a mental list of the schools you wish to receive your test scores (if you can't identify these when you take the test, you will have to pay $28 extra per school to get scores sent out later); a snack, and some water. You may also want to bring a reliable watch. (If you like, the testing computer will give you a constant digital readout of the time remaining in each section, but some students find this distracting.) Don't bother to bring a calculator—no calculators are permitted on the GMAT.

Once you have gathered everything you need, take the night off. Go to a movie. Relax. There is no point in last-minute cramming. You are as ready as you are going to be.

On the Day of the Test

If you are taking the test in the morning, get up early enough that you have time to eat breakfast, if that is your usual routine, and do a couple of GMAT questions you've already seen in order to get your mind working. If you are taking the test in the afternoon, make sure you get some lunch, and, again, do a few GMAT problems. You don't want to have to warm up on the test itself.

Bring a snack to the test center. You'll get two optional breaks during the test: one after the Essay section and one between the Verbal and the Quantitative sections. Some people spend the breaks comparing answers in the hallway and getting upset because not only didn't they get the same answers—they didn't even get the same questions. Ignore the people around you. Why assume that they know any more than you do? Use the breaks to eat the food you've brought.

At the Testing Center

Unlike testing sessions you may have attended in the past, where hundreds of people were lined up to take the same test, you may well be the only person at your testing center taking the GMAT. You'll be asked to present your government-issued ID, and an employee will take your photograph and digitally record your signature and fingerprint. Finally, you'll be led to the computer station where you will take the test. The station consists of a desk with a computer monitor, a keyboard, a mouse, and a scratch booklet. Before the test starts, make sure you're comfortable. Is there enough light? Is your desk sturdy? Don't be afraid to speak up; you're going to be spending four hours at that desk.

There will almost certainly be other people in the same room at other computer stations taking other computer-adaptive tests. You might be seated next to someone taking the licensing exam for architects or a test for school nurses, or even a test for golf pros.

None of the people in the room will have necessarily started at the same time. The testing center employee will show you how to begin the test, but the computer itself will be your proctor from then on. It will tell you how much time you have left in a section, when your time is up, and when to go on to the next section.

The test center employees will be available if you have a question. They will also monitor the room for security purposes. Just in case their eagle eyes aren't enough, video and audio systems will record everything that happens in the room.

The process sounds less human than it really is. Our students have generally found the test center employees to be quite nice.

WHAT YOUR SCREEN WILL LOOK LIKE

During most of the test, your screen will look a lot like this:

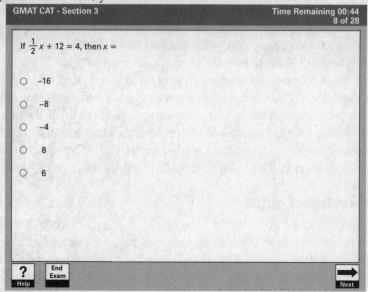

The problem you're working on at any particular moment will be near the top of the screen (by the way, the answer to this one is the first choice—what we call choice A). At the top right will be a readout of the time remaining in the section, the number of the question you're working on, and how many total questions there are in the section. At the bottom of the screen you'll see these buttons:

<u>End Exam</u>—By clicking on this button, you can end the test at any moment. We don't recommend that you do this unless you actually become ill. Even if you decide not to have your test scored (an option they will give you at the end of the exam), you might as well finish—it's great practice, and besides, GMAC has no intention of giving you a refund.

<u>Time</u>—The time you have left to complete the section is displayed in the upper right of the screen. You can hide the time by clicking on it, and you can make it reappear by clicking on the icon in its place. During the last few minutes of the test, the time is automatically displayed and you cannot hide it.

<u>Question Number</u>—The question number that you are on is also displayed in the upper right, and it works just like the time display: You can hide it by clicking on it or make it reappear by clicking on the icon. During the last few minutes of the test, the question number is automatically displayed and cannot be hidden.

<u>Help</u>—During the test this button provides test and section directions and information about using the software.

<u>Next</u>—When you've answered a question by clicking on the small bubble in front of the answer you think is correct, you press this button.

What Happens If You Get Stuck on a Question?

Everyone knows that sinking feeling of not knowing how to do a test problem—but before you start panicking, there are a few things to bear in mind about the GMAT.

First of all, as any Princeton Review graduate will tell you, seeing hard questions on the GMAT is a good sign. Because the test is interactive, you don't get a hard question until you've answered a bunch of increasingly difficult medium questions correctly—which means you are probably already on track for a good score.

Second, if you have gone through this book and taken the practice tests, then chances are good that if you reread the question and think about it for a few seconds, you may get an idea of how to start it (and starting is half the battle).

Third, you should remember that one-fourth of the questions on this test don't even count. They are "experimental questions" being tried out for future versions of the GMAT; it will turn out later that some of them do not even have a correct answer. So there's no point in getting too upset over a question that might not even get scored.

And fourth, if you are really stuck, then you can pull out the Princeton Review's arsenal of POE (Process of Elimination) techniques to do some very shrewd guessing.

What Happens If You Don't Get to Every Question in a Section?

If you run out of time without having answered all the questions in a section, the computer just moves you on to the next section. As we said earlier, the computer keeps a running score on you throughout each section. If you don't get to answer some questions, the computer deducts points (based on an algorithm that probably wouldn't survive rigorous scientific scrutiny) and gives you a score based on what you *have* answered. It would be theoretically possible to get a GMAT score on the computer-adaptive test by answering only one verbal question and one math question.

It Is Actually in Your Interest to Answer *All* the Questions—Even If You Have to Guess

You might think it would be better to skip any questions you don't have time to answer at the end of a section—but in fact, the reverse is true: If time is running out, you will probably get a slightly higher score by clicking through and answering any remaining questions at random. This is because the penalty for getting a question wrong diminishes sharply toward the end of each section (when the computer has already largely decided your score). The penalty for each question skipped at the end of a section is actually greater than the penalty for getting one of those last questions wrong.

But You Can Do Much Better Than Guessing at Random

In the following chapters, we will give you all the specific mathematical and verbal skills you need to ace the Math and Verbal sections. We will also raise the Process of Elimination to a fine art—in case you have to guess.

Zen and the Art of Test Taking

As you begin a new section, put the last one behind you. Don't get rattled if you think you've done poorly on one part of the test. Most people find that their impressions of how they did on certain sections is often worse than the reality.

At the End of the Test

When you finish, the computer will ask you if you want the test to count. If you say no, or you just walk away, the computer will not record your score, and no schools will ever see it. Of course, neither will you. GMAC will not let you look at your score and then decide whether or not you want to keep it. You should also know that if you do cancel your scores, your future score reports will show this.

If you tell the computer that you want the test to count, then it will give you your unofficial score right then and there on the screen. (You can also print out a copy.) Within 20 days, you'll receive your official results online. If you choose to cancel at the test site, you will not be able to change your mind later. By the same token, once you've chosen to see your score, you can't cancel it.

If Something Weird Happens at the Test Center...

Admissions Insight No. 3: When to Apply

Although many schools have a filing range that stretches from six to eight months, early applications often have a better chance. This is because there are more spots available in the beginning of the process.

We have found that almost nothing ever goes wrong at the test centers—they are professionally run. But in the unlikely event that there is a technical glitch with your assigned computer, or if you want to complain about test center conditions or some other anomaly, it is best to start the process before you leave the test center by filing a complaint immediately after the test is over. If possible, get the test center staff to corroborate your complaint. Then, as soon as possible after the test is over, send a letter describing the situation to Pearson VUE. It should be addressed to "Attention: GMAT Complaints" and sent either by fax (952-681-3681) or mail. The mailing address is:

Pearson VUE
5601 Green Valley Drive
Suite 220
Bloomington, MN 55437

One Final Thought Before You Begin

No matter how high or low you score on the test, and no matter how much you improve your performance with this book, you should *never* accept the score GMAC assigns you as an accurate assessment of your abilities. The temptation to see a high score as evidence that you're a genius, or a low score as evidence that you're an idiot, can be very powerful.

When you've read this book and practiced our techniques on real GMAT questions, you'll be able to judge for yourself whether the GMAT actually measures much besides how well you do on the GMAT.

Think of this as a kind of game—a game you can win.

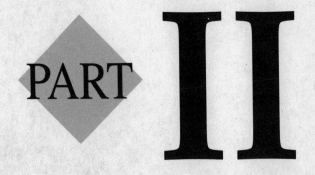

PART II

How to Crack the Math GMAT

7

GMAT Math:
Basic Principles

What's Covered in the Math Section

The 37 math questions on the GMAT come in two different formats. About half of the questions will be regular problem solving questions of the type you're familiar with from countless other standardized tests, such as the SAT. The other half of the questions, mixed in among the regular problem solving questions, will be of a type unique to the GMAT: They're called data sufficiency questions, and they will ask you to determine whether you can answer a math question based on two pieces of information. We've devoted an entire chapter to Data Sufficiency; it follows the math review.

But whether the question falls into the category of problem solving or data sufficiency, the GMAT questions will test your general knowledge of three subjects:

1. arithmetic

2. basic algebra

3. basic geometry

What Isn't Covered in the Math Section

The good news is that you won't need to know calculus, trigonometry, or any complicated geometry. The bad news is that the specialized, business-type math you're probably good at isn't tested, either. There will be no questions on computing the profit on three ticks of a particular bond sale, no questions about amortizing a loan, no need to calculate the bottom line of a small business.

Ancient History

For the most part, what you'll find on the GMAT is a kind of math that you haven't had to think about in years: junior high school and high school math. The GMAT is more difficult than your old nemesis, the SAT, but the problem solving on the GMAT tests the same general body of knowledge that's tested by the SAT. Because most people who apply to business school have been out of college for several years, high school math may seem a bit like ancient history. In the next few chapters, we'll give you a fast review of the important concepts, and we'll show you some powerful techniques for cracking the system.

Order of Difficulty

The first problem on the computer-adaptive Math test will be of medium difficulty. Based on your response to that first question, you will next be presented with an easier or a more difficult problem. GMAC says that within three or four problems, the computer will have honed in on your *approximate* score level. The other 33 questions you'll have to answer will be a mixture of experimental questions (which don't count toward your score) and questions that will allow GMAC to zero in on your exact score.

THE PRINCETON REVIEW APPROACH

Because it's probably been a long time since you've needed to reduce fractions or figure out how many degrees there are in a quadrilateral, the first thing to do is review the information tested on the GMAT by going through our math review. Along the way, you'll learn some valuable test-taking skills that will allow you to take advantage of some of the inherent weaknesses of standardized testing.

When you've finished the math review, you should read our chapter on data sufficiency and then take our diagnostic math test. Based on your approximate score on our diagnostic, you can then practice working through the problems at, or just above, your scoring range. By becoming familiar with the general level of difficulty of these problems and the number of steps required to solve them, you can increase your score on the real GMAT.

> Always keep in mind that if your purpose is to raise your GMAT score, it's a waste of time to learn math that won't be tested. Don't get us wrong, we think the derivation of π is fascinating, but...

EXTRA HELP

Although we can show you which mathematical principles are most important for the GMAT, this book cannot take the place of a basic foundation in math. We find that most people, even if they don't remember much of high school math, pick it up again quickly. Our drills and examples will refresh your memory if you've gotten rusty, but if you have serious difficulties with the following chapters, you should consider a more thorough review, like the *Math Workout for the GMAT*, also from The Princeton Review. This book will enable you to see where you need the most work. Always keep in mind, though, that if your purpose is to raise your GMAT score, it's a waste of time to learn math that won't be tested.

BASIC INFORMATION

Try the following problem:

> How many even integers are there between 17 and 27?
> ○   9
> ○   7
> ○   5
> ○   4
> ○   3

This is an easy GMAT question. Even so, if you don't know what an integer is, the question will be impossible to answer. Before moving on to arithmetic, you should make sure you're familiar with some basic terms and concepts. This material isn't difficult, but you must know it cold. (The answer, by the way, is C.)

INTEGERS

Integers are the numbers we think of when we think of numbers. They can be negative or positive. They do not include fractions. The positive integers are:

$$1, 2, 3, 4, 5, \text{etc.}$$

The negative integers are:

$$-1, -2, -3, -4, -5, \text{etc.}$$

Zero (0) is also an integer. It is neither positive nor negative.

Positive integers get bigger as they move away from 0; negative integers get smaller. Look at this number line:

Ancient History 101

The GMAT will test your (probably rusty) knowledge of high school math.

2 is greater than 1, but –2 is less than –1.

POSITIVE AND NEGATIVE

Positive numbers are to the right of zero on the number line. Negative numbers are to the left of zero on the number line.

There are three rules regarding the multiplication of positive and negative numbers:

> **positive × positive = positive**
>
> **positive × negative = negative**
>
> **negative × negative = positive**

If you add a positive number and a negative number, subtract the number with the negative sign in front of it from the positive number.

$$4 + (-3) = 1$$

If you add two negative numbers, you add them as if they were positive, then put a negative sign in front of the sum.

$$-3 + -5 = -8$$

DIGITS

There are ten digits:

$$0, 1, 2, 3, 4, 5, 6, 7, 8, 9$$

All integers are made up of digits. In the integer 246, there are three digits: 2, 4, and 6. Each of the digits has a different name:

6 is called the units (or ones) digit

4 is called the tens digit

2 is called the hundreds digit

A number with decimal places is also composed of digits, although it is not an integer. In the decimal 27.63 there are four digits:

2 is the tens digit

7 is the units digit

6 is the tenths digit

3 is the hundredths digit

ODD OR EVEN

Even numbers are integers that can be divided evenly by 2. Here are some examples:

−6, −4, −2, 0, 2, 4, 6, etc.

Any integer, no matter how large, is even if its last digit can be divided evenly by 2. Thus 777,772 is even.

Odd numbers are integers that cannot be divided evenly by 2. Here are some examples:

−5, −3, −1, 1, 3, 5, etc.

Any integer, no matter how large, is odd if its last digit cannot be divided evenly by 2. Thus 222,227 is odd.

There are several rules that always hold true with even and odd numbers:

> **even × even = even**
>
> **odd × odd = odd**
>
> **even × odd = even**
>
> **even + even = even**
>
> **odd + odd = even**
>
> **even + odd = odd**

It isn't necessary to memorize these, but you must know that the relationships always hold true. The individual rules can be derived in a second. If you need to know *even × even*, just try 2 × 2. The answer in this case is even, as *even × even* always will be.

REMAINDERS

If a number cannot be divided evenly by another number, the number that is left over at the end of division is called the **remainder**.

$$\frac{3 \ R1}{2 \overline{)7}}$$

Q: 20,179.01792
In the number above, which of the following two digits are identical?

(A) the tens digit and the hundredths digit

(B) the ones digit and the thousandths digit

(C) the hundreds digit and the tenths digit

(D) the thousands digit and the tenths digit

(E) the thousands digit and the hundredths digit

Consecutive Integers

Consecutive integers are integers listed in order of increasing size without any integers missing in between. For example, –3, –2, –1, 0, 1, 2, 3 are consecutive integers. The formula for consecutive integers is $n, n + 1, n + 2, n + 3$, etc., where n is an integer.

A: D. Both the thousands digit and tenths digit are 0.

> Some consecutive even integers: –2, 0, 2, 4, 6, 8, etc.
> Some consecutive odd integers: –3, –1, 1, 3, 5, etc.

Distinct Numbers

If two numbers are **distinct**, they cannot be equal. For example, if x and y are distinct, then they must have different values.

Prime Numbers

A **prime number** is a positive integer that can be divided evenly only by two numbers: itself and 1. Thus 2, 3, 5, 7, 11, 13 are all prime numbers. The number 2 is both the smallest and the only even prime number. Neither 0 nor 1 is a prime number. All prime numbers are positive.

Divisibility Rules

If a number can be divided evenly by another number, it is said to be **divisible** by that number.

Some useful shortcuts:

- A number is divisible by 2 if its units digit can be divided evenly by 2. Thus 772 is divisible by 2.

- A number is divisible by 3 if the sum of its digits can be divided evenly by 3. We can instantly tell that 216 is divisible by 3, because the sum of the digits (2 + 1 + 6) is divisible by 3.

- A number is divisible by 4 if the number formed by its last two digits is divisible by 4. 3,028 is divisible by 4, because 28 is divisible by 4.

- A number is divisible by 5 if its final digit is either 0 or 5. Thus, 60, 85, and 15 are all divisible by 5.

- A number is divisible by 6 if it is divisible by both 2 and 3, the factors of 6. Thus 318 is divisible by 6 because it is even, and the sum of 3 + 1 + 8 is divisible by 3.

- Division by zero is undefined. There is no answer. The test writers won't ever put a zero in the denominator. If you're working out a problem and you find yourself with a zero in the denominator of a fraction, you've done something wrong. By the way, a 0 in the numerator is fine. Any fraction with a 0 on the top is 0.

$$\frac{0}{1} = 0 \qquad \frac{0}{4} = 0$$

FACTORS AND MULTIPLES

A number is a **factor** of another number if it can be divided evenly into that number. Thus the factors of 15, for example, are 1, 3, 5, and 15.

A number, x, is considered to be a **multiple** of another number, y, if y times another integer equals x. For example, 15 is a multiple of 3 (3×5); 12 is also a multiple of 3 (3×4). When you think about it, most numbers have only a few factors, but an infinite number of multiples. The memory device you may have learned in school is "factors are few; multiples are many."

ABSOLUTE VALUE

The **absolute value** of a number is the distance between that number and 0 on the number line. The absolute value of 6 is expressed as $|6|$.

$$|6| = 6$$
$$|-5| = 5$$

STANDARD SYMBOLS

The following standard symbols are frequently used on the GMAT:

Symbol	Meaning
=	is equal to
≠	is not equal to
<	is less than
>	is greater than
≤	is less than or equal to
≥	is greater than or equal to

Q: Which of the following numbers is prime?
0, 1, 15, 23, 33

A: 23. Remember, neither 0 nor 1 is prime.

NOW LET'S LOOK AT THE INSTRUCTIONS

During the test, you'll be able to see test instructions by clicking on the "Help" button at the bottom of the screen. However, to avoid wasting time reading these during the test, read our version of the instructions for problem solving questions now:

Directions: For each problem solving question, solve the problem and choose the best of the answer choices provided.

Numbers: This test uses only real numbers; no imaginary numbers are used or implied.

Diagrams: All problem solving diagrams are drawn as accurately as possible UNLESS it is specifically noted that a diagram is "not drawn to scale." All diagrams are in a plane unless stated otherwise.

8

POE and GMAT Math

In Chapter 4, we introduced you to the Process of Elimination—a way to find correct answers by eliminating wrong answers. Now, we're going to show you how to turn POE into a science.

Here's an example of a typical medium-level problem—the sort of problem that the computer might give you for your very first math question:

> Twenty-two percent of the cars produced in America are manufactured in Michigan. If the total number of cars produced in America is 40 million, how many cars are produced outside of Michigan?
>
> ○
> ○
> ○   31.2 million
> ○
> ○

ZEN AND THE ART OF TEST WRITING

Let's put ourselves in the place of the GMAT test writer who has just written this medium-level math problem. He's finished with his question, and he has his correct answer (31.2 million), but he isn't done yet. He still has four empty slots to fill. He needs to come up with incorrect numbers for answer choices A, B, D, and E.

He could simply choose numbers at random, or numbers that are closely clustered around the correct answer. However, if he did either, test takers who didn't know how to do the problem wouldn't see an obvious answer and might therefore guess at random. The test writer does not want test takers to guess at random. If they did, they might actually pick the right answer. So our test writer comes up with incorrect answer choices that whisper seductively, "Pick me." If people who don't know how to do the problem are going to guess (and of course they have to guess if they don't know the answer in order to get to the next question), our test writer wants to make sure they guess wrong.

The test writers are very careful in creating incorrect answer choices. They try to figure out all the mistakes a careless test taker might make; then they include those answers among the choices. Here's that same question, now that the test writer has finished it:

> Twenty-two percent of the cars produced in America are manufactured in Michigan. If the total number of cars produced in America is 40 million, how many cars are produced outside of Michigan?
>
> ○   8.8 million
> ○   18 million
> ○   31.2 million
> ○   48.8 million
> ○   62 million

PARTIAL ANSWERS

People often go wrong on GMAT math problems by thinking that they are finished before they really are. The first step in this problem is to find out how many actual cars are produced in Michigan; in other words, we need to know what 22 percent of 40 million equals. If you aren't sure how to do this, don't worry; we'll show you how to do percent problems in the arithmetic chapter. For the moment, take our word for it that 22 percent of 40 million equals 8.8 million.

If you were feeling smug about having figured this out, you might just look at the answer choices, notice that the first answer choice (what we call choice A) says 8.8 million, and figure that you're done. Unfortunately, the problem didn't ask how many cars were produced in Michigan; it asked how many cars were *not* produced in Michigan.

GMAC provided answer choice A just in case you got halfway through the problem and decided you'd done enough work. It was a *partial* answer. To find the correct answer, you have to subtract 8.8 from 40 million. The correct answer is choice C, 31.2 million.

HOW DO YOU AVOID PICKING PARTIAL ANSWERS?

You can avoid this mistake by doing two things:

- When you finish a problem, always take two seconds to reread the problem to make sure you've actually answered the question.

- Always consider the level of the problem you're working on in order to determine whether you've done enough work for GMAC to think you "deserve" to get the problem right. For example, if this question were the very first one on the Math section of the GMAT, then you would know it is a medium problem—and medium problems always require more than one step. If this question were in the middle of your GMAT Math section, you would still have a pretty good idea of its level of difficulty—based on how you are scoring on practice GMATs. If you were normally scoring at around the 50th percentile in Math, then you would know that most of the questions you'd answer would be medium problems that require at least two steps. If you were normally scoring in the 30th percentile, you would know most of the questions you'd answer would be relatively easy problems that require only one or two simple steps. If you were normally scoring in the 80th percentile, you would know most of the questions you'd answer would be difficult problems that require at least three steps.

CRAZY ANSWERS

The GMAT test writers also know that people taking tests do crazy things under pressure. Thus, even though there is no good reason why a person would want to do this, some percentage of the test takers who see this question are going to correctly find 22 percent of 40, or 8.8, but then *add* it to the original 40. Thus, the test writer will want to include 48.8 among the answer choices. If it weren't there, test takers who'd gotten this answer might realize they had made a mistake and figure out the correct answer, but the test writer would prefer that they just get it wrong.

How else could a test taker go wrong on this problem?

JOE BLOGGS AND GMAT MATH

In Chapter 5 we introduced you to Joe Bloggs—the average test taker. Joe just does the first thing that comes into his head. On easy problems, this often gets him the right answer. On difficult questions, his first response is *always* wrong. On medium problems Joe Bloggs's first response is wrong about half the time. On this particular medium problem, what might Joe want to do?

What about just adding the two numbers in the problem together? 22 + 40 equals 62. Or subtracting 22 from 40, which gives you 18. If there's a chance that Joe might pick it, GMAC wants it to be there. So the test writers will probably include 62 and 40 among the answer choices. Again, there's no good mathematical reason why a test taker would want to do these things, but GMAC knows that you don't always need a good reason to go wrong.

It might strike you that this is pretty unfair. If GMAC just picked answers at random, Joe would be much less likely to fall into their traps. However, there is one positive side to GMAC's obsession with trap answers...

COMMON SENSE: THE ANTIDOTE TO TRAP ANSWERS

GMAC is so caught up in trying to provide answer choices that anticipate all the mistakes a test taker might make on a problem that it often forgets to make certain that all of these answer choices make sense. Let's just think about that problem again.

> Twenty-two percent of the cars produced in America are manufactured in Michigan. If the total number of cars produced in America is 40 million, how many cars are produced outside of Michigan?
>
> ○　　　8.8 million
> ○　　　18 million
> ○　　31.2 million
> ○　　48.8 million
> ○　　62 million

We want the number of cars produced in places other than Michigan. Forget about math for a moment. Let's just look at the answer choices in the cold light of day. Even if you're rusty on percentages, is there any way that the number of cars produced in the other states could be greater than the total number of cars produced altogether? No way. The answer has to be less than 40 million. Thus, in their zeal to anticipate your potential wrong answers, the test writers have given you two answer choices (48.8 and 62) that are just plain crazy.

SCRATCH WORK

If these two answers are crazy, then cross them off in your scratch booklet. It's psychologically very uplifting to see your possible answers narrowed down to only three. Here's what your scratch work should look like for this question:

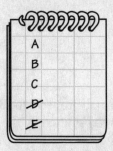

HOW DO YOU PREVENT YOURSELF FROM PICKING CRAZY ANSWERS?

You can prevent yourself from selecting crazy answers by doing two simple things:

- Before you even start doing any serious math, take a second to use common sense on the problem: Are there any answers that simply don't make sense? If so, cross them off in your scratch work. This will prevent you from picking them later through carelessness or desperation.

- If, based on your scores on practice tests, you expect to be seeing mainly medium and difficult problems on the Math section, take a second to see if there are any Joe Bloggs answers to cross off.

PSST! HEY, JOE...

To come up with answers that will appeal to Joe Bloggs, the GMAT test writer has to know how Joe thinks. Fortunately for the test writer, she can draw on more than 30 years of statistical information GMAC has compiled. From this, she knows that:

1. On difficult math problems, Joe Bloggs is always attracted to easy solutions that he can find in one step.

For example, Joe might just add together the numbers mentioned in the problem.

2. On difficult math problems, Joe Bloggs is attracted to numbers that he has already seen in the problem.

It's pretty silly, but frequently Joe picks a number simply because he remembers it from the problem itself.

Admissions Insight No. 4: How Criteria Are Weighted

Although requirements vary from school to school, most rely on some combination of the following criteria (although not necessarily in this order):
1) GMAT score
2) undergraduate grade point average
3) work experience
4) essays
5) letters of recommendation
6) interviews
7) extracurriculars

The advantage of this system is that it allows applicants to compensate for weaknesses in some areas with strengths in other areas. And the single easiest thing to change in your admissions "package" is your GMAT score.

Now, let's look at the upper-medium problem we showed you in Chapter 5, complete with answer choices:

> The output of a factory was increased by 10% to keep up with rising demand. To handle the holiday rush, this new output was increased by 20%. By approximately what percent would the output now have to be decreased in order to restore the original output?
>
> ○   20%
> ○   24%
> ○   30%
> ○   32%
> ○   70%

If the test writer has done her job properly, Joe Bloggs will never even consider the correct answer (24%). He's too smitten by the other answer choices.

Here's How to Crack It

As we said in Chapter 5, Joe's favorite answer to this question is undoubtedly 30 percent (what we call choice C). Joe notices that the output seems to have increased by 30 percent and figures that to get rid of that increase, you would have to decrease it by 30 percent. Joe just added together the two numbers he saw in the problem.

> On medium and difficult math problems, Joe Bloggs is attracted to easy solutions that he can find in one step.

Another answer Joe might be attracted to is choice A. Twenty (20%) is simply one of the numbers from the problem. There is no logical reason to think this is the correct answer, but Joe isn't always logical.

> On medium and difficult math problems, Joe Bloggs is attracted to answer choices that simply repeat numbers from the problem.

PUTTING EVERYTHING TOGETHER

Here's one last example of an upper medium problem to show how you can use both common sense and the Joe Bloggs principle to help eliminate answers:

> A student took 6 courses last year and received an average grade of 100. The year before, the student took 5 courses and received an average grade of 90. To the nearest tenth of a point, what was the student's average grade for the entire two-year period?
>
> ○   79
> ○   89
> ○   95
> ○   95.5
> ○   97.2

Here's How to Crack It

Don't worry if you aren't sure how to solve this problem right now; we'll cover average problems in the next chapter. Let's assume for a moment that you've done our math review and will be facing mostly medium questions on the Math portion of the GMAT.

Even if you knew exactly how to do this problem, it would still make sense for you to eliminate wrong answers before you begin using any serious math. Let's begin by thinking about what Joe Bloggs would like to pick on this question. Joe likes answer choice C a lot. He figures that to find the average of the entire two-year period, all he has to do is find that the average of 90 and 100 is 95. If this were an easy problem, he might be right, but we're assuming for the moment that you will be seeing mainly medium problems—so cross off choice C in your scratch booklet.

There are no other obvious Joe Bloggs answers, but it *is* possible to eliminate a couple of other choices by using common sense. The student's average for the first year was 90. The student's average for the second year was 100. Obviously the student's second-year grades are going to bring his average *up*. We may not be sure by exactly how much, but the average for the entire two-year period has to be higher than it was for the first year. Both choices A and B are less than the first year's average. We can therefore eliminate both of them.

We've eliminated three answer choices. If you know how to solve the problem, go to it. If not, you have a fifty-fifty shot at getting it right anyway. The correct answer is choice D, 95.5.

Admissions Insight No. 5: Online Applications

Schools and students alike prefer online applications more and more. The Princeton Review has online applications to more than 100 business schools. There are no extra fees to apply through our site, and the process is completely efficient: Once you fill out the applications profile, all subsequent applications will be pre-populated with that information. For access to these applications, go to www.PrincetonReview.com.

SUMMARY

1. The Process of Elimination allows you to eliminate answer choices even when you don't know how to do a problem. There are three types of answers to look for: partial answers, crazy answers, and Joe Bloggs answers.

2. **Partial answers:** GMAC likes to include, among the answer choices, answers that are partial completions of the problem. If you get halfway through a problem and decide that you're done, the number you have arrived at will likely be there, waiting to trip you up. The way to avoid partial answers is to reread the problem before you pick an answer to make sure you're answering the question it has asked.

3. **Crazy answers:** The test writers also like to include, among the answer choices, numbers that a test taker may arrive at—even though they don't make much sense. Crazy answer choices can be spotted by taking a step back and looking at the problem and its answers in the cold light of day.

4. **Joe Bloggs answers:** GMAC also likes to plant, among the answer choices, numbers that would appeal to Joe Bloggs, the average test taker. Joe is attracted to easy solutions that he can arrive at in one step and answers that repeat numbers from the problem.

9

Arithmetic

Although arithmetic is only one of the three types of math tested on the GMAT, arithmetic problems comprise about half of the total number of math questions. Here are the specific arithmetic topics tested on the GMAT:

1. Axioms and Fundamentals (properties of integers, positive and negative numbers, even and odd). These were covered in Chapter 7.

2. Arithmetic Operations

3. Fractions

4. Decimals

5. Ratios

6. Percentages

7. Averages

8. Exponents and Radicals

In this chapter we will first discuss the fundamentals of each topic and then show how the test writers construct questions based on that topic.

ARITHMETIC OPERATIONS

There are six arithmetic operations you will need for the GMAT:

1.	addition $(2 + 2)$	the result of addition is a sum or total
2.	subtraction $(6 - 2)$	the result of subtraction is a difference
3.	multiplication (2×2)	the result of multiplication is a product
4.	division $(8 \div 2)$	the result of division is a quotient
5.	raising to a power (x^2)	in the expression x^2 the little 2 is called an exponent
6.	finding a square root $\left(\sqrt{4}\right)$	$\sqrt{4} = \sqrt{2 \cdot 2} = 2$

WHICH ONE DO I DO FIRST?

In a problem that involves several different operations, the operations must be performed in a particular order, and occasionally GMAC likes to see whether you know what that order is. Here's an easy way to remember the order of operations:

Please Excuse My Dear Aunt Sally

or

PEMDAS

The first letters stand for Parentheses, Exponents, Multiplication, Division, Addition, Subtraction. Do operations that are enclosed in parentheses first; then take care of exponents; then multiply, divide, add, and subtract, from left to right.

DRILL 1

Just to get you started, solve each of the following problems by performing the indicated operations in the proper order. The answers can be found on page 300.

1. $74 + (27 - 24) =$

2. $(8 \times 9) + 7 =$

3. $2[9 - (8 \div 2)] =$

4. $2(7 - 3) + (-4)(5 - 7) =$

It is not uncommon to see a problem like this on the GMAT:

5. $4[-3(3 - 5) + 10 - 17] =$
   - ○ -27
   - ○ -4
   - ○ -1
   - ○ 32
   - ○ 84

There are two operations that can be done in any order, provided they are the only operations involved: *When you are adding or multiplying a series of numbers, you can group or regroup the numbers any way you like.*

$2 + 3 + 4$ is the same as $4 + 2 + 3$

and

$4 \times 5 \times 6$ is the same as $6 \times 5 \times 4$

This is called the **associative law**, but the name will not be tested on the GMAT.

Another law that GMAC likes to test states that

$$a(b + c) = ab + ac \text{ and } a(b - c) = ab - ac.$$

This is called the **distributive law** but, again, you don't need to know that for the test. Sometimes the distributive law can provide you with a shortcut to the solution of a problem. If a problem gives you information in "factored form"— $a(b + c)$—you should distribute it immediately. If the information is given in distributed form—$ab + ac$—you should factor it.

Q: According to the associative law, can you perform the following operations in any order you like?

2 divided by 6 divided by 3 divided by 4.

Hint: The answer is yes *and* no.

DRILL 2

If the following problems are in distributed form, factor them; if they are in factored form, distribute them. Then do the indicated operations. Answers are on page 300.

Answers are on page 300.

1. $8(10 + 5)$

2. $(55 \times 12) + (55 \times 88)$

3. $a(b + c - d)$

4. $abc + xyc$

A GMAT problem might look like this:

5. If $x = 6$ what is the value of $\dfrac{2xy - xy}{y}$?
   - ○   −30
   - ○   6
   - ○   8
   - ○   30
   - ○   It cannot be determined.

A: There are two ways to approach the problem. You can divide from left to right. Division *must* be performed from left to right. The second way is to convert the several division operations into multiplication:
$$2 \times \frac{1}{6} \times \frac{1}{3} \times \frac{1}{4}.$$
In this form, the operations can be performed in whatever order you find most convenient.

FRACTIONS

Fractions can be thought of in two ways:

- A **fraction** is just another way of expressing division. The expression $\dfrac{1}{2}$ is exactly the same thing as 1 divided by 2. $\dfrac{x}{y}$ is nothing more than x divided by y. In the fraction $\dfrac{x}{y}$, x is known as the **numerator** and y is known as the **denominator**.

- The other important way to think of a fraction is as $\dfrac{\text{part}}{\text{whole}}$. The fraction $\dfrac{7}{10}$ can be thought of as 7 parts out of a total of 10 parts.

ADDING AND SUBTRACTING FRACTIONS WITH THE SAME DENOMINATOR

To add two or more fractions that have the same denominator, simply add up the numerators and put the sum over the common denominator. For example:

$$\frac{1}{7} + \frac{5}{7} = \frac{(1+5)}{7} = \frac{6}{7}$$

Subtraction works exactly the same way:

$$\frac{6}{7} - \frac{2}{7} = \frac{6-2}{7} = \frac{4}{7}$$

ADDING AND SUBTRACTING FRACTIONS WITH DIFFERENT DENOMINATORS

Before you can add or subtract two or more fractions with different denominators, you must give all of them the same denominator. To do this, multiply each fraction by a number that will give it a denominator in common with the others. If you multiplied each fraction by any old number, the fractions wouldn't have their original values, so the number you multiply by has to be equal to 1. For example, if you wanted to change $\frac{1}{2}$ into sixths, you could do the following:

$$\frac{1}{2} \times \frac{3}{3} = \frac{3}{6}$$

We haven't actually changed the value of the fraction, because $\frac{3}{3}$ equals 1. If we wanted to add:

$$\frac{1}{2} + \frac{2}{3}$$

$$\frac{1}{2} \times \frac{3}{3} + \frac{2}{3} \times \frac{2}{2}$$

$$\frac{3}{6} + \frac{4}{6} = \frac{7}{6}$$

MULTIPLYING FRACTIONS

To multiply fractions, just multiply the numerators and put the product over the product of the denominators. For example:

$$\frac{2}{3} \times \frac{6}{5} = \frac{12}{15}$$

REDUCING FRACTIONS

When you add or multiply fractions, you often end up with a big fraction that is hard to work with. You can usually reduce such a fraction. To reduce a fraction, find a factor of the numerator that is also a factor of the denominator. It saves time to find the biggest factor they have in common, but this isn't critical. You may just have to repeat the process a few times. When you find a common factor, cancel it. For example, let's take the product we just found when we multiplied the fractions above:

$$\frac{12}{15} = \frac{4 \times \cancel{3}}{5 \times \cancel{3}} = \frac{4}{5}$$

Get used to reducing all fractions (if they can be reduced) *before* you do any work with them. It saves a lot of time and prevents errors in computation.

DIVIDING FRACTIONS

To divide one fraction by another, just invert the second fraction and multiply:

$$\frac{2}{3} \div \frac{3}{4}$$

which is the same thing as...

$$\frac{2}{3} \times \frac{4}{3} = \frac{8}{9}$$

You may see this same operation written like this:

$$\frac{\dfrac{2}{3}}{\dfrac{3}{4}}$$

Again, just invert and multiply. This next example is handled the same way:

$$\frac{6}{\dfrac{2}{3}} = \frac{6}{1} \times \frac{3}{2} = \frac{18}{2} = 9$$

When you invert a fraction, the new fraction is called a **reciprocal**. $\frac{2}{3}$ is the reciprical of $\frac{3}{2}$.

CONVERTING TO FRACTIONS

An integer can be expressed as a fraction by making the integer the numerator and 1 the denominator: $16 = \frac{16}{1}$.

The GMAT sometimes gives you numbers that are mixtures of integers and fractions, for example, $3\frac{1}{2}$. It's easier to work with these numbers if you convert them into ordinary fractions. Simply multiply the denominator by the integer, and then add the numerator. Because the fractional part of this number was expressed in halves, let's convert the integer part of the number into halves as well:

$$3 = \frac{6}{2}$$

Now just add $\frac{1}{2} + \frac{6}{2}$.

So, $3\frac{1}{2} = \frac{7}{2}$.

COMPARING FRACTIONS

In the course of a problem, you may have to compare two or more fractions and determine which is larger. This is easy to do as long as you remember that you can compare fractions directly only if they have the same denominator. Suppose you had to decide which of these three fractions is largest:

$$\frac{1}{2}, \frac{5}{9}, \text{ or } \frac{7}{15}$$

To compare these fractions directly you need a common denominator, but finding a common denominator that works for all three fractions would be complicated and time consuming. It makes more sense to compare these fractions two at a time. We showed you the classical way to find common denominators when we talked about adding fractions earlier.

Let's start with $\frac{1}{2}$ and $\frac{5}{9}$. An easy common denominator for these two fractions is 18 (9×2).

$$\frac{1}{2} \qquad \frac{5}{9}$$

$$\frac{1}{2} \times \frac{9}{9} \qquad \frac{5}{9} \times \frac{2}{2}$$

$$= \frac{9}{18} \qquad = \frac{10}{18}$$

Because $\frac{5}{9}$ is bigger, let's compare it with $\frac{7}{15}$. Here the easiest common denominator is 45.

Two Shortcuts

One good shortcut when comparing fractions is what we call the Bowtie. The idea is that if all you need to know is which fraction is bigger, you just have to compare the new numerators. To use the Bowtie, simply multiply the denominator of the first fraction by the numerator of the second, and the denominator of the second by the numerator of the first, as shown below.

$$9 \times 1 = \mathbf{9} \quad \frac{1}{2} \diagdown \frac{5}{9} \quad 2 \times 5 = \mathbf{10}$$

$$10 > 9, \text{ therefore } \frac{5}{9} > \frac{1}{2}$$

You could also have saved yourself some time on the last problem by a little fast estimation. Again, which is larger? $\frac{1}{2}$, $\frac{5}{9}$, or $\frac{7}{15}$?

Let's think about $\frac{5}{9}$ in terms of $\frac{1}{2}$. How many ninths equal a half? To put it another way, what is half of 9? 4.5. So $\frac{4.5}{9} = \frac{1}{2}$. That means $\frac{5}{9}$ is *bigger* than $\frac{1}{2}$.

Now let's think about $\frac{7}{15}$. Half of 15 is 7.5. $\frac{7.5}{15} = \frac{1}{2}$, which means that $\frac{7}{15}$ is less than $\frac{1}{2}$.

PROPORTIONS

A fraction can be expressed in many ways. $\frac{1}{2}$ also equals $\frac{2}{4}$ or $\frac{4}{8}$, etc. A **proportion** is just a different way of expressing a fraction. Here's an example:

> If 2 boxes hold a total of 14 shirts, how many shirts are contained in 3 boxes?

Half Empty or Half Full?

In the GMAT, always think about what's left over. If a pizza is three-quarters eaten, there's still one-quarter left.

Here's How to Crack It

The number of shirts per box can be expressed as a fraction. What you're asked to do is express the fraction $\frac{2}{14}$ in a different way.

$$\frac{2\,(\text{boxes})}{14\,(\text{shirts})} = \frac{3\,(\text{boxes})}{x\,(\text{shirts})}$$

To find the answer, all you need to do is find a value for x such that $\frac{2}{14} = \frac{3}{x}$. The easiest way to do this is to cross-multiply.

$2x = 42$, which means that $x = 21$. There are 21 shirts in 3 boxes.

DRILL 3

The answers to these questions can be found on page 300.

1. $5\frac{2}{3} + \frac{3}{8} =$

2. Reduce $\frac{12}{60}$

3. Convert $9\frac{2}{3}$ to a fraction

4. $\frac{9}{2} = \frac{x}{4}$

> Proportions are really ratios. Where a proportion question asks about the number of shirts *per* box, a ratio question might ask about the number of red shirts to blue shirts in a box.

A relatively easy GMAT fraction problem might look like this:

5. $\dfrac{\left(\dfrac{\frac{4}{5}}{\frac{3}{5}}\right)\left(\dfrac{\frac{1}{8}}{\frac{2}{3}}\right)}{\frac{3}{4}} =$

○ $\frac{3}{100}$

○ $\frac{3}{16}$

○ $\frac{1}{3}$

○ 1

○ $\frac{7}{16}$

FRACTIONS: ADVANCED PRINCIPLES

Now that you've been reacquainted with the basics of fractions, let's go a little further. More complicated fraction problems usually involve all of the rules we've just mentioned, with the addition of two concepts: $\frac{part}{whole}$, and the rest. Here's a typical medium fraction problem:

A cement mixture is composed of 3 elements. By weight, $\frac{1}{3}$ of the mixture is sand, $\frac{3}{5}$ of the mixture is water, and the remaining 12 pounds of the mixture is gravel. What is the weight of the entire mixture in pounds?

○ 11.2
○ 12.8
○ 36
○ 60
○ 180

Q: There are only roses, tulips, and peonies in a certain garden. There are three roses to every four tulips and every five peonies in the garden. Expressed as a fraction, what part of the flowers in the garden are tulips?

EASY ELIMINATIONS

Before we even start doing serious math, let's use some common sense. The weight of the gravel alone is 12 pounds. Because we know that sand and water make up the bulk of the mixture—sand $\frac{1}{3}$, water $\frac{3}{5}$ (which is a bit more than half)—the entire mixture must weigh a great deal more than 12 pounds. Answer choices A and B are out of the question. Eliminate them on an erasable board.

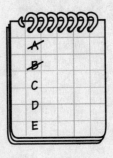

Here's How to Crack It

The difficulty in solving this problem is that sand and water are expressed as fractions, while gravel is expressed in pounds. At first there seems to be no way of knowing what fractional part of the mixture the 12 pounds of gravel represent; nor do we know how many pounds of sand and water there are.

The first step is to add up the fractional parts that we do have:

$$\frac{1}{3} + \frac{3}{5} = \frac{1}{3}\left(\frac{5}{5}\right) + \frac{3}{5}\left(\frac{3}{3}\right) = \frac{14}{15}$$

A: To find the answer, find the *whole*. We know the parts are 3 roses, 4 tulips, and 5 peonies. $3 + 4 + 5 = 12 =$ the whole. What fractional part of the flowers are tulips? 4 out of a total of 12, otherwise known as $\frac{4}{12}$, or $\frac{1}{3}$.

Sand and water make up 14 parts out of the whole of 15. This means that gravel makes up what is left over—the rest: 1 part out of the whole of 15. Now the problem is simple. Set up a proportion between parts and weights.

$$\frac{1}{15} = \frac{12}{x} \quad \begin{array}{l} \text{pounds (of gravel)} \\ \text{pounds (total pounds)} \end{array}$$

Cross-multiply: $x = 180$. The answer is choice E.

DECIMALS ARE REALLY FRACTIONS

A decimal can be expressed as a fraction, and a fraction can be expressed as a decimal.

$$0.6 = \frac{6}{10}, \text{ which can be reduced to } \frac{3}{5}$$

$$\frac{3}{5} \text{ is the same thing as } 3 \div 5$$

Which would you rather figure out—the square of $\frac{1}{4}$ or the square of 0.25? There may be a few of you out there who've had so much practice with decimals in your work that you prefer decimals to fractions, but for the rest of us, fractions are infinitely easier to deal with.

Occasionally, you will have to work with decimals. Whenever possible, however, convert decimals to fractions. It will save time and eliminate careless mistakes. In fact, it makes sense to memorize the fractional equivalent of some commonly used decimals:

$$0.2 = \frac{1}{5} \qquad\qquad\qquad 0.6 = \frac{3}{5}$$

$$0.25 = \frac{1}{4} \qquad\qquad\qquad 0.\overline{66} = \frac{2}{3}$$

$$0.\overline{33} = \frac{1}{3} \qquad\qquad\qquad 0.75 = \frac{3}{4}$$

$$0.4 = \frac{2}{5} \qquad\qquad\qquad 0.8 = \frac{4}{5}$$

$$0.5 = \frac{1}{2}$$

ADDING AND SUBTRACTING DECIMALS

To add or subtract decimals, just line up the decimal points and proceed as usual. Adding 6, 2.5, and 0.3 looks like this:

$$
\begin{array}{r}
6.0 \\
2.5 \\
+\ 0.3 \\
\hline
8.8
\end{array}
$$

MULTIPLYING DECIMALS

To multiply decimals, simply ignore the decimal points and multiply the two numbers. When you've finished, count all the digits that were to the right of the decimal points in the original numbers you multiplied. Now place the decimal point in your answer so that there are the same number of digits to the right of it. Here are two examples:

$0.3 \times 0.7 = 0.21$
There were a total of two digits to the right of the decimal point in the original numbers, so we place the decimal so that there are two digits to the right in the answer.

$14.3 \times .232 = 3.3176$
There were a total of four digits to the right of the decimal point in the original numbers, so we place the decimal so that there are four digits to the right in the answer.

DIVIDING DECIMALS

The best way to divide one decimal by another is to convert the number you are dividing by (in mathematical terminology, the **divisor**) into a whole number. You do this simply by moving the decimal point as many places as necessary. This works as long as you remember to move the decimal point in the number that you are *dividing* (in mathematical terminology, the **dividend**) the same number of spaces.

For example, to divide 12 by 0.6, set it up the way you would an ordinary division problem: $0.6\overline{)12}$.

To make 0.6 (the divisor) a whole number, you simply move the decimal point over one place to the right. You must also move the decimal one place to the right in the dividend. Now the operation looks like this:

$$6\overline{)120}$$

$$
\begin{array}{r}
20 \\
6\overline{)120}
\end{array}
$$

ROUNDING OFF DECIMALS

9.4 rounded to the nearest whole number is 9.
9.5 rounded to the nearest whole number is 10.

To round off a decimal, look at the digit to the right of the digits place you are rounding to. If that number is 0–4, there is no change. If that number is 5–9, round up.

When GMAC asks you to give an approximate answer on an easy question, it is safe to round off numbers. But you should be leery about rounding off numbers on a difficult question. If you're scoring in a high percentile, rounding off numbers will be useful to eliminate answer choices that are out of the ballpark, but not to decide between two close answer choices.

DRILL 4

The answers to these questions can be found on page 300.

1.
$$\begin{array}{r} 34.26 \\ -\ 0.96 \\ \hline \end{array}$$

2.
$$\begin{array}{r} 27.3 \\ \times\ 9.75 \\ \hline \end{array}$$

3. $\dfrac{19.6}{3.22}$

4. $\dfrac{\dfrac{4}{0.25}}{\dfrac{1}{50}}$

On the GMAT, there might be questions that mix decimals and fractions:

5. $\dfrac{\dfrac{3}{10}\times 4\times 0.8}{0.32}$

- ○ 0.96
- ○ 0.333
- ○ 3.0
- ○ 30.0
- ○ 96.0

RATIOS

Ratios are close relatives of fractions. A ratio can be expressed as a fraction and vice versa. The ratio 3 to 4 can be written as $\frac{3}{4}$ as well as in standard ratio format: 3 : 4.

THERE IS ONLY ONE DIFFERENCE BETWEEN A RATIO AND A FRACTION

One way of defining the *fraction* $\frac{3}{4}$ is to say that there are 3 equal parts out of a whole of 4. However, let's take the ratio of 3 women to 4 men in a room, which could also be expressed as $\frac{3}{4}$. Is 4 the whole in this ratio? Of course not. There are 3 women and 4 men, giving a total of 7 people in the room. The whole in a ratio is the sum of all the parts. If the ratio is expressed as a fraction, the whole is the sum of the numerator and the denominator.

> **Fraction:**
> $\dfrac{\text{part: 3 women}}{\text{whole: 7 people}}$
>
> **Ratio:**
> $\dfrac{\text{part: 3 women}}{\text{part: 4 men}}$ (The whole is 7.)

ASIDE FROM THAT, ALL THE RULES OF FRACTIONS APPLY TO RATIOS

A ratio can be converted to a percentage or a decimal. It can be cross-multiplied, reduced, or expanded—just like a fraction. The ratio of 1 to 3 can be expressed as:

$$\frac{1}{3}$$
$$1 : 3$$
$$0.333$$
$$33\frac{1}{3}\%$$
$$\frac{2}{6}$$
$$\frac{3}{9}$$

An Easy Ratio Problem

> The ratio of men to women in a room is 3 to 4.
> What is the number of men in the room if there are
> 20 women?

Here's How to Crack It

No matter how many people are actually in the room, the ratio of men to women will always stay the same: 3 to 4. What you're asked to do is find the numerator of a fraction whose denominator is 20, and which can be reduced to $\frac{3}{4}$. Just set one fraction equal to another and cross-multiply:

$$\frac{3}{4} = \frac{x}{20} \qquad 60 = 4x \qquad x = 15$$

The answer to the question is 15 men. Note that $\frac{15}{20}$ reduces to $\frac{3}{4}$. The two fractions are equal, which is just another way of saying that they're still in the same ratio.

A More Difficult Ratio Problem

> The ratio of women to men in a room is 3 to 4. If
> there are a total of 28 people in the room, how
> many women are there?

This problem is more difficult because, while we are given the ratio of women to men, we do not have a specific value for either women or men. If we tried to set this problem up the way we did the previous one, it would look like this:

$$\frac{3}{4} = \frac{x}{y}$$

You can't solve an equation if it has two variables.

Here's How to Crack It

The trick here is to remember how a ratio differs from a fraction. If the ratio is 3 parts to 4 parts, then there is a total of 7 parts. This means that the 28 people in that room are made up of groups of 7 people (3 women and 4 men in each group). How many groups of 7 people make up 28 people? 4 groups ($4 \times 7 = 28$).

If there are 4 groups—each made up of 3 women and 4 men—the total number of women would be 4×3, or 12. The number of men would be 4×4, or 16. To check this, make sure that $\frac{12}{16}$ equals $\frac{3}{4}$ (it does) and that 12 + 16 adds up to 28 (it does).

PERCENTAGES

A **percentage** is just a fraction in which the denominator is always equal to 100. Fifty percent means 50 parts out of a whole of 100. Like any fraction, a percentage can be reduced, expanded, cross-multiplied, converted to a decimal, or converted to another fraction. $50\% = \dfrac{1}{2} = 0.5$

AN EASY PERCENT PROBLEM

The number 5 is what percent of the number 20?

Here's How to Crack It

Whenever you see a percent problem, you should be thinking $\dfrac{\text{part}}{\text{whole}}$. In this case, the question asks you to expand $\dfrac{5}{20}$ into another fraction in which the denominator is 100.

$$\frac{\text{part}}{\text{whole}} = \frac{5}{20} = \frac{x}{100}$$

$$500 = 20x$$

$$x = 25$$

$$\frac{x}{100} = 25\%$$

PERCENT SHORTCUTS

In the last problem, reducing $\dfrac{5}{20}$ to $\dfrac{1}{4}$ would have saved you time if you knew that $\dfrac{1}{4} = 25\%$. Here are some fractions and decimals whose percent equivalents you should know:

$$\frac{1}{4} = 0.25 = 25\%$$

$$\frac{1}{2} = 0.50 = 50\%$$

$$\frac{1}{3} = 0.333... \text{ (a repeating decimal)} = 33\frac{1}{3}\%$$

$$\frac{1}{5} = .20 = 20\%$$

Some percentages simply involve moving a decimal point: To get 10 percent of any number, you simply move the decimal point of that number over one place to the left:

$$10\% \text{ of } 6 = 0.6$$

$$10\% \text{ of } 60 = 6$$

$$10\% \text{ of } 600 = 60$$

Q: What is $\dfrac{1}{4}\%$ of 40?

- To get 1 percent of any number, you just move the decimal point of that number over two places to the left:

$$1\% \text{ of } 600 = 6$$

$$1\% \text{ of } 60 = 0.6$$

$$1\% \text{ of } 6 = 0.06$$

- To find a more complicated percentage, it's easy to break the percentage down into easy-to-find chunks:

20% of 60: 10% of 60 = 6; 20% of 60 is double 10%, so the answer is 2 × 6, or 12.

30% of 60: 10% of 60 = 6; 30% of 60 is three times 10%, so the answer is 3 × 6, or 18.

3% of 200: 1% of 200 = 2; 3% of 200 is just three times 1%, so the answer is 3 × 2, or 6.

23% of 400: 10% of 400 = 40. Therefore 20% equals 2 × 40, or 80.

1% of 400 = 4. Therefore 3% equals 3 × 4, or 12.

Putting it all together, 23% of 400 equals 80 + 12, or 92.

A MEDIUM PERCENT PROBLEM

Like medium and difficult fraction problems, medium and difficult percent problems often involve remembering the principles of $\dfrac{\text{part}}{\text{whole}}$ and the rest.

A motor pool has 300 vehicles of which 30% are trucks. 20% of all the vehicles in the motor pool are diesel, including 15 trucks. What percent of the motor pool is composed of vehicles that are neither trucks nor diesel?

○   165%
○   90%
○   65%
○   55%
○   10%

Here's How to Crack It

Do this problem one sentence at a time.

1. A motor pool has 300 vehicles, of which 30% are trucks. 30% of 300 = 90 trucks, which means that 210 (the rest) are *not* trucks.

2. 20% of all the vehicles are diesel, including 15 trucks. 20% of 300 = 60 diesel vehicles, 15 of which are trucks, which means there are 45 diesel vehicles that are *not* trucks.

3. What percent of the motor pool is composed of vehicles that are neither truck nor diesel? We know from sentence number 1 that there are 210 nontrucks. We know from sentence number 2 that of these 210 nontrucks, 45 are diesel. Therefore 210 – 45, or 165, are neither diesel nor truck.

The question asks what percent of the entire motor pool these 165 nondiesel nontrucks are.

$$\frac{165}{300} = \frac{x}{100} \qquad 300x = 16,500$$

$x = 55$ and the answer is choice D.

> There's a handy formula for calculating mixed groups. It isn't a priority for you to memorize (you just saw the problem calculated without it), but the formula can be helpful on some questions. Here it is: Group 1 + Group 2 – both + neither = total. Here's what that looks like using the numbers from the vehicle problem. 90 trucks + 60 diesel – 15 diesel trucks + x = 300. 135 + x = 300. x = 165, or 55% of 300.

EASY ELIMINATIONS

1. Because the problem asks us to find a portion of the entire motor pool, it's impossible for that portion to be larger than the motor pool itself. Therefore answer choice A, 165%, is crazy. Also, answer choice A was a trap for people who successfully got all the way to the end of the problem and then forgot that the answer was supposed to be expressed as a percent, not as a specific number.

2. If the problem simply asked what percent of the motor pool was not made up of trucks, the answer would be 70%. But because there is a further condition (the vehicles must be both nontruck and nondiesel), the answer must be even less than 70%. This makes answer choice B impossible, too.

3. Answer choice C is probably a Joe Bloggs answer. You can get it simply by adding 30 + 20 + 15.

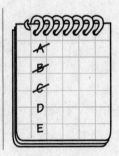

PERCENT INCREASE OR DECREASE

Another type of percent problem you may see on the GMAT has to do with *percentage increase* or *percentage decrease*. In these problems the trick is always to put the increase or decrease in terms of the *original* amount. See the following example:

The cost of a one-family home was $120,000 in 1980. In 1988, the price had increased to $180,000. What was the percent increase in the cost of the home?

○   60%
○   50%
○   55%
○   40%
○   33.3%

Here's How to Crack It

The actual increase was $60,000. To find the percent increase, set up the following equation:

$$\frac{\text{amount of increase}}{\text{original amount}} = \frac{x}{100}$$

In this case, $\dfrac{\$60,000}{\$120,000} = \dfrac{x}{100}$. So, $x = 50$ and the answer is choice B.

To solve a percentage *decrease* problem, simply put the amount of the decrease over the original amount.

COMPOUND INTEREST

Another type of percentage problem involves **compound interest**. If you kept $1,000 in the bank for a year at 6% simple interest, you would get $60 in interest at the end of the year. Compound interest would pay you slightly more. Let's look at a compound-interest problem:

Ms. Lopez deposits $100 in an account that pays 20% interest, compounded semiannually. How much money will there be in the account at the end of one year?

○ $118.00
○ $120.00
○ $121.00
○ $122.00
○ $140.00

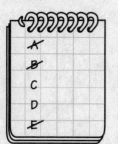

EASY ELIMINATIONS

Joe Bloggs doesn't know how to find compound interest, so he finds simple interest instead. In a compound-interest problem, always calculate simple interest first. $100 at 20% simple interest for one year would turn into $120, which is answer choice B. Because compound interest is always a *little bit* more than simple interest, we can eliminate answer choices A and B. Answer choice E is a great deal more than simple interest, so we can eliminate it, too. Only answer choices C and D are a *little bit* more than simple interest. We're down to a fifty-fifty guess.

Here's How to Crack It

To find compound interest, divide the interest into as many parts as are being compounded. For example, if you're compounding interest semiannually, you divide the interest into two equal parts. If you're compounding quarterly, you divide the interest into four equal parts.

When Ms. Lopez deposited $100 into her account at a rate of 20% compounded semiannually, the bank divided the interest into two equal parts. Halfway through the year, the bank put the first half of the interest into her account. In this case, because the full rate was 20% compounded semiannually, the bank deposited 10% of $100 (10% of $100 = $10). Halfway through the year, Ms. Lopez had $110.

For the second half of the year, the bank paid 10% interest on the $110 (10% of $110 = $11). At the end of the year, Ms. Lopez had $121.00 in her account. She earned $1 more than she would have earned if the account had paid only simple interest. The answer is choice C.

AVERAGES

To find the **average** of a set of n numbers, you simply add the numbers and divide by n. For example:

$$\text{The average of 10, 3, and 5 is } \frac{10+3+5}{3} = 6$$

A good way to handle average problems is to set them up in the same way every time. Whenever you see the word *average*, you should think:

$$\frac{\text{total sum of the items}}{\text{total number of the items}} = \text{average}$$

Reminder!

Averaging problems often have easy eliminations, so be sure to look for them—*before* you solve.

A ONE-STEP AVERAGE PROBLEM

In a simple problem, GMAC will give you two parts of this equation, and it will be up to you to figure out the third. For example, the test writers might ask:

What is the average of the numbers 3, 4, 5, and 8?

Here's How to Crack It

In this case they've given us the actual numbers, which means we know the total sum (3 + 4 + 5 + 8 = 20) and the total number of items (there are four numbers). What we're missing is the average.

$$\frac{\text{total sum of the items}}{\text{total number of the items}} = \text{average} \qquad \frac{20}{4} = x \qquad x = 5$$

Or the test writers might ask:

> If the average of 7 numbers is 5, what is the sum
> of the numbers?

Here's How to Crack It
In this case we know the total number of items and the average, but not the total sum of the numbers.

$$\frac{\text{total sum of the items}}{\text{total number of the items}} = \text{average} \qquad \frac{x}{7} = 5 \qquad x = 35$$

A TWO-STEP AVERAGE PROBLEM
This is the same problem you just did, made a little more difficult:

> The average of 7 numbers is 5. If two of the
> numbers are 11 and 14, what is the average of the
> remaining numbers?

Here's How to Crack It
Always set up an average problem the way we showed you above. With more complicated average problems, take things one sentence at a time. The first sentence yields:

$$\frac{\text{total sum of the items}}{\text{total number of the items}} = \text{average} \qquad \frac{x}{7} = 5 \qquad x = 35$$

The sum of *all* the numbers is 35. If two of those numbers are 11 and 14, then the sum of the remaining numbers is 35 − (11 + 14), or 10. The question asks, "what is the average of the remaining numbers?" Again, let's set this up properly:

$$\frac{\text{total sum of the remaining numbers}}{\text{total number of the remaining numbers}} = \text{average} \qquad \frac{10}{5} = y \quad y = 2$$

Why did we divide the total sum of the remaining numbers by 5? There were only 5 remaining numbers!

MEANS
When a question refers to an average, the words "arithmetic mean" will often follow in parentheses. This is not just to make the problem sound scarier. **Arithmetic mean** is the precise term for the process of finding an average that we've illustrated in the problems above.

MEDIANS AND MODES

Calculating the average of a set of numbers is one way to find the "middle" of these numbers, but there are two other ways that yield slightly different results. To find the **median** of a set of n numbers, just reorder the numbers from least to greatest, and pick the middle number.

If n is odd, this is a piece of cake:

The median of 4, 7, 12, 14, 20 = 12.

If n is even, just add the two middle numbers together and divide by 2:

The median of 4, 12, 14, 20 = $\dfrac{12+14}{2}$ = 13.

To find the **mode** of a set of n numbers, just pick the number that occurs most frequently...

The mode of 5, 6, 3, 9, 3, 28, 3, 5 = 3.

...but remember that a set of numbers *can* have more than one mode:

The modes of 3, 3, 3, 4, 5, 5, 5 = both 3 and 5.

Here's a relatively easy problem:

$$\{4, 6, 3, y\}$$

If the mode of the set of numbers above is 3, then what is the average (arithmetic mean) of the set of numbers?

- ○ 7
- ○ 3
- ○ 4
- ○ 9
- ○ 12

Here's How to Crack It

The mode of the set of numbers is 3, which means that y must also equal 3 (because the mode is the number that occurs most frequently in the set). So now all we have to do is find the average of 4, 6, 3, and 3. The correct answer is choice C.

RANGE AND STANDARD DEVIATION

To find the **range** of a set of n numbers, take the smallest number and subtract it from the largest number. This measures how widely the numbers are dispersed.

The range of 4, 3, 8, 12, 23, 37 = 37 − 3 = 34

Another way to measure the dispersion of a set of numbers is **standard deviation**, which measures the distance between the arithmetic mean and the set of numbers. Even if you think you've never heard of this concept before, you've actually seen one example of standard deviation in the form of a graph that is near and dear to the test writers' hearts: the bell-shaped curve.

On the approximate chart below, you'll notice that many people's GMAT scores are clustered around the mean (500), with some people's scores below and other's above. The standard deviation is a number that expresses the degree to which the set of numbers vary from the mean, either above it or below it. The greater the standard deviation, the greater the degree of variation.

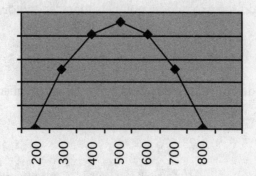

To calculate the standard deviation of a set of *n* numbers (not that the GMAT is likely to ask you to), first find the average (arithmetic mean) of the numbers. Then find the difference between that average and each number in the set and square each of the differences. And finally, find the average of the squared differences and take the square root of this average. The rather intimidating formula looks like this:

$$\sqrt{\frac{\sum(x - \bar{x})^2}{n-1}}$$

But you won't need it.

Standard deviation usually comes down to a single number such as 2.4 or 3.0. Most GMAT questions about standard deviation concern the difference between standard deviation and the mean. Here's a typical problem:

> If the arithmetic mean of a set of numbers is 12 and the standard deviation of that set of numbers is 1.3, then which of the following numbers would be more than two standard deviations from the mean?
>
> I. 14.7
> II. 12.3
> III. 9.3
>
> ○ I only
> ○ I and II only
> ○ II only
> ○ III only
> ○ I and III only

Here's How to Crack It

One standard deviation above the mean of 12 would be 13.3, and two standard deviations would be 14.6. So 14.7 (Statement I) is definitely more than two standard deviations. Is the correct answer choice A? We don't know yet—but we can definitely cross off choices C and D because they don't include statement I. Let's look at Statement II. 12.3 is definitely less than two standard deviations, so we can cross off choice B. Now, you may have wanted to cross off choice E as well, because 9.3 (Statement III) is much less than 14.6—but remember, standard deviation means a deviation either above *or below* the mean. Two standard deviations below 12 would be 9.4, so 9.3 is actually more than two standard deviations from the mean. The correct answer is choice E.

EXPONENTS

An **exponent** is a short way of writing the value of a number multiplied several times by itself. $4 \times 4 \times 4 \times 4 \times 4$ can also be written as 4^5. This is expressed as "four to the fifth power." The large number (4) is called the base, and the little number (5) is called the exponent.

There are several rules to remember about exponents:

- **Multiplying numbers with the same base:** When you multiply numbers that have the same base, you simply add their exponents.

$$6^2 \times 6^3 = 6^{(2+3)} = 6^5 \qquad (y^4)(y^6) = y^{(4+6)} = y^{10}$$

- **Dividing numbers with the same base:** When you divide numbers that have the same base, you simply subtract the bottom exponents from the top exponents.

$$\frac{3^6}{3^2} = 3^{(6-2)} = 3^4 \qquad \frac{x^7}{x^4} = x^{(7-4)} = x^3$$

- **Raising a power to a power:** When you raise a power to a power, you can simply multiply the exponents.

$$(4^3)^2 = 4^{(3 \times 2)} = 4^6 \qquad (z^2)^4 = z^{(2 \times 4)} = z^8$$

- **Distributing exponents:** When several numbers are inside parentheses, the exponent outside the parentheses must be distributed to all of the numbers within.

$$(4y)^2 = (4)^2(y)^2 = 4^2 \times y^2 = 16 \times y^2$$

There are several operations that *seem* like they ought to work with exponents but don't.

- Does $x^2 + x^3 = x^5$?　　　NO!

- Does $x^6 - x^2 = x^4$?　　　NO!

- Does $\dfrac{\left(x^2 + y^2 + z^2\right)}{\left(x^2 + y^2\right)} = z^2$?　　NO!

Means, Medians, and Modes, Oh My!

A: Always remember to reorder the numbers.
In the set of numbers:
{2, 2, 3, 5, 8, 16}
The mean is 6.
The mode is 2.
The median is 4.
The range is 14.

The Strange Powers of Powers

If you raise a positive integer to a power, the number gets larger. For example, $6^2 = 36$. However, raising a number to a power can sometimes have unexpected results:

- If you raise a positive fraction that is less than 1 to a power, the fraction gets *smaller*.

$$\left(\frac{1}{3}\right)^2 = \frac{1}{3} \times \frac{1}{3} = \frac{1}{9}$$

- If you raise a negative number to an odd power, the number gets *smaller*.

$(-3)^3 = (-3)(-3)(-3) = -27$
(Remember, -27 is smaller than -3.)

- If you raise a negative number to an even power, the number becomes positive.

$(-3)^2 = (-3)(-3) = 9$
(Remember, negative times negative = positive.)

- Any number to the first power = itself.

- Any number to the 0 power = 1.

- Any number to the negative power y is equal to the reciprocal of the same number to the positive power y.

  For example, $3^{-2} = \frac{1}{3^2} = \frac{1}{9}$.

Strange Powers Revealed!

Why is any number to the 0 power equal to 1, because any other time we multiply by 0 the result is 0? The answer is that we aren't multiplying by 0 at all. Watch closely now: 3^0 should equal $3^{-1} \times 3^1$, because when you add the exponents you get 3^0. Now, $3^{-1} \times 3^1$ can be rewritten $\frac{1}{3} \times 3 = \frac{3}{3} = 1$.

In other words, when a base is raised to the 0 power it means multiply the base by its reciprocal, an operation that will always equal 1.

RADICALS

The **square root** of a positive number x is the number that, when squared, equals x. For example, the square root of 9 is 3 or -3, because $3 \times 3 = 9$, and $-3 \times -3 = 9$. The symbol for a square root is $\sqrt{\ }$. A number inside the $\sqrt{\ }$ is called a **radical**. Thus, in $\sqrt{4} = 2$, 4 is the radical and 2 is its square root.

There are several rules to remember about radicals:

1. $\sqrt{x}\sqrt{y} = \sqrt{xy}$. For example, $\sqrt{12}\sqrt{3} = \sqrt{36} = 6$

2. $\sqrt{\frac{x}{y}} = \frac{\sqrt{x}}{\sqrt{y}}$. For example, $\sqrt{\frac{3}{16}} = \frac{\sqrt{3}}{\sqrt{16}} = \frac{\sqrt{3}}{4}$

3. To simplify a radical, try factoring. For example, $\sqrt{32} = \sqrt{16}\sqrt{2} = 4\sqrt{2}$

4. The square root of a positive fraction less than 1 is actually larger than the original fraction. For example, $\sqrt{\frac{1}{4}} = \frac{1}{2}$.

Even More Strange Powers

A radical can be rewritten as a fractional exponent, and vice versa. That is, $\sqrt[3]{5} = 5^{\frac{1}{3}}$.

If this all seems a little terrifying, realize that questions that deal with strange powers show up once in a blue moon and only on the very hardest questions.

SUMMARY

1. The six arithmetic operations are addition, subtraction, multiplication, division, raising to a power, and finding a square root.

2. These operations must be performed in the proper order (**Please Excuse My Dear Aunt Sally**).

3. If you are adding or multiplying a group of numbers, you can regroup them in any order. This is called the **associative law**.

4. If you are adding or subtracting numbers with common factors, you can regroup them in the following way:

$$ab + ac = a(b + c)$$
$$ab - ac = a(b - c)$$

This is called the **distributive law**.

5. A fraction can be thought of in two ways:

   A. another way of expressing division

   B. as a $\dfrac{part}{whole}$

6. You must know how to add, subtract, multiply, and divide fractions. You must also know how to raise them to a power and find their roots.

7. Always reduce fractions (when you can) before doing a complicated operation. This will reduce your chances of making a careless error.

8. In tough fraction problems always think $\dfrac{part}{whole}$ and *the rest.*

9. A decimal is just another way of expressing a fraction.

10. You must know how to add, subtract, multiply, and divide decimals.

11. In general it is easier to work with fractions than with decimals, so convert decimals to fractions.

12. A ratio is a fraction in all ways but one:

$$\text{A fraction is a } \dfrac{part}{whole}. \text{ A ratio is a } \dfrac{part}{part}.$$

   In a ratio, the whole is the sum of all its parts.

13. A percentage is just a fraction whose denominator is always 100.

14. You must know the percentage shortcuts outlined in this chapter.

15. In tough percent problems, like tough fraction problems, think $\dfrac{part}{whole}$ and *the rest.*

16. In a percentage increase or decrease problem, you must put the amount of the increase or decrease over the *original* amount.

17. In compound interest problems, the answer will always be *a little bit more* than it would be in a similar simple interest problem.

18. To find the average of several values, add the values and divide the total by the number of values.

19. Always set up average problems in the same way:

$$\frac{\text{total sum of the items}}{\text{total number of the items}} = \text{average}$$

20. To find the median of a set of n numbers, reorder the numbers from least to greatest, and pick the middle number if n is odd. Take the average of the two middle numbers if n is even.

21. To find the mode of a set of n numbers, pick the number that occurs most frequently.

22. To find the range of a set of n numbers, subtract the smallest number from the greatest number.

23. Standard deviation measures the distance between a set of numbers and its arithmetic mean. Most GMAT problems about this concept hinge on the difference between the standard deviation and the arithmetic mean.

24. An exponent is a shorter way of expressing the result of multiplying a number several times by itself.

25. When you multiply numbers with the same base, you simply add the exponents.

26. When you divide numbers with the same base, you simply subtract the exponents.

27. When you raise a power to a power, you multiply the exponents.

28. You *cannot* add or subtract numbers with the same or different bases by adding their exponents.

29. On the GMAT, the square root of a number x is the number that when multiplied by itself $= x$.

30. The two radical rules you need to know:

$$\sqrt{x}\sqrt{y} = \sqrt{xy} \qquad \sqrt{\frac{x}{y}} = \frac{\sqrt{x}}{\sqrt{y}}$$

31. There are some unusual features of exponents and radicals:

   A. The square root of a positive fraction that's less than 1 is larger than the original fraction.

   B. When you raise a positive fraction that's less than 1 to an exponent, the resulting fraction is smaller.

   C. When you raise a negative number to an even exponent, the resulting number is positive.

   D. When you raise a negative number to an odd exponent, the resulting number is still a negative number.

10

Algebra

More than one quarter of the problems on the computer-adaptive GMAT Math section will involve traditional algebra.

In this chapter we'll show you some powerful techniques that will enable you to solve these problems without using traditional algebra. The first half of this chapter will discuss these new techniques. The second half will show you how to do the few algebra problems that must be tackled algebraically.

Is It Worth It?

The average 1998 B-School grad almost tripled his or her pre-M.B.A. salary five years out of school, to $106,000.

Source: *Forbes*, 2003

NOT EXACTLY ALGEBRA: BASIC PRINCIPLES

There are certain problems in math that aren't meant to have just one specific number as an answer. Here's an example:

What is two more than 3 times a certain number x?

To find *one* specific number that answers this question, we would need to know the value of that "certain number x." Here's the way the GMAT would ask the same question:

What is two more than 3 times a certain number x?
- $3x - 2$
- $3x$
- $2x - 3$
- $2x + 3$
- $3x + 2$

COSMIC PROBLEMS

In other words, this is kind of a cosmic problem. GMAC asks you to write an equation that will answer this question no matter what the "certain number" is. x could be *any* number, and that equation would still give you the correct answer.

The test writers expect you to use algebra to answer this question, but there is a better way. Because the correct answer will work for *every* value of x, why not just pick *one* value for x?

We call this **Plugging In**. It is perhaps our most powerful math technique and will allow you to solve complicated problems more quickly than you might ever have thought possible. Plugging In is easy. There are three steps involved:

Plugging In

1. Pick numbers for the variables in the problem.

2. Using your numbers, find an answer to the problem. At The Princeton Review, we call this the target answer.

3. Plug your numbers into the answer choices to see which choice equals the answer you found in step 2.

Let's look at that same problem again:

What is two more than 3 times a certain number x?

- ○ $3x - 2$
- ○ $3x$
- ○ $2x - 3$
- ○ $2x + 3$
- ○ $3x + 2$

Here's How to Crack It

Let's pick a number for x. How about 4? In your scratch booklet, write down "$x = 4$" so you will remember what number you've plugged in. By substituting 4 for the x, we now have a specific rather than a cosmic problem. The question now reads,

"What is two more than 3 times 4?"

$3 \times 4 = 12$

What is 2 more than 12?

14

Using the number we chose for x, the answer to this question is 14. Write 14 down on the erasable board and circle it to indicate that it is your answer. All you need to do now is figure out which of the answer choices equals 14 when you substitute 4 for x.

When you're plugging values in for variables, always start with the first answer choice (what we call choice A). If that doesn't work, try the last choice (choice E), then B, then D, then C. In other words, start from the outside and work toward the center.

(Why do we tell you to do it this way? We've analyzed thousands of GMAT questions and have found that, when the answer choices contain variables, A and E turn out to be correct more often than B, C, and D do. Seem logical? Not at all. But trust us on this one. In general, you'll find the answers faster on these questions if you start with A and E.)

Let's start with choice A, $3x - 2$. Plugging in 4 for x, do we get 14? No, we get 10. Eliminate it.

Go to choice E, $3x + 2$. Plugging in 4 for x, we get $12 + 2$, or 14. This is the answer we wanted. To be absolutely sure, check all the answer choices, but choice E is the correct answer to this question.

WHY PLUG IN? BECAUSE IT MAKES DIFFICULT PROBLEMS EASY!

You might be thinking, "Wait a minute. It was just as easy to solve this problem algebraically. Why should I plug in?" There are two answers:

1. This was an easy problem, but Plugging In makes even difficult problems easy.

2. The test writers have spent hours coming up with all the possible ways you might screw this problem up using algebra. If you made one of these mistakes, your answer would be among the answer choices and you'll pick it and get the question wrong.

SCRATCH WORK

The students in our GMAT course learn to do scratch work automatically. When Plugging In, always write down the number you are plugging in for the variable, and then once you find the answer to the problem in terms of that number, write it down and circle it. Then try each of the answer choices, crossing them off as you eliminate them. Here's what your scratch work should have looked like for that last problem:

Plugging numbers into a problem is much more natural, for most folks, a way of thinking than algebra. Has anyone ever asked a bartender, "Say, could I get 6x of whiskey, where 6x equals a standard shot?" The bartender might comply, but you can be sure he'd ask for your car keys first. Complicate the question with y, the ounces of alcohol in a standard shot, and z, the number of ice cubes in the glass, and you've got a real headache. Essentially, Plugging In is a matter of putting numbers back into a form you are used to working with.

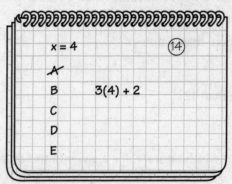

THERE ARE THREE KINDS OF COSMIC PROBLEMS—AND YOU CAN PLUG IN ON ALL OF THEM

You can plug numbers into any problem in which the answer choices are not specific numbers. Try Plugging In if you see:

1. variables in the answer choices

2. percents in the answer choices (when they are percents of some unspecified amount)

3. fractions or ratios in the answer choices (when they are fractional parts or ratios of unspecified amounts)

When you are deciding what number or numbers to plug in, the question to ask is: "What numbers make this problem easy for me?"

VARIABLES IN THE ANSWERS

GMAC wants you to use algebra on problems that have variables in the answers, but Plugging In is easier, faster, and less likely to produce errors. Here's an example:

At a photocopy center, the first 10 copies cost x cents each. Each of the next 50 copies costs 5 cents less per copy. From the 61st copy on, the cost is 2 cents per copy. In terms of x, how much does it cost in cents to have 200 copies made?

- ○ 60x + 30
- ○ 50x − 10
- ○ 50(x − 5)
- ○ 60x − 110
- ○ 10x + 490

Here's How to Crack It

Pick a number for x. How about 8?

The first 10 copies = $10 \times 8 = \underline{80 \text{ cents}}$

The next 50 copies each cost 5 cents less than the first 10, so each of these copies cost $8 - 5$, or 3 cents each.

The next 50 copies = $50 \times 3 = \underline{150 \text{ cents}}$

From now on, the cost is 2 cents for any additional copies. We need a total of 200 copies. So far, we've done 60 copies. We need an additional 140 copies.

The final 140 copies = $140 \times 2 = \underline{280 \text{ cents}}$

$$80 \text{ cents}$$
$$150 \text{ cents}$$

Let's add it all up. $\underline{+ \ 280 \text{ cents}}$

$$510 \text{ cents}$$

This is the answer to the question. All we have to do is find out which answer choice equals 510. Start with choice A, $60x + 30$, and remember that we plugged in 8 for x. Does $60(8) + 30 = 510$? Yes, it does. The answer to this question is choice A. (Try the other choices just to make certain.)

WHAT NUMBER SHOULD I PLUG IN?

While such a problem is designed to work with any number, you'll find that certain numbers work better than others. Plugging in a number that's simple to use is obviously a good idea. In general you should stick with small numbers. But if the problem concerns hours and days, it might make sense to pick 24. If the problem concerns minutes and hours, a good number would probably be 60. So remember, when you are deciding what number(s) to plug in, the question to ask is: "What number(s) make this problem easy for me?"

Avoid 0, 1, and numbers that are already in the problem or the answer choices. Why? If you plug in one of these numbers, you may find that more than one answer choice appears to be correct. We call these numbers "weird numbers" for this very reason.

Sometimes the best way to select a number is to use a little common sense. Here's an example:

> If Jim can drive the distance k miles in 50 minutes, how many minutes, in terms of k, will it take him to drive 10 miles at the same speed?
>
> ○ $\dfrac{500}{k}$
>
> ○ $\dfrac{k}{50}$
>
> ○ $60k$
>
> ○ $10k$
>
> ○ $\dfrac{50}{k}$

Checking Your Work

Because you're plugging in and using real numbers, it's much easier to catch a mistake should you make one. If the numbers you plug in are realistic, the answer should be realistic. If, in solving the copy shop problem, you came up with an answer that indicated making 200 copies cost $500, you'd know you'd taken a misstep. But when you are working with variables alone, it's almost impossible to see what a realistic answer might or might not be. In a sense, by plugging in you're checking your work as you go.

Q: If 80% of a certain number x is 50% of y and y is 20% of z, then what is x in terms of z?

A. $5z$

B. $3z$

C. $\dfrac{z}{4}$

D. $\dfrac{z}{5}$

E. $\dfrac{z}{8}$

Here's How to Crack It

GMAC wants you to write a complicated equation based on the formula *rate × time = distance*, or perhaps set up a proportion. But this isn't necessary. Because there are variables in the answer choices, you can simply plug in.

Any number you choose to plug in for *k* will eventually give you the answer to this problem, but there are some numbers that will make your task even easier.

> If it takes Jim 50 minutes to drive *k miles*, how long will it take him to drive *10 miles* at the same rate?

We need a number for *k*. What if we made *k* = half of 10? See how the question reads now:

> If it takes Jim 50 minutes to drive 5 miles, how long will it take him to drive 10 miles at the same rate?

Suddenly the problem is simple. It will take him twice as long: 100 minutes. Now all we need to know is which of the answer choices equals 100, given that *k* = 5. Start with answer choice A. Divide 500 by 5 and you have 100. Bingo! To double-check, plug 5 into the other answer choices as well. None of them give us the correct answer of 100.

The answer to this question is choice A.

PERCENTS IN THE ANSWERS

GMAC also expects you to use algebra on certain problems that have percents in the answers. Plugging In is the better method. Here's an example:

> A merchant was selling an item at a certain price, then marked it down 20% for a spring sale. During the summer, he marked the item down another 20% from its spring price. If the item sold at the summer price, what percent of the original price did it sell for?
>
> ○ 40%
> ○ 60%
> ○ 64%
> ○ 67%
> ○ 80%

EASY ELIMINATIONS

This is a difficult question. The first thing to do here is eliminate any answers that are too good to be true. The number 20 appears twice in this problem. Adding them together gives you answer choice A. Eliminate choice A. Joe's favorite answer is probably choice B. Joe reasons that if an item is discounted 20% and then another 20%, there must be 60% left. Eliminate choice B. Choice E seems too large. The answer is probably C or D.

Here's How to Crack It

You may have noticed that while this problem gave us lots of information, it never told us the original price of the item. This is another cosmic problem. GMAC wants you to write an equation that will work regardless of the original price of the item. But because this problem is supposed to work for any original amount, we may as well pick one amount.

Let's plug in 100. *When you are dealing with a percent problem, 100 is usually a convenient number.* The merchant was selling the item for $100. He discounted it by 20% for the spring sale. 20% of $100 is $20, so the spring price was $80. For the summer, he discounted it again, by 20% of the spring price. Twenty percent of $80 is $16. Therefore he took $20 and then $16 off the original price. The summer price is $64.

The question asks what percent of the original price the item sold for. It sold for $64. What percent of 100 is 64? 64%. The answer is choice C.

FRACTIONS OR RATIOS IN THE ANSWERS

You could use traditional math on certain problems with fractions or ratios in the answer choices, and that's what GMAC wants. However, as we've seen before, you'll work more quickly and make fewer mistakes if you use Plugging In. Here's an example:

> Half the graduating class of a college was accepted by a business school. One-third of the class was accepted by a law school. If one-fifth of the class was accepted to both types of school, what fraction of the class was accepted only by a law school?
>
> ○ $\dfrac{1}{60}$
>
> ○ $\dfrac{2}{15}$
>
> ○ $\dfrac{1}{3}$
>
> ○ $\dfrac{1}{2}$
>
> ○ $\dfrac{4}{5}$

Here's How to Crack It

You may have noticed that while this problem gave us lots of fractions to work with, it never told us how many people were in the graduating class. This is yet another cosmic problem. The test writers want you to find a fractional part without knowing what the specific whole is. Because this problem is supposed to work with any number of people in the graduating class, we may as well pick one number.

This problem will work with any number, but some numbers are easier to work with than others. For example, if we chose 47 for the number of people in the graduating class, that would mean that $23\frac{1}{2}$ people were accepted by a business school; while this might make a good plot for a Stephen King novel, wouldn't it be easier to pick a number that can be divided evenly by all the fractions in the problem? One number that is evenly divisible by 2, 3, and 5 is 30. So let's plug in 30 for the number of people in the graduating class.

One half of the class got into business school. $\left(\frac{1}{2} \text{ of } 30 = 15\right)$

One third of the class got into law school. $\left(\frac{1}{3} \text{ of } 30 = 10\right)$

One fifth of the class got into both. $\left(\frac{1}{5} \text{ of } 30 = 6\right)$

GMAC wants to know what fraction of the class was accepted only by a law school. Ten people were accepted by a law school, but 6 of those 10 were also accepted by a business school. Therefore 4 people out of 30 were accepted only by a law school. Reduced, $\frac{4}{30}$ is $\frac{2}{15}$, so the answer is choice B.

ANOTHER TYPE OF PLUGGING IN: PLUGGING IN THE ANSWER CHOICES

Any cosmic algebra problem can be solved, as we have seen, by plugging in numbers. But not all algebra problems are cosmic. What about a problem that asks for a specific numeric answer?

> A company's profits have doubled for each of the 4 years it has been in existence. If the total profits for those 4 years were $30 million, what were the profits in the first year of operation?

There is only one number in the whole world that will answer this question. If you tried plugging in amounts for the first year of operation in hopes of happening upon the correct answer, you would be busy for a very, very long time.

GMAC expects you to use algebra to answer this question. It wants you to assign a variable for the first year's profits, say x, in which case the second year's profits would be $2x$, the third year's profits would be $4x$, and the fourth year's profits would be $8x$. Altogether, we get $15x = 30$, and $x = 2$.

Unfortunately, it is extremely easy to make a mistake when you set up an equation. You could add up the number of x's incorrectly, or think that the profits of the third year were equal to $3x$. While this is not a difficult problem, it does represent the potential difficulties of using algebra.

So why not solve this problem a better way? Take advantage of the fact that each time GMAC asks you to find a specific numeric answer, it is forced to give you five clues. Here is how GMAC would ask this question:

> A company's profits have doubled for each of the 4 years it has been in existence. If the total profits for the last 4 years were $30 million, what were the profits in the first year of operation?
>
> ○ $1 million
> ○ $2 million
> ○ $4 million
> ○ $4.5 million
> ○ $6 million

Here's How to Crack It

Without answer choices this problem is complicated, and the only way to solve it is to use algebra. Now, however, there are only five possible answers. One of them has to be correct. Why not work backward and plug the answer choices back into the problem?

Plugging In the Answers is easy. There are three steps involved:

1. Numeric answers on the GMAT are always given in order of size (with one or two rare exceptions). Therefore, always start with the middle answer choice (what we call choice C). Plug that number into the problem and see whether it makes the problem work.

2. If choice C is too small, try the next larger number.

3. If choice C is too big, try the next smaller number.

Let's try answer choice C:

If the first year's profits were	$4 million
the second year's profits would be	$8 million
the third year's profits would be	$16 million
and the fourth year's profits would be	$32 million
the total profits =	$60 million

This is too big. The total profits were only $30 million. We don't even have to look at choice D or E, which are even bigger. We can eliminate choices C, D, and E.

Let's try answer choice B:

If the first year's profits were	$2 million
the second year's profits would be	$4 million
the third year's profits would be	$8 million
and the fourth year's profits would be	$16 million
the total profits =	$30 million

Bingo! The correct answer is choice B. Note that if choice B had been too big, the only possible answer would have been choice A.

Q: Patrick reads twice as much as Bob but only $\frac{1}{2}$ as much as Amy, and Doug reads as much as all three others put together. How many books did Bob read last week if Doug read 7 books?

A. $\frac{1}{4}$ book

B. $\frac{1}{2}$ book

C. 1 book

D. 2 books

E. 4 books

When to Plug In the Answers

You can work backward by Plugging In the Answers as long as:

1. The answer choices are numbers.

2. The question is relatively straightforward. For example, it's easy to plug in the answers on a question that asks, "What is x?" It's difficult and not worth the bother to plug in the answers on a problem that asks, "What is $(x + y)$?"

Let's try another example:

> If x is a positive number such that $x^2 + 5x - 14 = 0$, what is the value of x?
>
> ○ -7
> ○ -5
> ○ 0
> ○ 2
> ○ 5

A: The answer is C. Let's say Bob read 1 book. That means Patrick read 2 and Amy read 4. Doug is supposed to have read as many books as the others put together. Does $1 + 2 + 4$ equal 7? Yes, it does! Be sure to follow these questions carefully. It's Patrick who reads half as much as Amy, not Bob.

Here's How to Crack It

There is only one number in the world that will make this problem work, and fortunately it has to be one of the five answer choices. Let's plug them into the problem and see which one is correct. Start with the middle choice, C. (Zero squared) plus (zero times 5) minus 14 does *not* equal 0. Eliminate it. Let's try choice D. (Two squared) plus (5 times 2)—we're up to 14 so far—minus 14 *does* equal 0. The answer is choice D.

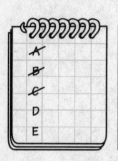

Easy Eliminations

Obviously, if x is a positive number, choices A, B, and C are out of the question.

Plugging In the Answers: Advanced Principles

Sometimes when you're Plugging In the Answers you'll be able to eliminate choice C, but you may not be sure whether you need a larger number or a smaller number. Rather than waste time trying to decide, just try all the answer choices until you hit the right one. You'll never have to try more than four of them.

Today Jim is twice as old as Fred, and Sam is 2 years younger than Fred. Four years ago Jim was 4 times as old as Sam. How old is Jim now?

- ○   8
- ○   12
- ○   16
- ○   20
- ○   24

Here's How to Crack It

One of these five answer choices is the right answer. Let's work backward and find out which one it is.

Start with C. Jim is 16 years old today. He is twice as old as Fred, so Fred is 8. Sam is 2 years younger than Fred, so Sam is 6. Therefore, 4 years ago Jim was 12 and Sam was 2. If these numbers agree with the rest of the problem, then choice C is the answer to this question. The problem says that 4 years ago Jim was 4 times as old as Sam. Does 2 times 4 equal 12? No. Choice C is the wrong answer. Does anybody want to guess which direction to go in now? Rather than hem and haw, just try the other answers until you get the right one.

Let's try choice D. Jim is 20 years old today. He is twice as old as Fred, so Fred is 10. Sam is 2 years younger than Fred, so Sam is 8. Therefore, 4 years ago Jim was 16 and Sam was 4. If these numbers agree with the rest of the problem, choice D is the right answer. The problem says that 4 years ago Jim was 4 times as old as Sam. Does 4 times 4 equal 16? Yes. The answer is choice D.

Must Be/Could Be

From time to time the test writers will give you a question that contains the words "must be," "could be," or "cannot be." This type of problem can almost always be solved by Plugging In, *but you may need to plug in more than one number*. Here's an example:

If x and y are consecutive positive integers, which of the following must be an even integer?

- ○ x

- ○ y

- ○ $\dfrac{xy}{2}$

- ○ $\dfrac{x}{y}$

- ○ xy

Here's How to Crack It

Plug in numbers for x and y. How about 2 for x and 3 for y? Now go through each of the answer choices. Using these numbers, choice A is even, but because of the words "must be," we cannot assume that it will *always* be even, or that this is necessarily the right answer. Keep going. Using the numbers we plugged in, choices B and C turn out to be odd, and D is not an integer. Because the question asks us for an answer that is *always* even, we can eliminate all of these. However, choice E is also even. We're down to either choice A or E. Which is correct?

Try Plugging In a different set of numbers. The problem concerns even and odd numbers, so this time let's try an odd number first. How about 3 and 4? This time choice A is odd. Eliminate it. Choice E is still even; this must be our answer. In "must be" or "could be" problems, it often helps to plug in "weird numbers" such as 1 or 0—the kind of numbers we told you to avoid in regular Plugging In problems. This is because, when solving these problems, we're often looking for a weird, exceptional answer.

BASIC ALGEBRA

Plugging In will take care of most of your algebraic needs, but there are a few other types of problems that require some knowledge of basic algebra. If after reading the next few pages and working out the problems you still feel rusty, you might want to dig out your old high-school algebra book.

SOLVING EQUALITIES

Even the simplest equalities can be solved by Plugging In the Answers, but it's probably easier to solve a simple equation algebraically. If there is one variable in an equation, isolate the variable on one side of the equation and solve it. Here's an example:

If $x - 5 = 3x + 2$, then $x =$

- ○ -8
- ○ $-\dfrac{7}{2}$
- ○ -7
- ○ $\dfrac{10}{3}$
- ○ $\dfrac{7}{5}$

Here's How to Crack It

Get all of the x's on one side of the equation. If we subtract x from both sides we have:

$$\begin{array}{rcl} x-5 & = & 3x+2 \\ -x & & -x \\ \hline -5 & = & 2x+2 \end{array}$$

Now subtract 2 from both sides:

$$\begin{array}{rcl} -5 & = & 2x+2 \\ -2 & & -2 \\ \hline -7 & = & 2x \end{array}$$

Finally, divide both sides by 2:

$$\frac{-7}{2} = \frac{2x}{2}$$

$$x = -\frac{7}{2}$$

The answer is choice B.

SOLVING INEQUALITIES

To solve inequalities, you must be able to recognize the following symbols:

>	is greater than
<	is less than
≥	is greater than or equal to
≤	is less than or equal to

As with an equation, you can add a number to or subtract a number from both sides of an inequality without changing it; you can collect similar terms and simplify them. In fact, an inequality behaves just like a regular equation except in one way:

If you multiply or divide both sides of an inequality by a negative number, the direction of the inequality symbol changes.

For example,

$$-2x > 5$$

To solve for x, you would divide both sides by –2, just as you would in an equality. But when you do, the sign flips:

$$\frac{-2x}{-2} < \frac{5}{-2}$$

$$x < -\frac{5}{2}$$

Q: Are the following equations distinct?
  (1) $3x + 21y = 12$
  (2) $x + 7y = 4$

SOLVING SIMULTANEOUS EQUATIONS

It's impossible to solve one equation with two variables. But if there are two equations, both of which have the same two variables, then it is possible to solve for both variables. An easy problem might look like this:

If $3x + 2y = 6$ and $5x - 2y = 10$, then $x = ?$

To solve simultaneous equations, add or subtract the equations so that one of the variables disappears.

$$\begin{array}{rcl} 3x + 2y & = & 6 \\ + \ 5x - 2y & = & 10 \\ \hline 8x \quad\;\; & = & 16 \end{array}$$

$$x = 2$$

In more difficult simultaneous equations, you'll find that neither of the variables will disappear when you try to add or subtract the two equations. In such cases you must multiply both sides of one of the equations by some number in order to get the coefficient in front of the variable that you want to disappear to be the same in both equations. This sounds more complicated than it is. A difficult problem might look like this:

If $3x + 2y = 6$ and $5x - y = 10$, then $x = ?$

Let's set it up the same way:

$$3x + 2y = 6$$
$$5x - y = 10$$

Unfortunately, in this example neither adding nor subtracting the two equations gets rid of either variable. But look what happens when we multiply the bottom equation by 2:

$$\begin{array}{ll} 3x + 2y = 6 & \qquad 3x + 2y = 6 \\ (2)5x - (2)y = (2)10 \quad\text{or} & \qquad \underline{+\ 10x - 2y = 20} \\ & \qquad 13x \quad\;\; = 26 \quad\; x = 2 \end{array}$$

QUADRATIC EQUATIONS

On the GMAT, quadratic equations always come in one of two forms: factored or unfactored. Here's an example:

$$\begin{array}{cc} \textit{factored} & \textit{unfactored} \\ (x + 2)(x + 5) & = x^2 + 7x + 10 \end{array}$$

The first thing to do when solving a problem that involves a quadratic equation is to see which form the equation is in. If the quadratic equation is in an unfactored form, factor it immediately. If the quadratic equation is in a factored form, unfactor it. The test writers like to see whether you know how to do these things.

To unfactor a factored expression, just multiply it out using FOIL (First, Outer, Inner, Last):

$$(x+2)(x+5) = (x+2)(x+5)$$

$$= (x \text{ times } x) + (x \text{ times } 5) + (2 \text{ times } x) + (2 \text{ times } 5)$$

$$= x^2 + x5 + 2x + 10$$

$$= x^2 + x7 + 10$$

To factor an unfactored expression, put it into the following format and start by looking for the factors of the first and last terms.

$$x^2 + 2x - 15$$
$$= (\quad)(\quad)$$
$$= (x \quad)(x \quad)$$
$$= (x \quad 5)(x \quad 3)$$
$$= (x + 5)(x - 3)$$

Quadratic equations are usually set equal to 0. Here's an example:

> What are all the values of x that satisfy the equation $x^2 + 4x + 3 = 0$?
> ○   −3
> ○   −1
> ○   −3 and −1
> ○   3 and 4
> ○   4

Here's How to Crack It

This problem contains an unfactored equation, so let's factor it.

$$x^2 + 4x + 3 = 0$$
$$(x \quad)(x \quad) = 0$$
$$(x \quad 3)(x \quad 1) = 0$$
$$(x + 3)(x + 1) = 0$$

In order for this equation to be correct, x must be either −3 or −1. The correct answer is choice C.

Note: This problem would also have been easy to solve by Plugging In the Answers. It asked a specific question, and there were five specific answer choices. One of them was correct. All you had to do was try the choices until you found the right one. Bear in mind, however, that in a quadratic equation there are usually two values that will make the equation work.

The Equation Rule

You must have as many equations as you have variables for the data to be sufficient. For example, $x = y + 1$ cannot be solved without another *distinct* equation.

FAVORITES OF GMAT TEST WRITERS

There are two types of quadratic equations the GMAT test writers find endlessly fascinating. These equations appear on the GMAT with great regularity in both the problem solving format and the data sufficiency format:

$$(x + y)^2 = x^2 + 2xy + y^2$$

$$(x + y)(x - y) = x^2 - y^2$$

Memorize both of these. As with all quadratic equations, if you see the equation in factored form, you should immediately unfactor it; if it's unfactored, factor it immediately. Here's an example:

If $\dfrac{x^2 - 4}{x + 2} = 5$, then $x =$

- ○ 3
- ○ 5
- ○ 6
- ○ 7
- ○ 9

Here's How to Crack It

It is unfactored, so let's factor it:

$$\frac{(x + 2)(x - 2)}{(x + 2)} = 5$$

The $(x + 2)$'s cancel out, leaving us with $(x - 2) = 5$. So $x = 7$, and the answer is choice D.

SUMMARY

1. Most of the algebra problems on the GMAT are simpler to solve *without* algebra, using two Princeton Review techniques: **Plugging In** and **Plugging In the Answers**.

2. Plugging In will work on any cosmic problem—that is, any problem that does not include specific numbers in the answer choices. You can usually Plug In if you see:

   - variables in the answer choices

   - fractional parts in the answer choices

   - ratios in the answer choices

   - percentages in the answer choices

3. Plugging In is easy. There are three steps:

   A. Pick numbers for the variables in the problem.

   B. Using your numbers, find an answer to the problem.

   C. Plug your numbers into the answer choices to see which choice equals the answer you found in Step B.

4. When you Plug In, try to choose convenient numbers—those that are simple to work with and make the problem easier to manipulate.

5. When you Plug In, avoid choosing 0, 1, or a number that already appears in the problem or in the answer choices.

6. On problems with variables in the answers that contain the words "must be" or "could be," you may have to Plug In more than once to find the correct answer.

7. Plugging In the Answers will solve algebra problems that are *not* cosmic— in other words, problems that are highly specific. You can always Plug In the Answers on an algebra problem if the answer choices contain specific numbers and if the question being asked is relatively straightforward.

8. Plugging In the Answers is easy. There are three steps:

   A. Always start with answer choice C. Plug that number into the problem and see whether it makes the problem work.

   B. If choice C is too small, try the next larger number.

   C. If choice C is too big, try the next smaller number.

9. If you see a problem with a quadratic equation in factored form, the easiest way to get the answer is to unfactor the equation immediately. If the equation is unfactored, factor it immediately.

10. Memorize the factored and unfactored forms of the two most common quadratic equations on the GMAT:

$$(x + y)^2 = x^2 + 2xy + y^2$$
$$(x + y)(x - y) = x^2 - y^2$$

11. On problems containing inequalities, remember that when you multiply or divide both sides of an inequality by a negative number, the sign flips.

12. In solving simultaneous equations, add or subtract one equation to or from another so that one of the two variables disappears.

11

Applied Arithmetic

It's time to look at some applied arithmetic subjects that GMAT test writers love to use. In this chapter, we'll cover:

1. Rate × Time problems

2. Work problems

3. Function problems

4. Probability problems

5. Permutation and Combination problems

RATE × TIME = DISTANCE

Any problem that mentions planes, trains, cars, bicycles, distance, miles per hour, or any other travel-related terminology is asking you to write an equation based on the formula *rate × time = distance*. This formula is easy to reconstruct if you forget it; just think of a real-life situation. If you drove at 50 miles per hour for 2 hours, how far did you go? That's right, 100 miles. We just derived the formula. The *rate* is 50 miles per hour. The *time* is 2 hours. The *distance* is 100 miles.

> Pam and Sue drove to a business meeting 120 miles away in the same car. Pam drove to the meeting, and Sue drove back along the same route. If Pam drove at 60 miles per hour and Sue drove at 50 miles per hour, how much longer, in minutes, did it take Sue to travel the distance than it did Pam?
>
> ○   4
> ○   10
> ○   20
> ○   24
> ○   30

Here's How to Crack It

As soon as you see the words "drove" and "travel," make a little chart for yourself:

	r	$\times$	t	$=$	d
Pam					
Sue					

The problem says the meeting was 120 miles away from wherever they started. This tells us not only how far Pam drove, but how far Sue drove as well, because she returned along the same route. We are also given the rates of both drivers.

$r \times t = d$ can also be written:

$$t = \frac{d}{r}$$

$$r = \frac{d}{t}$$

It may sometimes be easier, or faster, to start from one of these variations, but if you aren't sure, begin with the standard $r \times t = d$.

Let's fill in the chart with the information we have:

	r	$\times$	t	$=$	d
Pam	60		?		120
Sue	50		?		120

60 times what equals 120? It took Pam 2 hours to drive to the meeting. 50 times what equals 120? It took Sue 2.4 hours to drive back from the meeting. Sue took 0.4 hours longer, but the problem asks for the answer in minutes. 0.4 equals $\frac{4}{10}$ or $\frac{2}{5}$. There are 60 minutes in an hour, so just find $\frac{2}{5}$ of 60. The answer is choice D, 24 minutes.

See your DVD for more.

WORK PROBLEMS

Another type of GMAT problem that requires an equation is the work problem. It is easy to spot because it always involves two people (or factories or machines) working at different rates. In this problem the trick is not to think about how long it takes to do an entire job, but rather how much of the job can be done in *one hour*.

> If Sam can finish a job in 3 hours and Mark can finish a job in 12 hours, in how many hours could they finish the job if they worked on it together at their respective rates?
>
> ○ 1
>
> ○ $2\frac{2}{5}$
>
> ○ $2\frac{5}{8}$
>
> ○ $3\frac{1}{4}$
>
> ○ 4

Here's How to Crack It

If Sam can finish a job in 3 hours, then in one hour he can finish $\frac{1}{3}$ of the job. If Mark can finish a job in 12 hours, then in one hour he can finish $\frac{1}{12}$ of the job. Working together, how much of the job can they do in one hour?

$$\frac{1}{3} + \frac{1}{12} = \frac{1}{x}$$

Now we only need to solve for x. First, find a common denominator for $\frac{1}{3}$ and $\frac{1}{12}$.

$$\frac{1}{3} + \frac{1}{12} = \frac{1}{x}$$
$$\frac{4}{12} + \frac{1}{12} = \frac{1}{x}$$
$$\frac{5}{12} = \frac{1}{x}$$

Cross-multiply and divide.

$$5x = 12$$
$$x = \frac{12}{5} \text{ or } 2\frac{2}{5}$$

The answer is choice B.

Another way to look at this problem is to realize that the actual job is never specified. In other words, this is a cosmic problem, too, and you can plug in a number. Let's say the job is to make 12 widgets. If Sam can finish the job in three hours, how many does he make per hour? If you said 4, you're doing just fine. If Mark can finish the job in 12 hours, how many does he make per hour? That's right: He makes 1 per hour. Working together, they make a total of 5 per hour. Now, how long will it take them to make 12? To find out, simply divide 12 by 5. You get 2.4 altogether—which reduces to choice B.

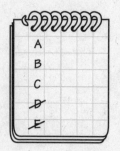

EASY ELIMINATIONS

It stands to reason that two men working together would take less time to finish a job than they would if each of them worked alone. Because Sam, working alone, could finish the job in 3 hours, it must be true that the two of them, working together, could do it in less time. The answer to this question has to be less than 3. Therefore we can eliminate answer choices D and E.

Functions? No Problem

If you can follow a recipe, you can do a GMAT function problem. Because function questions freak so many people out, they often show up in the medium to difficult area of a section. If you can become comfortable with function problems, you'll pick up a point on a question that you might otherwise feel tempted to guess on.

FUNCTIONS

You know you've hit a function problem by the sensation of panic and fear you get when you see some strange symbol ($ or # or * or Δ) and say, "I studied for two months for this test and somehow managed to miss the part where they told me about $ or # or * or Δ." Relax. Any strange-looking symbol on the GMAT is just a function, and on this test, functions are easy.

A function is basically a set of directions. Let's look at an example:

If $x * y = 3x - y$, then what is $4 * 2$?

What the first half of this problem says is that for any two numbers with a * between them, you must multiply the number on the left by 3 and then subtract the number on the right. These are the directions. The second half of the problem asks you to use these directions with two specific numbers: 4 * 2.

To solve this problem, all we need to do is plug the specific numbers into the set of directions:

$$x * y = 3x - y$$
$$4 * 2 = 3(4) - (2)$$
$$= 12 - 2$$
$$= 10$$

Functions don't always involve two variables. Sometimes, they look like this:

If $\Delta x = x$ if x is positive, or $2x$ if x is negative, what is $\dfrac{\Delta 30}{\Delta - 5}$?

- ○ −12
- ○ −6
- ○ −3
- ○ 6
- ○ 30

Let's take this one step at a time. In this case, the directions say that the function of any number x is simply that same number x if x is positive. However, if the number x is negative, then the function of that number is $2x$. Thus:

$$\frac{\Delta 30}{\Delta - 5} = \frac{30}{2(-5)} = \frac{30}{-10}$$ or −3. The answer is choice C.

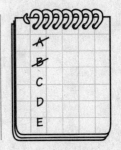

Don't Ignore the Function!

Joe Bloggs always tries to solve function problems as if the function just didn't exist. Eliminate answers to function problems that do this.

Easy Eliminations

Joe has no idea what to do with Δ, so he just ignores it. Because $\dfrac{30}{-5} = -6$, Joe picks answer choice B. On the other hand, Joe might also think he can reduce functions. In other words, he might think he could do this:

$$\frac{\Delta 30}{\Delta - 5} = \Delta - 6$$

The function of −6 = −12, so Joe might also select answer choice A.

One of the most often-used functions on the GMAT consists of a **factorial**: a number followed by an exclamation point. A factorial is the product of a positive integer and all the positive integers less than that number:

$$5! = 5 \times 4 \times 3 \times 2 \times 1 \qquad 3! = 3 \times 2 \times 1 \qquad 1! = 1$$

The only counterintuitive factorial is 0!, which equals 1. Nearly all factorials are positive, because virtually all of them have 2 as a factor. The only odd factorials: 0! and 1!.

PROBABILITY, PART 1

Just the word is enough to cause math phobes to run for the exits—but, at least as it appears on the GMAT, probability really isn't all that bad. Check out the easy example below:

> If you rolled a six-sided die (with faces numbered one through six) one time, what is the probability that it would land with the "2" side facing upward?

See your
DVD for
more.

Well, of course, there's only one possibility of this happening, and there are six possible outcomes, so there's a one-in-six chance. In essence, this is all that probability is about. On the GMAT, probability is usually expressed as a fraction: The total number of possibilities is always the denominator. The number of possibilities that match what you want is the numerator. In the example above, that translates to $\frac{1}{6}$.

Let's make this example a little harder:

> If you rolled a six-sided die (with faces numbered one through six) one time, what is the probability that it would land with either the "2" side facing upward or the "3" side facing upward?

The total number of possible outcomes (the denominator) is still the same: 6. But the numerator is different now. There are two possibilities that would match what we want, so the numerator becomes 2. The probability is $\frac{2}{6}$, or $\frac{1}{3}$.

Let's make the example a little harder still.

> If you rolled a six-sided die (with faces numbered one through six) two times, what is the probability that it would land with the "2" side facing up <u>both</u> times?

Obviously, the odds of this happening are much smaller. How do you figure out the probability of something happening over a series of events? It's actually pretty easy. To find the probability of a series of events, you multiply the probabilities of each of the individual events. Let's start with the first roll of the die. We already figured out that the probability of the die landing with its "2" side facing up on a single toss is $\frac{1}{6}$. Now, let's think about the second toss. Well, actually, the probability of this happening on the second toss is exactly the same: $\frac{1}{6}$.

However, to figure out the probability of the "2" side facing upward on *both* tosses, you multiply the first probability by the second probability: $\frac{1}{6} \times \frac{1}{6} = \frac{1}{36}$.

Here's an example of a moderately difficult GMAT problem.

> There are 8 job applicants sitting in a waiting room—4 women and 4 men. If 2 of the applicants are selected at random, what is the probability that both will be women?
>
> ○ $\frac{1}{2}$
>
> ○ $\frac{3}{7}$
>
> ○ $\frac{1}{4}$
>
> ○ $\frac{3}{14}$
>
> ○ $\frac{1}{10}$

Here's How to Crack It

Let's take the first event in the series. The total number of possibilities for the first selection is 8, because there are 8 applicants in the room. Of those 8 people, 4 are women, so the probability that the first person chosen will be a woman is $\frac{4}{8}$, or $\frac{1}{2}$. You might think that the probability would be exactly the same for the second choice (in which case you would multiply $\frac{1}{2} \times \frac{1}{2}$ and choose answer choice C), but in fact, that's not true. Let's consider: The first woman has just left the room, and they are about to choose another applicant at random. How many total people are now in the room? Aha! Only 7. And how many of those 7 are women? Only 3. So the probability that the second choice will be a woman is actually only $\frac{3}{7}$, which is choice B. But we aren't done yet. We have to figure out the probability that BOTH choices in this series of two choices will be women. The probability that the first will be a woman is $\frac{1}{2}$. The probability that the second will be a woman is $\frac{3}{7}$. The probability that they both will be women is $\frac{1}{2} \times \frac{3}{7}$, or $\frac{3}{14}$. The answer is choice D.

PROBABILITY, PART 2: ONE THING OR ANOTHER

So far, we've been dealing with the probability of one event happening and then another event happening (for example, in that last problem, the first event was choosing a female job applicant; the second event was choosing ANOTHER female job applicant). But what if you are asked to find the probability of either one thing OR another thing happening? To solve this type of problem, you simply add the probabilities. Here's an example:

> 18 children, including Sally and Sam, are watching a magician. The magician summons children up to the stage to assist one at a time. What is the probability that Sally or Sam will be chosen first?

By this point, you should have no problem figuring out that the probability of Sally being chosen first is $\frac{1}{18}$. And the probability of Sam being chosen first? That's right: $\frac{1}{18}$. So what is the probability of Sally or Sam being chosen first?

$$\frac{1}{18} + \frac{1}{18} = \frac{2}{18} \ or \ \frac{1}{9}$$

PROBABILITY, PART 3: THE ODDS THAT SOMETHING DOESN'T HAPPEN

But what if you are asked to find the probability that something will NOT happen? Well, think of it this way: If the probability of snow is 70%, what's the probability that it won't snow? That's right: 30%. To figure out the probability that something won't happen, simply figure out the probability that it WILL happen, and then subtract that fraction from 1. Here's an example:

> 18 children, including Sally and Sam, are watching a magician. The magician summons children up to the stage to assist one at a time. What is the probability that neither Sally nor Sam will be chosen first?

As we already know, the probability that Sally will be chosen first is $\frac{1}{18}$. The probability that Sam will be chosen first is also $\frac{1}{18}$. So what is the probability that neither Sally nor Sam will be chosen first?

$$1 - \frac{2}{18} = \frac{16}{18} = \frac{8}{9}$$

Probability, Part 4: The Odds That at Least One Thing Will Happen

What if the problem asks the probability of something happening at least once? To calculate the probability of at least one thing happening, just use this equation: The probability of what you WANT to happen plus the probability of what you DON'T want to happen equals one. Here's an example:

> 18 children, including 9 girls and 9 boys, are watching a magician. The magician summons a total of 4 children, one at a time, up to the stage to assist. Once a child is finished assisting, he or she returns to the audience, and can potentially be chosen over again. What is the probability that a girl is chosen at least once?

To find out the odds of a girl being chosen at least once, let's begin by figuring out the odds that a girl isn't chosen at all. The magician will make a total of four choices. What are the odds that the magician will not pick a girl in the first round? If you said $\frac{9}{18}$ *or* $\frac{1}{2}$, you are doing just fine. And what are the odds that the magician will not pick a girl the second, third, and fourth round? Each time, the odds of not picking a girl stay the same, because the children are returned to the pool of possible candidates, so each time the odds will be $\frac{9}{18}$ *or* $\frac{1}{2}$. The probability of not picking a girl all four times is:

$$\frac{1}{2} \times \frac{1}{2} \times \frac{1}{2} \times \frac{1}{2} = \frac{1}{16}$$

But we aren't done. The probability of a girl being picked at least once is 1 minus the probability that she will not be picked. So the correct answer is:

$$1 - \frac{1}{16} = \frac{15}{16}$$

PERMUTATIONS AND COMBINATIONS

In general, permutation and combination problems tend to show up as medium-hard to hard problems on the GMAT.

Here's a very simple example of a combination problem:

> At a restaurant, you must choose an appetizer, a main course, and a dessert. If there are 2 possible appetizers, 3 possible main courses, and 5 possible desserts, how many different meals could you order?
>
> ○   60
> ○   30
> ○   10
> ○   6
> ○   3

Here's How to Crack It

You could just carefully write down all the different combinations:

Shrimp cocktail with meatloaf with cherry pie
Shrimp cocktail with meatloaf with ice cream
Shrimp cocktail with meatloaf with…

You get the idea. But first of all, this is too time-consuming, and second of all, there's a much easier way.

> For a problem that asks you to choose a number of items to fill specific spots, when each spot is filled from a different source, all you have to do is multiply the number of choices for each of the spots.

So, because there were 2 appetizers, 3 main courses, and 5 possible desserts, the total number of combinations of a full meal at this restaurant would be $2 \times 3 \times 5$, or 30. The answer is choice B.

PERMUTATIONS: SINGLE SOURCE, ORDER MATTERS

The same principle applies when you're choosing from a group of similar items—with one slight wrinkle. Take a look at this easy permutation problem:

> Three basketball teams play in a league against each other. At the end of the season, how many different ways could the 3 teams end up ranked against each other?
>
> ○   1
> ○   3
> ○   6
> ○   36
> ○   72

Here's How to Crack It

You could just carefully write down all the different combinations. If we call the three teams A, B, and C, then here are the different ways they could end up in the standings:

ABC   ACB   BAC   BCA   CAB   CBA

But again, this approach is time-consuming (even more so for more difficult problems). As you probably suspected, there's a simpler and faster way to solve this problem.

> For a problem that asks you to choose from the same source to fill specific spots, all you have to do is multiply the number of choices for each of the spots—but the number of choices keeps getting smaller.

Let's think for a moment about how many teams could possibly end up in first place. If you said 3, you're doing just fine.

Now, let's think about how many teams could finish second. Are there still 3 possibilities? Not really, because one team has already finished first. There are, in fact, only 2 possible teams that could finish second.

And finally, let's think about how many teams could finish third. In fact, there is only 1 team that could finish third.

To find the number of different ways these teams could end up in the rankings, just multiply the number of choices for first place (in this case, 3) times the number of choices for second place (in this case, 2) times the number of choices for third place (in this case, 1).

$$3 \times 2 \times 1 = 6$$

The correct answer is choice C.

In general, no matter how many items there are to arrange, you can figure out the number of permutations of a group of n similar objects with the formula:

$$n(n-1)(n-2)\ldots \times 3 \times 2 \times 1, \text{ or } n!$$

So if there were 9 baseball teams, the total number of permutations of their standings would be $9 \times 8 \times 7 \times 6 \times 5 \times 4 \times 3 \times 2 \times 1$, also sometimes written as 9!. If 4 sailboats sailed a race, the total number of permutations of the orders in which they could cross the finish line would be $4 \times 3 \times 2 \times 1$, also sometimes written as 4!

SINGLE SOURCE, ORDER MATTERS BUT ONLY FOR A SELECTION

The problems we've shown you so far were necessary to show you the concepts behind permutation problems—but were much too easy to be on the GMAT.

Here's a problem that would be more likely to appear on the test:

> Seven basketball teams play in a league against
> each other. At the end of the season, how many
> different permutations are there for the top 3
> teams in the rankings?
>
> ○   6
> ○   42
> ○   210
> ○   5,040
> ○   5,045

EASY ELIMINATIONS

If you were to see this problem on the actual GMAT, you should first stop and give yourself a pat on the back, because it means you're doing pretty well—permutation and combination problems usually only show up only among the more difficult problems. But after you've congratulated yourself, stop and think for a moment. Could the answer to this difficult problem simply be a matter of finding $7 \times 6 \times 5 \times 4 \times 3 \times 2 \times 1$, choice D? Too easy. Because the question is asking for the permutations for only 3 of the 7 slots, the number must be less than that. So get rid of choices D and E.

Here's How to Crack It

To find all the possible permutations of the top 3 out of 7 baseball teams, simply multiply the number of combinations for each spot in the standings. How many teams are possibilities for the first place slot? If you said 7, you're right. How about for the second slot? Well, one team is already occupying the first place slot, so there are only 6 contenders left. And for the third place slot? That's right: 5.

So, the correct answer is $7 \times 6 \times 5 = 210$, or choice C.

In general, no matter how many items there are to arrange, you can figure out the number of permutations of r objects chosen from a set of n objects with the formula:

$$n(n-1)(n-2)\ldots \times (n-r+1)$$

So if there were 9 baseball teams (n), the total number of permutations of the top 4 teams (r) would be $9 \times 8 \times 7 \times 6$. If 4 sailboats sailed a race (n), the total number of permutations of the first 3 boats to cross the finish line (r) would be $4 \times 3 \times 2$. Another way to write this same formula is found on the following page:

$$\frac{n!}{(n-r)!}$$

(where n = total items and r = the number selected).

Because $9 \times 8 \times 7 \times 6$ is the same as $\dfrac{9 \times 8 \times 7 \times 6 \times \cancel{5}!}{\cancel{5}!}$

COMBINATIONS: SINGLE SOURCE, ORDER DOESN'T MATTER

In the previous problems, the order in which the items are arranged actually matters to the problem. For example, if the order in which the three teams finish a season is Yankees, Red Sox, Orioles—that's entirely different than if the order were Red Sox, Yankees, Orioles.

But combination problems don't care about the order of the items.

> Six horses are running in a race. How many different groups of horses could make up the first 3 finishers?
>
> ○   6
> ○   18
> ○   20
> ○   120
> ○   720

EASY ELIMINATIONS

If we cared about the order in which the top 3 horses finished the race, then the answer would be the number of permutations: $6 \times 5 \times 4$, or 120. But in this case, we only care about the number of *unique* permutations, and that means the number will be smaller because we don't have to count the set of, for example, (Secretariat, Seattle Slew, and Affirmed) and the set of (Seattle Slew, Secretariat, and Affirmed) as two different permutations. If the correct answer must be smaller than 120, then we can eliminate choices D and E—they're too big.

Here's How to Crack It

To find the number of combinations, first find the number of permutations. If 6 horses run in the race, and we are interested in the top 3 finishers, then the number of permutations would be $6 \times 5 \times 4$, or 120. But if we don't care about the order in which they finished, then a bunch of these 120 permutations turn out to be duplicates.

How many? Let's think of one of those permutations. Let's say the first 3 finishers were Secretariat, Seattle Slew, and Affirmed. How many different ways could we arrange these 3 horses? If you said 6, you're thinking like a probability master. There are 3!, or $3 \times 2 \times 1$ permutations of any 3 objects. So, of those 120 permutations of the top 3 horses, each combination is being counted 3!, or 6 times. To find the number of combinations, we need to divide 120 by 6. The correct answer is choice C.

In general, no matter how many items there are to arrange, you can figure out the number of combinations of r objects chosen from a set of n objects with the formula:

$$\frac{n(n-1)(n-2)\ldots\times(n-r+1)}{r!}$$

So if there were 9 baseball teams, the total number of combinations of the top 4 teams would be:

$$\frac{9\times8\times7\times6}{4\times3\times2\times1}$$

Another way to write this same formula is:

$$\frac{n!}{r!(n-r)!}$$

because $\dfrac{9\times8\times7\times6}{4\times3\times2\times1}$ is the same as $\dfrac{9\times8\times7\times6\times5!}{(4\times3\times2\times1)\times5!}$

SUMMARY

1. Any travel-related problem is probably concerned with the formula *Rate × Time = Distance*.

2. The key to work problems is to think about how much of the job can be done in one hour.

3. A function problem may have strange symbols like $, Δ, or *, but it is really just a set of directions.

4. Probability problems can be solved by putting the total number of possibilities in the denominator, and the number of possibilities that match what you are looking for in the numerator.

5. Permutation and combination problems ask you to choose or arrange a group of objects.

   A. To choose a number of items to fill specific spots, when each spot is filled from a different source, all you have to do is multiply the number of choices for each of the spots.

   B. To choose from a set of n objects from the same source to fill specific spots, when order matters, all you have to do is multiply the number of choices for each of the spots—but the number of choices keeps getting smaller, according to the formula:

   $$n(n-1)(n-2)\ldots\times3\times2\times1, \text{ or } n!$$

C. To find the number of permutations of r objects chosen from a set of n objects, when order matters, use the formula:

$$n(n-1)(n-2)\ldots \times (n-r+1), \text{ also expressed as } \frac{n!}{(n-r)!}$$

D. To find the number of combinations of r objects chosen from a set of n objects, use the formula:

$$\frac{n(n-1)(n-2)\ldots \times (n-r+1)}{r!}$$

12

Geometry

Fewer than one-quarter of the problems on the computer-adaptive GMAT will involve geometry. And while this tends to be the math subject most people remember least from high school, the good news is that the GMAT tests only a small portion of the geometry you used to know. It will be relatively easy to refresh your memory.

The bad news is that unlike some standardized tests, such as the SAT, the GMAT does not provide you with the formulas and terms you'll need to solve the problems. You'll have to memorize them.

The first half of this chapter will show you how to eliminate answer choices on certain geometry problems without using traditional geometry. The second half will review all the geometry you need to know in order to answer the problems that must be solved using more traditional methods.

CRAZY ANSWERS

Eliminating choices that don't make sense has already proven to be a valuable technique on arithmetic and algebra questions. On geometry questions you can develop this technique into an art form. The reason for this is that many geometry problems come complete with a diagram *drawn to scale*.

Most people get so caught up in solving a geometry problem geometrically that they forget to look at the diagram to see whether their answer is reasonable.

CRAZY ANSWERS ON EASY QUESTIONS

How big is angle *x*?

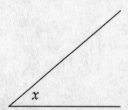

Obviously you don't know exactly how big this angle is, but it would be easy to compare it with an angle whose measure you *do* know exactly. Let's compare it with a 90-degree angle:

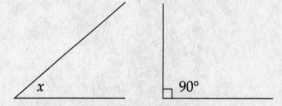

Angle *x* is less than 90 degrees. How much less? It looks as though it's about half of a 90-degree angle, or 45 degrees. Now look at the problem on the next page, which asks about the same angle, *x*.

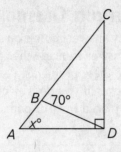

In the figure above, if $BC = CD$, and angle $ADC = 90$ degrees, then what is the value of x?

- ○ 45
- ○ 50
- ○ 70
- ○ 75
- ○ 100

EASY ELIMINATIONS

This is a relatively easy problem, but before you launch into solving it, it's still a good idea to take a moment to decide whether any of the answer choices are clearly unreasonable. We've already decided that angle x is less than 90 degrees, which means that the last answer choice (what we call choice E) can be eliminated. How much less is it? Well, we estimated before that it was about half, which rules out answer choices C and D as well.

There is another way to eliminate choices C and D. We can compare angle x with the other marked angle in the problem—angle DBC. If the answer to this problem is choice C, then angle x should look like angle DBC. Does it? No. Angle x looks a little bit smaller than angle DBC, which means that both choices C and D can be eliminated.

Eliminating crazy answers will prevent you from making careless mistakes on easy problems. (By the way, we'll show you how to solve this problem using geometry later on page 144.)

CRAZY ANSWERS ON DIFFICULT QUESTIONS

If it's important to cross off crazy answer choices on easy questions, it's even more important to eliminate crazy answer choices when you're tackling a medium or difficult geometry problem. On these problems, you may not know how to find the answer geometrically, and even if you do, you could still fall victim to one of the traps the test writers have placed in your path. Take a look at the following difficult geometry problem:

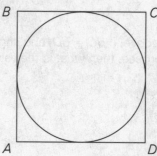

In the figure above, circle C is inscribed inside square $ABCD$ as shown. What is the ratio of the area of circle C to the area of square $ABCD$?

○ $\dfrac{\pi}{2}$

○ $\dfrac{4}{\pi}$

○ $\dfrac{\pi}{3}$

○ $\dfrac{\pi}{4}$

○ $\dfrac{\pi}{5}$

EASY ELIMINATIONS

This is a difficult problem, but before you start guessing at random, let's see whether you can eliminate any of the answer choices just by looking at the diagram and using some common sense.

The problem asks you for the ratio of the area of the circle to the area of the square. Just by looking at the diagram, you can tell that the circle is smaller than the square. The correct answer to this question has to be the ratio of a smaller number to a bigger number. Let's look at the answer choices.

In choice A, the ratio is π over 2. An approximate value of π is 3, so this really reads $\dfrac{3}{2}$.

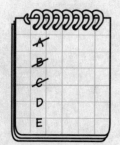

Is this the ratio of a smaller number to a bigger number? Just the opposite. Therefore choice A is a crazy answer. Eliminate it.

In choice B, the ratio is 4 over π. This really reads $\frac{4}{3}$.

Is this the ratio of a smaller number to a bigger number? No. Choice B is a crazy answer. Eliminate it.

In choice C, the ratio is π over 3. This really reads $\frac{3}{3}$.

Is this the ratio of a smaller number to a bigger number? No. Choice C is a crazy answer. Eliminate it.

Answer choices D and E both contain ratios of smaller numbers to bigger numbers, so they're both still possibilities. However, we've eliminated three of the answer choices without doing any math. If you know how to solve the problem geometrically, then proceed. If not, guess and move on. (By the way, we will show you how to solve this problem using geometry later in the chapter.)

THE BASIC TOOLS

In eliminating crazy answers, it helps to have the following approximations memorized.

$$\pi \approx 3$$
$$\sqrt{1} = 1$$
$$\sqrt{2} \approx 1.4$$
$$\sqrt{3} \approx 1.7$$

It's also useful to have a feel for the way certain common angles look:

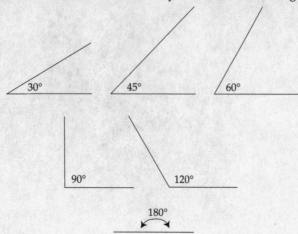

GETTING MORE PRECISE

Q: Is using your marker as a ruler cheating?

When a geometry problem contains a diagram that's drawn to scale, you can get even more precise in eliminating wrong answer choices.

How? By measuring the diagram.

The instructions to the GMAT say that unless a diagram is marked "not drawn to scale," it is drawn "as accurately as possible" in regular problem solving questions. GMAT diagrams can be drawn very accurately indeed. All you need now is something with which to measure the diagram. Fortunately the folks at GMAC provide you with a ruler—the marker that comes with your scratch booklet. By holding it up to the computer screen, you can roughly measure the diagram.

Look at the problem below:

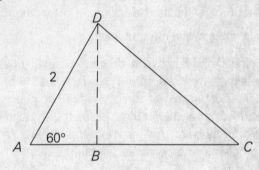

In the figure above, if a line segment connecting points B and D is perpendicular to AC and the area of triangle ADC is $\dfrac{3\sqrt{3}}{2}$, then $BC = ?$

○ $\sqrt{2}$

○ $\sqrt{3}$

○ 2

○ $3\sqrt{3}$

○ 6

Here's How to Crack It

Practice measuring the diagram with your pen or pencil. If you measure carefully, you'll notice that the distance between *A* and *D* is the same as the distance between *B* and *C*—exactly 2. Let's look at the answer choices. Because you memorized the values we told you to memorize earlier, you know that answer choice A is equal to 1.4. Eliminate it. Answer choice B is equal to 1.7. This is close enough for us to hold on to it while we look at the other choices. Choice C is exactly what we're looking for—2. Choice D is 3 times 1.7, which equals 5.1. This is much too large. Choice E is even larger. Eliminate D and E. We're down to choices B and C. The correct answer is choice C.

A: No.

Three Important Notes

1. Diagrams in questions using the problem-solving format may be drawn to scale (unless otherwise indicated), but they are not all drawn to the same scale.

2. Diagrams marked "not drawn to scale" cannot be measured. In fact, the drawings in these problems are often purposely misleading to the eye.

3. Drawings in questions using the Data Sufficiency format of the GMAT are not drawn to scale. They cannot be estimated with your eye or with a ruler.

WHAT SHOULD I DO IF THERE IS NO DIAGRAM?

Draw one. It's always difficult to imagine a geometry problem in your head. The first thing you should do with any geometry problem that doesn't have a diagram is sketch it out in your scratch booklet. And when you draw the diagram, try to draw it to scale. That way, you'll be in a position to estimate.

Geometry Hint

If there's no diagram, draw one yourself.

WHAT SHOULD I DO IF THE DIAGRAM IS NOT DRAWN TO SCALE?

The same thing you would do if there were no diagram at all—draw it yourself. Draw it as accurately as possible so you'll be able to see what a realistic answer should be.

BASIC PRINCIPLES: FUNDAMENTALS OF GMAT GEOMETRY

The techniques outlined above will enable you to eliminate many incorrect choices on geometry problems. In some cases, you'll be able to eliminate every choice but one. However, there will be some geometry problems in which you will need geometry. Fortunately, GMAC chooses to test only a small number of concepts.

For the sake of simplicity, we've divided GMAT geometry into five basic topics:

1. degrees and angles
2. triangles
3. circles
4. rectangles, squares, and other four-sided objects
5. solids and volume
6. coordinate

The 180° Rule, Part I

When you see a geometry problem that asks about angles, always look to see if two angles add up to a line, which tells you that the total of the two angles is 180 degrees. This is often the crucial starting point on the road to the solution. The test writers like to construct problems in such a way that it is very easy to miss this.

DEGREES AND ANGLES

There are 360 degrees in a circle. No matter how large or small a circle is, it still has precisely 360 degrees. If you drew a circle on the ground and then walked a quarter of the distance around it, you would have traveled 90 degrees of that circle. If you walked halfway around the circle, you would have traveled 180 degrees of it.

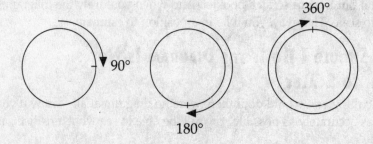

An angle is formed when two line segments extend from a common point. If you think of that point as the center of a circle, the measure of the angle is the number of degrees enclosed by the lines when they pass through the edge of the circle.

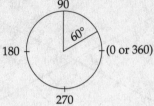

A line is just a 180-degree angle.

Triangles

Triangles are by far the test writers' favorite geometric shape. If you get stuck on a geometry problem that doesn't have triangles in it, ask yourself: Can the figure in this problem be divided into triangles (especially right triangles) that I can work with? This will sometimes be the key to the solution.

ℓ is the symbol for a line. A line can be referred to as ℓ or by naming two points on that line. For example, in the diagram below, both points A and B are on the line ℓ. This line could also be called line AB. Also, the part of the line that is between points A and B is called a line segment. A and B are the end points of the line segment.

If a line is cut by another line, as in the diagram below, angle x and angle y add up to one straight line, or 180 degrees. So, for example, if you know that angle x equals 120 degrees, you can find the measure of angle y by subtracting 120 degrees from 180 degrees. Thus angle y would equal 60 degrees.

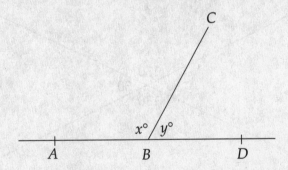

Note that in the diagram above, angle x could also be called angle ABC, with B being the point in the middle.

When two lines intersect—as in the diagram below—four angles are formed. The four angles are indicated by letters.

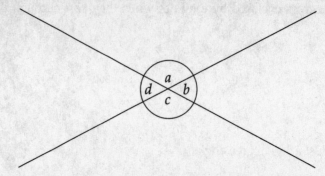

The four angles add up to 360 degrees (remember the circle).

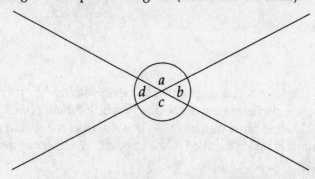

$a + b + c + d = 360$. Angle a + angle b, because they add up to a straight line, are equal to 180 degrees. Angle b + angle c also add up to a straight line, as do $c + d$ and $d + a$. Angles that are opposite each other are called *vertical angles* and have the same number of degrees. For example, in the diagram above, angle a is equal to angle c. Angle d is equal to angle b.

Therefore, when two lines intersect, there appear to be four different angles, but there are really only two:

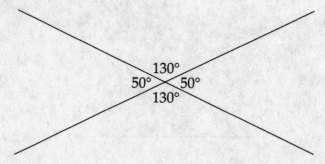

Two lines in the same plane are said to be parallel if they extend infinitely in both directions without touching. The symbol for parallel is ||.

Look at the diagram below:

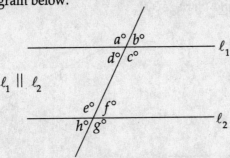

When two parallel lines are cut by a third line, there appear to be eight different measurements angle, but there are really only two.

There is a big one (greater than 90°) and a little one (less than 90°). Angle *a* (a big one) is equal to angles *c*, *e*, and *g*. Angle *b* (a little one) is equal to angles *d*, *f*, and *h*.

If two lines intersect in such a way that one line is perpendicular to the other, all the angles formed will be 90-degree angles. These are also known as right angles:

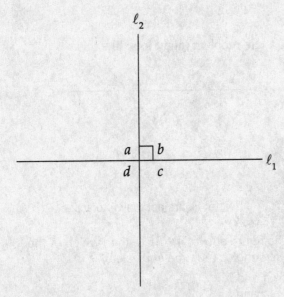

Angles *a*, *b*, *c*, and *d* each equal 90 degrees. The little box at the intersection of the two lines is the symbol for a right angle.

DRILL 5 (ANGLES AND LENGTHS)

In the following figures, find numbers for all the variables. The answers to these problems can be found on page 300.

In a problem solving question, if it doesn't say *not drawn to scale* then it *is* drawn to scale. When they give you a scaled drawing, use it to eliminate answers that are out of proportion.

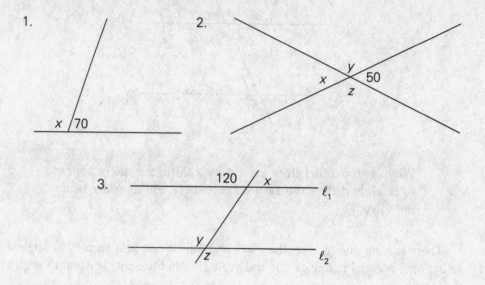

1.

2.

3.

4. If a driver has traveled 270 degrees around a circular race track, what fractional part of the track has he driven?

A real GMAT angle problem might look like this:

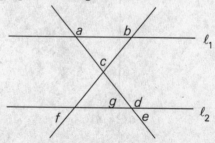

Note: Figure not drawn to scale.

5. In the figure above, if $\ell_1 \parallel \ell_2$, then which of the following angles must be equivalent?
   - ○ *a* and *b*
   - ○ *g* and *f*
   - ○ *d* and *e*
   - ○ *a* and *d*
   - ○ *f* and *d*

TRIANGLES

A triangle is a three-sided figure that contains three interior angles. The interior angles of a triangle always add up to 180 degrees. Several kinds of triangles appear on the GMAT:

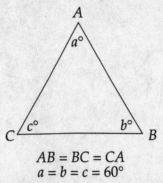

$$AB = BC = CA$$
$$a = b = c = 60°$$

An **equilateral triangle** has three sides that are equal in length. Because the angles opposite equal sides are also equal, all three angles in an equilateral triangle are equal.

An **isosceles triangle** has two sides that are equal in length. The angles opposite the two equal sides are also equal.

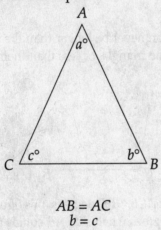

$$AB = AC$$
$$b = c$$

A **right triangle** has one interior angle that is equal to 90 degrees. The longest side of a right triangle (the one opposite the 90-degree angle) is called the *hypotenuse.*

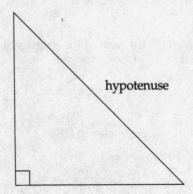

The 180° Rule, Part II

When a question involving angles has a triangle or several triangles in it, remember that the interior angles of a triangle add up to 180 degrees. Apply that rule in every possible way you can. It is one of the things that the GMAT writers love to test most.

EVERYTHING ELSE YOU NEED TO KNOW ABOUT TRIANGLES

1. The sides of a triangle are in the same proportion as its angles. For example, in the triangle below, which is the longest side?

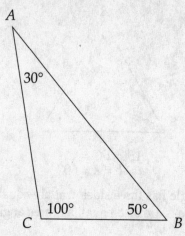

The longest side is opposite the largest angle. The longest side in the triangle above is *AB*. The next longest side would be *AC*.

2. One side of a triangle can never be longer than the sum of the lengths of the other two sides of the triangle, or less than their difference. Why? Look at the diagrams below:

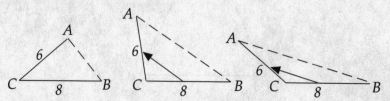

At the point where angle *ACB* = 180 degrees, this figure ceases to be a triangle. Angle *ACB* becomes 180 degrees when side *AB* equals the sum of the other two sides, in this case 6 + 8. Side *AB* can never quite reach 14.

By the same token, if we make angle *ACB* smaller and smaller, at some point, when angle *ACB* = 0 degrees, the figure also ceases to be a triangle. Angle *ACB* becomes 0 degrees when side *AB* equals the difference of the other two sides, in this case 8 − 6. So *AB* can never quite reach 2.

3. The *perimeter* of a triangle is the sum of the lengths of the three sides.

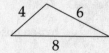

perimeter = 18

4. The *area* of a triangle is equal to $\dfrac{height \times base}{2}$.

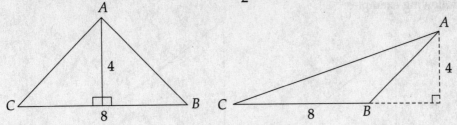

In both of the above triangles, the area = $\dfrac{4 \times 8}{2}$ = 16.

In a right triangle, the height also happens to be one of the sides of the triangle:

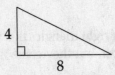

5. Don't expect triangles to be right side up:

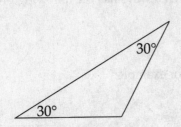

This is an isosceles triangle.

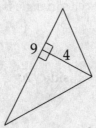

The area of this triangle is $\dfrac{9 \times 4}{2}$, or 18.

6. In a right triangle, the square of the hypotenuse equals the sum of the squares of the other two sides. In the triangle below:

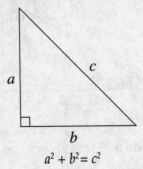

$$a^2 + b^2 = c^2$$

This is called the **Pythagorean theorem**. The test writers love to test this theorem, but usually you won't actually have to make use of it if you've memorized a few of the most common right-triangle proportions.

Pythagoras's Other Theorem

Pythagoras also developed a theory about the transmigration of souls. So far, this theory has not been proven.

The Pythagorean triangle that comes up most frequently on the GMAT is one that has sides of lengths 3, 4, and 5, or multiples of those numbers. Look at the following examples:

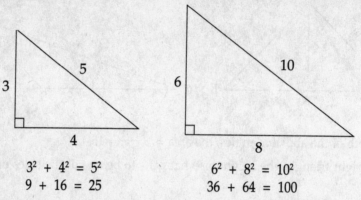

$$3^2 + 4^2 = 5^2$$
$$9 + 16 = 25$$

$$6^2 + 8^2 = 10^2$$
$$36 + 64 = 100$$

There are two other kinds of right triangles that GMAC loves to test. These are a little complicated to remember, but they come up so often that they're worth memorizing.

7. A right isosceles triangle is one that always has the following proportions:

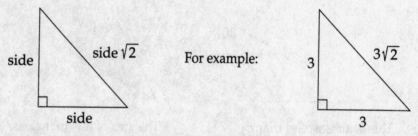

For example:

8. The second special right triangle is called the **30-60-90** right triangle. The ratio between the lengths of the sides in a 30-60-90 triangle is constant. If you know the length of any of the sides, you can find the lengths of the others. Here's the ratio of the sides:

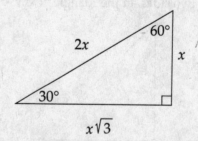

Remembering how to order the 1, 2, $\sqrt{3}$ sides of a 30-60-90 triangle is easy if you remind yourself that the largest side goes opposite the largest angle and the smallest side opposite the smallest angle, *and* if you remind yourself that $\sqrt{3}$ is roughly 1.7, okay?

That is, if the shortest side is length x, then the hypotenuse is $2x$, and the remaining side is $x\sqrt{3}$.

DRILL 6 (TRIANGLES)

Find the value of the variables in the following problems. The answers can be found on page 300.

1.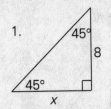

2.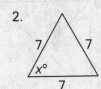

3.

4. What value must x be less than in the triangle below? What value must x be greater than?

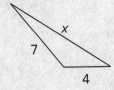

5. In the square $ABCD$ below, what is the value of line segment AC?

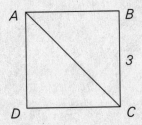

6. In the triangle below, what is the value of the line segment BC?

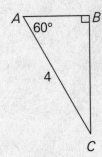

A real GMAT triangle problem might look like this:

7. In the diagram below, if the area of triangle *LNP*
   is 32, then what is the area of triangle *LMN*?

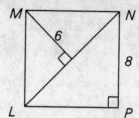

Note: Figure not drawn to scale.

○   24

○ $24\sqrt{2}$

○ $24\sqrt{3}$

○   32

○   48

CIRCLES

A line connecting any two points on a circle is called a **chord**. The distance from the center of the circle to any point on the circle is called the **radius**. The distance from one point on the circle through the center of the circle to another point on the circle is called the **diameter**. The diameter is equal to twice the radius.

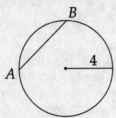

radius = 4
diameter = 8
AB is a chord.

The rounded portion of the circle between points *A* and *B* is called an **arc**.
The **area** of a circle is equal to πr^2.
The **circumference** (the length of the entire outer edge of the circle) is equal to $2\pi r$ or πd.

DRILL 7 (CIRCLES)

Answer the following questions. The answers can be found on page 300.

1. In the circle below with center *O*, what is the area of the circle? What is the circumference?

    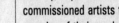

2. If the area of a circle is 36π, what is the circumference?

3. In the circle below with center *O*, if the arc *RT* is equal to $\dfrac{1}{6}$ of the circumference, what is the value of angle *x*?

    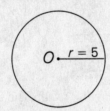

A real GMAT circle problem might look like this:

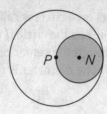

4. In the figure above, *P* is the center of the larger circle, and *N* is the center of the smaller, shaded circle. If the radius of the smaller circle is 5, what is the area of the unshaded region?

○ 100π
○ 75π
○ 25π
○ 20π
○ 10π

RECTANGLES, SQUARES, AND OTHER FOUR-SIDED OBJECTS

A four-sided figure is called a **quadrilateral**. The perimeter of any four-sided object is the sum of the lengths of its sides. A **rectangle** is a quadrilateral whose four interior angles are each equal to 90 degrees.

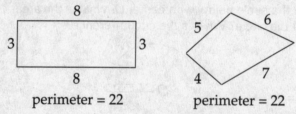

The area of a rectangle is *length × width*. The area of the rectangle above is therefore 3×8, or 24.

A **square** is a rectangle whose four sides are all equal in length. The *perimeter* of a square is therefore just four times the length of one side. The *area* of a square is the *length* of one of its sides squared. For example:

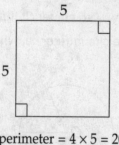

perimeter = 4×5 = 20
area = 5×5 = 25

A **parallelogram** is a quadrilateral in which the two pairs of opposite sides are parallel to each other and equal to each other, and in which opposite angles are equal to each other. A rectangle is obviously a parallelogram, but so is a figure like this:

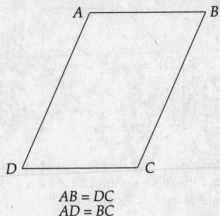

$$AB = DC$$
$$AD = BC$$

Angle ADC = angle ABC, and angle DAB = angle DCB. The area of a parallelogram equals *base* × *height*.

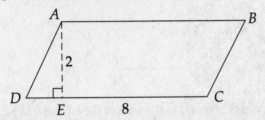

The area of parallelogram $ABCD$ = $8 \times 2 = 16$. (If you are having trouble picturing this, imagine cutting off the triangular region ADE and sticking it onto the other end of the figure. What you get is a rectangle with dimensions 8 by 2.)

SOLIDS, VOLUME, AND SURFACE AREA

The GMAT will occasionally ask you to find the *volume* or *surface area* of a three-dimensional object.

Advance!

With GMAT geometry, just get going. Wade in there and do something. With each piece you add to the puzzle the next piece to look for becomes evident.

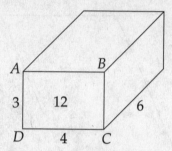

The volume of the *rectangular solid* above is equal to the area of the rectangle *ABCD* times the depth of the solid—in this case, 12×6, or 72. Another way to think of it is *length* × *width* × *depth* = $3 \times 4 \times 6$, or 72.

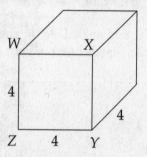

The volume of a *cube* is equal to the area of the square *WXYZ* times the depth of the cube, or again, *length* × *width* × *depth*. In the case of a cube, the length, width, and depth are all the same, so the volume of a cube is always the length of any side, cubed. The volume of this cube is $4 \times 4 \times 4$, or 64.

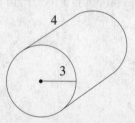

The volume of a *cylinder* is equal to the *area* of the circular base times the *depth*. The area of this circle is 9π. Thus the volume of the cylinder is 36π.

You may need to find the surface area of a solid. Surface area is just the sum of the areas of all the two-dimensional outer surfaces of the object. So, for example, the surface area of a rectangular solid is the sum of the areas of the solid's six faces. Take a look at how you'd calculate the surface area of the rectangular solid on the next page:

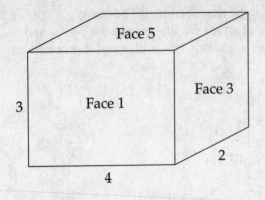

Face 1:	3×4	=	12
Face 2:	3×4	=	12
Face 3:	3×2	=	6
Face 4:	3×2	=	6
Face 5:	4×2	=	8
Face 6:	4×2	=	8
Surface Area:		=	52

COORDINATE GEOMETRY

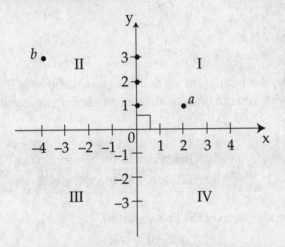

A coordinate plane, like the one above, lets you plot out lines and objects in two-dimensions. If you played the game Battleship as a child, this should feel very familiar—even if you don't remember learning about it in high school. The horizontal line is called the x-axis. The vertical line is called the y-axis. The axes divide the plane into four quadrants as shown above.

Every point on the plane has an ordered pair of numbers (x, y) that describes it. For example, in the plane above, point a is represented by the ordered pair $(2, 1)$ which simply means starting from 0, count over 2 to the right along the x-axis and then up 1. Point b above is represented by the ordered pair $(-4, 3)$, which simply means starting from 0, count over -4 (to the left) along the x-axis, and up 3.

Any straight line on this plane can be described by the equation $y = mx + b$, where b is the y-intercept (the point at which the line crosses the y-axis) and m is the slope of the line. Slope defines whether a line is diagonal, horizontal, or vertical and to what degree.

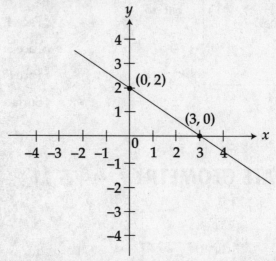

For example, the y-intercept of the line shown above is 2 (that's where it crosses the y-axis). You can find the slope of any line if you know any two points on that line:

$$\text{slope} = \frac{\text{the difference in the } y\text{-coordinates}}{\text{the difference in the } x\text{-coordinates}}$$

For example, the slope of the line above is

$$\frac{2-0}{0-3} \text{ or } \frac{2}{-3}$$

So the equation of this line can be written as $y = \dfrac{2}{-3}x + 2$

Let's see how this might show up in a fairly tough GMAT problem:

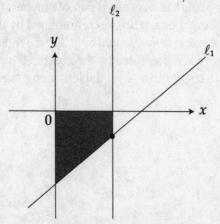

In the coordinate plane above, if the equation of ℓ_1 is $y = x - 3$ and the equation of ℓ_2 is $x = 2$, then what is the area of the shaded region?

(A) 3

(B) 4

(C) $3\sqrt{2}$

(D) 4.5

(E) 5

Here's How to Crack It

First, draw your own coordinate axes. The equation for ℓ_1 is $y = x - 3$, which means that the y-intercept is –3 and the slope is 1. That means the bottommost point of the large triangle is point $(0, -3)$, and the rightmost point of the large triangle is $(3, 0)$. What we have here is an upside-down right triangle with base 3 and height 3. The area of this entire triangle is $\dfrac{b \times h}{2}$ or $\dfrac{9}{2}$, which is choice D, but we aren't done yet. Now we have to find the area of the small triangle, and subtract it from the large triangle. What remains will be the shaded region.

The equation for ℓ_2 is $x = 2$, which means that ℓ_2 is a vertical line running parallel to the y-axis. The small triangle therefore must also be an upside-down right triangle. Its base is 1 (from point $(2, 0)$ to point $(3, 0)$). Eyeballing it, you might decide that its height is 1, too. The way to know for sure is to realize that these two right triangles (the small one and the large one) share an angle formed by the x-axis and ℓ_1. The large triangle is isosceles, so its angles must measure 90-45-45. And since the small triangle shares one of the large triangle's 45-degree angles, we know that the small triangle's third angle must be 45 degrees as well. That means that the small triangle is an isosceles triangle, too, and that its height equals 1, the length of its base. Equipped with this information, we can calculate that the small triangle's area is $\dfrac{1}{2}$. Thus, the area of the shaded region is $\dfrac{9}{2} - \dfrac{1}{2}$, or 4. The best answer is choice B.

GMAT GEOMETRY: ADVANCED PRINCIPLES

All geometry problems (even easy ones) involve more than one step. Remember the first problem we looked at in this chapter?

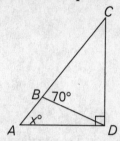

In the figure above, if *BC* = *CD* and angle *ADC* = 90 degrees, then what is the value of *x*?

- ○ 45
- ○ 50
- ○ 70
- ○ 75
- ○ 100

Here's How to Crack It

Just by looking at the figure, we were able to eliminate answer choices C, D, and E. Now let's solve the problem using geometry. The figure includes two—actually three—different triangles: *ABD*, *BCD*, and *ACD*. The test writers want even this easy problem to be a little challenging; there must be more than one step involved. To find angle *x*, which is part of triangles *ABD* and *ACD*, we must first work on triangle *BCD*.

What do we know about triangle *BCD*? The problem itself tells us that *BC* = *CD*. This is an isosceles triangle. Because angle *DBC* equals 70, so does angle *BDC*. Angle *BCD* must therefore equal 180 minus the other two angles. Angle *BCD* = 40.

Now look at the larger triangle, *ACD*. We know that angle *ACD* = 40, and that angle *ADC* = 90. What does angle *x* equal? Angle *x* equals 180 minus the other two angles, or 50 degrees. The answer is choice B.

With GMAT geometry you shouldn't expect to be able to see every step a problem involves before you start solving it. Often, arriving at the right answer involves saying, "I have no idea how to get the answer, but because the problem says that *BC* = *CD*, let me start by figuring out the other angle of that triangle. Now what can I do?" At some point the answer usually becomes obvious. The main point is not to stare at a geometry problem looking for a complete solution. Just wade in there and start.

WALKING AND CHEWING GUM AT THE SAME TIME

Most GMAT geometry problems involve more than one geometric concept. A problem might require you to use both the properties of a triangle and the properties of a rectangle, or you might need to know the formula for the volume of a cube in order to find the dimensions of a cube's surface area. The difficult geometry problems do not test more complicated concepts—they just pile up easier concepts.

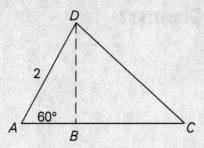

In the figure above, if a line segment connecting points B and D is perpendicular to AC, and the area of triangle ADC is $\frac{3\sqrt{3}}{2}$, then $BC =$

○ $\sqrt{2}$

○ $\sqrt{3}$

○ 2

○ $3\sqrt{3}$

○ 6

Here's How to Crack It

We already got an approximate answer to this question by measuring; now let's solve it using geometry. If we draw in the line DB (which is perpendicular to line AC), we form a 30-60-90 triangle on the left side of the diagram (triangle ADB). The hypotenuse of this triangle is 2. Using the rules we've learned about 30-60-90 triangles, we can conclude that the measurements of triangle ADB are as follows:

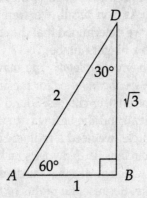

Thus $DB = \sqrt{3}$. At first you might think we're no closer to the solution, but don't despair. Just look for somewhere else to start. The problem tells us that the area of triangle ADC is $\frac{3\sqrt{3}}{2}$. The area of a triangle is $\frac{\text{base} \times \text{height}}{2}$. DB is the height. Let's find out what the base is. In other words, $\frac{\text{base} \times \sqrt{3}}{2} = \frac{3\sqrt{3}}{2}$, so the base equals 3. We know from the 30-60-90 triangle that $AB = 1$. What is BC? 2.

The answer is choice C.

PLUGGING IN ON GEOMETRY?

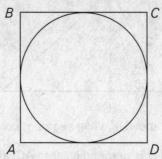

In the figure above, circle C is inscribed inside square $ABCD$ as shown. What is the ratio of the area of circle C to the area of square $ABCD$?

○ $\dfrac{\pi}{2}$

○ $\dfrac{4}{\pi}$

○ $\dfrac{\pi}{3}$

○ $\dfrac{\pi}{4}$

○ $\dfrac{\pi}{5}$

Here's How to Crack It

We already saw this problem in the first half of the chapter when we discussed eliminating crazy answers. As you recall, we were able to eliminate answer choices A, B, and C because we determined that the correct answer had to be the ratio of a smaller number to a bigger number.

Now let's solve this problem completely. You may have noticed that the answer choices do not contain *specific numbers* for the areas of the two figures—all we have here are *ratios* in the answer choices. Sound familiar? That's right! This is just another cosmic problem, and the best way to solve it is to Plug In.

To find the area of the circle, we need a radius. Let's just pick one—3. If the radius is 3, the area of the circle is 9π. Now let's tackle the square. The circle is inscribed inside the square, which means that the diameter of the circle is also the length of a side of the square. Because the radius of the circle is 3, the diameter is 6. Therefore the side of the square is 6, and the area is 36.

The problem asks for the ratio of the area of the circle to the area of the square:

$$\frac{9\pi}{36} = \frac{\pi}{4}$$

The answer is choice D.

SUMMARY

1. While the geometry found on the GMAT is rudimentary, you will have to memorize all of the formulas that you'll need because they are not provided on the test.

2. Always study any problem drawn to scale very closely in order to eliminate crazy answer choices.

3. You must know the following approximate values: $\pi \approx 3$, $\sqrt{2} \approx 1.4$, and $\sqrt{3} \approx 1.7$.

4. You must be familiar with the size of certain common angles:

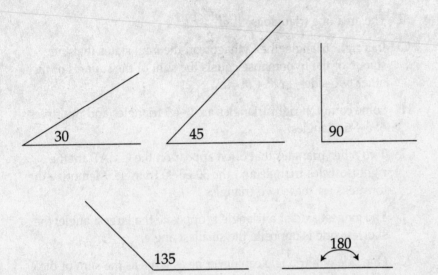

5. You can estimate problem solving diagrams drawn to scale very precisely by using the marker that comes with your scratch booklet.

6. You can *never* estimate from drawings on data sufficiency problems.

7. When no diagram is provided, draw your own, and make it to scale.

8. When the diagram is not drawn to scale, redraw it.

9. Degrees and angles:

    A. A circle contains 360 degrees.

    B. When you think about angles, remember circles.

    C. A line is a 180-degree angle.

    D. When two lines intersect, four angles are formed, but in reality there are only two pairs of identical angles.

    E. When two parallel lines are cut by a third line, eight angles are formed, but in reality there are only two sets of identical angles: a set of big ones and a set of little ones.

10. Triangles:

  A. Every triangle contains 180 degrees.

  B. An equilateral triangle has three equal sides and three equal angles, each of which measures 60 degrees.

  C. An isosceles triangle has two equal sides, and the angles opposite those sides are also equal.

  D. A right triangle contains one 90-degree angle.

  E. The perimeter of a triangle is the sum of the lengths of its sides.

  F. The area of a triangle is $\dfrac{height \times base}{2}$.

  G. In a right triangle, the Pythagorean theorem states that the square of the hypotenuse equals the sum of the squares of the other two sides, or $a^2 + b^2 = c^2$.

  H. Some common right triangles are 3-4-5 triangles and multiples of 3-4-5 triangles.

  I. Two other triangles that often appear on the GMAT are the right isosceles triangle and the 30-60-90 triangle. Memorize the formulas for these two triangles.

  J. The longest side of a triangle is opposite the largest angle; the shortest side is opposite the smallest angle.

  K. One side of a triangle can never be as large as the sum of the two remaining sides, nor can it ever be as small as the difference of the two remaining sides.

11. Circles:

  A. The circumference of a circle is $2\pi r$ or πd, where r is the radius of the circle and d is the diameter.

  B. The area of a circle is πr^2, where r is the radius of the circle.

12. Rectangles, squares, and other four-sided objects:

    A. Any four-sided object is called a quadrilateral.

    B. The perimeter of a quadrilateral is the sum of the lengths of the four sides.

    C. The area of a rectangle, or of a square, is equal to *length × width*.

    D. The area of a parallelogram is equal to *height × base*.

13. Solids and volume:

    A. The volume of most objects is equal to their two-dimensional *area* × their *depth*.

    B. The volume of a rectangular solid is equal to *length × width × depth*.

    C. The volume of a cylinder is equal to the *area* of the circular base × *depth*.

14. GMAT geometry problems always involve more than one step, and difficult GMAT geometry problems may layer several concepts. Don't be intimidated if you don't see the entire process that's necessary to solve the problem. Start somewhere. You'll be amazed at how often you arrive at the answer.

13

Data Sufficiency

As we mentioned earlier, about half of the 37 math questions on the GMAT will be data sufficiency questions.

WHAT IS DATA SUFFICIENCY?

See your DVD for more.

These questions exist on no other test in the world and definitely require some getting used to. When you take the exam, you may notice that some of the people sitting at computers nearby will spend the first ten minutes of the Math section just reading the directions for data sufficiency. To avoid being among the unfortunate few, look at the problem below:

What is x?

(1) $x + y = 7$
(2) $2x + 4 = 14$

Every data sufficiency problem consists of a question followed by two statements. You have to decide NOT what the answer is, but WHETHER the question can be answered based on the information in the two statements. There are five possible answers:

Curiosity Killed the Clock

Data sufficiency means just that, sufficiency: Is there enough data to solve the problem? It does not mean *problem solving*. If a question asks, "What is x?" it means, can a single value for x be found? Once you know the data is sufficient (or not) *stop* solving. It is pointless to find out what x actually is. Don't get curious.

○ Statement (1) ALONE is sufficient, but statement (2) alone is not sufficient.

○ Statement (2) ALONE is sufficient, but statement (1) alone is not sufficient.

○ BOTH statements TOGETHER are sufficient, but NEITHER statement alone is sufficient.

○ EACH statement ALONE is sufficient.

○ Statements (1) and (2) TOGETHER are NOT sufficient.

Here's How to Crack It

The best way to answer data sufficiency problems is to look at *one statement at a time*. So cover up Statement (2) with your hand. Now read Statement (1) as if it were part of the problem. Based on Statement (1) $x + y = 7$ can we answer the question "What is x?"

No way. If $x + y = 7$, there are many possible values of x: If y equals 2, then x could equal 5. On the other hand, if y equals 3, then x could equal 4. Statement (1) is *not* sufficient to give us a single value for x.

Now forget you ever saw Statement (1). Cover it up with your finger and look only at Statement (2) $2x + 4 = 14$. This time, read Statement (2) as if it were part of the problem. Based on Statement (2) *alone*, can we find a single value for x?

Yes. Using algebraic manipulation, we can do the following:

$$2x + 4 = 14$$
$$\underline{-\quad 4 \quad -4}$$
$$2x = 10$$

So, $x = 5$.

Note that the question isn't asking us what x equals. The question asks only whether the information provided is sufficient to find out what x equals.

In this case it is. Statement (2) gives us enough information to answer the question "What is x?"

Because (2) is sufficient and (1) is not, the answer to this question is

○　Statement (2) ALONE is sufficient, but statement (1) alone is not sufficient.

DATA SUFFICIENCY: BASIC PRINCIPLES

Now that you've seen one example, it's time to learn how to take this weird question type and make it your own. The first step is to streamline the answer choices. As we've recommended throughout this book, think of the five answer choices as A through E. Here's the down-and-dirty definition of what they mean:

(A)　The first statement ALONE answers the question.

(B)　The second statement ALONE answers the question.

(C)　You need both statements TOGETHER to answer the question

(D)　Both statements SEPARATELY answer the question.

(E)　Neither statement together or separately answers the question.

The good news is that with a bit of practice, you won't have to think consciously about what the answer choices mean; they will be ingrained in your memory—but there's even better news: Every time you find out almost *anything* about a data sufficiency question, you automatically eliminate several answer choices.

To see how this works, let's look at another simple example:

What is x?

(1) $x - 3 = 2$
(2) $3x = 15$

○   Statement (1) ALONE is sufficient, but statement (2) alone is not sufficient.

○   Statement (2) ALONE is sufficient, but statement (1) alone is not sufficient.

○   BOTH statements TOGETHER are sufficient, but NEITHER statement alone is sufficient.

○   EACH statement ALONE is sufficient.

○   Statements (1) and (2) TOGETHER are NOT sufficient.

As always, cover up Statement (2) and look only at Statement (1). By itself, is Statement (1) sufficient to answer the question? Of course. Simply add three to both sides of the equation and you get $x = 5$. Because Statement (1) is sufficient, the answer to this question must be either:

(A) Statement (1) ALONE is sufficient

or

(D) EACH statement ALONE is sufficient

By simply looking at Statement (1), you've narrowed your choice down to two possibilities. You now have a fifty-fifty chance of getting this question correct, even if you never looked at Statement (2).

See your DVD for more.

EASY ELIMINATIONS

Just by figuring out whether or not the first statement answers the question, you have already done some great eliminating. If the first statement works, you are always down to A or D. If it doesn't, you're always down to the remaining choices: B, C, or E.

AD or BCE. Memorize it; these are *always* your options. And it makes sense to write it down this way in your scratch work. If the first statement answers the question by itself, write down AD. Then cover up Statement (1) and look at Statement (2). If (2) also answers the question, circle D and mark it on your computer screen. If it doesn't, circle A and mark it on your screen.

If the first statement does NOT answer the question, then write down BCE in your scratch work. Then cover up Statement (1) and look at Statement (2). If (2) answers the question by itself, you're done: Circle B and pick it on your screen. If (2) does not answer the question by itself, cross off B. You're down to C or E.

In the problem we're working on from the preceding page, we're already down to AD, but which is it? To find out, cover up Statement (1) and look only at Statement (2). Does this statement answer the question? It sure does. Dividing both sides by 3 gives you $x = 5$. Because we were down to A or D, and Statement (2) DOES answer the question, the answer to the problem must be D.

Note that Statement (1) and Statement (2) agree with each other: In both cases, x equals 5. While correctly solving a data sufficiency problem does not rely on finding the exact answer to the question, it is worth noting that we have never yet found a GMAT data sufficiency question where the correct answer was D and the two statements did not yield the same answer.

Try another example:

If $x + y = 3$, what is the value of xy?

(1) x and y are integers
(2) x and y are positive

○ Statement (1) ALONE is sufficient, but statement (2) alone is not sufficient.

○ Statement (2) ALONE is sufficient, but statement (1) alone is not sufficient.

○ BOTH statements TOGETHER are sufficient, but NEITHER statement alone is sufficient.

○ EACH statement ALONE is sufficient.

○ Statements (1) and (2) TOGETHER are NOT sufficient.

Remember:

Just because there is only one variable doesn't mean an equation has *just one solution*. For example, if $x^2 = 4$, then x could equal either 2 or –2. When an equation has one variable and that variable is to an *odd* power, the equation has only one solution.

Here's How to Crack It

As always, cover up Statement (2) and look only at Statement (1). If x and y are integers and $x + y = 3$, do we know what they are? Not really—x could be 1 and y could be 2 (in which case, xy would be 2). But x could also be 0 (yes, 0 is an integer) and y could be 3 (in which case, xy would be 0). Because Statement (1) alone does not answer the question definitively, we are down to BCE, a one in three shot. Write it down in your scratch booklet.

Now, cover up Statement (1) and look at Statement (2). By itself, this statement doesn't begin to give us values for x and y—x could be 1 and y could be 2, but x could just as easily be 1.4 and y could be 1.6. Because there is still more than one possible value for xy, cross off answer choice B.

We're down to C or E. Let's look at the two statements at the same time. Because we know from the first statement that x and y are integers, and from the second statement that they must be positive, do we now know specific values for x and y?

Well, we *do* know that there are only two positive integers in the world that add up to 3: 2 and 1. (Remember, zero is an integer but it is neither positive nor negative.) Do we know if $x = 1$ and $y = 2$, or vice versa? Not really, but frankly, it doesn't matter in this case. The question is asking us the value of xy.

Because neither statement by *itself* is sufficient, but both statements *together* are sufficient, the answer is choice C.

DRILL 8 (AD/BCE)

In the following drill, each question is followed by only one statement. Based on the first statement, decide if you are down to AD or BCE. The answers can be found on page 301.

1. What is the value of x?
   - (1) $y = 4$
   - (2) ????

2. Is y an integer?
   - (1) $2y$ is an integer.
   - (2) ????

3. A certain room contains 12 children. How many more boys than girls are there?
   - (1) There are three girls in the room.
   - (2) ????

4. What number is x percent of 20?
   - (1) 10 percent of x is 5.
   - (2) ????

Data Sufficiency Math Versus Problem Solving Math

In terms of mathematical content, data sufficiency questions test the same kinds of topics tested by problem solving questions. You'll find problems involving integers, percents, averages, ratios, algebra, and geometry. Only the format is different.

Let's do a "regular" math problem and then turn it into a data sufficiency problem.

A certain factory has filled 92 orders. If the total number of orders on file is 230, what percent of the orders have been filled?

- ○ 20%
- ○ 30%
- ○ 40%
- ○ 50%
- ○ 60%

If you've already done the math review in the preceding chapters, this problem should be pretty easy. It's a percent problem, and as soon as you see the word "percent," you should immediately be thinking:

$$\frac{\text{part}}{\text{whole}} = \frac{92}{230} = \frac{x}{100}$$

(The answer, by the way, is C, 40%.)

Now let's turn this same problem into a data sufficiency problem.

If a certain factory has filled 92 orders, what percent of the total number of orders has been filled?

(1) The total number of orders on file is 230.
(2) The number of orders the factory has already filled represents two-fifths of the total number of orders.

- ○ Statement (1) ALONE is sufficient, but statement (2) alone is not sufficient.
- ○ Statement (2) ALONE is sufficient, but statement (1) alone is not sufficient.
- ○ BOTH statements TOGETHER are sufficient, but NEITHER statement alone is sufficient.
- ○ EACH statement ALONE is sufficient.
- ○ Statements (1) and (2) TOGETHER are NOT sufficient.

Here's How to Crack It

Although the problem is now in a different format, the math involved is exactly the same. Again, as soon as you see the word "percent," you should be thinking:

$$\frac{\text{part}}{\text{whole}}$$

Without looking at the two statements, let's look at the information contained in the question itself and set that up as a part-over-whole equation:

$$\frac{\text{part}}{\text{whole}} = \frac{92}{?} = \frac{x}{100}$$

As this equation stands, there is no way to find a value for x. We have the part (the number of orders that have already been filled), but we do not have the whole (total number of orders).

Cover up Statement (2). Think of Statement (1) as the next sentence in the problem. Does Statement (1) alone give us the missing whole? Yes, it does. Therefore, the answer to this question is either choice A or D.

Now cover up Statement (1) and read Statement (2) as if it were the next sentence in the problem. Statement (2) expresses the number of orders already filled as a fraction of the total number of orders. *Remember*, a fraction is *also* a part over whole. Let's see what we have:

$$\frac{\text{part}}{\text{whole}} = \frac{2}{5} = \frac{x}{100}$$

Can we find a value for x in this equation? Of course. Therefore Statement (2) is also sufficient, and the answer to this question is choice D.

DRILL 9 (DATA SUFFICIENCY PARTS AND WHOLES)

The answers can be found on pages 301–302.

1. If only people who paid deposits attended the Rose Seminar, how many people attended this year?

    (1)   70 people sent in deposits to attend the Rose Seminar this year.

    (2)   60% of the people who sent deposits to attend the Rose Seminar this year actually went.

    ○   Statement (1) ALONE is sufficient, but statement (2) alone is not sufficient.

    ○   Statement (2) ALONE is sufficient, but statement (1) alone is not sufficient.

    ○   BOTH statements TOGETHER are sufficient, but NEITHER statement alone is sufficient.

    ○   EACH statement ALONE is sufficient.

    ○   Statements (1) and (2) TOGETHER are NOT sufficient.

2. Luxo paint contains only alcohol and pigment. What is the ratio of alcohol to pigment in Luxo paint?

(1) Exactly 7 ounces of pigment are contained in a 12-ounce can of Luxo paint.

(2) Exactly 5 ounces of alcohol are contained in a 12-ounce can of Luxo paint.

○ Statement (1) ALONE is sufficient, but statement (2) alone is not sufficient.

○ Statement (2) ALONE is sufficient, but statement (1) alone is not sufficient.

○ BOTH statements TOGETHER are sufficient, but NEITHER statement alone is sufficient.

○ EACH statement ALONE is sufficient.

○ Statements (1) and (2) TOGETHER are NOT sufficient.

3. A car drives along a straight road from Smithville to Laredo, going through Ferristown along the way. What is the total distance by car from Smithville to Laredo?

(1) The distance from Smithville to Ferristown is $\frac{3}{5}$ of the entire distance.

(2) The distance from Ferristown to Laredo is 12 miles.

○ Statement (1) ALONE is sufficient, but statement (2) alone is not sufficient.

○ Statement (2) ALONE is sufficient, but statement (1) alone is not sufficient.

○ BOTH statements TOGETHER are sufficient, but NEITHER statement alone is sufficient.

○ EACH statement ALONE is sufficient.

○ Statements (1) and (2) TOGETHER are NOT sufficient.

DATA SUFFICIENCY AND GEOMETRY: CAN YOU MEASURE THE DIAGRAMS?

Unlike regular problem solving questions, data sufficiency diagrams cannot be measured. This is because the two statements may *change* the shape of the diagram.

DATA SUFFICIENCY AND THE STRANGE POWERS OF POWERS

The data sufficiency question type is particularly well-suited to testing your knowledge of the rules of equations and the strange powers of powers. Let's review this important information:

1. For a data sufficiency statement to be sufficient, there must be as many equations as there are variables.

   - A single equation with two variables cannot be solved,

   - but two distinct equations with the same two variables *can* be solved, using simultaneous equations, as you learned in Chapter 10.

For example, $x = y + 1$ cannot be solved, but $x = y + 1$ and $2x = -y - 6$ can be added together, eliminating one variable so the other may be solved.

2. Just because there is only one variable doesn't mean an equation has just one solution.

   - An equation with a variable raised to an *even* power may have more than one solution.

   - An equation with a variable raised to an odd power will have only one solution.

For example, if $x^2 = 4$, then x could equal either 2 or –2. If $x^3 = 8$, then x can only equal 2.

DRILL 10 (STRANGE POWERS OF POWERS)

The answers can be found on page 302.

The answers can be found on page 302.

Equation Tricks and Traps

Some equations are not distinct, such as when one equation can be multiplied to equal the other equation. For example:
$$x + y = 4$$
$$4x + 4y = 16$$
These are not distinct equations. There is not enough data yet to solve for x or y.

1. What is the value of x?

   (1) $x^2 = 4$
   (2) $x < 0$

   ○   Statement (1) ALONE is sufficient, but statement (2) alone is not sufficient.

   ○   Statement (2) ALONE is sufficient, but statement (1) alone is not sufficient.

   ○   BOTH statements TOGETHER are sufficient, but NEITHER statement alone is sufficient.

   ○   EACH statement ALONE is sufficient.

   ○   Statements (1) and (2) TOGETHER are NOT sufficient.

2. What is the value of xy?

    (1)　$x^2 = 4$
    (2)　$y = 0$

    ○　Statement (1) ALONE is sufficient, but statement (2) alone is not sufficient.

    ○　Statement (2) ALONE is sufficient, but statement (1) alone is not sufficient.

    ○　BOTH statements TOGETHER are sufficient, but NEITHER statement alone is sufficient.

    ○　EACH statement ALONE is sufficient.

    ○　Statements (1) and (2) TOGETHER are NOT sufficient.

3. What is the value of xy?

    (1)　$x^2 = 4$
    (2)　$y^2 = 9$

    ○　Statement (1) ALONE is sufficient, but statement (2) alone is not sufficient.

    ○　Statement (2) ALONE is sufficient, but statement (1) alone is not sufficient.

    ○　BOTH statements TOGETHER are sufficient, but NEITHER statement alone is sufficient.

    ○　EACH statement ALONE is sufficient.

    ○　Statements (1) and (2) TOGETHER are NOT sufficient.

DANISH DATA SUFFICIENCY

In the examples above you may have noticed that you were already using the Process of Elimination. In Data Sufficiency a little knowledge goes a long way. Suppose you saw the following data sufficiency problem:

How tall is Frank?

(1)   Frank is 6'2".
(2)   Frank er en stor mand.

○   Statement (1) ALONE is sufficient, but statement (2) alone is not sufficient.

○   Statement (2) ALONE is sufficient, but statement (1) alone is not sufficient.

○   BOTH statements TOGETHER are sufficient, but NEITHER statement alone is sufficient.

○   EACH statement ALONE is sufficient.

○   Statements (1) and (2) TOGETHER are NOT sufficient.

When we don't know something about a problem, our first impulse is just to skip the whole thing. Of course, on the GMAT, you can't do that; to get to the next question, you have to answer this one. So, should you guess at random?

Because you probably don't speak Danish, you have no idea whether the second statement is sufficient to answer the question.

However, it would be a mistake to guess at random.

Heads You Win, Tails You Lose

Let's focus on what you DO know. Cover up Statement (2). Based on Statement (1) *alone*, do you know how tall Frank is? Of course. He is 6'2". Because Statement (1) is sufficient, the answer to this question is either:

(A)   Statement (1) ALONE is sufficient

or

(D)   EACH statement ALONE is sufficient

By using POE, you've narrowed your choice down to two possibilities. You now have a fifty-fifty chance of getting this question correct, even though you know absolutely nothing about Statement (2).

More Danish Data Sufficiency

As long as you know something about a data sufficiency problem, you can do some shrewd guessing. Look at the following problem:

How tall is Frank?

(1) Frank is pretty tall.
(2) Frank er en stor mand.

○ Statement (1) ALONE is sufficient, but statement (2) alone is not sufficient.

○ Statement (2) ALONE is sufficient, but statement (1) alone is not sufficient.

○ BOTH statements TOGETHER are sufficient, but NEITHER statement alone is sufficient.

○ EACH statement ALONE is sufficient.

○ Statements (1) and (2) TOGETHER are NOT sufficient.

Because Statement (1) does not give you a specific height, it is not sufficient to answer the question. So what are you down to? BCE. Write it down in your scratch booklet. Now, let's cover it up and look at Statement (2). Based on Statement (2) alone, can you tell exactly how tall Frank is? No, not unless you speak Danish.

By using POE in this case, you've narrowed your choice down to three possibilities—a one-in-three shot—even though the only thing you knew for certain about this problem was that one of the statements did not work.

Can't Make Heads or Tails of the First Statement?

If you're having trouble understanding the first statement, skip it for a minute and look at the second statement. If Statement (2) is sufficient, you can eliminate answer choices A, C, and E and be down to a fifty-fifty guess—choice B or D. If it is not sufficient, you can eliminate answer choices B and D, and have a one-in-three shot at getting the problem right.

Look at the following problem:

How tall is Frank?

(1) Frank er en stor mand.
(2) Frank is pretty tall.

○ Statement (1) ALONE is sufficient, but statement (2) alone is not sufficient.

○ Statement (2) ALONE is sufficient, but statement (1) alone is not sufficient.

○ BOTH statements TOGETHER are sufficient, but NEITHER statement alone is sufficient.

○ EACH statement ALONE is sufficient.

○ Statements (1) and (2) TOGETHER are NOT sufficient.

Because we have no idea what Statement (1) says, let's cover it up and look at Statement (2). Based on Statement (2) alone, can you tell exactly how tall Frank is? Of course not. Because Statement (2) is not sufficient, you can rule out choices B and D.

By using POE in this case, you've narrowed your choice down to three possibilities—a one-in-three shot—even though the only thing you knew for certain about this problem was that one of the statements did not work.

MATH IS MATH IS MATH

All data sufficiency problems are just standard math problems in a new format. Look for the clue that tells you what to do, then see whether the two statements provide you with enough information to answer the question.

EXCEPT ON YES OR NO QUESTIONS

Leave it to GMAC to come up with a way to give you five different answer choices on a yes-or-no question. Let's look at an example:

Did candidate x receive more than 40% of the 30,000 votes cast in the general election?

(1)   Candidate y received 45% of the votes.
(2)   Candidate x received exactly 11,000 votes.

○   Statement (1) ALONE is sufficient, but statement (2) alone is not sufficient.

○   Statement (2) ALONE is sufficient, but statement (1) alone is not sufficient.

○   BOTH statements TOGETHER are sufficient, but NEITHER statement alone is sufficient.

○   EACH statement ALONE is sufficient.

○   Statements (1) and (2) TOGETHER are NOT sufficient.

Here's How to Crack It

When all is said and done, the answer to this question is either yes or no. Cover up Statement (2). Does Statement (1) alone answer the question? If you were in a hurry, you might think so. Many people just assume that Statement (1) is talking about candidate x—in which case they get the problem wrong. Other people notice that Statement (1) is talking about candidate y but assume that these are the only two candidates running in the election (in which case, because candidate y received 45%, candidate x must have received 55%). Because the problem doesn't *say* that there were only two candidates, Statement (1) doesn't answer the question.

Now cover up Statement (1) and let's look at Statement (2). This seems more promising. Like the problem we saw earlier involving factory orders, this problem is also about percents, so again we think:

$$\frac{\text{part}}{\text{whole}} = \frac{11,000}{30,000} = \frac{x}{100}$$

By multiplying, we learn that $x = 36.6\%$. At which point many people say, "The guy got less than 40%—this statement doesn't answer the question, either." But they're wrong.

JUST SAY NO

Broken down to its basics, the question we were asked was, "Did he get more than 40% of the vote—yes or no?"

Statement (2) *does* answer the question. The answer is, "No, he didn't." The answer is choice B.

On a yes-or-no data sufficiency problem, if a statement answers the question in the affirmative *or* in the negative, it is sufficient.

HOW TO KEEP IT ALL STRAIGHT

Because as many as half of the data sufficiency problems you'll see on the GMAT will be yes-or-no problems, it's a good idea to have a strategy. When yes-or-no questions involve variables, there's a good way to keep everything straight. Here's an example:

> Is x an integer?
>
> (1) $5x$ is a positive integer.
> (2) $5x = 1$
>
> ○ Statement (1) ALONE is sufficient, but statement (2) alone is not sufficient.
>
> ○ Statement (2) ALONE is sufficient, but statement (1) alone is not sufficient.
>
> ○ BOTH statements TOGETHER are sufficient, but NEITHER statement alone is sufficient.
>
> ○ EACH statement ALONE is sufficient.
>
> ○ Statements (1) and (2) TOGETHER are NOT sufficient.

Here's How to Crack It

As always, cover up Statement (2). Look only at Statement (1). Let's plug in a value for x, a number that anyone, even Joe Bloggs, might pick. How about 2? We know that $5 \times 2 = 10$, which is a positive integer. Is 2 an integer? Yes.

What we've just found is *one case* in which the answer to the question, 10, is yes. If x is *always* an integer, then the answer is always yes, and Statement (1) is sufficient. If x is *never* an integer, the answer would always be no, and Statement (1) would *still* be sufficient (remember, the answer to a yes-or-no question can be no).

But if Statement (1) gives us an answer that is sometimes yes and sometimes no, then the statement is no good.

By Plugging In, we found *one case* in which the answer to the question is yes. Now all we need to do is see whether we can find *one case* in which the answer to the question is no. The statement says,

> (1) $5x$ is a positive integer.

Most numbers we could plug in for x to make the statement true are integers. Is there ANY value of x that makes the statement true, but isn't an integer itself? What if x were $\frac{1}{5}$?

We know that $5 \times \frac{1}{5} = 1$, which *is* a positive integer; but now x is *not* an integer. By plugging in $\frac{1}{5}$, we have found one case in which the answer is no. Because Statement (1) gives us an answer that is sometimes yes and sometimes no, the statement is not sufficient. Now we're down to B, C, or E.

Cover up Statement (1) and look at Statement (2):

(2) $5x = 1$

To make this statement true, x *must* equal $\frac{1}{5}$. Is x an integer? No. We have now found *one case* in which the answer is no. Is there any other number we could plug in for x that would make the statement true? No.

Because Statement (2) gives us an answer that is *always* no, the statement is sufficient, and the answer to this question is choice B.

YES OR NO PLUGGING IN CHECKLIST

- First, try plugging in a normal number for your variable. The number will yield an answer to the question—either yes or no. But you're not done yet.

- Now, try plugging in a different number for your variable. This time, you might try one of the "weird" numbers, such as 0, 1, a negative number, or a fraction. If the statement still answers the question the same way, then you can begin to suspect that the statement yields a consistent answer, and that you're down to AD.

- If you plug in a different number and get a different answer this time (a "yes" after getting a "no," or a "no" after getting a "yes") then the statement does NOT definitively answer the question, and you're down to BCE.

- Now, repeat this checklist with Statement (2).

DRILL 11 (YES OR NO)

The answers can be found on page 303.

1. If x is a positive number, is $x < 1$?

    (1) $2x < 1$
    (2) $2x \leq 2$

    ○   Statement (1) ALONE is sufficient, but statement (2) alone is not sufficient.

    ○   Statement (2) ALONE is sufficient, but statement (1) alone is not sufficient.

    ○   BOTH statements TOGETHER are sufficient, but NEITHER statement alone is sufficient.

    ○   EACH statement ALONE is sufficient.

    ○   Statements (1) and (2) TOGETHER are NOT sufficient.

2. Is x positive?

    (1) $xy = 6$
    (2) $x(y^2) = 12$

    ○   Statement (1) ALONE is sufficient, but statement (2) alone is not sufficient.

    ○   Statement (2) ALONE is sufficient, but statement (1) alone is not sufficient.

    ○   BOTH statements TOGETHER are sufficient, but NEITHER statement alone is sufficient.

    ○   EACH statement ALONE is sufficient.

    ○   Statements (1) and (2) TOGETHER are NOT sufficient.

3. Are x and y integers?

    (1)   The product xy is an integer.
    (2) $x + y$ is an integer.

    ○   Statement (1) ALONE is sufficient, but statement (2) alone is not sufficient.

    ○   Statement (2) ALONE is sufficient, but statement (1) alone is not sufficient.

    ○   BOTH statements TOGETHER are sufficient, but NEITHER statement alone is sufficient.

    ○   EACH statement ALONE is sufficient.

    ○   Statements (1) and (2) TOGETHER are NOT sufficient.

Dr. Livingstone, I Presume?

Sir Henry Stanley would not have done well on the GMAT with that kind of careless presumption. The test writers love to try to trick you into assuming something that isn't necessarily true. Here's an example:

> Two people went into an executive trainee program at the same time. How much more money per week does trainee A now earn than trainee B?
>
> (1) Trainee A earns $300 per week more than she did when she began the program.
> (2) Trainee B earns $100 more per week than she did when she began the program.
>
> ○ Statement (1) ALONE is sufficient, but statement (2) alone is not sufficient.
>
> ○ Statement (2) ALONE is sufficient, but statement (1) alone is not sufficient.
>
> ○ BOTH statements TOGETHER are sufficient, but NEITHER statement alone is sufficient.
>
> ○ EACH statement ALONE is sufficient.
>
> ○ Statements (1) and (2) TOGETHER are NOT sufficient.

Never Assume

In this problem almost everyone's first impression is that the answer is choice C (both statements together are sufficient). Most people make the perfectly natural assumption that both trainees started at the same salary. But do we know this?

If you are answering medium or difficult questions, you can never assume anything. The answer to this question is choice E because the two trainees may have had different starting salaries.

Here's another exmple:

> At a business dinner, people were offered coffee
> or tea. If all the diners had either coffee or tea, how
> many of the diners had tea?
>
> (1)   Of the 60 people at the dinner, 10% had tea.
> (2)   Fifty-four people had coffee.
>
> ○   Statement (1) ALONE is sufficient, but state-
>   ment (2) alone is not sufficient.
> ○   Statement (2) ALONE is sufficient, but state-
>   ment (1) alone is not sufficient.
> ○   BOTH statements TOGETHER are sufficient,
>   but NEITHER statement alone is sufficient.
> ○   EACH statement ALONE is sufficient.
> ○   Statements (1) and (2) TOGETHER are NOT
>   sufficient.

Here's How to Crack It

Statement (1) is sufficient because 10% of 60 = 6. Now look at Statement (2). At first glance this seems sufficient as well. We just found out from Statement (1) that there were a total of 60 people at the dinner. If 54 of them had coffee, then the other 6 had tea, which agrees with the number we got in Statement (1). There is only one hitch: Statement (2) by itself does not tell us the total number of people at the dinner. We are subconsciously relying on information in Statement (1).

Just Because One Statement Seems to Agree with the Other Doesn't Mean They Are Necessarily Saying the Same Thing

If Statement (2) had said "two people had coffee," you would have eliminated it right away. But because it seemed to agree with Statement (1), it became much more tempting. Just remember: When you look at Statement (2), *always cover up Statement (1) and forget you ever saw it*. The answer to this question is choice A.

CRACKING DATA SUFFICIENCY: ADVANCED PRINCIPLES

It is particularly important to know your approximate GMAT scoring level when you're doing data sufficiency questions. If you will mainly be answering easy questions, then by concentrating on the principles we've shown you so far, you will get most of these questions right.

But if you will be answering mainly medium and difficult questions, then you have to learn to anticipate the level of complexity of medium and difficult data sufficiency problems. Some of the medium problems will contain traps that the test writers hope will trip you up. We'll show you some of their favorite traps in just a minute.

On the difficult problems, virtually every question contains a trap. By learning to recognize the traps GMAC has set for you, you can eliminate them. Sometimes all that remains is the correct answer.

JOE'S FAVORITE ANSWERS

Joe Bloggs's initial reaction to a difficult data sufficiency question is, "I don't know how to do this." This statement doesn't seem to help Joe in answering the question. Therefore on questions he perceives to be difficult, Joe's favorite answer is usually choice E (Statements (1) and (2) TOGETHER are NOT sufficient).

His second favorite answer is choice C (BOTH statements TOGETHER are sufficient, but neither statement alone is sufficient). Joe likes choice C because he assumes that a difficult question will need a lot of information.

Joe's favorite answers on tough data sufficiency questions are choices E and C, but that doesn't mean these will never be the answer to difficult questions. It simply means that you should be wary if your first impulse is to choose choice C or E—don't fall into the same traps Joe does.

Take a look at the following problem:

If $xyz \neq 0$, what is the value of $\dfrac{x^4 y^3 z^2}{y^2 x^2 y^1 z^2}$?

(1) $x = 3$
(2) $y = 5$

○ Statement (1) ALONE is sufficient, but statement (2) alone is not sufficient.

○ Statement (2) ALONE is sufficient, but statement (1) alone is not sufficient.

○ BOTH statements TOGETHER are sufficient, but NEITHER statement alone is sufficient.

○ EACH statement ALONE is sufficient.

○ Statements (1) and (2) TOGETHER are NOT sufficient.

Here's How to Crack It

This is a tough problem. Of course, we won't be able to tell you that during the test, but your performance on practice tests will provide a rough idea of what difficulty level to expect. Joe's *first* impulse here might be to pick answer choice E. He sees an expression with x's, y's, and z's, but the two statements underneath give values only for x and y.

If Joe thinks for a minute, he might realize that there is a z^2 in the numerator and a z^2 in the denominator. These cancel out, eliminating all the z's in the expression. Joe's *second* impulse might be to pick answer choice C. He now sees an equation with x's and y's, and assumes he will need values for both in order to answer the question.

Knowing that Joe will be inclined to pick C or E on this problem, we can eliminate these answer choices. That leaves us with choices A, C, or D. If that's as far as you have time to get on this problem, guess and move on. You have a one-in-three shot of getting it right—good odds.

The correct answer is answer choice A. The y^2 and the y^1 in the denominator can be consolidated to form y^3. The y's cancel out.

WHEN JOE THINKS A TOUGH QUESTION IS EASY

The only time the correct answer to a tough data sufficiency question will actually turn out to be E or C is when Joe is convinced that the question is easy.

What was the combined average attendance at Memorial Stadium for the months of June and July?

(1)   The average attendance for the month of June was 23,100, and the average attendance for the month of July was 25,200.

(2)   There were 20 games played in June at the stadium and 22 games played in July.

○   Statement (1) ALONE is sufficient, but statement (2) alone is not sufficient.

○   Statement (2) ALONE is sufficient, but statement (1) alone is not sufficient.

○   BOTH statements TOGETHER are sufficient, but NEITHER statement alone is sufficient.

○   EACH statement ALONE is sufficient.

○   Statements (1) and (2) TOGETHER are NOT sufficient.

Here's How to Crack It

Joe thinks this is an easy one. Statement (1) gives us the average attendance for June and the average attendance for July. Joe probably decides this is sufficient by itself. He thinks you can get the total average of the two months by averaging the two averages. (You—having completed our chapter on arithmetic—know better.) Joe looks at Statement (2) and doesn't see any attendance figures at all. He picks answer choice A.

Because he is convinced that this is an easy question and that the answer is choice A, Joe Bloggs never even considers his two favorite answers—choices E and C. *This* time he *knows* he's right!

But, of course, he is wrong. The answer to this question is choice C. An average is the *total* sum of values divided by the total number of values. We need to know the number of games in each month in order to find out the *total* number of people attending. Remember, data sufficiency questions most likely are not as easy as they seem.

PUTTING IT ALL TOGETHER

Eliminating Joe Bloggs answers gives you an enormous advantage on data sufficiency problems. But by coupling this technique with POE, you can do even better. Remember our Danish question?

> How tall is Frank?
>
> (1)   Frank is 6'2".
> (2)   Frank er en stor mand.
>
> ○   Statement (1) ALONE is sufficient, but statement (2) alone is not sufficient.
>
> ○   Statement (2) ALONE is sufficient, but statement (1) alone is not sufficient.
>
> ○   BOTH statements TOGETHER are sufficient, but NEITHER statement alone is sufficient.
>
> ○   EACH statement ALONE is sufficient.
>
> ○   Statements (1) and (2) TOGETHER are NOT sufficient.

Using POE and completely ignoring Statement (2), we were able to get down to a fifty-fifty choice. Because Statement (1) unequivocably answers the question, we knew the answer had to be choice A or D. Now suppose you also knew this was a tough question. Aside from just having seen enough questions like it, how would you know? Because your scores on practice tests indicate that the GMAC computer will mainly be throwing medium and difficult questions at you.

Now, consider for a moment: Which of the two remaining choices—A or D—does Joe like?

Because Joe doesn't know anything about Statement (2), he'll probably choose A. If this is a tough question, there's no way Joe's answer could be correct. In that case we'd better pick answer choice D.

Here's one last example:

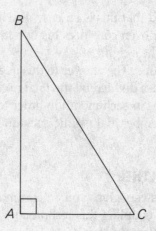

If the perimeter of right triangle *ABC* above is $3 + 3\sqrt{3}$, what is the area of the triangle?

(1)   side *AC* ≠ side *AB*
(2)   angle *ABC* = 30 degrees

○   Statement (1) ALONE is sufficient, but statement (2) alone is not sufficient.

○   Statement (2) ALONE is sufficient, but statement (1) alone is not sufficient.

○   BOTH statements TOGETHER are sufficient, but NEITHER statement alone is sufficient.

○   EACH statement ALONE is sufficient.

○   Statements (1) and (2) TOGETHER are NOT sufficient.

Here's How to Crack It

The area of a triangle is $\dfrac{base \times height}{2}$. Joe looks at Statements (1) and (2) and sees neither the length of the base nor the length of the height. Joe likes choice E a lot on this problem. He doesn't see how he can get the area of the triangle from this information. Joe might also be tempted by choice C just because it seems like he is being given an awful lot of information; maybe, he reasons, there's some formula he doesn't know about.

Let's look at the problem seriously now. Cover up Statement (2). Statement (1) tells us only that two of the sides of the triangle are not equal. Is there any conceivable way this information could help us find the base and the height of the triangle? No, Statement (1) alone doesn't give us enough information to answer the question. Because Statement (1) is not sufficient by itself, we can eliminate answer choices A and D.

We are left with three choices: B, C, or E.

Are any of these choices Joe Bloggs answers? Well, yes. We decided a moment ago that choice E was definitely Joe Bloggs and that, in fact, choice C might be as well. It therefore seems quite likely that the answer is choice B.

Here's How GMAC Wants You to Crack It

Statement (2) tells us that the right triangle is a 30-60-90 triangle. If you have already read our chapter on geometry, you know that the dimensions of a 30-60-90 triangle are always in the same proportion: The short side (the side opposite the 30-degree angle) is always equal to half the hypotenuse, and the middle side is always equal to the short side times $\sqrt{3}$. If we call the short side x, then the hypotenuse is $2x$ and the middle side is $x\sqrt{3}$. Thus the formula for the perimeter of a 30-60-90 triangle is $3x + x\sqrt{3}$, where x is the side opposite the 30-degree angle. If we set this equal to the actual perimeter of the triangle, we can solve for x.

$$3x + x\sqrt{3} = 3 + 3\sqrt{3}$$

After we do a lot of work solving for x, it turns out that $x = \sqrt{3}$. This is equal to the base of our triangle. We can now figure out the height, which would be the short side ($\sqrt{3}$) times $\sqrt{3}$, or 3. If we know the base and the height, we can figure out the area, which means that Statement (2) is sufficient, and the answer is choice B.

Wait a minute! If the base is $\sqrt{3}$ and the height is 3, doesn't this agree with Statement (1) that $AC \neq AB$? Sure, but so what? Just because Statement (1) seems to *agree* with Statement (2) doesn't mean that it says the same thing.

That Was a Lot of Work

This problem was very difficult and took a long time if you actually tried to solve it mathematically, the way the test writers wanted you to. You will notice that we got the same answer within only a few seconds by using a combination of POE and the Joe Bloggs technique.

Using our method isn't infallible, but if you know you will mostly be answering tough questions, this technique will help you on problems you have neither the time nor the inclination to figure out mathematically.

SUMMARY

1. The instructions for data sufficiency questions are very complicated. Memorize them now. Here is a pared-down checklist:

   (A) The first statement ALONE answers the question.
   (B) The second statement ALONE answers the question.
   (C) You need both statements TOGETHER to answer the question.
   (D) Both statements SEPARATELY answer the question.
   (E) Neither statement together or separately answers the question.

2. To aid in scratch booklet eliminations, think of these answer choices as A, B, C, D, and E.

3. Use Process of Elimination to narrow down the field. If you know that Statement (1) is sufficient, you are already down to a fifty-fifty guess: A or D. If you know that Statement (1) is not sufficient, you are already down to a one-in-three guess: B, C, or E.

4. If you are stuck on Statement (1), skip it and look at Statement (2). POE will be just as helpful.

5. The math content of the data sufficiency questions is exactly the same as it is on the regular math questions.

6. As you would in the regular math problems, look for the clues that tell you how to solve data sufficiency problems.

7. When a problem asks a yes-or-no question, remember that the answer can be no.

8. In yes-or-no questions, a statement is sufficient if it always gives us the *same* answer: always yes or always no. If the answer is sometimes yes and sometimes no, the statement is insufficient.

9. In medium and difficult data sufficiency problems, you must be on guard against careless assumptions.

10. In *difficult* data sufficiency problems:

   • If Joe Bloggs *thinks* the problem is difficult, his favorite answers are choices E ("there isn't enough information") or C ("this problem needs all the information it can get").

   • If Joe Bloggs thinks the problem is easy, he will be drawn to choices A, B, or D.

11. On difficult data sufficiency problems, Joe's answer is always wrong.

PART ◆ III

How to Crack the Verbal GMAT

14

Sentence Correction

B-School Lingo

finheads: finance heads
(see *Sharks*)

four Ps: elements of marketing
strategy—Price, Promotion,
Place, Product

fume date: the date a
company will run out of cash

Sentence corrections make up a little more than one-third of the 41 questions on the Verbal portion of the GMAT—approximately 17 questions that will be interspersed throughout. A sentence correction question consists of one long sentence that is either partially or completely underlined. You have to decide whether the sentence is grammatically correct as it's written, or if it is not, which of the answer choices best replaces the underlined portion.

Before we begin, take a moment to read the following instructions. They are a close approximation of the instructions you'll see on the real GMAT. Be sure you know and understand these instructions before you take the GMAT. If you learn them ahead of time, you won't have to waste valuable seconds reading them on the day of the test.

> Directions: Each sentence correction question refers to a sentence, a portion or all of which has been underlined. If you think the sentence is correct as written, pick the first answer choice, which simply repeats the underlined portion exactly. If you think there is something wrong with the sentence as written, choose the answer choice that best replaces the underlined portion of the sentence.
>
> Sentence correction questions are designed to measure your correct use of grammar, your ability to form clear and effective sentences and your capacity to choose the most appropriate words. Pick the answer that best states what was meant in the original sentence while adhering to the requirements of standard written English. Avoid constructions that are awkward, unclear, or redundant.

THE BAD NEWS

It's important to understand the fine print of the instructions you've just read. The test writers ask you to choose the "best" answer, by which they mean the answer that they think is right. The bad news is that some of the "correct" answer choices for the GMAT's sentence correction questions will probably not sound correct to you. The rules of English as interpreted by the GMAT are very different from the rules of English that govern what we read in newspapers, hear on television, or speak in our everyday lives.

How many times have you heard your boss, or a television anchorperson, or a president of the United States, make the following statement?

"Hopefully, we will know the answer to that question, tomorrow."

While you probably don't want to make a habit of correcting people's grammar, you should know that this sentence is not technically correct. According to the arbiters of grammar at GMAC, the president was supposed to say, "We hope that we will know the answer to that question tomorrow." It may be of some comfort to you that your boss, the television anchorperson, and a president of the United States would all get a question like this wrong if they took the GMAT.

GMAT English

GMAT English should be studied the same way you would approach any other foreign language. It has its own rules and its own internal logic. GMAT English has much in common with American English, but if you rely solely on your ear, you may get into trouble.

Confronted with a poorly constructed sentence, most of us could find *a* way to fix it. Most of the time we would probably break the sentence into two separate sentences (GMAT sentences are often too long and unwieldy). Unfortunately, on this test we are forced to find *the* way to fix the sentence; that is to say, GMAC's way to fix it.

To do well on sentence corrections, you will have to learn GMAT English.

The Good News

The people who write the GMAT try to stick to the basics. If they tested a controversial point of grammar, they might be proven wrong. They don't want to have to change their minds after a test is given and mail 20,000 letters explaining why they're changing the answer key (something that has happened from time to time in the past). The easiest way to avoid trouble is to test a handful of the rules of standard written English.

There are huge books devoted exclusively to the correct use of English. You could spend the next six weeks just studying grammar and never even scratch the surface of the subject. The good news is that this won't be necessary. Although there are hundreds of rules of standard written English that could be tested, the GMAT concentrates on only a few.

In other words, GMAT English is fairly easy to learn.

SENTENCE CORRECTION: CRACKING THE SYSTEM

In this chapter, we'll show you the most common types of errors that are tested in GMAT sentences and how to spot them. We'll show you how the test writers choose the four incorrect choices for each question, and we'll show you how to use Process of Elimination to make your life a lot easier.

See your DVD for more.

To forestall the objections of the expert grammarians out there, let us say at the outset that this discussion is not designed to be an all-inclusive discussion of English grammar. You are reading this chapter to do well on sentence correction *as it appears on the GMAT*. Thus, if we seem to oversimplify a point or ignore an arcane exception to a rule, it is because we do not feel that any more detail is warranted. Remember, this isn't English; it's GMAT English.

Order of Difficulty

The computer-adaptive GMAT will be choosing questions for you from a large pool based on your responses to previous questions. Theoretically, the computer knows which questions in its pool are easy and which are difficult. However, when it comes to sentence corrections, most of our students find that they can't tell the difference; "easy" questions often seem as poorly worded as "difficult" questions. You will discover that The Princeton Review techniques make the relative difficulty of sentence correction questions pretty meaningless.

PROCESS OF ELIMINATION

See your
DVD for
more.

Most people approach sentence correction questions the same way. They read the original sentence and then read the entire sentence again, substituting the first answer choice for the underlined part. Then they go back and do the same thing for the second, third, and fourth answer choices. This approach is both laborious and confusing. It's hard to keep five different versions of the same sentence straight, especially when all five of them are awkward.

The Princeton Review approach uses Process of Elimination to narrow down the choices before you have to start reading the answers carefully. Because there are relatively few types of errors that appear in sentence correction questions, we will focus on teaching you how to spot these errors. Once you've spotted the error in a sentence you'll be able to go through the answer choices and eliminate any that also contain that error. Then you can decide among the remaining choices.

WRITE IT DOWN

Effective use of POE on the GMAT always involves your scratch booklet, and *always* involves thinking of the answer choices as A, B, C, D, and E, even though they are not labeled that way onscreen. As you eliminate answer choices, you should cross them off in your scratch booklet.

BASIC PRINCIPLES

Let's look at a sentence correction question that's written in a way that you will unfortunately never see on the real GMAT—with only the correct answer listed:

> Registered brokerage firms have been required to record details of all computerized program trades made in the past year so that government agencies <u>will be able to decide whether they should be banned</u>.
> ○
> ○
> ○
> ○
> ○ will be able to decide whether program trades should be banned

Piece of cake, right? It gets a little harder when they throw in the other four answer choices. Don't worry if you aren't sure why the last answer choice—what we call answer choice E—is better than the original sentence. We will cover how to spot this type of error (pronoun reference) a little later in the chapter. For now, it's enough to know that the "they" in the underlined portion of the sentence was ambiguous. It wasn't clear whether "they" referred to "registered brokerage firms," "details," or the "computerized program trades."

Don't bother saying it was perfectly obvious that "they" referred to the program trades. This is GMAT English, remember? It doesn't matter if you knew what the sentence meant. The sentence had to be clear to the GMAT test writer who wrote it.

ZEN AND THE ART OF TEST WRITING

Let's put ourselves in the place of the GMAT test writer who wrote this question. He has just finished his sentence and he has his correct answer, but he isn't finished yet. He still has to write four other answer choices. It's actually kind of difficult to come up with four answer choices that seem plausible but are wrong. If the test writer makes the incorrect choices too obviously wrong, Joe Bloggs might be able to pick the correct answer without having really understood the rule of grammar involved. If the test writer makes the incorrect answer choices too subtle, Joe won't find one that seems right to him, and therefore might guess at random. The test writer does not want Joe to guess at random. If Joe guesses at random, he might actually pick the right answer.

ONE DOWN, FOUR TO GO

Coming up with the correct answer is easy for our test writer—after all, he wrote the question. He will probably spend much more time on the incorrect answer choices.

Answer Choice A

Composing the first wrong answer choice is also easy for our test writer; the first of the answer choices (what we call answer choice A) is always a repeat of the underlined part of the original sentence. Obviously, this is the choice to select if you think that the sentence is correct as it's written. Two down, three to go.

IF YOU CAN'T SELL A LEMON, REPACKAGE IT

To see whether Joe has spotted the error in the sentence, the GMAT test writer will include the same error in at least one, and usually two, of the other answer choices. If Joe didn't like the error in the original sentence, maybe he'll like it better surrounded by different words. Look at the same sentence again, this time with two incorrect answer choices that include the error found in the original sentence:

> Registered brokerage firms have been required to record details of all computerized program trades made in the past year so that government agencies <u>will be able to decide whether they should be banned</u>.

- ○ will be able to decide whether they should be banned
- ○ should be able to decide whether they should be banned
- ○ should be able to decide whether they can be banned
- ○
- ○ will be able to decide whether program trades should be banned

The GMAT on the GMAT:

"The GMAT has two primary limitations: (1) it cannot and does not measure all the qualities important for graduate study in management and other pursuits; (2) there are psychometric limitations to the test—for example, only score differences of certain magnitudes are reliable indicators of real differences in performance. Such limits should be taken into consideration as GMAT scores are used."
Source: A previous edition of *The Official Guide for GMAT Review*

Joe Bloggs has no idea what point of grammar is tested in this question. He picks answers because they sound good. Our test writer hopes that one of these answer choices will sound better to Joe than the correct answer. Both choices change the sentence, but both also still contain the ambiguous word "they," so both are still wrong.

ALMOST RIGHT

Our test writer has one more kind of trap to insert into a question. This time the trap isn't for Joe Bloggs; it's for the person who has spotted the error in the sentence but is in too big a hurry to make fine distinctions.

Usually one of the incorrect answer choices will actually fix the original error—*but will create some new error in the process.*

Spotting the original error is all well and good, but our test writer wants to make sure you really "deserve" to get this one right, so he includes an answer choice that's almost right. It will be a close variation of the "best" answer; it will correct the mistake in the original sentence, but it will be *wrong.*

Here's the same sentence with an answer choice that fixes the original mistake but creates a new one:

> Registered brokerage firms have been required to record details of all computerized program trades made in the past year so that government agencies <u>will be able to decide whether they should be banned</u>.
>
> ○ will be able to decide whether they should be banned
>
> ○ should be able to decide whether they should be banned
>
> ○ should be able to decide whether they can be banned
>
> ○ **will be able to decide whether program trades should be able to be banned**
>
> ○ will be able to decide whether program trades should be banned

Answer choice D fixes the original problem; there is no longer an ambiguous "they" in the sentence. Our test writer is hoping that anyone who has spotted the original error will read just far enough to see that answer choice D fixes it, but not far enough to see that there is something else wrong. What's wrong? On the GMAT, only animate objects are "able" to do anything.

THREE DOWN, TWO TO GO

Let's look at the entire problem, now that our test writer has finished it, and count our blessings.

Registered brokerage firms have been required to record details of all computerized program trades made in the past year so that government agencies <u>will be able to decide whether they should be banned</u>.

- ○ will be able to decide whether they should be banned
- ○ should be able to decide whether they should be banned
- ○ should be able to decide whether they can be banned
- ○ will be able to decide whether program trades should be able to be banned
- ○ will be able to decide whether program trades should be banned

Here's How to Crack It

By spotting what was wrong in the original sentence, we could have eliminated three of the five answer choices. Choice A merely repeats the original sentence word for word. Choices B and C contain the same error that was found in the original sentence.

We're down to choice D or E. Both fix the original error. What's the difference between them? Three words. If you don't see why one is correct and the other isn't, don't soul-search. Just click on one answer and move on. The correct answer is choice E.

OUR BASIC APPROACH

To use POE, you must be able to spot the errors in the original sentences. Fortunately, as we said before, GMAC leans heavily on only a few major types of errors. Just recognizing these errors should enable you to answer many of the sentence correction problems. There are two ways to do this.

Plan A

The first step in your sentence correction strategy should be to read the original sentence, looking for the very specific errors that the test writers like to test. As soon as you spot an error, you can eliminate any answer choices that repeat this error. Then, having gotten rid of several choices, you can actually read the remaining choices carefully to see which is best.

But what happens if you finish the sentence without spotting one of these errors? Unfortunately, you can't skip the question and come back to it later. So what do you do?

Plan B

If you don't spot the error as you read the original sentence, then the second step in your sentence correction strategy is to go straight to the answer choices to look for clues. Here are the answer choices to a real GMAT problem:

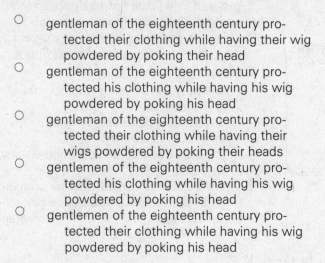

- ○ gentleman of the eighteenth century protected their clothing while having their wig powdered by poking their head
- ○ gentleman of the eighteenth century protected his clothing while having his wig powdered by poking his head
- ○ gentleman of the eighteenth century protected their clothing while having their wigs powdered by poking their heads
- ○ gentlemen of the eighteenth century protected his clothing while having his wig powdered by poking his head
- ○ gentlemen of the eighteenth century protected their clothing while having his wig powdered by poking his head

Forget about the original sentence entirely for a moment (pretty easy, because we didn't give it to you). Just look at the first word of each of the choices. Does anything strike you?

The differences in the answer choices are excellent hints as to what kind of error you might be looking for in the original sentence. For example, in the answers above, the test writer is offering you a choice of the singular noun "gentleman" or the plural noun "gentlemen." A further fast scan of the answer choices reveals a choice of pronouns referring back to the nouns. What type of error might be involved if we're seeing singular and plural nouns, along with singular and plural pronouns? Aha—pronoun reference.

Even if the answer choices do not provide a clue, all is not lost. Remember how our GMAT test writer constructs wrong answer choices: The test writer likes to throw in one or more answer choices that fix the original error but create new errors in the process. You may not have been able to spot the original error, but you'll probably see the *new* errors in the bogus answer choices.

As you read the remaining answer choices, look for differences. Sometimes the realization that one answer choice is exactly the same as another with the exception of a couple of words will enable you to choose between them.

When you've eliminated everything you can, guess and move on.

The combination of Plan A and Plan B should allow you to get most of the sentence completion questions correct—once you've learned one other important concept…

B-School Lingo

I-bankers: investment banking analysts coming out of a two-year training program and into B-School

incentivize: a verb form of the word *incentive*

The Most Common Error Is *No* Error

While we are going to teach you to spot the eight most common errors used by the GMAT test writers, you should know that about one-fifth of the sentence correction sentences are fine just the way they are. If a sentence is correct as is, the "best" answer is the first answer choice (what we call choice A), which repeats the original sentence. According to the law of averages, two or three of the sentence correction questions you will see on the GMAT will contain no error.

How do you tell when there is nothing wrong with a sentence?

You can tell that a sentence is correct by the absence of any of the other types of errors that we're going to show you how to spot. Try not to use your ear —at least not at first. As you're reading each sentence, you'll mark off a mental checklist of likely errors. If you come to the end of the list without having found a specific error, go to Plan B and look for differences in the answer choices. If you still haven't found an error in the original sentence, chances are very good that there was none.

We'll come back to answer choice A later in the chapter, after you've learned how to spot the major errors.

Before We Start, Some Basic Terminology

You won't be asked to name the parts of speech on the GMAT. However, an acquaintance with some of these terms is necessary to understand the techniques we're about to show you.

- A *noun* is a word that's used to name a person, place, thing, or idea.

- A *verb* is a word that expresses action.

Here is a very basic sentence:

> *Sue opened the box.*

In this sentence, *Sue* and *box* are both nouns, and *opened* is a verb. *Sue* is considered the subject of this sentence because it is the person, place, or thing doing the verb. *Box* is considered the object of the sentence because it receives the action of the verb.

- An *adjective* is a word that modifies a noun.

- An *adverb* is a word that modifies a verb, adjective, or another adverb.

- A *preposition* is a word that notes the relation of a noun to an action or a thing.

- A *phrase* is a group of words acting as a single part of speech. A phrase is missing either a subject or a verb or both.

- A *prepositional phrase* is a group of words beginning with a preposition. Like any phrase, a prepositional phrase does not contain both a subject and a verb.

Here's a more complicated version of the same sentence:

> *Sue quickly opened the big box of chocolates.*

Here's Where Recruiters Look for Marketing Whizzes

Northwestern
Harvard
Michigan
Cornell
Duke
Source: *BusinessWeek*, 2004

In this sentence, *quickly* is an adverb modifying the verb *opened*. *Big* is an adjective modifying the noun *box*. *Of* is a preposition because it shows a relation between *box* and *chocolates*. *Of chocolates* is a prepositional phrase that acts like an adjective by modifying *box*.

- A *pronoun* is a word that takes the place of a noun.

B-School Lingo

net net: end result

- A *clause* is a group of words that contains a subject and a verb.

Here's an even more complicated version of the same sentence:

> *Because she was famished, Sue quickly opened the big box of chocolates.*

There are two clauses in this sentence. *Sue quickly opened the big box of chocolates* is considered an *independent clause* because it contains the main idea of the sentence and could stand by itself. *Because she was famished* is also a clause (it contains a subject and a verb), but it cannot stand by itself. This is known as a *dependent clause*. The word *she* is a pronoun referring to the noun *Sue*.

THE MAJOR ERRORS OF GMAT ENGLISH

1. PRONOUN ERRORS

There are two main types of pronoun errors. The first is called *pronoun reference*. You saw an example of this in the sentence about program trading. Take a look at a simple example:

> *Samantha and Jane went shopping, but she couldn't find anything she liked.*

This type of mistake used to drive Harold Ross, the founding editor of *The New Yorker*, crazy. He was famous for scrawling *Who he?* in the margins of writers' manuscripts. It is supposed to be absolutely clear who is being referred to by a pronoun. In the example above, the pronoun *she* could refer to either Samantha or Jane. The pronoun is ambiguous and must be fixed. You can fix it in three different ways:

> *Samantha and Jane went shopping, but Samantha couldn't find anything she liked.*

> *Samantha and Jane went shopping, but Jane couldn't find anything she liked.*

> *Samantha and Jane went shopping, but they couldn't find anything they liked.*

The second type of pronoun error is called *pronoun number* (singular or plural). Here is a simple example:

> *The average male moviegoer expects to see at least one scene of violence per film, and they are seldom disappointed.*

In this case, the pronoun *they* clearly refers to the average male moviegoer, so there is no ambiguity of reference. However, *the average male moviegoer* is singular. *They* cannot take the place of a singular noun. There is really only one way to fix this sentence.

> *The average male moviegoer expects to see at least one scene of violence per film, and he is seldom disappointed.*

The people who write the GMAT are very fond of both of these types of errors, and routinely make use of them. By the way, as we mentioned earlier, you don't have to memorize any of the terminology we use. You simply have to recognize a GMAT English error when you see it.

HOW DO YOU SPOT A PRONOUN ERROR?

That's easy. Look for pronouns.

A pronoun is a word that replaces a noun. Here's a list of common pronouns. (You don't need to memorize these—just be able to recognize them.)

Singular	Plural
I, me	we, us
he, him	they, them
she, her	both
it	these
each	those
another	
one	
other	**Can Be Singular or Plural**
mine	**Depending on Context**
yours	some
his, hers	none
this	ours
either	you
neither	who
each	which
everyone	what
everybody	that
nobody	
no one	

Every single time you spot a pronoun, you should immediately ask yourself the following two questions:

- Is it completely clear, not just to me but to a pedantic GMAT test writer, who or what the pronoun is referring to?

- Does the pronoun agree in number with the noun it is referring to?

Let's look at an example:

> While Brussels has smashed all Western European tourism revenue records <u>this year, they still lag well behind in exports</u>.

- ○ this year, they still lag well behind in exports
- ○ in the past year, they still lag well behind in exports
- ○ in the past year, it lags still well behind in exports
- ○ this year, they lag still well behind in exports
- ○ this year, it still lags well behind in exports

Here's How to Crack It

Plan A: As you read the sentence for the first time, look to see if there is a pronoun. There is: *they*. Let's make sure the pronoun is used correctly. Who is the *they* supposed to refer to? *Brussels*. Is *Brussels* plural? No, it's the name of a city.

Now that you've spotted the problem, go through the answer choices. Any answer choice with the pronoun *they* in it has to be wrong. You can cross off answer choices A, B, and D. You're down to answer choices C and E.

Both of the remaining answer choices solve the original problem. Read them carefully. If you aren't sure, take a guess. If you said answer choice E, you were right. The adverb *still* in answer choice C should go in front of the verb.

Plan B: Now, what if Plan A lets you down, and you don't spot the error as you read the sentence in the first place? There is always Plan B. Go straight to the answer choices and ask yourself how they are different. Obviously, they differ in several ways—but one huge difference is that some answer choices use the pronoun *they*, while others use the pronoun *it*. This is a clue that will remind you to check pronoun reference and number.

2. MISPLACED MODIFIERS

Misplaced modifiers come in several forms, but the test writers' favorite looks like this:

> *Coming out of the department store, John's wallet was stolen.*

When a sentence begins with a *participial phrase* (just a fancy term for a phrase that starts with a verb ending in *ing*), that phrase is supposed to modify the noun or pronoun immediately following it.

Was the *wallet* coming out of the department store? No.

There are two ways to fix this sentence. First, we could change the second half of the sentence so that the noun or pronoun that comes after the participial phrase is actually what the phrase is supposed to refer to:

> *Coming out of the department store, John was robbed of his wallet.*

Or, we could change the first half of the sentence into an adverbial clause (which contains its own subject) so that it is no longer necessary for the first half of the sentence to modify the noun that follows it:

> *As John was* coming out of the department store, his wallet was stolen.

Other forms of misplaced modifiers include:

A. participial phrases preceded by a preposition:

> *On leaving the department store, John's wallet was stolen.*

(**Correct:** *On leaving the department store, John was robbed of his wallet.*)

B. adjectives:

> *Frail and weak, the heavy wagon could not be budged by the old horse.*

(**Correct:** *Frail and weak, the old horse could not budge the heavy wagon.*)

C. adjectival phrases:

> *An organization long devoted to the cause of justice, the mayor awarded a medal to the American Civil Liberties Union.*

(**Correct:** *An organization long devoted to the cause of justice, the American Civil Liberties Union was awarded a medal by the mayor.*)

In each of these examples, the modifying phrase modified the wrong noun or pronoun.

How Do You Spot a Misplaced Modifier?

That's easy. Whenever a sentence begins with a modifying phrase that's followed by a comma, the noun or pronoun right after the comma should be what the phrase is referring to. Every single time you see a sentence that begins with a modifying phrase, check to make sure that it modifies the right noun or pronoun. If it doesn't, you've spotted the error in the sentence.

The correct answer choice will either change the noun that follows the modifying phrase (the preferred method) or change the phrase itself into an adverbial clause so that it no longer needs to modify the noun.

Let's look at two examples:

Written in 1961, Joseph Heller scored a literary hit with his comedic first novel, *Catch-22.*

○ Written in 1961, Joseph Heller scored a literary hit with his comedic first novel, *Catch-22.*

○ Written in 1961, Joseph Heller scored a literary hit with *Catch-22*, his comedic first novel.

○ Written in 1961, *Catch-22*, the comedic first novel by Joseph Heller, was a literary hit.

○ *Catch-22*, which was written in 1961 by Joseph Heller, scored a literary hit with his comedic first novel.

○ *Catch-22*, the comedic first novel, scored a literary hit for Joseph Heller by its being written in 1961.

Here's How to Crack It

Plan A: As you read the sentence for the first time, go through your checklist. Is there a pronoun error in the sentence? No. Does the sentence begin with a modifying phrase? Yes. Now we're getting somewhere. Let's check to see if the modifying phrase actually modifies what it is *supposed to*. Does it? No. "Joseph Heller" is not what was written in 1961. This is a misplaced modifier.

Now that you've spotted the error, look through the other answer choices and eliminate any that contain the same error. Choice B contains the same error. Get rid of it. You're down to choices C, D, and E.

Now, there are really only two ways to fix this kind of error, as you know. Do any of the answer choices change the noun that follows the modifying phrase? Yes, answer choice C. This is probably the right answer. Read through the other two choices just to make sure there's nothing better. Choices D and E contain awkward constructions. Choice C is the "best" answer.

Plan B: If you don't spot the error as you read the sentence for the first time, you have a second chance to spot it by looking for differences in the answer choices. Several contain a participial phrase followed by the noun the phrase is supposed to modify. But in one of those choices, the noun following the phrase is different. Hmmm. Could this sentence be a case of a misplaced modifier?

<u>Although not quite as liquid an investment as</u> a money-market account, financial experts recommend a certificate of deposit for its high yield.

- ○   Although not quite as liquid an investment as
- ○   Although it is not quite as liquid an investment as
- ○   While not being quite as liquid an investment as
- ○   While it is not quite as liquid as an investment
- ○   Although not quite liquid an investment as

Here's How to Crack It

Plan A: Go through your checklist. Is there a pronoun in this sentence? Yes, the third to last word of the sentence is a pronoun, but it clearly refers back to the certificate of deposit. False alarm. Does the sentence begin with a modifying phrase? Yes. Now we're getting warmer. Check to see whether the modifying phrase modifies what it's supposed to modify. Does *although not quite as liquid an investment*…refer to financial experts? No. This is a misplaced modifier.

The clearest way to fix this sentence would be to change the noun that follows the modifying phrase:

> *Although not quite as liquid an investment as a money-market account, a* certificate of deposit *is recommended by financial experts for its high yield.*

However, you can't fix *this* sentence that way for the very good reason that only the first phrase of the sentence was underlined. This time, you'll have to find a way to fix the modifying phrase itself. Look for an answer choice that changes the modifying phrase into an adverbial clause with its own subject and verb.

Choices A, C, and E do not have subjects and therefore can be eliminated immediately. Choices B and D each have a subject—in both cases, the word *it* turns the modifying phrase into an adverbial clause. However, choice D contains a new error: The word *as* has been moved, leaving *money-market* stranded in the middle of the sentence with no function. While it may sound atrocious, choice B is the "best" answer.

Plan B: Again, if you didn't spot the error as you read the original sentence, the answer choices were there to provide you with a clue. Of the five answer choices, two turned the beginning phrase into a clause by means of the pronoun *it*. By noticing this, you might be reminded to check for a misplaced modifier.

A close relative of a misplaced modifier is a *dangling modifier*. You can spot the two errors in the same way. Here's a simple example:

> *Before designing a park, the public must be considered.*

Q: What is a tip-off to a misplaced modifier error?

Again, this sentence starts with a modifying phrase followed by a comma. The noun following the comma is what the modifying phrase is supposed to modify. Does it? No! *The public* didn't design the park. So who did? A dangling modifier differs from a misplaced modifier in that a dangling modifier doesn't just modify the wrong word—it doesn't modify any word.

To fix this sentence, we would have to insert whoever is designing the park into the sentence:

> *Before designing a park,* the architect *must consider the public.*

3. PARALLEL CONSTRUCTION

There are two kinds of GMAT sentences that test parallel construction. The first is a sentence that contains a list, or has a series of actions set off from one another by commas. Here's an example:

> *Among the reasons cited for the city councilwoman's decision not to run for reelection were the high cost of a campaign, the lack of support from her party, and desiring to spend more time with her family.*

When a main verb controls several phrases that follow it, each of those phrases has to be set up in the same way. In the sentence above, three reasons were listed. The three reasons *were* (main verb):

> the high cost of a campaign,
> the lack of support from her party,
> and
> desiring to spend more time with her family.

The construction of each of the three reasons is supposed to be parallel. The first two items on the list are phrases that are essentially functioning as nouns: the high *cost* (of a campaign); the *lack* (of support from her party). However, the third item on the list seems more like a verb than a noun. How could we change the word *desiring* to a noun? If you said, "the desire," you were absolutely correct. It should read:

> the high cost of a campaign,
> the lack of support from her party,
> and
> *the desire* to spend more time with her family.

A: A modifying phrase followed by a comma. To correct it, make sure that what comes after the comma is modified by what comes before it.

The second kind of GMAT sentence that tests parallel construction is a sentence that's divided into two parts. Here's an example:

> *To say that the song patterns of the common robin are less complex than those of the indigo bunting is doing a great disservice to both birds.*

If the first half of a sentence is constructed in a particular way, the second half must be constructed in the same way. The first half of this sentence begins, "To…"; therefore, the second half has to begin the same way:

> *To say that the song patterns of the common robin are less complex than those of the indigo bunting is* to do *a great disservice to both birds.*

HOW DO YOU SPOT PARALLEL CONSTRUCTION?

That's easy. Every time you read a sentence correction problem, look to see if you can find a series of actions, a list of several things, or a sentence that is divided into two parts.

Here's an example:

> In a recent survey, the Gallup poll discovered that the average American speaks 1.3 languages, buys a new car every 5.2 years, <u>drinks 14 gallons of alcoholic beverages every year, and forgot to pay at least one bill per quarter</u>.

- ○ drinks 14 gallons of alcoholic beverages every year, and forgot to pay at least one bill per quarter
- ○ drinks 14 gallons of alcoholic beverages every year, and forgets to pay at least one bill per quarter
- ○ can drink 14 gallons of alcoholic beverages every quarter and forgot to pay at least one bill per quarter
- ○ drinks 14 gallons of alcoholic beverages every year, and forgets at least to pay one bill per quarter
- ○ drank 14 gallons of alcoholic beverages every year, and forgets to pay at least one bill per quarter

Here's How to Crack It

Plan A: As you read the sentence for the first time, run through your checklist. Is there a pronoun? No. Does the sentence begin with a modifying phrase? Yes, but the word after the phrase is what is supposed to be modified, so this is not a misplaced modifier. Is there a series or list of three things or a series of actions? Yes. Let's see if all the actions are parallel. The average American…

> speaks (1.3 languages)
> buys (a new car…)
> drinks (14 gallons…)
> and
> forgot (to pay…)

The first three verbs are all in the present tense, but the fourth one is in the past tense. The problem in this sentence is a lack of parallel construction.

Now that you know what the error is, go through the answer choices. Any choice that contains the word *forgot* is wrong. We can eliminate choices A and C. Choice E, even though it fixes the parallel construction of the fourth verb, changes the construction of the third verb. Eliminate it.

Choices B and D have perfect parallel construction. If you aren't sure which one is correct, guess and move on. If you picked choice B, you were right. In choice D, the adjectival phrase *at least* had to be in front of *one bill*.

Plan B: The error on which this question hinges is easy to spot if you use Plan B. Clearly, what is at issue is the verb that begins the underlined portion of the sentence. Why would the test writers change around the form of this verb? Aha! They do it in order to create a parallel construction problem.

4. PARALLEL COMPARISON

Another form of parallel construction error that appears on the GMAT is what we call faulty comparison sentences. Here's a simple example:

> *The people in my office are smarter than other offices.*

Taken literally, this sentence compares *the people in my office* with *other offices*. Therefore, it's an example of faulty comparison—it compares two dissimilar things (in this case, *people* and *offices*). To fix this sentence, we need to make the comparison clear, or parallel. There are two ways to do this:

> *The people in my office are smarter than* the people *in other offices.*

or

> *The people in my office are smarter than* those *in other offices.*

We hope that you recognized *those* as a pronoun that takes the place of *the people*. The correct answer to a parallel comparison question on the GMAT almost invariably involves the use of a pronoun (*that* or *those*) rather than a repetition of the noun.

Parallel comparison problems also come up when you compare two actions:

Synthetic oils burn less efficiently than natural oils.

In this case, what is compared is not the two types of oil, but how well each type of oil *burns.* You could fix this by changing the sentence to read,

Synthetic oils burn less efficiently than natural oils burn.

However, the GMAT test writers would rather that you fix it by replacing the second verb (in this case, *burn*) with a replacement verb (*do* or *does*.) Here is how GMAC would like to see this sentence rewritten:

Synthetic oils burn less efficiently than do *natural oils.*

How Do You Spot Parallel Comparison?

Look for sentences that make comparisons. These sentences often include words such as *than, as, similar to,* and *like.* When you find one of these comparison words, check to see whether the two things compared are really comparable.

Let's look at an example:

Q: What is an indication of a parallel comparison error?

> Doctors sometimes have difficulty diagnosing viral pneumonia because the early symptoms of this potentially deadly illness <u>are often quite similar to the common cold.</u>
>
> ○　are often quite similar to the common cold
> ○　often resemble that of the common cold
> ○　are often quite similar to those of the common cold
> ○　are often quite similar to the common cold's symptom
> ○　quite often are, like the common cold, similar

Here's How to Crack It

Plan A: Go through your checklist: Do you see any suspicious pronouns, misplaced modifiers, or unparallel constructions? Good. There aren't any. Do you see any comparison words? Yes, the sentence uses "are" "similar to." Let's see exactly what is being compared. The symptoms of one illness are being compared directly to...another illness. Aha! This is a parallel comparison error. To make this sentence correct, we need to compare the "symptoms" of one illness to the "symptoms" of the other, and the way GMAC would prefer that we do it is by using a replacement pronoun.

If we look at the answer choices, we can eliminate choices A and E because neither makes any attempt to compare symptoms to symptoms. Choice B looks promising because it uses the replacement pronoun "that"; however, "symptoms" is plural and therefore can't be replaced by the singular "that." Choice D seems promising because it looks like it's trying to compare symptoms to symptoms—but if you look more closely, you'll notice that the last word of choice D is "symptom," which is singular. The correct answer is choice C.

Plan B: There are often clues to parallel comparison questions in the answer choices as well. Just as you should be on the lookout for words like *similar to* in the sentences themselves, you can also often spot faulty comparison problems by looking for replacement nouns such as *that of* and *those of*, or replacement verbs such as *than do* and *than does* in the answer choices.

5. Tense

On the GMAT, tense problems are often just a matter of parallel construction. In general, if a sentence starts out in one tense, it should probably stay there. Let's look at an example:

> *When he was younger he walked three miles every day and has lifted weights, too.*

The clause *when he was younger* puts the entire sentence firmly in the past. Thus the two verbs that follow should be in the past tense as well. You may not have known the technical term for *has lifted* (the present perfect tense), but you probably noticed that it was inconsistent with *walked* (the simple past tense). The sentence should read:

> *When he was younger he walked three miles every day and lifted weights, too.*

Here are the tenses that come up on the GMAT:

Tense	Example
present	He *walks* three miles a day.
simple past	When he was younger, he *walked* three miles a day.
present perfect	He *has walked* three miles a day for the last several years.
past perfect	He *had walked* three miles a day until he bought his motorcycle.
future	He *will walk* three miles a day, starting tomorrow.

It isn't important that you know the names of these tenses as long as you understand how they're used. As we said before, a sentence that begins in one tense should generally stay in that tense. For example, a sentence that begins in the present perfect (which describes an action that has happened in the past, but is potentially going on in the present as well) should stay in the present perfect.

> *He has walked three miles a day for the last several years and has never complained.*

One exception to this rule is a sentence that contains the past perfect (in which one action in the past happened before another action in the past). By definition, any action set in the past perfect must have another action that comes after it, set in the simple past.

> *He had ridden his motorcycle for two hours when it ran out*
> *of gas.*

The only other exceptions to this rule come up when one action in a sentence clearly precedes another.

> *The dinosaurs are extinct now, but they were once present on*
> *the earth in large numbers.*

In this case, the sentence clearly refers to two different time periods: *now*, which requires the present tense, and a period long ago, which requires the past tense.

How Do You Spot Tense Errors?

By now, you probably have a pretty good sense of what to do. Using Plan A, look for changes in verb tense in the sentence. Or, using Plan B, look for changes in verb tense in the answer choices. If the answer choices give you several versions of a particular verb themselves, then you should be looking to see which one is correct. Here's an example:

> A doctor at the Amsterdam Clinic maintains that if
> children eat a diet high in vitamins and <u>took vitamin</u>
> <u>supplements, they will be less likely to catch</u> the
> common cold.
>
> ○   took vitamin supplements, they will be less
>   likely to catch
> ○   took vitamin supplements, they are less likely
>   to catch
> ○   take vitamin supplements, they were less
>   likely of catching
> ○   take vitamin supplements, they will be less
>   likely of catching
> ○   take vitamin supplements, they are less likely
>   to catch

Here's How to Crack It

Plan A: As you read the sentence, go through your checklist. There is one pronoun (*they*) in the sentence, but in this case it clearly refers only to the children. Is there a modifying phrase? No. Is there a list of things or a series of actions? Not really. Are the verb tenses inconsistent? Hmm. Now we're getting somewhere. The first verb, "maintains," is in the present tense. So is the verb "eat." But the third verb, "took," which is supposed to be a parallel action with "eat," is in the past tense.

Look at the dependent clause that is partially underlined.

> *...that if children* eat *a diet high in vitamins and* <u>*took vita-*</u>
> <u>*min supplements*</u>...

Obviously, the two verbs are inconsistent with each other, and because only one of them is underlined, that's the one that must be wrong. The correct sentence must have a *take* in it, so we can eliminate choices A and B. Choice C puts the rest of the sentence in the past tense, so scratch C. Choice D puts the rest of the sentence in the future tense. This *might* be acceptable, but the choice also uses the incorrect idiomatic expression *likely of catching*. The correct answer to this question is E, which keeps the entire sentence in the present tense.

Plan B: If you don't spot the error as you read the original sentence, look at the answer choices. Aha! A and B offer us *took*, while D and E offer us *take*. One of these two alternatives must be right. Why would the test writers be offering us this choice of present- and past-tense verbs? Clearly, this is a tense question.

6. SUBJECT-VERB AGREEMENT ERRORS

A verb is supposed to agree with its subject. Let's look at an example:

> *The number of arrests of drunken drivers are increasing every year.*

GMAT test writers like to separate the subject of a sentence from its verb with several prepositional phrases, so that by the time you get to the verb you've forgotten whether the subject was singular or plural.

The subject of the sentence above is *number*, which is singular. The phrase *of arrests of drunken drivers* modifies the subject. The verb of this sentence is *are*, which is plural. If we set off the prepositional phrase with parentheses, this is what the sentence looks like:

> *The number (of arrests of drunken drivers) are...*

To fix this sentence we need to make the verb agree with the subject.

> *The number (of arrests of drunken drivers) is increasing every year.*

HOW TO SPOT SUBJECT-VERB AGREEMENT ERRORS

Cover up the prepositional phrases between the subject and the verb of each clause of the sentence so you can see whether there is an agreement problem. You should also be on the lookout for nouns that sound plural but are in fact singular:

Nouns That Sound Plural (But Aren't)

The Netherlands (the name of any city, state, or country)
Tom or John (any two singular nouns connected by *or*)
the family
the audience
politics
measles
the number
the amount

Singular or Plural?

"The number of..." is singular.
"A number of..." is plural.

You are already on the lookout for pronouns because they're first on your checklist. Sometimes pronouns can be the subject of a sentence, in which case the verb has to agree with the pronoun. There are some pronouns that people tend to think are plural when they are in fact singular:

Q: A parallel construction error can be recognized by what giveaways?

Pronouns That Sound Plural (But Aren't)

everyone	no one	anyone	none
everybody	nobody	anybody	each
everything	nothing	anything	

Let's look at an example of a subject-verb error as it might appear on the GMAT:

Many political insiders now believe that the dissension in Congress over health issues <u>decrease the likelihood for significant action being</u> taken this year to combat the rising costs of healthcare.

- ○ decrease the likelihood for significant action being
- ○ decrease the likelihood that significant action will be
- ○ decrease the likelihood of significant action to be
- ○ decreases the likelihood for significant action being
- ○ decreases the likelihood that significant action will be

Here's How to Crack It

Plan A: As you read the sentence for the first time, run through your mental checklist. Is there a pronoun, a modifying phrase, a list of several things, a series of parallel actions, or a change in tense? Not this time. Let's check for subject-verb agreement. The subject of the independent clause is "insiders" and the correct verb, "believe," follows almost immediately, so there's no problem in the main clause.

However, let's look at the dependent clause that follows: "that the dissension in Congress over health issues decrease the likelihood...."

In this clause, the subject is "dissension," not "health issues." Remember to imagine that there are parentheses around any prepositional phrases, as if the clause looked like this:

...the dissension (in Congress over health issues) decrease...

Is this correct? No, the singular "dissension" needs the singular verb "decreases." Looking at the answers, we can immediately eliminate choices A, B, and C. Now let's examine choices D and E. Both fix the subject-verb error, but choice D uses the unidiomatic expression "likelihood for," and it also uses "being" instead of "will be." The correct answer is choice E.

Plan B: If you don't spot the error as you read the sentence the first time, it takes only a second to look at the answer choices and see that one big difference in the answer choices is the form of the verb "decrease," which means this is a subject-verb issue.

7. IDIOM

GMAC likes to test certain idiomatic expressions. Here's an easy example:

> *There is little doubt that large corporations are indebted for the small companies that broke new ground in laser optics.*

It is incorrect to say you are indebted *for* someone.

> *There is little doubt that large corporations are indebted* to *the small companies that broke new ground in laser optics.*

Idiomatic errors are difficult to spot because there is no one problem to look for. In fact, there are really no rules. Each idiom has its own particular usage. There is no real reason an idiomatic expression is correct. It is simply a matter of custom.

However, you haven't been speaking English for the past 20 years for nothing. The main similarity between GMAT English and American English is that they both use the same idiomatic expressions.

You probably already know them.

HOW DO YOU SPOT IDIOMATIC ERRORS?

If you've gone through the first six items on your checklist—pronouns, misplaced modifiers, parallel construction, faulty comparison, tense, and subject-verb agreement—and still haven't found an error, try pulling any idiomatic expressions out of the sentence so that you can see whether they're correct.

Then make up your own sentence using the suspect idiom:

> *I am indebted for my parents for offering to help pay for graduate school.*

Does that sound right? Of course not. I am indebted *to* my parents. Usually if you take the expression out of the long and awkward sentence and use it in an everyday sentence, the error (if there is one) will be obvious. Here's what an idiom question might look like on the GMAT:

> The administration of a small daily dose of aspirin has not only been shown to lower the risk of heart attack, <u>and it has also been shown to help</u> relieve the suffering of arthritis.
>
> ○ and it has also been shown to help
> ○ and it has also been shown helpful to
> ○ but it has also been shown to help
> ○ but it has been shown helpful in addition for
> ○ in addition it has also been shown helping

Here's How to Crack It

Plan A: As always, run through your checklist. Is there a pronoun in the sentence? Yes, but if you check the answer choices, you'll discover that the same pronoun appears in each one. Obviously, pronoun error is *not* what is tested this time. Is there a modifying phrase? No. So much for misplaced modifiers. Is there a list of things or a series of actions? No. To be sure that there really is no parallel construction problem, we should look at the two halves of the sentence as well. The first half, "… has been shown," matches the second half, "… has also been shown," and both are in the same tense, so there is no problem with either parallel construction or tense. There are no comparison words either, so we don't have to worry about faulty comparison. Could there be something wrong with an idiomatic expression in the original sentence? Let's try a sentence of our own.

Not only is he nasty…

How would you finish this sentence? If you said something like "… but he is also disgusting," you would be absolutely correct. In GMAT English, "not only…" is always followed somewhere in the same sentence by "but also…." Let's look at the answer choices to see which can be eliminated. A, B, and E all use some other conjunction instead of "but," which means that the only possible answers are C and D. Choice D uses "in addition" instead of "also." This *might* not be fatal, but then keep reading after the underlining: "<u>helpful in addition for</u> relieve the suffering of arthritis." If the word "for" seems to stick out, it is because we need to form the infinitive case of "relieve" by using "to." Thus, the correct answer is C.

Plan B: If you didn't spot the idiomatic error in the sentence itself, the first word of each of the answer choices gives you a clue. Does the sentence need an "and," a "but," or an "in addition"?

Q: What is the rule when looking for tense errors?

THE IDIOMS MOST COMMONLY TESTED ON THE GMAT

There are, of course, thousands of idiomatic expressions that could be tested on the GMAT. But here are a handful that seem to come up all the time.

not only...but also...	according to
not so much...as...	agree with
defined as	appear to
regard as	because of
neither...nor...	choose from
modeled after	conclude that
based on	contribute to
a result of	depend on
to result in	due to
a debate over	in order to
a dispute over	instead of
a responsibility to	rather than
responsible for	subject to
different from	worry about
a consequence of	think of...as
so...as to be...	see...as
so (adjective) that	target...as
depicted as	prohibit from
define as	distinguish between...and...
as great as	distinguish...from...
as good as, or better than	
attributed to	
credited with	

THE MINOR ERRORS OF GMAT ENGLISH

The seven errors you've just learned to spot will enable you to answer most of the sentence correction problems that come up on the GMAT. However, there is one more error that shows up often enough that you will probably want to be looking out for it.

8. QUANTITY WORDS

GMAC likes to see if you know how to indicate quantity. Here's an example:

> On the flight to Los Angeles, Nancy had to choose among two dinner entrees.

If there were more than two items being compared, then "among" would be correct. However, if there are only two choices available, the correct quantity word would be "between."

> On the flight to Los Angeles, Nancy had to choose between two dinner entrees.

Below are the comparison quantity words that come up on the GMAT most frequently:

If two items	If more than two items
between	among
more	most
better	best
less	least

Another type of quantity word that shows up on the GMAT from time to time involves things that can be counted as opposed to things that can't. For example, if you were standing in line at a buffet, and you didn't want as big a serving of soup as the person in front of you received, which of the following would be correct?

Could I have fewer soup, please?

or

Could I have less soup, please?

If an item can't be counted, the correct adjective would be "less." However, if we were talking about french fries (which can be counted), the correct adjective would be "fewer."

Countable items	Uncountable items
fewer	less
number	amount, quantity
many	much

HOW DO YOU SPOT QUANTITY WORD ERRORS?

That's easy. Look for quantity words. Whenever you see a "between," check to see if there are only two items discussed in the sentence. (If there are more, you'll need an "among.") Whenever you see an "amount," make sure that whatever is discussed cannot be counted. (If the sentence is talking about the "amount" of people, then you'll need to change it to "number.")

Here's what a "between–among" quantity word error might look like on the GMAT:

Of the many decisions facing the energy commission as it meets to decide on new directions for the next century, the question of the future of nuclear energy <u>is for certain the more perplexing</u>.

- ○ is for certain the more perplexing
- ○ is certainly the most perplexing
- ○ it seems certain, is the most perplexed
- ○ is certainly the more perplexing
- ○ it seems certain, is perplexing the most

Here's How to Crack It

Plan A: If your checklist includes quantity words, the word "more" will set off red flags as you read the sentence. If there were two decisions facing the energy commission, then "the more perplexing" would be correct. However, the sentence says there are "many" decisions. Therefore the sentence must read, "the most perplexing."

This allows us to eliminate choices A and D immediately. Choice C gives the impression that it is the *question* that is perplexed. Eliminate it. Choice E incorrectly positions "the most" after the word it is supposed to modify. The correct answer is choice B.

Plan B: If you don't notice the quantity word in the question itself, you'll probably notice the series of different quantity words ("more" and "most") in the answer choices.

ONE LAST EXAMPLE

The foresight <u>that was evident in the court's selection of an independent trustee</u> to oversee the provisions of the agreement will probably go unremarked by the press.

○ that was evident in the court's selection of an independent trustee

○ that was evident by the court's selection of an independent trustee

○ evidenced with the court's selection of an independent trustee

○ evidenced of the court's selection of an independent trustee

○ that was evident of the court's selection of an independent trustee

Here's How to Crack It

Plan A: As you read the sentence, go through your checklist. Is there a pronoun? No. Does the sentence begin with a modifying phrase? No. Is there a list of several things or a series of actions? No. Is there a tense error? No. Is there a subject-verb problem? No. Is there a comparison word such as "similar" or "than"? No. Are there any quantity words to check? No. Do any expressions in the sentence seem suspicious? No.

We have checked off all of the items on our list. Maybe nothing is wrong with this sentence. The "best" answer to this question is choice A.

Plan B: In cases like this in which there is nothing wrong, you want to be careful not to go off on a wild goose chase. The idea behind Plan B is to look for clues that will lead you to spot one of the major errors that the test writers like to test. If all you're doing is trying out each of the answers in turn to see which one sounds better, you aren't really using Plan B. If you can't spot one of the major errors in the sentence or in the answer choices, you have to start considering that the sentence might be correct as written.

IF YOU'RE REALLY GUNG HO

You can expand your checklist to include as many types of errors as you like. Obviously the more types of errors you can identify, the better prepared you'll be to take the test. But you should bear in mind that while there are other types of errors that we haven't discussed, these errors don't come up very often on the GMAT. Some of the errors to consider: redundant words, misuse of the subjunctive mood, and the use of the passive voice when the active voice is possible. If you're seriously gunning to get every sentence correction question correct, you should dig out your old grammar book from high school and study it carefully. You should also do as many of the real GMAT sentence correction questions in *The Official Guide for GMAT Review* as you can; pay special attention to the idiomatic expressions that come up in these sections, because these are sometimes repeated.

SUMMARY

1. GMAT English is different from American English, and you have to learn the rules of GMAT English to do well on the test.

2. Fortunately, sentence correction questions test only a handful of rules. Once you learn them, you will be able to score quite well on this type of question.

3. There are two Princeton Review techniques that together will help you to ace Sentence Correction: Plan A, in which you look for specific errors as you read the sentence, and Plan B, in which you treat differences among the answer choices as clues that will help you spot the error.

4. Make a checklist of errors to look for when you read a sentence correction question. The most common are:

    A. **Pronouns:** If a sentence contains a pronoun, check to see whether it clearly refers to the noun it is replacing; also check to see whether the pronoun agrees in number with the noun to which it refers.

    B. **Misplaced modifiers:** If the sentence begins with a modifying phrase, check to make sure that the noun it modifies comes directly after the modifying phrase.

    C. **Parallel construction:** If a sentence contains a list of things, or actions, or is broken up into two halves, check to make sure the parts of the sentence are parallel.

    D. **Parallel comparison:** When a sentence makes a comparison, check to see whether the two things compared are really comparable.

    E. **Tense:** If the answer choices contain different verb tenses, make sure that the tense of the verb or verbs in the original sentence is correct. For the most part, verb tense should be consistent throughout a sentence.

    F. **Subject-verb agreement:** GMAT test writers sometimes put extraneous prepositional phrases between the subject and the verb. Cover up or ignore these phrases so that you can see whether the subject and the verb of each clause in the sentence agree with each other.

    G. **Idiom:** If a sentence contains an idiomatic expression that seems wrong to you, try taking the expression out of the sentence and creating a sentence of your own with the suspect expression.

    H. **Quantity words:** Whenever you see a quantity word (countable vs. uncountable; two vs. three or more), check to see if it is used correctly.

5. If you've spotted the error, go through the answer choices and eliminate any that contain the same error. Then look at the remaining answer choices and find the one that fixes the sentence.

6. If you can't find the error, look to the answer choices for clues. Then consider the possibility that there might not be an error.

7. About one-fifth of the sentences are correct as they are. When a sentence is correct, the answer is choice A, which simply repeats the sentence word for word.

8. Once you've gained confidence in your ability to spot the major errors, you should expand your checklist to include other types of errors.

15

Reading
Comprehension

Reading comprehension questions make up roughly one-third of the 41 questions on the Verbal section of the GMAT—approximately 14 questions. Unlike the other questions on the test, reading comprehension questions come in clumps of three or four, and are based on reading passages that range from 200 to 350 words in length.

Before we begin, take a moment to read the following instructions, which are a close approximation of the instructions you will find on the real GMAT.

> <u>Directions</u>: Every reading comprehension question refers to a passage. Answer the questions based on your knowledge of what has been directly said in the passage or what can be inferred from it. You may have to use the scroll bar to see the entire passage. Answer each question by clicking the oval in front of the best response.

Be sure you know and understand these instructions before you take the GMAT. If you learn them ahead of time, you won't have to waste valuable seconds reading them on the day you take the test.

GMAT READING COMPREHENSION: CRACKING THE SYSTEM

See your DVD for more.

It's important to know the instructions for reading comprehension questions on the GMAT, but it's much more important to understand what these instructions mean; they don't tell you everything you need to know about GMAT reading comprehension questions. The rest of this chapter will teach you what you do need to know.

Our techniques will enable you to:

1. Read quickly in a way that will allow you to understand the main idea of the passage.

2. Eliminate answer choices that could not possibly be correct.

3. Take advantage of outside knowledge.

4. Take advantage of inside information (about the way the test writers think).

5. Find answers in some cases *without reading the passage*.

BASIC PASSAGE TYPES

There are only three types of passages on the GMAT:

1. **The social science passage:** This usually concerns a social or historical issue. For example, you might see a passage about world food shortages or the history of a civil rights movement.

2. **The science passage:** This might describe a scientific phenomenon, such as gravitation or plate tectonics.

3. **The business passage:** This usually discusses a business-related topic. For example, you might see a passage about the privatization of state-owned industries or the causes of inflation.

The subject matter for one of the passages on each test may concern a minority group. There are certain useful techniques that can be used on this passage. We'll tell you more about that later in the chapter.

ORDER OF DIFFICULTY

The level of difficulty of the passages you see will depend on how you are doing on the exam—but unlike all the other questions on the GMAT, the three to four reading comprehension questions based on each passage are *not* arranged in order of difficulty. You will see the same questions based on this passage, regardless of how you answer them. The test writers found it too hard to create lots of different questions based on such brief passages.

WHAT YOU WILL SEE ON YOUR SCREEN

The reading passage appears on the left side of the screen. The questions appear one at a time on the right side of the screen, so you can always refer back to the passage. You can't see the next question until you answer the one before, and as always, you can't go back to a previous question once you've moved on.

When you are working on a reading comprehension question, your screen will look a lot like this:

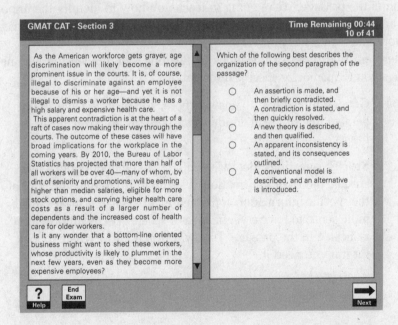

The reading passages come in two lengths—the shorter passages usually fit completely on the computer screen, but the longer passages will require you to use the scroll bar to read them entirely.

Sentence Correction Review

Q: How do you find quantity word mistakes?

Is This Like Normal Reading?

GMAT reading has nothing to do with normal reading. For one thing, no one in his right mind would ever read one of these passages of his own free will. They are almost always boring.

Is This Like Business Reading?

GMAT reading has even less to do with business reading. If your boss asked you to analyze a quarterly report and make a presentation of all the points it raised, you would go home and spend hours going over it. You would look for important information, anticipate questions, and memorize statistics. In short, business reading is a careful, painstaking process. Reading on the GMAT is different.

How to Succeed on the GMAT

If you try to read GMAT passages the way you read quarterly reports, you'll never have time for the questions. Worse, you'll have spent a lot of time absorbing information that you don't need to know.

Reading Comprehension Questions Cover Only a Tiny Fraction of the Material in the Passage

Each reading passage comes with three or four questions. You probably assumed that to answer these questions correctly you would need to know all of the information in the passage, but this isn't true. The questions cover only a small portion of the passage. We're going to teach you how to identify the important parts and ignore most of the rest. The less time you spend reading the passage, the more time you'll have for earning points.

There are two types of questions in Reading Comprehension and neither requires you to memorize specific information:

1. **General questions:** To answer these, you need to have an understanding of the main idea and, perhaps, the *structure* of the passage.

2. **Specific questions:** Because you'll be asked about only a few specific pieces of information, it's silly to try to remember all of the specific information contained in a passage. It makes much more sense to have a vague idea of where specific information is located in the passage. That way you'll know where to look for it if you need it.

Sentence Correction Review

A: Look for quantity words and know whether the noun they modify is countable or not. (See the lists on page 207.)

GMAT READING: THE PRINCETON REVIEW METHOD

Think of a GMAT reading passage as a house. The main idea of the passage is like the overall plan of the house; the main idea of each paragraph is like the plan of each room. Reading the passage is like walking quickly through the house. You don't want to waste time memorizing every detail of every room; you want to develop a general sense of the layout of the house.

Later, when you're asked what was sitting on the table beside the chair in the master bedroom, you won't know the answer off the top of your head, but you will know exactly where to look for it. And you'll be able to answer more questions in less time than someone who has tried to memorize every detail.

Sentence Correction Review

Q: How do you spot an idiom error?

TAKING NOTES

As you make your fast read, you'll probably want to write a one- or two-word summary of each paragraph in your scratch booklet. This is partly to make yourself articulate what the main idea of each paragraph is—but it is also to help you remember them. Have you ever had the experience of reading an entire passage, getting to the end, and then saying, "I have no idea what I just read"?

Most GMAT passages inspire exactly that thought.

STEP ONE: READ FOR THE MAIN IDEA

Take a look at the first paragraph of a sample GMAT passage:

> Biologists have long known that some types of electromagnetic radiation such as X rays and gamma rays can be dangerous to human beings. Operating at a frequency of 10^{18} through 10^{22} mHz, these rays, which are well above the visible light spectrum, were first detected in the early years of the twentieth century.

Here's How to Crack It

You should always read the first sentence of a paragraph carefully because it is often the key to understanding the entire paragraph. The first sentence of the paragraph you just read is no exception: It tells you that the paragraph is about two types of radiation and their danger to humans. When you've identified the main idea, it's a good idea to jot down a couple of key words to encapsulate it.

Once you know what the paragraph is about, it isn't necessary to pay a lot of attention to the other sentences in the paragraph. For example, you probably noticed that while the second sentence included some specific facts, it added nothing to our understanding of the main point of the paragraph. Later, if GMAC asks you a specific question about this radiation, you can go back and find the answer; it will still be there.

Think of This As *Variable* Speed Reading

Until you know what the main idea of a paragraph is, you want to read very carefully. However, as soon as you've got a handle on what's going on, you can speed up. Let your eyes glaze over when you get to the small details. Until GMAC asks you about them, who cares?

The goal is to spend no more than a minute or two "reading" the entire passage. Impossible? Sure, if you're going to insist on reading the way you normally do. Just remember that you don't get any points for reading the passages; when you take the real GMAT the proctor will *not* be walking around the test room awarding extra points for great reading technique. You get points for *answering questions*.

Try reading the second paragraph in the way we've suggested above:

Sentence Correction Review

A: Become familiar with the list of idioms most commonly tested on the GMAT on page 206.

> However, until now, no one has ever suggested that microwave radiation might also be harmful. In preliminary laboratory results, Cleary and Milham have found elevated growth rates in cancer cells exposed to low doses of microwaves. Cleary exposed cancer cells to levels of radiation that are commonly found in microwave ovens and found that the abnormal cells grew 30 percent faster than did unexposed cells. Milham's study focused on ham radio operators who are commonly exposed to levels of radiation slightly higher than those emitted by cellular telephones. He discovered elevated levels of myeloid leukemia.

Here's How to Crack It

Reading the first sentence carefully, we realize that this paragraph is going off on a tangent thought. In fact, the passage is *not* going to be about the dangers of X rays or gamma rays; it is going to be about the possible dangers of microwaves. Now that we have the main idea, we can afford to skim or skip over the rest of the paragraph. If the test writers ask us later about Cleary or Milham, we'll know where to find them, but until then, we can let this part of the passage pass in a blur.

Now try reading the last paragraph of the passage:

> The methodology of Cleary and Milham has been questioned by other scientists in the field. However, no one seriously disputes that their preliminary findings must be taken seriously or that new studies should be set up to try to duplicate their results. Although federal guidelines for how much electromagnetic energy can be allowed to enter the work and home environment have been made more stringent since they were first implemented in 1982, the recent studies pose troubling questions about the safety of microwaves.

Here's How to Crack It

The first word of the second sentence ("however") lets us know that the author was going to come back to the original point: Microwaves may be dangerous. Was this a conclusion? You bet.

In retrospect, the organization of the passage is pretty clear.

- The **first** paragraph states the known dangers of electromagnetic radiation.

- The **second** paragraph talks about the possible dangers of microwaves as shown by two studies.

- The **third** questions the two studies, but decides that, on balance, microwaves may indeed be dangerous.

STEP TWO: AS YOU READ, LOOK FOR STRUCTURAL SIGNPOSTS

Certain words instantly tell you a lot about the structure of a passage. For example, if you were reading a paragraph that began, *There are three reasons the Grand Canyon should be strip-mined*, at some point in the paragraph you would expect to find three reasons listed. If a sentence begins, *On the one hand*, you would expect to find an *on the other hand* later in the sentence. These structural signposts show an alert reader what's going to happen later in a passage. Here are some structural signposts to look out for on the GMAT.

TRIGGER WORDS

The second paragraph you just read began with a word that probably automatically clued you in to the fact that a change was on its way: The word was "however."

Trigger words (such as "however" and "but") always signal a change in the direction of a passage. Here's a simple example:

First paragraph: Most economists believe that the budget deficit will take years to remedy…

Second paragraph: HOWEVER (trigger word), some economists believe there may a fast solution to the problem.

In this example, the trigger word signals that the second paragraph will modify or qualify what has gone before. A trigger word at the beginning of any paragraph is a sure sign that this paragraph will disagree with what was stated in the preceding one.

Trigger words are important even if they do not appear at the beginning of a paragraph; they always signal a change of meaning, even if it is only within a sentence.

Here are the trigger words that often appear on the GMAT:

but	nonetheless
although (even though)	notwithstanding
however	except
yet	while
despite (in spite of)	unless
nevertheless	on the other hand

CONTINUING-THE-SAME-TRAIN-OF-THOUGHT WORDS

Some structural signposts let you know that there will be no contradiction, no change in path. If you see a *first of all*, it stands to reason that there will be a *second of all* and perhaps a *third*. Other signs of continuation:

in addition
by the same token
likewise
similarly
this (implies a reference to preceding sentence)
thus (implies a conclusion)

One other continuing structural element that appears on the GMAT is not a word. Sentences or fragments that appear inside *parentheses* often contain information you'll need to answer a question. You should make a mental note of any sentence or fragment that is enclosed in parentheses.

YIN-YANG WORDS

One of the test writers' all-time favorite types of passage contrasts two opposing viewpoints, and certain words immediately give this away. See if you can supply the second half of the following sentences:

> *The traditional view of the causes of global warming focuses on the burning of fossil fuel…*

(Second half: However, the *new* view is that there is some other cause.)

> *Until recently, it was thought that the Mayan civilization was destroyed as a result of drought…*

(Second half: However, *now* we believe that it was destroyed by space invaders.)

> *The classical model of laissez-faire capitalism does not even admit the possibility of government intervention…*

(Second half: But the *rock'n'roll* version of laissez-faire capitalism says, "Let me just get my checkbook.")

> Before 1960, *it was commonly assumed that the atom was the smallest particle in the universe…*

(Second half: However, *after 1960* scientists began to suspect that there was something even smaller.)

Whenever you spot a "yin" word, you should realize that there is a "yang" on the way. Some other yin-yang words:

Yin	Yang
generally	(however, this time…)
the old view	(however, the new view…)
the widespread belief	(but the in-crowd believes…)
most scientists think	(but Doctor Spleegle thinks…)
on the one hand	(on the other hand…)

Sentence Correction Review: Quantity Comparison Words

Comparing two items
between
more
better
less

Comparing more than two items
among
most
best
least

GETTING THROUGH THE PASSAGE FASTER

Structural elements like these can help you understand a passage more quickly, with less "reading" and less wear and tear on your brain. When you spot one of these signposts, make a mental note. If it actually starts a paragraph, you might begin your three-word synopsis of the paragraph with a big "but." A structural signpost is usually more important to your understanding of a passage than any individual fact within that passage.

STEP THREE: ATTACK THE QUESTIONS

Once you've grasped the main ideas of the paragraphs, you can attack the questions aggressively. As we noted earlier, each passage is followed by up to four questions of varying levels of difficulty. These questions *generally* follow the organization of the passage. In other words, a question about the first paragraph will probably come before a question about the second paragraph.

GENERAL QUESTIONS

- "What is the primary purpose of this passage?"

- "What is the author's tone?"

- "Which of the following best describes the structure of the passage?"

Each of the questions above is a general question. A two-minute "read" using the techniques we've shown you over the last few pages should be all that you need to answer the general questions—without going back to the passage. Always try to answer a general question in your own words *before* you look at the answer choices.

Using POE to Eliminate Wrong Answers on General Questions

Once you have your *own* idea of what the answer should be, it's time to use POE to zero in on GMAC's answer. In the chapter on Sentence Correction, you learned that it's often easier to eliminate incorrect answers than to select the correct answers. The Process of Elimination is just as useful on reading comprehension questions. How can you use POE to eliminate wrong answers to general questions?

General questions have general answers. Thus, we can eliminate any answer to a general question that focuses on only one part of the passage or is too specific in some other way. We can also eliminate answers that cite information that's not in the passage at all. For example, here's a question based on the passage you have already read:

> The main topic of the passage is
> - the health hazards of X rays and gamma rays on humans
> - the overly severe federal guidelines on radiation
> - the potential dangers of microwaves
> - to compare and contrast the work of Cleary and Milham
> - the limits of study methodology in science

Here's How to Crack It

In spite of the fact that X rays and gamma rays were mentioned in the first sentence, we know that this was just an introductory thought to get to the real idea of the passage—the danger of microwaves. So eliminate choice A. The federal guidelines in choice B were mentioned in the passage, but only at the very end. Could this be the main idea of the entire passage? No way. Choice C is the best answer and exactly what we should be expecting from our fast "read." Although Cleary and Milham are discussed several times, they are never compared, so we can eliminate choice D. And even though the passage mentions that the methodologies of the two scientists have been questioned, choice E goes much further than that to question the methodology of *all* science.

Specific Questions

- "The passage suggests which of the following about the laboratory results on microwaves mentioned in the highlighted section?"

- "According to the passage, a study of ham radio operators might be expected to find which of the following?"

Each of the questions above is a specific question. Specific questions have specific answers which you'll now need to find. Naturally, your two-minute "read" has not equipped you with the answers to these questions, but every specific question gives you a clue about where to look for the answer.

LINE REFERENCES

Some questions refer to a highlighted portion of the passage. The highlighting will be visible only when you're working on the question that it pertains to. In this book we'll use line numbers instead of highlighting, so you don't have to look at the highlighting when you're trying to answer other questions.

So, how do you find the answer to the following question?

> The passage suggests which of the following about the federal guidelines on microwaves mentioned in line 12?

That's easy: It has a line reference. All you have to do is go back to the cited (or, on the GMAT, the highlighted) line or lines. You should start reading a little above them until you come to the answer to the question.

LEAD WORDS

How do you find the answer to *this* question?

> "According to the passage, a study of ham radio operators might be expected to find which of the following?"

When a question seems to be specific but is not highlighted, look for a catchy word or phrase in the question. For example, in this question, there's a very clear specific reference: "ham radio operators." We call this a **lead** phrase. Now that you know what you're looking for, run your finger down the passage on the screen as you scroll until you see your lead word or phrase. When you find it, you will have almost certainly found your answer.

Try this technique out right now by running your finger down the passage below until you find "ham radio operators." Don't read; just look:

> Biologists have long known that some types of electromagnetic radiation such as X rays and gamma rays can be dangerous to human beings. Operating at a frequency of 10^{18} through 10^{22} mhz, these rays, which are well above the visible light spectrum, were first detected in the early years of the twentieth century.
>
> However, until now, no one has ever suggested that microwave radiation might also be harmful. In preliminary laboratory results, Cleary and Milham have found elevated growth rates in cancer cells exposed to low doses of microwaves. Cleary exposed cancer cells to levels of radiation that are commonly found in microwave ovens and found that the abnormal cells grew 30 percent faster than did unexposed cells. Milham's study focused on ham radio operators who are commonly exposed to levels of radiation slightly higher than those emitted by cellular telephones. He discovered elevated levels of myeloid leukemia.

Sentence Correction Review: Countability

Different words are used depending on whether you are talking about things that you can count (french fries) or things that are not countable (water).

Countable
fewer
number
many

Not countable
less
amount, quantity
much

The methodology of Cleary and Milham has been questioned by other scientists in the field. However, no one seriously disputes that their preliminary findings must be taken seriously or that new studies should be set up to try to duplicate their results. Although federal guidelines for how much electromagnetic energy can be allowed to enter the work and home environment have been made more stringent since they were first implemented in 1982, the recent studies pose troubling questions about the safety of microwaves.

USING POE TO ELIMINATE WRONG ANSWERS ON SPECIFIC QUESTIONS

Specific questions have very specific answers. Before you even go to the answer choices, you should usually be able to point to the exact spot in the passage where the answer to the question is to be found.

Once you go to the answer choices, you'll probably be able to eliminate several right away. However, if you are down to two possibilities, don't try to prove one of the answers right. Look for something in the passage that will make one of the answers *wrong*. It's often easier to find the flaw in an incorrect answer. For example, here's a question (complete with answer choices) based on the passage you have already read:

> According to the passage, a study of ham radio operators might be expected to find which of the following?
>
> ○ The presence of X rays and gamma rays
> ○ Unusual cells growing 30% faster than normal
> ○ A level of radiation exposure similar to that found in users of microwave ovens
> ○ Higher levels of a particular type of leukemia
> ○ Levels of radiation identical to those emitted by cellular phones

Here's How to Crack It

The lead words "ham radio operators" led us to the second half of the second paragraph. If you haven't already, read the relevant sentences and get an idea of what you might expect the answer to be.

Now, go to the answer choices. Would a study of ham radio operators find the presence of X rays and gamma rays? Well, neither are mentioned in *this* paragraph. The *first* paragraph did mention these rays—but only to introduce the dangers of microwaves. So much for choice A.

Both choices B and C were mentioned in this paragraph, but only in connection with *Cleary's* work—which had nothing to do with ham radio operators.

General or Specific?

When you read a reading comprehension question, determine whether it is general or specific. To answer general questions, you need to have an understanding of the main idea and the structure of the passage. To answer specific questions, you need to have a vague sense of where to find the information based on your knowledge of the passage's structure.

You might have been torn between choices D and E because both come from the right place in the passage. Don't try to decide which is best. Look for a reason one of them is *wrong*. Let's attack choice E. It says that ham operators were exposed to levels of radiation identical to those emitted by cellular phones. Is that *exactly* what the passage said? Well, no. According to the passage, ham radio operators were exposed to slightly *higher* levels. Choice E is history. The correct answer must be choice D.

Q: What is the purpose of skimming the passage?

INFERENCE QUESTIONS

> Which of the following can be inferred from the passage about the level of radiation from cellular telephones?

Although this question asks you to draw an inference, you'll find that GMAC's idea of an inference will be much more timid than yours. GMAT inferences go at most a *tiny* bit further than the passage itself. If your thoughts about this type of question becomes too subtle, you'll get it wrong. Here's an example:

> Which of the following can be inferred from the passage about the studies conducted by Cleary and Milham?
>
> ○   Cleary's results were better documented than Milham's.
> ○   Neither study is scientifically valid.
> ○   Both studies indicated that microwaves were more harmful than X rays.
> ○   The final results were not in at the time the article was written.
> ○   The results of both studies were based on the same scientific data.

Here's How to Crack It

The passage never said that one study was better than the other, so eliminate answer choice A. While both studies were questioned in the third paragraph, it would be inferring far too much to say that neither was scientifically valid. Eliminate choice B. The passage never said that microwaves were more harmful than X rays. It seems likely that they are less harmful. Eliminate choice C. The results of both studies were called "preliminary" in paragraph two. Thus, choice D seems so obvious that you might almost hesitate to call it an inference. This is exactly the kind of inference that the GMAT test writers feel comfortable making. Not only was choice E not stated, but it is likely to be false. Cleary concentrated on cancerous cells exposed to levels of radiation equivalent to microwave ovens. Milham studied ham radio operators. The best answer is D.

ADVANCED POE: ATTACKING DISPUTABLE ANSWER CHOICES

Say you've eliminated two answer choices on a reading comprehension question, but you can't decide which of the remaining three choices is best. All three seem to say the same thing. How do you choose among them? The test writers and GMAC want their correct answers to be indisputable so that no one will ever be able to complain.

Here are three statements. Which of them is indisputable?

- ○ Shaw was the greatest dramatist of his time.
- ○ Shaw's genius was never understood.
- ○ Shaw was a great dramatist, although some critics disagree.

Shaw's status as a playwright will always be a matter of opinion. If GMAC made the first statement the correct answer to a reading comprehension question, people who got the question wrong might argue that not everyone considers Shaw the greatest dramatist of his time.

If GMAC made the second statement the best answer to a reading comprehension question, people who got the question wrong could argue that someone, somewhere in the world, must have understood poor old Shaw.

The third statement, by contrast, is indisputable. Most critics would agree that Shaw was *a* great dramatist. If there are any critics who do not, the test writers cover themselves with a little disclaimer: "although some critics disagree." The third statement is so vague that no one could possibly argue with it.

In general, an answer choice that is highly specific and unequivocal is *disputable* and is therefore usually not the best answer.

> An answer choice that is general and vague is *indisputable* and is therefore often the correct answer.

HOW TO *PICK* AN INDISPUTABLE ANSWER CHOICE

Certain words make a statement so *vague* that it is almost impossible to dispute. Here are some of these words:

usually	can
sometimes	some
may	most

If a statement says that Shaw is *sometimes* considered the greatest dramatist ever, who can dispute that?

A: To gain basic familiarity with the topic and to sum up each paragraph. Devote only about two minutes to skimming; do not get caught up in details or difficult concepts. Remember, you get points for answering the questions, not reading the passage.

HOW TO *AVOID* A DISPUTABLE ANSWER CHOICE

Certain words make a statement so *specific* that it's easy to dispute. Here are some of these words:

always	all
must	complete
everybody	never

If a statement says that Shaw is *always* considered the greatest dramatist ever, who couldn't dispute that?

RESPECT FOR PROFESSIONALS

GMAC has tremendous respect for all professionals—doctors, scientists, economists, writers, and artists. It is very unlikely that the test writers would create a right answer that implies anything negative about a professional.

By the same token, it would be unusual to find a best answer choice that took any but the lightest digs at America. Our country is pretty much beyond GMAC's reproach.

MODERATE EMOTION

The test writers avoid using passages that convey strong emotions on the GMAT. The author's tone might be "slightly critical," but it will not be "scornful and envious." The author's tone might be "admiring," but it will never be "overly enthusiastic." If you see strong words like these in an answer choice, it's probably wrong and can be eliminated.

THE DIVERSITY PASSAGE

For many years minority groups have complained—justifiably—that standardized tests like the GMAT discriminate against them. GMAC responded to this criticism by adding a diversity passage to many of its tests. One of the reading passages on the GMAT you take will almost certainly be about some marginalized group—African-Americans, Mexican-Americans, women.

Designed to answer charges that the GMAT is biased, the diversity passage is invariably positive in tone. This doesn't make the test any fairer to minorities, but it does sometimes make the test easier to beat. Any answer choice that expresses negative views of the marginalized group in question is almost certainly wrong. Try the following example:

The author considers women's literature to be

- ○ derivative
- ○ lacking in imagination
- ○ full of promise and hope
- ○ much better than the literature being written by men today
- ○ uninteresting

Reading Comprehension

Trigger words that signal a change in meaning:
- but
- although (even though)
- however
- yet
- despite (in spite of)
- nevertheless
- nonetheless
- notwithstanding
- except
- while
- unless
- on the other hand

Here's How to Crack It

You don't need to see the passage to answer this question. The whole purpose of the diversity passage is to illustrate to everyone how broad-minded and unbiased the GMAT really is. "Derivative," "lacking in imagination," and "uninteresting" all express negative opinions of literature written by (what the test writers consider to be) a minority group.

Answer choice D goes too far in the other direction. As far as the test writers are concerned, women's literature is just as good as, but no better than, anyone else's. The answer must be choice C.

PUTTING ALL THIS TO WORK

Now that you know something about how to tackle GMAT passages and what to look for in them, try the sample passage below. Find the main idea of each paragraph (and if you like, jot down a few key words about each one); look for structural signposts along the way.

Try to spend no more than two minutes "reading." Remember, you only get points for answering questions. (At the end of this chapter, you will find the notes that one of our teachers made when she "read" the passage.)

Remember, on the GMAT, you'll have no more than four questions per passage. We've included a few extra questions just for practice.

Until recently, corporate ideology in the United States has held that bigger is better. This traditional view of the primacy of big, centralized companies is now being challenged as some
(5) of the giants of American business are being outperformed by a new generation of smaller, streamlined businesses. If it was the industrial revolution that spawned the era of massive industrialized companies, then perhaps it was the
(10) information revolution of the 1990s that spawned the era we're now in—the era of the small company.

For most of the 20th century, big companies dominated an American business scene that
(15) seemed to thrive on its own grandness of scale. The expansion westward, the growth of the railroad and steel industries, an almost limitless supply of cheap raw materials, plus a population boom that provided an ever-increasing demand
(20) for new products (although not a cheap source of labor) all coincided to encourage the growth of large companies.

But rapid developments in the marketplace have begun to change the accepted rules of
(25) business and have underscored the need for fast reaction times. Small companies, without huge overhead and inventory, can respond quickly to a technologically advanced age in which new products and technologies can become outmoded
(30) within a year of their being brought to market.

Of course, successful emerging small companies face a potential dilemma in that their very success will tend to turn them into copies of the large corporate dinosaurs they are now supplant-
(35) ing. To avoid this trap, small companies may look to the example of several CEOs of large corporations who have broken down their sprawling organizations into small, semi-independent divisions capable of surviving in today's market-
(40) place.

ATTACKING THE QUESTIONS

1. The primary purpose of the passage is to
   ○ present evidence that resolves a contra-
       diction in business theory
   ○ discuss reasons an accepted business pat-
       tern is changing
   ○ describe a theoretical model and a method
       whereby that model can be tested
   ○ argue that a traditional ideology deserves
       new attention
   ○ resolve two conflicting explanations for a
       phenomenon

Sentence Structure

While you skim a passage, be aware of its structure. Is one theory presented and then discounted? Are there lists of items? Does it provide two schools of thought? Trigger words, which act as structural signposts, can help you uncover a passage's structure.

Here's How to Crack It

This is a general question, and general questions always reflect the structure of the passage. The first words of the passage were "until recently." We hope you recognized right away that this was "yin-yang" terminology, as was "this tradi-tional view." Obviously this passage is about to present a *new* view.

The old view, according to the passage, was that in America large companies were always better off than small companies. Of course, the new view is that smaller companies are now doing better than big companies. This was probably enough for you to answer all the general questions in this section, but let's look quickly at the rest of the passage: Paragraph two gives historical reasons why big-ger used to be better; paragraph three explains why this is no longer true today; and paragraph four concludes by talking about how small companies can stay successful as they inevitably get bigger. Let's analyze the answer choices:

(A) In yin-yang passages, new is virtually always better than old. There is really no contradiction here. Also, GMAT passages hardly ever "resolve" anything definitively. How could they in only 250 words? Eliminate this answer.

(B) This is the best answer. It mirrors the yin-yang structure of the passage—the accepted pattern of almost a century is now changing.

(C) If you picked this one, you were thinking too hard. Perhaps you thought the primacy of the small company was the new theoretical model, about to be tested. However, the passage seems to imply that the decline of large companies and the ascendancy of small companies started before anyone even real-ized what was happening, let alone came up with some smart theory about it.

(D) Was the author arguing that in fact the traditional view that "bigger is better" is actually correct after all? Nope. Eliminate it.

(E) Again, GMAT passages rarely "resolve" anything. Also, while there are two conflicting elements in this passage, they are not conflicting explanations for a single phenomenon.

2. According to the passage, all of the following are examples of developments that helped promote the growth of large companies earlier in this century EXCEPT

- ○ the growth of the railroad industry
- ○ America's westward expansion
- ○ an almost inexhaustible source of raw materials
- ○ the existence of an inexpensive source of labor
- ○ the development of an industry to produce steel

Here's How to Crack It

This is a specific question without a line number, but you probably knew just where to look. Which paragraph gives historical background on the growth of large companies? If you said paragraph two, you are absolutely correct.

The first time you "read" this passage, you may have skipped over the specifics in this paragraph because they weren't necessary to understand the purpose of the paragraph. Now, of course, you are interested. But even if you had spent 20 minutes (you didn't really have) memorizing the entire passage, wouldn't you still have wanted to peek back at this paragraph just to make sure you remembered it correctly? Because you were going to have to look back anyway, it made sense to skip over the details the first time around. Remember, there was no guarantee that there would even be a question about this information. It is not unusual to find GMAT passages whose questions completely ignore whole paragraphs at a time.

This is an "except" question, which means that every answer choice is correct but one. The answer to this question was buried inside the parentheses in lines 20–21: ("although not a cheap source of labor"). The answer to this question is choice D.

3. The author's attitude toward the traditional view expressed in lines 1–7 can best be described as

- ○ scornful and denunciatory
- ○ dispirited and morose
- ○ critical but respectful
- ○ admiring and deferential
- ○ uncertain but interested

Here's How to Crack It

You could eliminate two of these answer choices without even reading the passage. GMAC would never include a passage in which the author's attitude toward companies like General Motors is "scornful and denunciatory" or "dispirited and morose." Both choices A and B are so strong and out in left field that we can safely eliminate them. As far as the passage is concerned, the traditional ideology no longer works, so we can pretty much rule out choice D, "admiring and deferential." Choice E is a little too vague. The only possible answer is choice C.

4. It can be inferred from the passage that which of the following actions would be most consistent with the traditional ideology described in the passage?

    ○   Splitting a manufacturing company into several smaller divisions
    ○   Bringing a new product to market within a year
    ○   Creating a department to utilize new emerging technologies
    ○   Expanding an existing company in anticipation of growing demand
    ○   Cutting inventory and decreasing overhead

Here's How to Crack It

The trick in inference questions is to infer as little as possible. The traditional ideology is that bigger is better. Which of the answer choices shows a situation getting bigger? The best answer is choice D. Choices A and E both illustrate the process of downsizing as described in the passage. Choices B and C illustrate the lean-and-mean tactics attributed in the passage to small companies.

5. According to the passage, to avoid the trap posed by "a potential dilemma" mentioned in line 33, emerging successful small companies will have to do which of the following?

    ○   Turn for advice to the industry analysts who earlier predicted the problems of large companies
    ○   Avoid taking paths that will make them too successful
    ○   Learn to embrace the traditional ideology of large corporations
    ○   Create small interconnected divisions rather than expanding in traditional ways
    ○   Hire successful CEOs from other firms

Here's How to Crack It

Whenever you see a specific question with a line reference (indicated on the test by highlighting, or in this book by line numbers), always remember to read a little above and a little below the referenced line. In this case, we are not interested so much in the "dilemma" as we are in avoiding the trap posed by the dilemma. The answer to this question is in the last three lines of the passage.

Let's analyze the answer choices:

(A) This is an interesting idea, but it is not said in the passage, so we can eliminate it.

(B) The right idea, but takes it too far. It is practically un-American to think that a company would try not to become too successful.

(C) The traditional ideology is what got the big companies into trouble. Eliminate it.

(D) This is the best answer and a nice paraphrase of what was said in the last three lines of the passage.

(E) The passage suggests that small companies could learn from these CEOs, but does not suggest that the small companies *hire* the CEOs.

6. Which of the following best describes the organization of the first paragraph of the passage?
   ○ A conventional model is described and an alternative is introduced.
   ○ An assertion is made and a general supporting example is given.
   ○ Two contradictory points of view are presented and evaluated.
   ○ A historical overview is given to explain a phenomenon.
   ○ A new theory is described and then qualified.

Here's How to Crack It
This is a structure question, pure and simple. Let's interpret the answers:

(A) correctly describes this yin-yang paragraph

(B) ignores the structure of the passage

(C) is close, but fails to show that one point of view is considered superior to the other

(D) describes paragraph two instead of paragraph one

(E) The word "qualified" means "limited." The author seems to like the idea of the small company and certainly doesn't qualify it in the first paragraph.

B-School Lingo

run the numbers: analyze
quantitatively

7. It can be inferred from the passage that small companies are better able to adapt to the new business climate due to which of the following factors?

    I. low overhead and inventory
    II. the ability to predict when new products will become outmoded
    III. the capacity to change quickly to meet new challenges

- ○ I only
- ○ II only
- ○ III only
- ○ I and III only
- ○ I, II, and III

Here's How to Crack It

I, II, III–type questions are nasty because you have to answer three questions in order to get one right. Where in the passage were small companies actually described? If you said paragraph three, you were absolutely correct. Because this is an inference question, we need to make sure we don't infer too far. Let's look at Statement I. Can we infer that small companies are better able to adapt because of low inventory? Sure. In lines 26–27 the passage reads, "Small companies, without huge overhead and inventory…"

Because we know that Statement I works, we can cross off choices B and C; why? Because neither includes Statement I. Let's look at Statement II. While it seems likely that the ability to predict ahead of time which products are going to become outmoded would help small companies adapt faster, there is no indication in the passage that anyone has the ability to predict ahead. If you aren't sure about Statement II, you can skip it and go on to Statement III. This statement is definitely true. It is a paraphrase of lines 26–27. The best answer is choice D.

HERE'S WHAT YOUR NOTES SHOULD LOOK LIKE AFTER YOU'VE FINISHED READING THIS PASSAGE

1) Traditional view: bigger is better
    New view: smaller is better

2) Hist. reasons for big companies' success

3) Reasons for small companies' success

4) Danger for small companies: getting too big

SUMMARY

1. Reading comprehension questions make up roughly one-third of the 41 questions on the Verbal section of the GMAT—approximately 13 questions. The three types of passages that may appear on the test are social science, science, and business.

2. Reading comprehension questions are not presented in any order of difficulty.

3. GMAT reading has little to do with regular reading, and even less to do with business reading. GMAT passages contain many more pieces of information than you'll be tested on. Trying to remember all this useless information is silly.

4. Read a passage for its main idea. This will enable you to answer the general questions, and give you a good idea of where to look for the answers to specific questions. When you read, jot down a few words summarizing each paragraph.

5. Structural signposts can help you see how a passage is organized. Look for trigger words, continuing-the-same-train-of-thought words, and yin-yang constructions.

6. Answers to specific questions can be found either through highlighted **line references** or **lead words**. When line references are given, read a little above and a little below them.

7. Attack answer choices that are disputable. Specific, strong statements are often wrong. Vague, wimpy statements are often correct.

8. The tone of a minority passage is invariably positive. This can sometimes help you to answer questions even if you haven't had time to read the entire passage.

9. The test writers typically do not create right answers that:

    A. are disrespectful to professionals
    B. are too strong
    C. condone prejudicial attitudes

10. I, II, III–type questions are best tackled by POE.

16

Critical Reasoning

Critical reasoning questions make up a little less than one-third of the 41 questions on the Verbal section of the GMAT—approximately 11 questions. They consist of very short reading passages (typically 20 to 100 words). Each of these passages is followed by one or two questions, which are supposed to test your ability to think clearly. When this section was first introduced, the test writers said that "no knowledge of the terminology and of the conventions of formal logic is presupposed." Nevertheless, you'll find that while it may not be presupposed, some knowledge of the rudiments of formal logic—as applied by The Princeton Review—can substantially increase your score.

THE HISTORY OF CRITICAL REASONING

Over the years the test writers have tried several different formats in an attempt to test reasoning ability.

The original GMAT contained a section called "Best Arguments." In 1961, this section was replaced with something called "Organization of Ideas." In 1966, this section was also phased out, and for six years reasoning ability went unmeasured. In 1972, GMAC tried again, with a section called "Analysis of Situations." Finally, on the October 1988 version of the GMAT, the test writers unveiled Critical Reasoning for the first time.

WELL, NOT EXACTLY THE *FIRST* TIME

In fact, Critical Reasoning looks a lot like Best Arguments. Test writers have used this type of question for years on the LSAT (Law School Admission Test) and, until recently, on the GRE (Graduate Record Exam).

Before we begin, take a moment to read a close approximation of the instructions for critical reasoning questions:

> Directions: Every critical reading question refers to a brief argument or set of statements. Pick the best answer among the choices given.

Obviously you won't need to read these instructions again.

HOW TO ATTACK THE CRITICAL REASONING QUESTIONS

The terseness of these instructions implies that all you need on these questions is common sense. Common sense will certainly help, but you should also understand a bit about the formal logic on which Critical Reasoning is based.

Like the other types of questions found on the GMAT, critical reasoning questions tend to be predictable. There are only a few question types, and as you learn how the test writers use their smattering of formal logic to write critical reasoning questions, you'll be able to anticipate the answers to certain of those questions. In this chapter we'll teach you how to:

1. Use clues in the questions to anticipate the kind of answer you're looking for in a passage.

2. Analyze and attack the passages in an organized
    fashion.

3. Understand the basic structure of the passages.

4. Use Process of Elimination to eliminate wrong choices.

A Word About GMAT Logic

GMAT logic is different from the formal logic you may have studied in college. Our review of GMAT logic is not intended to be representative of logic as a whole. We don't intend to teach you logic; we're going to teach you *GMAT* logic.

The Passage

Most critical reasoning passages are in the form of *arguments* in which the writer tries to convince the reader of something. Here's an example:

> In the past 10 years, advertising revenues for the magazine *True Investor* have fallen by 30%. The magazine has failed to attract new subscribers, and newsstand sales are down to an all-time low. Thus, sweeping editorial changes will be necessary if the magazine is to survive.

There are three main parts to an argument:

the Conclusion: This is what the author is trying to persuade us to accept.

the Premises: These are the pieces of evidence the author gives to support the conclusion.

the Assumptions: These are unstated ideas or evidence without which the entire conclusion might be invalid.

In the passage above, the author's *conclusion* is found in the last line:

> *Thus, sweeping editorial changes will be necessary if the magazine is to survive.*

To support this, the author gives three pieces of evidence, or *premises*: Advertising revenue is down; there are no new subscribers; and very few people are buying the newspaper at the newsstand.

Are there any *assumptions* here? Well, not in the passage itself. Assumptions are never stated by the author. They are parts of the argument that have been left out. Even the best thought-out argument has assumptions. In this case, one important assumption the author seems to make is that it was the old editorial policy that caused the problems the magazine is now encountering. Another assumption is that editorial changes alone will be enough to restore the magazine's financial health.

Reading Comprehension Review

Q: What should you keep in mind with reading comprehension inference questions?

A critical reasoning passage is not necessarily made up of only these three parts. The passage might contain other information as well—extraneous ideas, perhaps, or statements of an opposing point of view. This is why it's so important to find and identify the conclusion and the premises (as well as the argument's underlying assumptions).

- Look for conclusions at the beginning and end of a passage. Most arguments follow one of two common structures:

    premise, premise, premise, conclusion
    or
    conclusion, premise, premise, premise

    Therefore the conclusion can often be found in the first or last sentence of the passage.

A: Do not infer too much! Stick to the passage as closely as possible.

- Look for the same kinds of structural signposts we showed you in the Reading Comprehension chapter (Chapter 15). Words like the following often signal that a conclusion is about to be made:

    therefore   hence
    thus   implies
    so   indicates that

- Look for a statement that cannot stand alone; in other words, a statement that needs to be supported by premises.

- If you can't find the conclusion, look for the premises instead. These are the parts of the argument that support the conclusion.

    Premises are often preceded by another kind of signpost. Words like the following signal that evidence is about to be given to support a conclusion:

    because   in view of
    since   given that

THIS IS NOT LIKE READING COMPREHENSION

Reading comprehension passages are long and filled with useless facts. By now you've gotten used to reading these passages for their structure, letting your eyes skip over factual data you probably won't be tested on anyway.

By contrast, critical reasoning passages are quite short, and every single word should be considered carefully; shades of meaning are very important. Because the passages are relatively short, you will probably never have to use the scroll bar to see them in their entirety.

THE QUESTION

Immediately after the passage, there will be a question. There is usually only one question per passage—which means it is essential that you *always read the question first*.

The question contains important clues that will tell you what to look for as you read the passage.

THERE ARE EIGHT QUESTION TYPES

Here are examples of the eight major question types you'll see (we'll go into much greater detail later in the chapter):

   1. The passage above assumes that…

We call these **assumption questions**. As you read the passage in question, you will be looking for an unstated premise on which the argument depends.

Reading Comprehension Review

Trigger words that signal a conclusion:
therefore
thus
so
hence
implies
indicates

   2. Which of the following, if true, would most strengthen the conclusion drawn above?

We call these **strengthen-the-argument questions**. This type of question is like an assumption question in that it asks you to find an unstated premise on which the argument depends, and then bolster it.

   3. Which of the following, if true, would most seriously weaken the conclusion of the passage above?

We call these **weaken-the-argument questions**. This type of question, like an assumption question, asks you to find an unstated premise of the argument and poke holes in it.

   4. Which of the following can best be inferred from the passage above?

We call these **inference questions**. This question, like inference reading comprehension questions, is at most asking you to go a tiny, tiny bit further than the passage does.

   5. Which of the following most resembles the method used by the author to make the point above?

We call these **parallel-the-reasoning questions**. This type of question asks you to find a new argument among the answer choices that mimics the original argument.

   6. Which of the following best resolves the apparent contradiction in the passage above?

We call these **resolve/explain questions**. This type of question asks you to pick an answer choice that explains an inconsistency between two incompatible facts.

   7. Which of the following would be most useful in evaluating the logic of the argument above?

We call these **evaluate-the-argument questions**. This type of question asks you to pick an answer choice that would help to "assess" or "evaluate" part of an argument.

8. The bolded phrase plays which of the following roles in the argument above?

We call these **identify-the-reasoning questions**. This type of question asks you to identify the method or technique the author is using.

While the wording of the questions may vary, these are the question types you'll see—there are only eight. Each type of question has its own strategy, as we'll show you.

SCOPE

As you read through this chapter you will notice that certain sentences keep coming up again and again in our discussions of how to eliminate wrong answers.

The ones you'll see most often are:

"This answer choice goes too far."

"That choice is out of the scope of the argument."

Why do these sentences appear so frequently? Because scope is one of the test writers' favorite topics for critical reasoning questions. It takes a little practice to figure out how scope works. We'll give you an introduction to the concept here, but you'll need to work through the entire chapter (and practice on the questions in our online tests or in *The Official Guide for GMAT Review*) to understand it completely.

Here's an example:

> In an effort to save money, a country's government is considering reducing its military spending. However, without military contracts, crucial industries in that country face bankruptcy, which could disrupt the economy. Thus, the same government that is reducing its military spending will eventually have to provide these industries with money for peacetime research and development.
>
> Which of the following states the conclusion of the passage above?
> ○ The necessity of providing money to keep crucial industries from going bankrupt will discourage the government from reducing its military budget.
> ○ If the government decreases its military budget, it will eventually be forced to increase its military budget to its former level.
> ○ The industries that receive research and development money will be successful in their efforts to convert to peacetime manufacturing.
> ○ In the event of war, this country would be unprepared for military conflict.
> ✓ Reducing military spending to save money will result in some increases in other types of spending.

We will discuss how to do this type of question (inference) shortly, but for now we're going to summarize the argument and skip right to the answer choices in order to illustrate how to use scope as an elimination technique. The argument states that a country wants to save money by decreasing its military budget; however, in order to keep the industries that depend on military contracts from collapsing, the country will have to *spend* some additional money as well.

THE GMAT REWARDS NARROW MINDS

Q: What is the very first thing you should do when starting a critical reasoning passage?

In the Critical Reasoning section it is easy to think too much. The first answer choice (what we call answer choice A) might look very tempting at first, because it seems to take the argument to its logical conclusion: "Hey, if cutting military spending is going to end up *costing* the country money, they may as well not do it." But the test writers consider answer choice A to be outside the scope of this argument. In fact, if you think about it, we have no idea whether or not the government will be discouraged, or even whether the costs of supplying research and development money will be greater than the savings in military spending. This answer goes much further than the argument itself.

Choice B goes too far as well. Perhaps cutting military spending will turn out to be a bad idea, but even if that is true, how do we know that the country will then eventually decide to increase military spending? What might happen in the future is well outside the scope of this argument.

We can eliminate choice C for the same reason, because it merely goes off on a tangent to speculate as to the ultimate fate of the industries mentioned in the passage. Whether these industries succeed in making the transition to peacetime manufacturing is not crucial to this argument.

If you are tempted by choice D, you're still thinking too much. When a country reduces its military spending, you could argue that it might be less prepared for war—but that is way outside the scope of this passage. Be careful not to impose your own value judgments or thought processes on these questions.

Choice E may have seemed simplistic when you first read it. You might even have thought that it wasn't really a conclusion at all, that it was more like a summary. However, this is the answer the test writer would choose. And remember, *she's* the one who makes up the answer key. Choice E stays within the scope of the argument.

KEEPING TRACK OF POE

As you eliminate answer choices, it's vital that you physically cross them off in your scratch booklet. This will prevent you from wasting time rereading answer choices you've already eliminated.

Now let's look at the eight types of critical reading questions.

1. ASSUMPTION QUESTIONS

An assumption question asks you to identify an *unstated* premise of the passage from among the answer choices. As you read the passage, what you will be looking for is a gap in the underlying logic of the argument—a gap that can only be closed by stating out loud what is now only being assumed. There are many different kinds of assumptions the GMAT test writers can use, but let's get you started by identifying three: causal assumptions, statistical assumptions, and analogy assumptions.

A: Read the question! This will allow you to focus on what the question is asking when you read the passage.

CAUSAL ASSUMPTIONS

The test writers are extremely fond of these and make use of them several times on every GMAT. Causal assumptions take an effect and suggest a cause for it. Take a look at the simplified example below.

> *Every time I wear my green suit, people like me. Therefore, it is my green suit that makes people like me.*

The author's conclusion (it is the green suit that makes people like him) is based on the premise that every time he wears it, he has observed that people like him. But this argument relies on the assumption that there is no other possible cause for people liking him. Perhaps he always wears a red tie with his green suit, and it's really the tie that people like.

Whenever you spot a cause being suggested for an effect, ask yourself if the cause is truly the reason for the effect, or if there might be an alternate cause.

ANALOGY ASSUMPTIONS

An argument by analogy compares one situation to another, ignoring the question of whether the two situations are comparable.

> *Use of this product causes cancer in laboratory animals. Therefore, you should stop using this product.*

The author's conclusion (you should stop using the product) is based on the premise that the product causes cancer in laboratory animals. This argument is not really complete. It relies on the assumption that because this product causes cancer in laboratory animals, it will also cause cancer in humans.

Whenever you see a comparison in a critical reasoning passage, you should ask yourself: Are these two situations really comparable?

STATISTICAL ASSUMPTIONS

A statistical argument uses statistics to "prove" its point. Remember what Mark Twain said: "There are lies, damned lies, and statistics."

> *Four out of five doctors agree: The pain reliever in Sinutol is the most effective analgesic on the market today. You should try Sinutol.*

The conclusion (you should try Sinutol) is based on the premise that four out of five doctors found the pain reliever in Sinutol to be the most effective. However, a literal reading of the passage tells us that the statistic that the author uses in support of his conclusion is only based on the opinions of five doctors (all of whom may be on the board of directors of Sinutol). The author's conclusion is based on the *assumption* that four out of *every* five doctors will find Sinutol to be wonderful. This may be correct, but we do not know for sure. Therefore, the most we can say about the conclusion is that it may be true.

Whenever you see statistics in an argument, always be sure to ask yourself the following question: Are the statistics representative?

Neither analogy nor statistical arguments are as prevalent on the GMAT as causal arguments.

How to Recognize an Assumption Question

Assumption questions generally contain one of the following wordings:

- Which of the following is an assumption on which the argument depends?

- The argument above assumes which of the following?

- The claim above rests on the questionable presupposition that…

How to Attack the Answer Choices on an Assumption Question

Assumptions plug holes in the argument and help make a conclusion true. Here are some guidelines for spotting assumptions among the answer choices:

- Assumptions are never stated in the passage. If you see an answer choice that comes straight from the passage, it is **not** correct.

- Assumptions support the conclusion of the passage. Find the conclusion in the passage, then try out each answer choice to see whether it makes the conclusion stronger.

- Assumptions frequently turn on the gaps of logic we've just discussed. If the argument proposes a cause for an effect, you should ask yourself whether there might be some other cause. If the argument uses statistics, you should probably ask yourself whether the statistics involved are representative. If the argument offers an analogy, you should ask yourself whether the two situations are analogous.

Now Let's Try the Passage

Many people believe that gold and platinum are the most valuable commodities. To the true entrepreneur, however, gold and platinum are less valuable than opportunities that can enable him to further enrich himself. Therefore, in the world of high finance, information is the most valuable commodity.

The author of the passage above makes which of the following assumptions?

○ Gold and platinum are not the most valuable commodities.
○ Entrepreneurs are not like most people.
○ The value of information is incalculably high.
✓ Information about business opportunities is accurate and will lead to increased wealth.
○ Only entrepreneurs feel that information is the most valuable commodity.

Assumption Guidelines

1) Assumptions are never stated in the passage.
2) An assumption must support the conclusion; eliminate answer choices that do not strengthen the conclusion.
3) Assumptions frequently work to fill in gaps in the reasoning of the argument.
4) Look to see if the assumption, whether it is statistical, analogical, or causal, links the evidence to the conclusion.

Here's How to Crack It

The question tells you that you are looking for an assumption, which means that as you read, you'll be looking for a hole in the argument.

Because an assumption supports the conclusion, it's a good idea to know what the conclusion is. Can you identify it? It was in the last sentence, preceded by "therefore": "In the world of high finance, information is the most valuable commodity."

As you read the passage, keep your eyes open for potential holes in the argument. For example, as you read it might occur to you that the author is assuming that there is no such thing as bad information. Anyone who has ever taken a stock tip knows the error in that assumption.

Don't be upset if you can't find a hole in the argument as you read. The answer choices will give you a clue.

Let's attack the answer choices:

○ Gold and platinum are not the most valuable commodities.

Does this support the conclusion? In a way, it does. If information is supposed to be the most valuable commodity, it might help to know that gold and platinum are not the most valuable commodities.

However, saying that gold and platinum are *not* the most valuable commodities does not necessarily mean that information *is* the most valuable commodity.

○ Entrepreneurs are not like most people.

If most people find gold and platinum to be the most valuable commodities, while entrepreneurs prefer information, then it *could* be inferred that entrepreneurs are not like most people. Does this support the conclusion, though? Not really. Remember, the GMAT rewards narrow thinking.

○   The value of information is incalculably high.

This answer merely restates the conclusion. Remember, we're looking for an assumption, which is an *unstated* premise. In addition, this answer goes beyond the scope of the argument. To say that information is valuable does not mean that its value is "incalculable."

Q: Most arguments can be divided into what three parts?

○   Information about business opportunities is accurate and will lead to increased wealth.

This is the best answer. If the business information is not accurate, it could not possibly be valuable. Therefore this statement supports the conclusion by plugging a dangerous hole in the argument.

○   Only entrepreneurs feel that information is the most valuable commodity.

Does this statement strengthen the conclusion? Actually, it might weaken it. The conclusion states that "in the world of high finance, information is the most valuable commodity." Presumably the world of high finance is not composed exclusively of entrepreneurs. If only entrepreneurs believed information to be the most valuable commodity, then not everyone in the world of high finance would feel the same way.

2. STRENGTHEN-THE-ARGUMENT QUESTIONS

If a question asks you to strengthen an argument, it is saying that the argument can be strengthened; in other words, again, you're going to be dealing with an argument that has a gap in its logic.

Like assumption questions, strengthen-the-argument questions are really asking you to find this gap and then fix it with additional information. Here are some guidelines for spotting strengthen-the-argument statements among the answer choices:

- The best answer will strengthen the argument with *new* information. If you see an answer choice that comes straight from the passage, it's wrong.

- The new information you're looking for will support the conclusion of the passage. Find the conclusion in the passage, then try out each answer choice to see whether it makes the conclusion stronger.

- Strengthen-the-argument questions frequently turn on the gaps of logic we've already discussed. If the argument proposes a cause for an effect, you should ask yourself whether there might be some other cause. If the argument uses statistics, you should probably ask yourself whether the statistics involved are representative. If the argument offers an analogy, you should ask yourself whether the two situations are analogous.

HOW TO RECOGNIZE A STRENGTHEN-THE-ARGUMENT QUESTION

Strengthen-the-argument questions generally contain one of the following wordings:

- Which of the following, if true, most strengthens the author's argument?

- Which of the following, if true, most strongly supports the author's hypothesis?

NOW LET'S TRY THE PASSAGE

It has recently been proposed that we adopt an all-volunteer army. This policy was tried on a limited basis several years ago and was a miserable failure. The level of education of the volunteers was unacceptably low, while levels of drug use and crime soared among army personnel. Can we trust our national defense to a volunteer army? The answer is clearly "No."

Which of the following statements, if true, most strengthens the author's claim that an all-volunteer army should not be implemented?

○ The general level of education has risen since the first time an all-volunteer army was tried.

○ The proposal was made by an organization called Citizens for Peace.

◉ The first attempt to create a volunteer army was carried out according to the same plan now under proposal and under the same conditions as those that exist today.

○ A volunteer army would be less expensive than an army that relies on the draft.

○ The size of the army needed today is smaller than that needed when a volunteer army was first tried.

Here's How to Crack It

You know from reading the question first that you're expected to fix a flaw in the argument. Even better, the question itself tells you the conclusion of the passage: "An all-volunteer army should not be implemented."

Because the reasoning in a strengthen-the-argument question is going to contain gaps, it pays to see whether the argument is statistical, causal, or analogous. You may have noticed that the argument does, in fact, use an analogy. The author bases his conclusion on the results of one previous experience. In effect he says, "The idea didn't work then, so it won't work now." This is the potential flaw in the argument.

If you didn't spot the argument by analogy, don't worry. You would probably have seen it when you started attacking the answer choices:

> ○ The general level of education has risen since the first time an all-volunteer army was tried.

Does this support the author's conclusion? Actually, it may weaken the conclusion. If the general level of education has risen, it could be argued that the level of education of army volunteers is also higher. This would remove one of the author's objections to a volunteer army. Eliminate it.

> ○ The proposal was made by an organization called Citizens for Peace.

This is irrelevant to the author's conclusion. You might have wondered whether a group called "Citizens for Peace" was the right organization to make suggestions about the army. Attacking the reputation of a person in order to cast doubt on that person's ideas is a very old pastime. There's even a name for it: an ad hominem fallacy. An ad hominem statement does not strengthen an argument. Eliminate it.

> ○ The first attempt to create a volunteer army was carried out according to the same plan now under proposal and under the same conditions as those that exist today.

This is the best answer. The passage as it stands is potentially flawed because we cannot know that a new attempt to institute an all-volunteer army would turn out the same way it did before. This answer choice provides new information that suggests that the two situations *are* analogous.

> ○ A volunteer army would be less expensive than an army that relies on the draft.

Does this support the conclusion? No. In fact, it makes a case *for* a volunteer army. Eliminate it.

> ○ The size of the army needed today is smaller than that needed when a volunteer army was first tried.

Like answer choice D, this answer contradicts the conclusion of the passage. If we need a smaller army today, maybe we would be able to find enough smart and honest volunteers to make a volunteer army work. Eliminate it.

Strengthen the Conclusion

Always stick to the passage. The easiest way to strengthen an argument is to strengthen the conclusion. You can do this by presenting new evidence that strengthens the underlying assumptions. Any answer choice that comes from the passage will probably be wrong. New evidence or assumptions, whether statistical, analogical, or causal, must support the conclusion.

A: Causal assumptions. If an argument states that one event caused another, always ask yourself if there could have been an alternate cause.

3. WEAKEN-THE-ARGUMENT QUESTIONS

If a question asks you to weaken an argument, it implies that the argument can be weakened; in other words, once again you're going to be dealing with unstated premises and a logical gap.

Like assumption questions and strengthen-the-argument questions, weaken-the-argument questions really ask you to find a hole in the argument. This time, however, you don't need to fix the hole. All you have to do is expose it. Here are some guidelines for finding weaken-the-argument statements among the answer choices:

- The statement you'll look for should weaken the *conclusion* of the passage. Find the conclusion in the passage, then try out each answer choice to see whether it makes the conclusion less tenable.

- Weaken-the-argument questions frequently trade on the gaps of logic that we've already discussed. If the argument proposes a cause for an effect, ask yourself whether there might be some other cause. If the argument uses statistics, ask yourself whether the statistics involved are representative. If the argument offers an analogy, ask yourself whether the two situations are analogous.

How to Recognize a Weaken-the-Argument Question

Q: What are some helpful approaches to finding the conclusion?

Weaken-the-argument questions usually contain one of the following wordings:

- Which of the following, if true, most seriously weakens the conclusion drawn in the passage?

- Which of the following indicates a flaw in the reasoning above?

- Which of the following, if true, would cast the most serious doubt on the argument above?

Now Let's Try the Passage

The recent turnaround of the LEX Corporation is a splendid example of how an astute chief executive officer can rechannel a company's assets toward profitability. With the new CEO at the helm, LEX has gone, in only three business quarters, from a 10 million dollar operating loss to a 22 million dollar operating gain.

A major flaw in the reasoning of the passage above is that

○ the passage assumes that the new CEO was the only factor that affected the corporation's recent success

○ the recent success of the corporation may be only temporary

○ the chief executive officer may be drawing a salary and bonus that will set a damaging precedent for this and other corporations

○ the author does not define "profitability"

○ rechanneling assets is only a short-term solution

Here's How to Crack It

You know from reading the question that you'll need to find a flaw in the reasoning of the argument. As you read the passage, look for the conclusion. The correct answer choice will weaken this conclusion. In this passage the conclusion is in the first sentence: "The recent turnaround of the LEX Corporation is a splendid example of how an astute chief executive officer can rechannel a company's assets toward profitability."

Because this is a weaken-the-argument question that will almost certainly contain a gap in its reasoning, you should look to see whether the argument is causal, statistical, or analogical. In this case the argument is causal. The passage implies that the sole cause of the LEX Corporation's turnaround is the new CEO. While this *may* be true, it is also possible that there are other causes. If you didn't spot the causal argument, don't worry. You would probably have seen it when you attacked the answer choices. Let's do that now:

○ the passage assumes that the new CEO was the only factor that affected the corporation's recent success

This is the best answer. The new chief executive officer may not have been the cause of the turnaround—there may have been some other cause we don't know about.

○ the recent success of the corporation may be only temporary

It may be hasty to crown LEX with laurels after only three economic quarters, but this statement doesn't point out a flaw in the *reasoning* of the passage. Eliminate it.

A: Look at the beginning or end of the passage and be familiar with conclusion flag words (see list on page 240).

○   the chief executive officer may be drawing a
      salary and bonus that will set a damaging
      precedent for this and other corporations

This answer choice may seem tempting because it's not in favor of the new CEO. But this alone doesn't represent a major flaw in the reasoning of the passage. Eliminate it.

○   the author does not define "profitability"

An author can't define every word he uses. Profitability seems a common enough word, and a change in the balance sheet from minus 10 million to plus 22 million seems to qualify. Eliminate it.

○   rechanneling assets is only a short-term solu-
      tion

Like the second answer choice, this statement implies that all the votes aren't in yet. This does not affect the reasoning of the argument, however. Eliminate it.

WEAKEN-THE-ARGUMENT QUESTIONS COME IN DIFFERENT FLAVORS

GMAT test writers use a variety of different wordings to ask the same question. One variation on the weaken-the-argument question might look like this:

A telephone poll conducted over two states asked respondents whether their homes were ever cold during the winter months. 99% of respondents said they were never cold during the winter months. The pollsters published their findings, concluding that 99% of all homes in the United States have adequate heating.

Which of the following most accurately describes what might be a questionable technique employed by the pollsters in drawing their conclusion?

○   The poll wrongly ascribes the underlying
      causes of the problem.
○   The poll assumes conditions in the two states
      are representative of the entire country.
○   The pollsters conducted the poll by tele-
      phone, thus relying on the veracity of the
      subjects they spoke to.
○   The pollsters did not go to the houses in
      person, thus precluding the actual mea-
      surement of temperatures in the subjects'
      homes.
○   The pollsters never defined the term "cold" in
      terms of a specific temperature.

Here's How to Crack It

Whether a question contains the words "weakens the argument," or "undermines the conclusion," or even "describes a questionable technique"—what it is really asking you to do is find a hole in the logic of the argument. And, as usual, there are three types of holes that the GMAT test writers are very fond of: statistical, causal, and analogical. Did you spot one of these as you read the passage? Whenever you see an actual statistic in an argument (in this case, 99 percent), you should examine it closely: The pollsters are basing a statistic for the entire country on a poll conducted in only two states. If you didn't spot this as you read the passage, don't worry; you'll spot it as you read the answer choices.

    ○   The poll wrongly ascribes the underlying causes of the problem.

This answer choice says there might be an alternate cause for the conclusion—but does this feel like a causal argument? Let's hold onto this and keep reading.

    ○   The poll assumes conditions in the two states are representative of the entire country.

Aha! This choice is saying there is a statistical flaw in the argument. What if the two states were located in the southern part of the United States? If the residents of Florida were warm in January, would that be representative of the rest of the country who might be freezing? This seems like it must be the best answer, but let's keep reading to make sure.

    ○   The pollsters conducted the poll by telephone, thus relying on the veracity of the subjects they spoke to.

While this might represent a weakness in their interviewing technique, the question to ask yourself is whether this is an inherent weakness in the way the pollsters *drew their conclusion*. It is not; eliminate it.

    ○   The pollsters did not go to the houses in person, thus precluding the actual measurement of temperatures in the subjects' homes.

Again, if the pollsters had measured the temperature in each of the houses they went to, their information would probably have been more accurate, but does this constitute a flaw in the way the conclusion was drawn? Nope. Cross this one off.

    ○   The pollsters never defined the term "cold" in terms of a specific temperature.

This choice is nitpicking. While it might have been better if the pollsters had asked the respondents what temperature they considered cold, this wouldn't really weaken the conclusion. The best answer is the second one.

4. INFERENCE QUESTIONS

Like inference questions in reading comprehension, critical reasoning inference questions do not really ask you to make an inference. In fact, you will often find that the answer to a critical reasoning inference question is so basic that you won't believe it could be correct the first time you read it. Inference questions often have little to do with the conclusion of the passage; instead they might ask you to make inferences about one or more of the premises.

HOW TO RECOGNIZE AN INFERENCE QUESTION

Inference questions typically contain one of the following wordings:

- Which of the following can be inferred from the information above?

- Which of the following must be true on the basis of the statements above?

- Which of the following conclusions is best supported by the passage?

- Which of the following conclusions could most properly be drawn from the information above?

You'll note that the last two questions seem to ask about the conclusion—but, as you'll see, they in fact ask for an inference.

Let's try an example:

> In film and videotape, it is possible to induce viewers to project their feelings onto characters on the screen. In one study, when a camera shot of a woman's face was preceded by a shot of a baby in a crib, the audience thought the woman's face was registering happiness. When the same shot of the woman's face was preceded by a shot of a lion running toward the camera, the audience thought the woman's face was registering fear. Television news teams must be careful to avoid such manipulation of their viewers.

Which of the following can be inferred from the passage?

○ Television news teams have abused their position of trust in the past.
○ The expression on the woman's face was, in actuality, blank.
○ A camera shot of a baby in a crib provoked feelings of happiness in the audience.
○ Audiences should strive to be less gullible.
○ The technique for manipulating audiences described in the passage would work with film or videotape.

Here's How to Crack It

This is an inference question. The test writers are probably not interested in the conclusion of the passage. You'll look for a statement that seems so obvious that it almost doesn't need saying. Let's attack the answer choices:

> ○ Television news teams have abused their position of trust in the past.

If you chose this answer, you inferred too much. The passage doesn't say that news teams have ever abused their position of trust. Eliminate it.

> ○ The expression on the woman's face was, in actuality, blank.

The audience had no idea what the expression on the woman's face was, and neither do we. It would make sense for the woman's face to be blank, but we don't know whether this is so. This answer goes too far.

> ○ A camera shot of a baby in a crib provoked feelings of happiness in the audience.

This is the best answer. The passage says that the audience projects its own feelings onto characters on the screen. If the audience believes the woman's face reflects happiness, then that must have been its own reaction.

> ○ Audiences should strive to be less gullible.

This statement goes way beyond the intent of the passage. Eliminate it.

> ○ The technique for manipulating audiences described in the passage would work with film or videotape.

Again, this statement goes too far to be the correct answer to an inference question. Eliminate it.

ANOTHER TYPE OF INFERENCE QUESTION

Inference questions come in one other form—and as you read them, you might think you are being asked to supply a conclusion rather than an inference: Almost invariably, the question asks you to find a "conclusion that is best supported by the passage above." But, in fact, this is really nothing more than an inference question. And again, the key is not going too far.

Here's an example:

> Fewer elected officials are supporting environmental legislation this year than at any time in the last decade. In a study of 30 elected officials, only five were actively campaigning for new environmental legislation. This comes at a time when the public's concern for the environment is growing by leaps and bounds.
>
> Which of the following conclusions is best supported by the passage above?
>
> ○   More elected officials are needed to support environmental legislation.
>
> ○   Elected officials have lost touch with the concerns of the public.
>
> ○   The five elected officials who actively campaigned for new environmental legislation should be congratulated.
>
> ○   If the environment is to be saved, elected officials must support environmental legislation.
>
> ○   If elected officials are truly to represent their constituents, many of them must increase their support of environmental legislation.

Here's How to Crack It

Because you read the question first, you know that this is really just an inference question—and, as always with inference questions, the main thing is not to go too far. Be wary of answer choices that go further than the scope of the original argument. For example, if the passage has given you several noncontroversial facts about advertising, do not select an answer choice that says advertising is a waste of time.

Let's attack the answer choices:

> ○   More elected officials are needed to support environmental legislation.

This statement ignores the last premise of the passage—that the public is becoming more and more concerned about the environment. Eliminate it.

> ○   Elected officials have lost touch with the concerns of the public.

This clearly goes beyond the scope of the argument and ignores parts of the first two premises that relate to the environment.

      ○   The five elected officials who actively cam-
            paigned for new environmental legislation
            should be congratulated.

This statement, while consistent with the sentiments of the author, again does not deal with the last premise, relating to the concerns of the public.

      ○   If the environment is to be saved, elected offi-
            cials must support environmental legislation.

This answer choice again ignores the last premise in the passage and goes too far. Eliminate it.

      ○   If elected officials are truly to represent their
            constituents, many of them must increase
            their support of environmental legislation.

Bingo. This answer is supported by all the premises, and it does not go beyond the scope of the argument.

FOUR DOWN—FOUR TO GO

As you begin working through the practice questions in this book or in *The Official Guide to GMAT Review,* you will quickly realize that most critical reasoning questions turn out to be one of the four major question types you have just learned: assumption, weaken-the-argument, strengthen-the-argument, or inference. The four remaining question types appear much less often. However, because of the somewhat random nature of the CAT, one of these less frequently asked questions could easily be the first one you see on the Verbal portion of the GMAT; therefore it is just as important to be familiar with all eight.

5. PARALLEL-THE-REASONING QUESTIONS

Parallel-the-reasoning questions ask you to recognize the reasoning in a passage and follow the same line of reasoning in one of the answer choices. The best way to understand the passage associated with a reasoning question is to simplify the terms. Here's an example: "If it rains, I will stay home today." We could simplify this by saying, "If A, then B."

HOW TO RECOGNIZE A PARALLEL-THE-REASONING QUESTION

Parallel-the-reasoning questions will usually contain one of the following word-ings:

- Which of the following most closely parallels the reasoning used in the argument above?

- Which of the following supports its conclusion in the same manner as the argument above?

- Which of the following is most like the argument above in its logical structure?

Q: What is the most effective way to eliminate answer choices in critical reasoning assumption questions?

Here's an example:

> World-class marathon runners do not run more than six miles per day when they are training. Therefore, if you run more than six miles per day, you are not world-class.
>
> Which of the following statements supports its conclusion in the same manner as the argument above?
>
> ○ Sprinters always run in the morning. If it is morning, and you see someone running, it will not be a sprinter.
> ○ Paint never dries in less than three hours. If it dries in less than three hours, it is not paint.
> ○ Little League games are more fun for the parents than for the children who actually play. Therefore, the parents should be made to play.
> ○ If a car starts in the morning, chances are it will start again that evening. Our car always starts in the morning, and it always starts in the evening as well.
> ○ If you sleep less than four hours per night, you may be doing yourself a disservice. Studies have shown that the most valuable sleep occurs in the fifth hour.

Here's How to Crack It

First, simplify the argument in the passage. World-class marathon runners do not run more than six miles per day when they are training. (If A, then B.) Therefore, if you run more than six miles per day, you are not world-class. (If not B, then not A.)

Now let's attack the answer choices:

> ○ Sprinters always run in the morning. If it is morning, and you see someone running, it will not be a sprinter.

Just because this answer choice is also about running doesn't mean the reasoning will be the same. In fact, it is unlikely that the test writers would use the same subject matter for the correct answer. If we simplify this argument, we get: If A, then B. If B, then not A. Is this the same reasoning used in the passage? No. Eliminate it.

> ○ Paint never dries in less than three hours. If it dries in less than three hours, it is not paint.

If we simplify this argument, we get: If A, then B. If not B, then not A. This is the best answer.

A: Because assumptions are unstated, eliminate any answer choices that are stated in the passage. Also, look for the three types of reasoning—statistical, analogical, and causal—each of which may be used as an assumption.

    ○   Little League games are more fun for the
               parents than for the children who actu-
               ally play. Therefore, the parents should be
               made to play.

Simplifying this argument, we get…not much. The reasoning here is totally different. Also, note that the subject matter here is still about sports. Eliminate it.

    ○   If a car starts in the morning, chances are
               it will start again that evening. Our car
               always starts in the morning, and it always
               starts in the evening as well.

If we simplify this argument, we get: If A, then B. If always A, then always B. That doesn't sound right. Eliminate it.

    ○   If you sleep less than four hours per night,
               you may be doing yourself a disservice.
               Studies have shown that the most valu-
               able sleep occurs in the fifth hour.

Simplifying this argument, we get…again, not much. The reasoning in this answer choice is very different from the reasoning in the passage. Eliminate it.

6. RESOLVE/EXPLAIN QUESTIONS

Some GMAT questions ask you to resolve an apparent paradox or explain a possible discrepancy. In these questions, the passage will present you with two seemingly contradictory facts. Your job is to find the answer choice that allows both of the facts from the passage to be true.

How to Recognize a Resolve/Explain Question

Resolve/Explain questions will usually contain one of the following wordings:

- Which of the following, if true, resolves the apparent contradiction presented in the passage above?

- Which of the following, if true, best explains the discrepancy described above?

- Which of the following, if true, forms a partial explanation for the paradox described above?

Here's an example:

> In 1994, TipTop Airlines reported an increase in the total number of passengers it carried from the year before, but a *decrease* in total revenues— even though prices for its tickets on all routes remained unchanged during the two-year period.
>
> Which of the following, if true, best reconciles the apparent paradox described above?
>
> ○ TipTop Airlines was a victim of a mild recession in 1994.
> ○ Total passenger miles were up in 1994.
> ○ Fuel costs remained constant during the two-year period.
> ○ Passengers traveled shorter (and thus less expensive) distances in 1994.
> ○ TipTop did not buy any new airplanes or equipment in 1994.

Q: How do you tackle an assumption question?

Here's How to Crack It

First, restate the contradiction in your own words.

"TipTop's profits went down even though they flew more passengers."

Now, let's see which of the answer choices makes both of the facts in the argument true.

> ○ TipTop Airlines was a victim of a mild recession in 1994.

If TipTop was affected by a recession, that might explain a loss of revenues. But because ticket prices remained the same, it would not explain how the number of passengers could have increased at the same time. Eliminate it.

> ○ Total passenger miles were up in 1994.

If total passenger miles were up, and prices remained the same, there is no way that there could have been a loss of revenues. We can eliminate this choice as well.

> ○ Fuel costs remained constant during the two-year period.

If fuel costs had *not* remained constant, the company's profits might have fallen. An increase in fuel prices could have increased its costs and cut into profits. But it would not have cut into total *revenues*, which is what we are concerned with in this passage. Of course, because choice C told us that the costs remained constant, this choice has no bearing on the argument at all. Eliminate it.

> ○ Passengers traveled shorter (and thus less expensive) distances in 1994.

Bingo! If passengers traveled on short, inexpensive flights, then they paid less money. In spite of the increase in number of passengers, the money they paid could have added up to less than that of the year before. This is the best answer, but always remember to read all the choices anyway.

> ○ TipTop did not buy any new airplanes or equipment in 1994.

This answer is much like the third choice, which we call choice C. If TipTop *had* bought new planes, it might have cut into its profits, but it would not have had any bearing on revenues. Of course, because this choice told us that TipTop did not buy any planes, there is no relevance at all. Eliminate it

7. EVALUATE-THE-ARGUMENT QUESTIONS

A few GMAT critical reasoning questions will ask you to pick an answer choice that would help to "evaluate" or "assess" part of an argument. Like assumption questions, evaluate-the-argument questions revolve around understanding the unspoken gap in the logic of an argument.

HOW TO RECOGNIZE AN EVALUATE-THE-ARGUMENT QUESTION

Evaluate-the-argument questions generally contain one of the following wordings:

- The answer to which of the following questions would be most useful in evaluating the significance of the author's claims?

- Which of the following pieces of information would be most useful in assessing the logic of the argument presented above?

Take a look at the following example:

> Following a period of lingering malaise after a recent remarkable economic upturn in the solar-powered energy sector, Company X, a major maker of solar-powered generators, claimed that its rapid upturn resulted from the inventory still on hand in its warehouse.
>
> Which of the following, if it could be carried out, would be most useful in evaluating the company's hypothesis as to the causes of its rapid economic upturn?
>
> ○ Comparing the length of the economic downturn experienced by Company X to the length of the upturn later experienced by Company X
>
> ○ Comparing the rapidity of the economic upturn for Company X to that of other major makers of solar-powered generators, which did not have inventory on hand
>
> ○ Calculating the average sales increases within the individual business units of Company X
>
> ○ Comparing the total number of solar-powered generator sales by Company X just before the economic upturn to the total number of solar-powered generator sales by Company X just after the economic upturn
>
> ○ Using economic theory to predict the most likely date of the next economic upturn for Company X

A: Scope! If something is out of scope—if it is not closely tied to what's said in the passage—then you should eliminate it.

Here's How to Crack It

As always, you should begin by reading the question first—and the key word that should jump out at you in this question is "evaluate." In this particular passage, the conclusion is in the second half of the argument: Company X claims that its economic upturn was particularly fast-moving because the company already had existing inventory on hand.

This is an evaluate-the-argument question and will almost certainly contain a gap in its reasoning. You should, as always, look to see whether the argument is causal, statistical, or analogical. Take a moment before you keep reading, and look at the passage again to see if you can spot which type of argument this is.

In this case, the argument was causal. Company X says the cause of its rapid turnaround was the inventory it had in its warehouses—which presumably let the company immediately take advantage of the new demand for its product. The company implies that the sole cause of the rapidity of its economic upturn was its inventory. While this may be true, it is also possible that there are other causes. If you didn't spot the causal argument, don't worry. You would probably have seen it when you attacked the answer choices. Let's look at them now:

> ○ Comparing the length of the economic down-turn experienced by Company X to the length of the upturn later experienced by Company X

The length of the economic downturn that preceded the upturn seems like it would be outside the scope of this argument, and, in any case, would not have much to do with whether the speed of Company X's upturn had anything to do with the inventory it had on hand once the upturn began. If you were thinking that the length of time would matter because the inventory might be out of date, you overthought the problem. Eliminate it.

> ○ Comparing the rapidity of the economic up-turn for Company X to that of other major makers of solar-powered generators, which did not have inventory on hand

If Company X's competitors, which did not have inventory on hand, did just as well or better during the economic upturn, then Company X's explanation for its speedy upturn might be incorrect. In other words, there might be some other cause. Would this comparison be useful in evaluating Company X's argument? This seems like it would be very useful, but let's hold onto it while we look at the other answer choices.

> ○ Calculating the average sales increases within the individual business units of Company X

This answer choice might help us to understand in more detail the extent of the upturn at Company X, but it gives us no insights into the causes behind the rapidity of their economic upturn. Let this one go.

○ Comparing the total number of solar-powered generator sales by Company X just before the economic upturn to the total number of solar-powered generator sales by Company X just after the economic upturn

A: Expose the assumption and build it up to strengthen the argument or tear it down to weaken the argument.

Like the comparison in the previous answer choice, this comparison would no doubt detail exactly the extent of the rapid economic upturn for Company X, but not explain the cause of the rapid upturn. Eliminate it.

○ Using economic theory to predict the most likely date of the next economic upturn for Company X

A future economic upturn (presumably preceded by a downturn) is surely well beyond the scope of this question. We are concerned only with evaluating the reason that Company X believes is the cause of its speedy economic upturn. Eliminate it.

Given the fact that we've eliminated all the other possible answers, choice B looks even better.

8. IDENTIFY-THE-REASONING QUESTIONS

Occasionally, a critical reasoning question will ask you to identify a method, technique, or strategy used in the passage, or to identify the role of a bolded phrase in the passage. Either way, the best technique for answering this rare question type is to do what you would do to answer any of the other question types: identify the conclusion and the premise and think about how they are related.

HOW TO RECOGNIZE AN IDENTIFY-THE-REASONING QUESTION

Identify-the-reasoning questions generally contain one of the following wordings:

- The bolded phrase plays which of the following roles in the argument above?

- The argument uses which of the following methods of reasoning?

Here's a typical example:

> Although measuring the productivity of outside consultants is a complex endeavor, **Company K, which relies heavily on consultants for long-term projects, must find ways to assess the performance of these workers.** The risks to a company that does not review the productivity of its human resources are simply too great. **Last year, Company L was forced into receivership after its productivity declined for the third straight quarter.**

The bolded phrases play which of the following roles in the argument above?

- ○ The first phrase states the author's conclusion, and the second phrase refutes that conclusion.
- ○ The first phrase states an assumption of the argument, and the second phrase provides evidence to undermine that position.
- ○ The first phrase states one of the author's premises, and the second phrase provides the argument's conclusion.
- ○ The first phrase states a position, and the second phrase refutes that position.
- ○ The first phrase states the conclusion, and the second phrase supports the conclusion with an analogy.

Here's How to Crack It

As you read the question, the first things that should jump out at you are the words "bolded phrases," which signal that this is an identify-the-reasoning question. And the first thing to do in an identify-the-reasoning question is to find the conclusion. Where is it? If you said "in the second half of the first sentence," then you are doing just fine. Company K, according to the argument, should find a way to measure the productivity of its consultants. The second sentence merely reiterates the first, and the third sentence supports the conclusion with what appears to be an analogous situation.

As you look at the answer choices, look for an answer that correctly explains the purpose of the two bolded phrases. Now, let's look at the answer choices:

- ○ The first phrase states the author's conclusion, and the second phrase refutes that conclusion.

The first bolded phrase is, in fact, the conclusion of the passage; so far, so good. But does the second phrase refute that conclusion? Not at all. In fact, it seems to be supporting it. Eliminate it.

○ The first phrase states an assumption of the argument, and the second phrase provides evidence to undermine that position.

We've already determined that the first bolded phrase is the conclusion of the argument—but even if we weren't sure of that, we could rule out this answer choice because an assumption is never stated in the passage. Even if you missed that, you would probably be able to eliminate this answer choice because the second bolded phrase seems to be supporting the first phrase, not undermining it. Eliminate it.

○ The first phrase states one of the author's premises, and the second phrase provides the argument's conclusion.

A premise is evidence in support of a conclusion. The first bolded phrase (about Company K) seems less a piece of evidence, than the conclusion itself. The second bolded phrase is about another company entirely and seems to be offered in support of the first sentence; in other words, it is not likely to be the conclusion of the argument. Eliminate it.

○ The first phrase states a position, and the second phrase refutes that position.

Like answer choices A and B, this says the second bolded phrase refutes the first. Because this is clearly not so, we can forget about this answer choice as well. Eliminate it.

○ The first phrase states the conclusion, and the second phrase supports the conclusion with an analogy.

Because we have eliminated all the other possibilities, you should feel hopeful that this is the best answer, but never skip the final step and decide choice E must be right without reading it. Does the first bolded phrase state the conclusion of the argument? Yes, it does. Does the second phrase support the conclusion with an analogy? Yes, in fact it does. The argument compares Company K's situation to that of Company L. If this were a weaken-the-argument question, you would need to be asking yourself if these two companies were actually analogous. However, in this case, all we have to do is pick answer choice E and move on.

PUTTING IT ALL TOGETHER

Now that you know how to spot and how to approach each of the eight question types, the best way to proceed is to practice. As you do each critical reasoning question, force yourself to spot what type of question it is before you start reading the passage. Once identified, a critical reasoning question isn't a mystery anymore—it will adhere to the conventions you've learned, and you will have a much easier time choosing the best answer.

To get you started, here's a drill to see how you are doing at spotting the different critical reasoning question types.

DRILL 12 (SPOTTING CRITICAL REASONING QUESTION TYPES)
The answers can be found on page 304.

For each of the questions below, decide which question type it belongs to. For extra credit, list what you should look for in the passage that would normally precede the question.

1. Which of the following, if true, gives the most support to the recommendations above?

2. If the statements above are true, which of the following can properly be inferred on the basis of them?

3. The answer to which of the following questions would be most useful in evaluating the significance of the counter-claimant's charge?

4. The argument in the passage depends on which of the following assumptions?

5. Which of the following statements, if true, provides the best evidence that the CEO's reasoning is flawed?

6. Which of the following, if true, best reconciles the seeming discrepancy described above?

7. The bolded phrase plays which of the following roles in the argument?

8. Which of the following most closely parallels the reasoning used in the argument above?

SUMMARY

1. Critical Reasoning is made up of short passages. Each of these passages is followed by one or two questions, for a total of roughly 11 questions.

2. The test writers have said that no formal logic is required to answer these questions, but in fact some knowledge of the rudiments of GMAT logic *will* increase your score.

3. There are three parts to an argument:

   A. the conclusion
   B. the premises
   C. assumptions

4. Critical reasoning is **not** like reading comprehension:

   A. You should never skim; each word is important.

   B. Most of the reading comprehension techniques we have shown you are inappropriate for critical reasoning.

5. Always read the question first because it will contain clues that will help you to find the answer as you read the passage. As you eliminate answer choices, cross them off in your scratch booklet.

6. In Critical Reasoning, the most important POE technique is eliminating answers that are outside the scope of the argument.

7. There are eight question types. Each type has its own strategy.

   A. assumption questions

      Assumptions are unstated premises that support the conclusion. Look for a flaw in the argument that is fixed by the assumption.

   B. strengthen-the-argument questions

      Look for an answer choice with information that supports the conclusion.

   C. weaken-the-argument questions

      These questions ask you to find the answer choice that points out flaws in the reasoning of passages.

   D. inference questions

      Like reading comprehension inference questions, these questions do not actually want you to infer. Unlike most critical reasoning questions, these questions typically concern the *premises*, not the conclusion.

E. parallel-the-reasoning questions

This type of question asks you to find an argument in one of the answer choices that mimics the method of reasoning used in the original argument. Most of these questions can be answered by simplifying (if A, then B).

F. resolve/explain questions

This type of question asks you to pick an answer choice that explains an apparent contradiction between two incompatible facts.

G. evaluate-the-argument questions

This type of question asks you to pick an answer choice that would help to evaluate an unspoken assumption about the argument.

H. identify-the-reasoning questions

This type of question asks you to pick an answer choice that identifies the purpose of a word or phrase or the type of reasoning used in an argument.

8. In assumption questions, weaken-the-argument questions, and strengthen-the-argument questions, there are three types of assumptions that students should be on the lookout for. These are (in order of frequency):

A. causal assumptions—Ask yourself whether there might be an alternate cause.

B. assumptions of analogy—Ask yourself whether the two situations are analogous.

C. statistical assumptions—Ask yourself whether the statistics are representative.

PART ◆ IV

How to Crack the
Writing Assessment

17
Writing Assessment

The very first thing you will be asked to do on the GMAT is to write two essays using a word-processing program. You will have 30 minutes for each essay. You will not be given the essay topic in advance, nor will you be given a choice of topics. However, there is a complete list of all the possible writing assessment topics available for you to download on the GMAC website. Simply go to www.mba.com/mba/TaketheGMAT/Tools/AWATopics.htm. Oh, and just in case you are wondering, it's free!

WHY HAVE ESSAYS ON THE GMAT?

The business schools themselves asked for them. Recent studies have indicated that success in business (and in business school) actually depends more on verbal skills than has been traditionally thought.

The business schools have also had to contend with a huge increase in the number of applicants from overseas. Admissions officers at the business schools were finding that the application essays they received from outside the United States did not always accurately reflect the abilities of the students who were supposed to have written them. To put it more bluntly, some of these applicants were paying native English speakers to write their essays for them.

The GMAT Writing Assessment is thus at least partly a check on the writing ability of foreign applicants who now make up more than one-third of all applicants to American business schools.

At the business schools' request, all schools to which you apply now receive, in addition to your Writing Assessment score, a copy of the actual essays you wrote.

HOW DO THE SCHOOLS USE THE WRITING ASSESSMENT?

If you are a citizen of a non-English-speaking country, you can expect the schools to look quite closely at both the score you receive on the essays you write and the essays themselves. If you are a native English speaker with reasonable Verbal scores and English grades in college, then the Writing Assessment is not likely to be a crucial part of your package.

On the other hand, if your verbal skills are *not* adequately reflected by your grades in college, or in the other sections of the GMAT, then a strong performance on the Writing Assessment could be extremely helpful.

HOW WILL THE ESSAYS BE SCORED?

When you get your GMAT score back from GMAC, you will also receive a separate score for the Writing Assessment. Each essay is read by two readers, each of whom will assign your writing a grade from 0–6, in half-point increments (6 being the highest score possible). If the two scores are within a point of each other, they will be averaged. If there is more than a one-point spread, the essays will be read by a third reader, and scores will be adjusted to reflect the third scorer's evaluation.

The essay readers use the "holistic" scoring method to grade essays; your writing will be judged not on small details but rather on its overall impact. The readers are supposed to ignore small errors of grammar and spelling. Considering that these readers are going to have to plow through more than 600,000 essays each year, this is probably just as well.

Who Are These Readers Anyway?

Well, let's talk about the first reader first. We'll put this in the form of a multiple-choice question:

Your essays will initially be read by:

(A) captains of industry

(B) leading business school professors

(C) college TAs working part time

If you guessed C, you're doing just fine. Each essay will be read first by part-time employees of the testing company, mostly culled from graduate school programs. However, you might have a hard time guessing who (or should we say, what) will read your essays second.

What Are These Readers Anyway?

The second reader of your essays will be a computer. Yes, you read right. That well-known arbiter of creative writing and syntax, a software program called the "E-rater," will read and grade your essay. If the computer and the human reader disagree, the essay in question will be read by a third (human) reader, who will make the final decision.

How Much Time Do They Devote to Each Essay?

The human graders get two minutes, tops. They work in eight-hour marathon sessions (nine to five, with an hour off for lunch). The humans are each required to read 30 essays per hour. Obviously, these poor graders do not have time for an in-depth reading of your essay. They probably aren't going to notice how carefully you thought out your ideas or how clever your analysis was. Under pressure to meet their quota, they are simply going to be giving it a fast skim. By the time your reader gets to your essay, she will probably have already seen more than a hundred—and no matter how ingenious you were in coming up with original ideas, she's already seen them.

The computer grader, of course, takes even less time. It scores your essay by comparing it to other essays on the same topic. In other words, if you actually did come up with an original point, the computer not only wouldn't recognize it—it would probably penalize you for not coming up with one of the more obvious points it was programmed to find.

So How Do You Score High on the GMAT Essays?

On the face of it, you might think it would be pretty difficult to impress these jaded human readers and rote computer readers, but it turns out that there are some very specific ways to persuade them of your superior writing skills.

Admissions Insight No. 10: Financial Aid, Part 1

The perception is that there is no financial aid available for business school. While this is generally true in the case of grants (money you don't have to pay back), it is not true about government-subsidized student loans. Right now, about 70 percent of graduate students receive some form of aid.

What GMAC Doesn't Want You to Know

In a 1982 internal study, two researchers from one of the big testing companies analyzed a group of essays written by actual test takers and the grades that those essays received. The most successful essays had one thing in common. Which of the following characteristics do you think it was?

- good organization
- proper diction
- noteworthy ideas
- good vocabulary
- sentence variety
- length
- number of paragraphs

GMAC describes an "outstanding" Analysis of an Issue essay as one that "explores ideas and develops a position on the issue with insightful reasons and/or persuasive examples; is clearly well organized; demonstrates superior control of language, including diction and syntactic variety; demonstrates superior facility with the conventions of standard written English..." You can check out an example of what GMAC thinks is an outstanding Analysis of an Issue essay at www.mba.com.

What Your Essay Needs in Order to Look Like a Successful Essay

The ETS researchers discovered that the essays that received the highest grades from ETS essay graders had one single factor in common.

Length.

To ace the Writing Assessment, you need to take one simple step: *Write as much as you possibly can*. Each essay should include at least four indented paragraphs.

How Does the Word-Processing Program Work?

The test makers have created a simple word-processing program to allow students to compose their essays on the screen.

Here's what your screen will look like during the essay portion of the test:

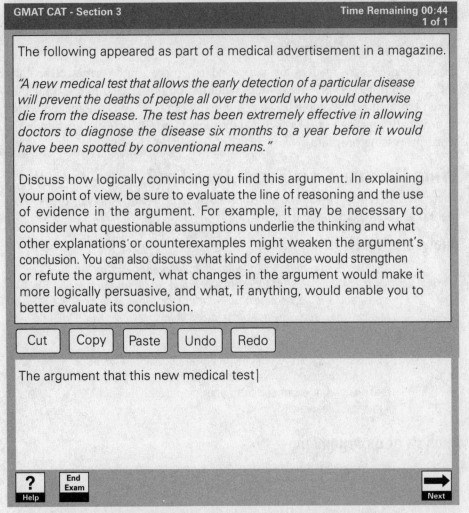

The following appeared as part of a medical advertisement in a magazine.

"A new medical test that allows the early detection of a particular disease will prevent the deaths of people all over the world who would otherwise die from the disease. The test has been extremely effective in allowing doctors to diagnose the disease six months to a year before it would have been spotted by conventional means."

Discuss how logically convincing you find this argument. In explaining your point of view, be sure to evaluate the line of reasoning and the use of evidence in the argument. For example, it may be necessary to consider what questionable assumptions underlie the thinking and what other explanations or counterexamples might weaken the argument's conclusion. You can also discuss what kind of evidence would strengthen or refute the argument, what changes in the argument would make it more logically persuasive, and what, if anything, would enable you to better evaluate its conclusion.

| Cut | Copy | Paste | Undo | Redo |

The argument that this new medical test|

? Help   End Exam   → Next

Admissions Insight No. 11: Financial Aid, Part 2

The best kind of student loans: low-cost Stafford loans (which don't have to be repaid until the student has graduated or left the program and which generally have much lower rates than regular unsecured loans). Graduate students can borrow up to $18,500 per year in Stafford loans (of which at least $10,000 must be unsubsidized, so you'll pay interest from the start). If necessary, borrow the rest through private educational loans.

The question always appears at the top of your screen. Below it, in a box, will be your writing area (where you can see a partially completed sentence). When you click inside the box with your mouse, a winking cursor will appear, indicating that you can begin typing. The program supports the use of many of the normal computer keys, plus the following shortcuts:

Cut: Ctrl + X and Alt + T

Copy: Ctrl + C and Alt + C

Paste: Ctrl + V and Alt + A

Undo: Ctrl + Z and Alt + U

Redo: Ctrl + Y and Alt + R

You can also use the icons above the writing area to copy and paste words, sentences, or paragraphs and to undo and redo actions.

Obviously, this small box is not big enough to display your entire essay. However, you can see your entire essay by using the scroll bar, the up and down arrows, or the Page Up and Page Down keys.

DOES SPELLING COUNT?

Officially, no. Essay readers are supposed to ignore minor errors of spelling and grammar. However, the readers wouldn't be human (so to speak) if they weren't influenced favorably by an essay that had no obvious misspelled words or unwieldy constructions. Unfortunately, there is no spell-check function in the word-processing program.

WHAT WILL THE ESSAY TOPICS LOOK LIKE?

There are two types of essay topics: Analysis of an Issue and Analysis of an Argument. Here's an example of each:

Analysis of an Issue

> *"Some believe that violent television programs and music lyrics are the cause of increased violence and crime in our cities, and should be censored—but in fact, there is no correlation between violence in popular culture and violence in real life."*
>
> Discuss the extent to which you agree or disagree with the opinion expressed above. Support your point of view with reasons and/or examples from your own experience, observations, or reading.

The key to an Analysis of an Issue essay is to choose a side and make a persuasive case for your argument.

Analysis of an Argument

> *The following appeared as part of a medical advertisement in a magazine.*
>
> *"A new medical test that allows the early detection of a particular disease will prevent the deaths of people all over the world who would otherwise die from the disease. The test has been extremely effective in allowing doctors to diagnose the disease six months to a year before it would have been spotted by conventional means."*
>
> Discuss how logically convincing you find this argument. In explaining your point of view, be sure to evaluate the line of reasoning and the use of evidence in the argument. For example, it may be necessary to consider what questionable assumptions underlie the thinking and what other explanations or counterexamples might weaken the argument's conclusion. You can also discuss what kind of evidence would strengthen or refute the argument, what changes in the argument would make it more logically persuasive, and what, if anything, would enable you to better evaluate its conclusion.

You will have to write one essay on each topic.

THE WRITING ASSESSMENT: BASIC PRINCIPLES

You might think that there is really no way to prepare for the Writing Assessment (other than by practicing writing over a long period of time, and by practicing your typing skills). After all, you won't find out the topic of the essay they'll ask you to write until you get there, and there is no way to plan your essays in advance.

However, it turns out there are some very specific ways to prepare for GMAT essays. Let's take a look.

CREATE A TEMPLATE

When a builder builds a house, the first thing he does is construct a frame. The frame supports the entire house. After the frame is completed, he can nail the walls and windows to the frame. We're going to show you how to build the frame for the perfect GMAT essay. Of course, you won't know the exact topic of the essay until you get there (just as the builder may not know what color his client is going to paint the living room), but you will have an all-purpose frame on which to construct a great essay no matter what the topic is.

We call this frame the *template*.

PRECONSTRUCTION

Just as a builder can construct the windows of a house in his workshop weeks before he arrives to install them, so can you pre-build certain elements of your essay.

We call this *preconstruction*.

In the rest of this chapter we'll show you how to prepare *ahead of time* to write essays on two topics you won't see until they appear on your screen. Let's begin with the Analysis of an Issue essay.

THE FIRST TOPIC: ANALYSIS OF AN ISSUE

Writing the Analysis of an Issue essay requires the following steps:

Step 1: Read the topic.

Step 2: Decide the general position you are going to take—you need to take a stand on the issue.

Step 3: Brainstorm. Come up with a bunch of supporting ideas or examples. It helps to write these down in your scratch booklet, or even to type them in the space where you will eventually write your essay. (If you type them, remember to erase them later.) These supporting statements are supposed to help persuade the reader that your main thesis is correct.

Step 4: Look over your supporting ideas and throw out the weakest ones. There should be three to five left over.

Step 5: Write the essay on screen, using all the preconstruction and template tools you're going to learn in this chapter.

Admissions Insight No. 12: Financial Aid, Part 3

To get student loans, you will probably have to fill out both the FAFSA form (available at www.fafsa.gov) and the PROFILE form (available at www.collegeboard.com). For simple and straightforward advice about making your way through all of that financial aid paperwork, visit www.PrincetonReview.com.

Step 6: Read over the essay and do some editing. The GMAT readers will not take away points for spelling or grammatical mistakes, but you want your organization to be as well-reasoned as possible.

WHAT THE READERS LOOK FOR

The essay topic for the Analysis of an Issue will ask you to choose a side on an issue and develop coherent reasons or examples in defense of your position. You aren't required to know any more about the subject than would any normal person. As far as the essay graders are concerned, it doesn't even matter which side of the argument you take—as long as your essay is well written. So what constitutes a well-written essay?

The essay readers will look for four characteristics as they skim at the speed of light through your Analysis of an Issue essay. According to GMAC, "an outstanding essay…

- explores ideas and develops a position on the issue with insightful reasons and/or persuasive examples,

- is clearly well organized,

- demonstrates superior control of language, including diction and syntactic variety,

- demonstrates superior facility with the conventions of standard written English, but may have minor flaws."

To put it more simply, they'll look for good organization, good supporting examples for whatever position you've taken, and reasonable use of the English language. Let's start with good organization and the easiest way to accomplish it—the template.

A SAMPLE TEMPLATE

You will want to come up with your own template, but here is an elementary example of one, just to get you started:

Paragraph 1:

The issue of _____

is a controversial one. On the one hand, _____

_____ .

On the other hand, _____

_____ .

However, in the final analysis, I believe that _____

_____ .

Paragraph 2:

One reason for my belief is that _____

_____

_____

_____ .

Paragraph 3:

Another reason for my belief is _____

_____

_____

_____ .

Paragraph 4:

Perhaps the best reason is _____

_____

_____

_____ .

Paragraph 5:

For all these reasons, I therefore believe that _____

_____

_____

_____ .

Let's try fitting the Analysis of an Issue topic we've already seen into this organizational structure.

Essay Topic 1:

> *"Some believe that violent television programs and music lyrics are the cause of increased violence and crime in our cities, and should be censored—but in fact, there is no correlation between violence in popular culture and violence in real life."*
>
> Discuss the extent to which you agree or disagree with the opinion expressed above. Support your point of view with reasons and/or examples from your own experience, observations, or reading.

How would this topic fit into the first paragraph of our template? Take a look.

The issue of censorship of popular TV programs and music lyrics is a controversial one. On the one hand, increased crime and violence are causing a disintegration of the framework of our society. On the other hand, free speech is one of our most important freedoms, guaranteed by the constitution. However, in the final analysis, I believe that the dangers of subjecting impressionable young minds to questionable values makes self-censorship by the entertainment industry a viable alternative.

If we were writing the rest of this essay, we would start giving supporting examples and reasons for our position, but for now, let's concentrate on the first paragraph. Could we have used this template to take the other side of the argument? Sure. Here's how that would look:

The issue of censorship of popular TV programs and music lyrics is a controversial one. On the one hand, free speech is one of our most important freedoms, guaranteed by the constitution. On the other hand, increased crime and violence are causing a disintegration of the framework of our society. However, in the final analysis, I believe that the principle of free speech is too precious to allow censorship in any form.

OKAY, IT WORKS WITH THAT TOPIC, BUT WILL IT WORK WITH ANOTHER?

Of course. Let's try the same template with another topic.

Essay Topic 2:

> *"Critics who blame government bureaucracy for the increasing costs of our country's infrastructure say our federal bureaucracy needs to be overhauled. However, these increasing costs are only to be expected in a growing state."*

> Discuss the extent to which you agree or disagree with the opinion expressed above. Support your point of view with reasons and/or examples from your own experience, observations, or reading.

The issue of the overhaul of our federal bureaucracy **is a controversial one. On the one hand,** federal jobs employ a huge number of Americans, making any attempt to prune the federal payroll both difficult and painful. **On the other hand,** the percentage of our tax dollars spent simply on the upkeep of this huge bureaucratic juggernaut is rising at an alarming rate. **However, in the final analysis, I believe that** the political and financial price of bureaucratic reform would be too high.

As you can see, this template will fit practically any situation. To prove it, let's try it out on one of the great philosophical arguments of our time.

TASTES GREAT/LESS FILLING

Essay Topic X:

> *"Some people say that they drink light beer because it tastes great. However, the true reason people drink light beer is that it is less filling."*

> Discuss the extent to which you agree or disagree with the opinion expressed above. Support your point of view with reasons and/or examples from your own experience, observations, or reading.

The issue of whether light beer is so popular because of its taste or because you can drink more of it without it filling you up **is a controversial one. On the one hand,** light beer does have a pleasingly mild taste. **On the other hand,** light beer also offers a sharply reduced number of calories. **However, in the final analysis, I believe that** light beer is so popular because of its great taste.

B-School Lingo

three Cs: three primary business forces—Customer, Competition, Company

Total Quality Management: the Edward Demming method of management that caught on with the Japanese and is currently hot in American business—managing the quality of service, process, people, and objectives

Now You Try It

Read the following topic carefully. Decide which side of the argument you want to be on, and then fill in the blanks of the first paragraph of this template.

You may have noticed in the previous examples that to make this particular template work most effectively, the first "on the one hand" should introduce the argument that you are ultimately going to support. The "on the other hand" should be the argument you are going to disprove. The sentence beginning "however, in the final analysis" will return to the point of view that you believe in.

Essay Topic 3:

> *"Capping monetary awards in medical malpractice cases would result in lower costs for patients and a better health-care system."*
>
> Discuss the extent to which you agree or disagree with the opinion expressed above. Support your point of view with reasons and/or examples from your own experience, observations, or reading.

The issue of _____

_____ is a controversial one. On the one hand,

_____

_____.

On the other hand, _____

_____.

However, in the final analysis, I believe that _____

_____.

If you were completing the entire essay now, you would write paragraphs giving support to your belief, but for right now let's concentrate on that first paragraph. Here's one way Topic 3 could have gone:

The issue of capping malpractice awards is a controversial one. On the one hand, health-care costs are rising so quickly that drastic measures are needed to contain them. On the other hand, when an individual's life is ruined as a result of a doctor's negligence, that individual deserves fair recompense. However, in the final analysis, I believe that by capping the awards at a reasonable amount we can both lower the cost of health care and protect the rights of victims of malpractice.

ARE THERE OTHER TEMPLATES?

There are many ways to organize an Analysis of an Issue essay, and we'll show you a few variations, but the important thing is that you bring with you to the exam a template you have practiced using and are comfortable with. Whatever the topic of the essay and whatever your personal mood that day, you don't want to have to think for a second about how your essay will be organized. By deciding on a template in advance you will already have your organizational structure down before you get there.

That said, it's important that you develop your *own* template, based on your own preferences and your own personality. Of course, yours may have some similarities to one of ours, but it should not mimic ours exactly—for one thing, because it's pretty likely that when this edition of our book comes out, the folks who write the GMAT will read it, and they might take a dim view of anyone who blatantly copies one of our templates word-for-word.

CUSTOMIZING YOUR TEMPLATE

Your organizational structure may vary in some ways, but it will always include the following elements:

- The *first paragraph* should illustrate to the reader that you have understood the topic, and that you have chosen a position. To do this, first restate the topic, then say how you feel about it. The first paragraph does not have to be more than a couple of sentences.

- In the *second, third, and fourth paragraphs* you will develop examples and ideas to support your thesis.

- The *last paragraph* should sum up your position on the topic, using slightly different wording from the first paragraph.

> **The Analysis of an Issue Essay in Six Steps**
>
> **Step 1:** Read the topic.
> **Step 2:** Decide your position, for or against.
> **Step 3:** Brainstorm for three to five minutes.
> **Step 4:** Select the strongest three to four supporting ideas.
> **Step 5:** Write the essay, using preconstruction and template tools.
> **Step 6:** About two minutes before time is up, read over your essay and correct for spelling or grammar mistakes.

Here are some alternate ways of organizing your essay:

Variation 1:

1st paragraph: State both sides of the issue briefly before announcing what side you are on

2nd paragraph: Support your position

3rd paragraph: Further support

4th paragraph: Further support

5th paragraph: Conclusion

Variation 2:

1st paragraph: State your position

2nd paragraph: Acknowledge the arguments in favor of the *other* side

3rd paragraph: Rebut each of those arguments

4th paragraph: Conclusion

Variation 3:

1st paragraph: State the position you will eventually contradict, i.e., "Many people believe that…"

2nd paragraph: Contradict that first position, i.e., "However, I believe that…

3rd paragraph: Support your position

4th paragraph: Further support

5th paragraph: Conclusion

SO MUCH FOR ORGANIZATION. NOW, WHAT ABOUT SUPPORT?

We've shown you how templates and structure words can be used to help the organization of your essay. However, organization is not the only important item on the essay reader's checklist. You will also be graded on how you support your main idea.

THE KEY TO GOOD SUPPORT: BRAINSTORMING

Learning to use the structural words we've just discussed is in fact a way to bring pre-built elements into the GMAT examination room with you. Along with a template, they will enable you to concentrate on your ideas without worrying about making up a structure from scratch. But what about the ideas themselves?

After reading the essay topic, you should take a couple of minutes to plan out your essay. First, decide which side of the issue you're going to take. Then, begin brainstorming. Write down all the reasons and persuasive examples you can think of in support of your essay. Don't stop to edit yourself; just let them flow out.

If you think better on the computer, you can write out your outline and supporting ideas directly on the screen. Just remember to erase them before the time for that essay is over.

Then go through what you've written to decide on the order in which you want to make your points. You may decide, on reflection, to skip several of your brainstorms—or you may have one or two new ones as you organize.

Here's an example of what some brainstorming might produce in the way of support for Analysis of an Issue topic #1:

Main Idea: Censorship of television programs and popular music lyrics would be a mistake.

Support:

1. Freedom of speech was one of the founding principles of this country. It has been too hard won for us to give it up.

2. Who would perform this censorship, and how would we ensure that there was no political agenda attached to it?

3. Once started, censorship of violent content is hard to stop or to curb. Where would we draw the line? *Hamlet*? *Bambi*?

4. So far, the evidence of different studies is contradictory. The causal link between violence on television and real violence has not yet been persuasively proven.

5. While upsetting to many, the lyrics of such entertainers as Snoop Dogg continue a long tradition of protest of social conditions that has stretched over the centuries and has included such artists as Bob Dylan and Woody Guthrie.

> Before beginning any essay, always brainstorm! Write your ideas out in your scratch booklet.

After you've finished brainstorming, look over your supporting ideas and throw out the weakest ones. In general, examples from your personal life are less compelling to readers than examples from history or current events. There should be three to five ideas left over. Plan the order in which you want to present these ideas. You should start with one of your strongest ideas.

GETTING SPECIFIC

The GMAT readers are looking for supporting ideas or examples that are, in their words, "insightful" and "persuasive." What do they mean? Suppose you asked your friend about a movie she saw yesterday, and she said, "It was really cool."

Well, you'd know that she liked it, and that's good—but you wouldn't know much about the movie. Was it a comedy? An action adventure? Were the characters sexy? Did it make her cry?

The GMAT readers don't want to know that the movie was cool. They want to know that you liked it because:

"It traced the development of two childhood friends as they grew up and grew apart."

or because:

"It combined the physical comedy of the Three Stooges with the action adventure of *Raiders of the Lost Ark.* "

You want to make each example as precise and compelling as possible. After you have brainstormed a few supporting ideas, spend a couple of moments on each one, making it as specific as possible. For example, let's say we are working on an essay supporting the idea that the United States should stay out of other countries' affairs.

> **Too vague**: When the United States sent troops to Vietnam, things didn't work out too well. (*How* didn't they work out? What were the results?)

> **More specific**: Look at the result of the United States sending troops to Vietnam. After more than a decade of fighting in support of a dubious political regime, American casualties numbered in the tens of thousands, and we may never know how many Vietnamese lost their lives as well.

ANALYSIS OF AN ISSUE: FINAL THOUGHTS

You've picked a position, you've brainstormed, you've brought with you a template and some structure words; brainstorming should have taken about five minutes. Now it's time to write your essay. Start typing, indenting each of the four or five paragraphs. Use all the tools you've learned in this chapter. Remember to keep an eye on the time. You have only 30 minutes to complete the first essay.

If you have a minute at the end, read over your essay and do any editing that's necessary.

Then, during the next 30 minutes, you'll turn to the second essay topic.

THE SECOND TOPIC: ANALYSIS OF AN ARGUMENT

You'll be able to use all the skills we've just been discussing on the second type of essay as well—with one major change. The Analysis of an Argument essay must initially be approached just like a logical argument in the Critical Reasoning section.

An Analysis of an Argument topic requires the following steps:

Step 1: Read the topic and separate out the conclusion from the premises.

Step 2: Because they're asking you to critique (i.e., weaken) the argument, concentrate on identifying its assumptions.

Brainstorm as many different assumptions as you can think of. Again, it helps to write or type these out.

Step 3: Look at the premises. Do they actually help to prove the conclusion?

Step 4: Choose a template that allows you to attack the assumptions and premises in an organized way.

Step 5: At the end of the essay, take a moment to illustrate how these same assumptions could be used to make the argument more compelling.

Step 6: Read over the essay and do some editing.

WHAT THE READERS LOOK FOR

An Analysis of an Argument topic presents you with an argument. Your job is to critique the argument's line of reasoning and the evidence supporting it and suggest ways in which the argument could be strengthened. Again, you aren't required to know more about the subject than would any normal person—but you must be able to spot logical weaknesses. This should start to remind you of Critical Reasoning.

The essay readers will look for four things as they skim through your Analysis of an Argument essay at the speed of light. According to GMAC, "an outstanding argument essay…

- clearly identifies and insightfully analyzes important features of the argument;

- develops ideas cogently, organizes them logically, and connects them smoothly with clear transitions;

- effectively supports the main points of the critique; and

- demonstrates superior control of language, including diction, syntactic variety, and the conventions of standard written English. There may be minor flaws."

To put it more simply, the readers will look for all the same things they looked for in the Analysis of an Issue essay, plus one extra ingredient: a cursory knowledge of the rules of logic.

Q: What are the most important aspects of writing a good Analysis of an Issue essay?

CRITICAL REASONING IN ESSAY FORM

In any GMAT argument, the first thing to do is to separate the conclusion from the premises.

Let's see how this works with an actual essay topic. Check out the Analysis of an Argument topic you saw before on the next page.

Topic:

The following appeared as part of a medical advertisement in a magazine.

"A new medical test that allows the early detection of a particular disease will prevent the deaths of people all over the world who would otherwise die from the disease. The test has been extremely effective in allowing doctors to diagnose the disease six months to a year before it would have been spotted by conventional means."

Discuss how logically convincing you find this argument. In explaining your point of view, be sure to evaluate the line of reasoning and the use of evidence in the argument. For example, it may be necessary to consider what questionable assumptions underlie the thinking and what other explanations or counterexamples might weaken the argument's conclusion. You can also discuss what kind of evidence would strengthen or refute the argument, what changes in the argument would make it more logically persuasive, and what, if anything, would enable you to better evaluate its conclusion.

The conclusion in this argument comes in the first line:

A new medical test that allows the early detection of a particular disease will prevent the deaths of people all over the world who would otherwise die from that disease.

The premises are the evidence in support of this conclusion.

The test has been extremely effective in allowing doctors to diagnose the disease six months to a year before it would have been spotted by conventional means.

The assumptions are the *unspoken* premises of the argument—without which the argument would fall apart. Remember that assumptions are often causal, analogical, or statistical. What are some assumptions of *this* argument? Let's brainstorm.

BRAINSTORMING FOR ASSUMPTIONS

You can often find assumptions by looking for a gap in the reasoning:

Medical test → early detection: According to the conclusion, the medical test leads to the early detection of the disease. There doesn't seem to be a gap here.

Early detection → nonfatal: In turn, the early detection of the disease allows patients to survive the disease. Well, hold on a minute. Is this necessarily true? Let's brainstorm:

1. First of all, do we know that early detection will necessarily lead to survival? We don't even know if this disease is *curable*. Early detection of an incurable disease is not going to help someone survive it.

2. Second, will the test be widely available and cheap enough for general use? If the test is expensive or only available in certain parts of the world, people will continue to die from the disease.

3. Will doctors and patients interpret the tests correctly? The test may be fine, but if doctors misinterpret the results or if patients ignore the need for treatment, then the test will not save lives.

THE USE OF THE EVIDENCE

Okay, we've uncovered some assumptions. Now, the essay graders also want to know what we thought of the argument's "use of evidence." In other words, did the premises help to prove the conclusion? Well, in fact, no, they didn't. The premise here (the fact that the test can *spot* the disease six months to a year earlier than conventional tests) does not really help to prove the conclusion that the test will save *lives*.

ORGANIZING THE ANALYSIS OF AN ARGUMENT ESSAY

We're ready to put this into a ready-made template. In any Analysis of an Argument essay, the template structure will be pretty straightforward: You're simply going to reiterate the argument, attack the argument in three different ways (one to a paragraph), summarize what you've said, and mention how the argument could be strengthened. From an organizational standpoint, this is pretty easy. Try to minimize your use of the word "I." *Your* opinion is not really the point in an Analysis of an Argument essay.

A SAMPLE TEMPLATE

Of course, you will want to develop your *own* template for the Analysis of an Argument essay, but to get you started, here's one possible structure:

The argument that   (restatement of the conclusion)   is not entirely logically

convincing, because it ignores certain crucial assumptions.

First, the argument assumes that _____

_____ .

Second, the argument never addresses _____

_____ .

Finally, the argument omits _____

_____ .

Thus, the argument is not completely sound. The evidence in support of the

conclusion _____ .

Ultimately, the argument might have been strengthened by_____

_____ .

> The key to an Analysis of an Argument essay is to critique the weaknesses in the argument clearly.

How Would Our Brainstorming Fit into the Template?

Here's how the assumptions we came up with for this argument would have fit into the template:

The Analysis of an Argument Essay in Six Steps

Step 1: Read the topic. Isolate the conclusion and premises.

Step 2: Identify its assumptions. Brainstorm for five minutes.

Step 3: Look at the assumptions. Do they help to prove the conclusion?

Step 4: Choose a template that allows you to attack the assumptions in an organized way.

Step 5: Illustrate how these same assumptions could be used to make the argument more compelling.

Step 6: Do some editing to correct spelling or grammar mistakes.

The argument that *the new medical test will prevent deaths that would have occurred in the past* is not entirely logically persuasive, because it ignores certain crucial assumptions.

First, the argument assumes that *early detection of the disease will lead to a reduced mortality rate. There are a number of reasons this might not be true. For example, the disease might be incurable (etc.).*

Second, the argument never addresses *the point that the existence of this new test, even if totally effective, is not the same as the widespread use of the test (etc.).*

Finally, *even supposing the ability of early detection to save lives and the widespread use of the test, the argument still depends on the doctors' correct interpretation of the test and the patients' willingness to undergo treatment. (etc.)*

Thus, the argument is not completely sound. The evidence in support of the conclusion *(further information about the test itself) does little to prove the conclusion—that the test will save lives—because it does not address the assumptions already* raised. Ultimately, the argument might have been strengthened by *making it plain that the disease responds to early treatment, that the test will be widely available around the world, and that doctors and patients will make proper use of the test.*

Customizing Your Analysis of an Argument Template

Your organizational structure may vary in some ways, but it will always include the following elements:

- The *first paragraph* should sum up the argument's conclusion.

- In the *second, third, and fourth paragraphs*, you should attack the argument and the supporting evidence.

- In the *last* paragraph, you should summarize what you've said and state how the argument could be strengthened. Here are some alternate ways of organizing your essay.

Variation 1:

1st paragraph: Restate the argument.

2nd paragraph: Discuss the link (or lack of one) between the conclusion and the evidence presented in support of it.

3rd paragraph: Show three holes in the reasoning of the argument.

4th paragraph: Show how each of the three holes could be plugged up by explicitly stating the missing assumptions.

Variation 2:

1st paragraph: Restate the argument and say it has three flaws.

2nd paragraph: Point out a flaw and show how it could be plugged up by explicitly stating the missing assumption.

3rd paragraph: Point out a second flaw and show how it could be plugged up by explicitly stating the missing assumption.

4th paragraph: Point out a third flaw and show how it could be plugged up by explicitly stating the missing assumption.

5th paragraph: Summarize and conclude that because of these three flaws, the argument is weak.

ANALYSIS OF AN ARGUMENT: FINAL THOUGHTS

You've separated the conclusion from the premises. You've brainstormed for the gaps that weaken the argument. You've noted how the premises support (or don't support) the conclusion. Now it's time to write your essay. Start typing, indenting each of the four or five paragraphs. Use all the tools you've learned in this chapter. Remember to keep an eye on the time.

Again, if you have a minute at the end, read over your essay and do any editing that's necessary.

Q: What are the most important aspects of writing a good Analysis of an Argument essay?

PRECONSTRUCTION

In both essays, the readers will look for evidence of your facility with standard written English. This is where preconstruction comes in. It's amazing how a little elementary preparation can enhance an essay. We'll look at three tricks that almost instantly improve the appearance of a person's writing:

- structure words

- sentence variety

- the impressive book reference

STRUCTURE WORDS

In Chapter 14, we brought up a problem that most students encounter when they get to the Reading Comprehension section: There isn't enough time to read the passages carefully and answer all the questions. To get around this problem, we showed you some ways to spot the overall organization of a dense reading passage in order to understand the main idea and to find specific points quickly.

When you think about it, the essay readers face almost the identical problem: They have less than two minutes to read your essay and figure out if it's any good. There's no time to appreciate the finer points of your argument. All they want to know is whether it's well organized and reasonably lucid—and to find out, they will look for the *same* structural clues you have learned to look for in the reading comprehension passages. Let's mention them again:

- If you have three points to make in a paragraph, it helps to point this out ahead of time:

  There are three reasons why I believe that the Grand Canyon should be strip-mined. First...Second...Third...

- If you want to clue the reader in to the fact that you are about to support the main idea with examples or illustrations, the following words are useful:

  for example
  to illustrate
  for instance
  because

- To add yet another example or argument in support of your main idea, you can use one of the following words to indicate your intention:

  furthermore
  in addition
  similarly
  just as
  also
  moreover

- To indicate that the idea you're about to bring up is important, special, or surprising in some way, you can use one of these words:

  surely
  truly
  undoubtedly
  clearly
  certainly
  indeed
  as a matter of fact
  in fact
  most important

A: Write at least four or five well-organized paragraphs (an introduction in which you state that you will analyze the reasoning of the topic; a middle, to pick apart the argument by exposing assumptions; and a conclusion in which you state how the argument could be strengthened and sum up your position). Remember, this essay uses the same skills and approach you developed for the Critical Reasoning section of the test.

- To signal that you're about to reach a conclusion, you might use one of these words:

  therefore
  in summary
  consequently
  hence
  in conclusion
  in short

How It Works

Here's a paragraph that consists of a main point and two supporting arguments:

> I believe he is wrong. He doesn't know the facts. He isn't thinking clearly.

Watch how a few structure words can make this paragraph classier and clearer at the same time:

> I believe he is wrong. **For one thing**, he doesn't know the facts. **For another**, he isn't thinking clearly.

> I believe he is wrong. **Obviously**, he doesn't know the facts. **Moreover**, he isn't thinking clearly.

> I believe he is wrong **because, first**, he doesn't know the facts, and **second**, he isn't thinking clearly.

> **Certainly**, he doesn't know the facts, and he isn't thinking clearly **either**. **Consequently**, I believe he is wrong.

The Appearance of Depth

You may have noticed that much of the structure we have discussed thus far has involved contrasting viewpoints. Nothing will give your writing the *appearance* of depth faster than learning to use this technique. The idea is to set up your main idea by first introducing its opposite.

> It is a favorite ploy of incoming presidents to blame the federal bureaucracy for the high cost of government, but I believe that bureaucratic waste is only a small part of the problem.

Percentage of MBA Grads Interested in Investment Banking

10%

Source: *BusinessWeek*, 2003

You may have noticed that this sentence contained a "trigger word." In this case, the trigger word *but* tells us that what was expressed in the first half of the sentence is going to be contradicted in the second half. We discussed trigger words in the Reading Comprehension chapter of this book. Here they are again:

but	however
on the contrary	although
yet	while
despite	in spite of
rather	nevertheless
instead	

By using these words, you can instantly give your writing the appearance of depth.

Example:

> Main thought: *I believe that television programs should be censored.*
>
> *While many people believe in the sanctity of free speech, I believe that television programs should be censored.*
>
> *Most people believe in the sanctity of free speech, but I believe that television programs should be censored.*

In addition to trigger words, here are a few other words or phrases you can use to introduce the view you are eventually going to decide *against*:

admittedly	true
certainly	granted
obviously	of course
undoubtedly	to be sure
one cannot deny that	it could be argued that

Also, don't forget about yin-yang words, which can be used to point directly to two contrasting ideas:

> on the one hand/on the other hand
> the traditional view/the new view

Contrasting Paragraphs

Trigger words can be used to signal the opposing viewpoints of entire paragraphs. Suppose you saw an essay that began:

> *Many people believe that youth is wasted on the young. They point out that young people never seem to enjoy, or even think about, the great gifts they have been given but will not always have: Physical dexterity, good hearing, good vision. However...*

What do you think is going to happen in the second paragraph? That's right, the author is now going to disagree with the *many people* of the first paragraph.

Setting up one paragraph in opposition to another lets the reader know what's going on right away. The organization of the essay is immediately evident.

SENTENCE VARIETY

Many people think good writing is a mysterious talent that you either have or don't have, like good rhythm. In fact, good writing has a kind of rhythm to it, but there is nothing mysterious about it. Good writing is a matter of mixing up the different kinds of raw materials that you have available to you—phrases, dependent and independent clauses—to build sentences that don't all sound the same.

The graders won't have time to savor your essay, but they will look for variety in your writing. Here's an example of a passage in which all the sentences sound alike:

> *Movies cost too much. Everyone agrees about that.*
> *Studios need to cut costs. No one is sure exactly how*
> *to do it. I have two simple solutions. They can cut*
> *costs by paying stars less. They can also cut costs by*
> *reducing overhead.*

Why do all the sentences sound alike? Well, for one thing, they are all about the same length. For another thing, the sentences are all made up of independent clauses with the same exact setup: Subject, verb, and sometimes object. There are no dependent clauses, almost no phrases, no structure words, and, frankly, no variety at all.

Now let's take a look at the same passage, with some minor modifications.

> *Everyone agrees that movies cost too much. Clearly,*
> *studios need to cut costs, but no one is sure exactly*
> *how to do it. I have two simple solutions: They can cut*
> *costs by paying stars less and by reducing overhead.*

In this version of the passage, we've combined some clauses and used conjunctions. This helped to add variety in both sentence structure and sentence length. We also threw in a few structure words as well. As you can see, simple techniques like these can make your writing appear stronger and more polished.

THE IMPRESSIVE BOOK REFERENCE

In any kind of writing, it pays to remember who your audience will be. In this case, the essays are first going to be graded by college teaching assistants. They wouldn't be TAs if they didn't have a soft spot in their heart for someone who can refer to a well-known, nonfiction book or a famous work of literature.

What book should you pick? Obviously it should be a book that you have actually read and liked. We do not advise picking a book if you've only seen the movie. Hollywood has a habit of changing the endings.

You might think that it would be impossible to pick a book to use as an example for an essay before you even know the topic of the essay, but it's actually pretty easy. Just to give you an idea of how it's done, let's pick a famous work of literature that most people have read at some point in their lives: Shakespeare's *Hamlet*.

Safety in Numbers?

More people signed up for the GMAT in 2002 than at any time in its history.

Source: *U.S. News & World Report*, 2003

Now let's take each of the topics we've used in this chapter, and see how we could work in a reference to *Hamlet*.

Essay Topic 1:

> *"Should television and song lyrics be censored in order to curb increasing crime and violence?"*
>
> *...Where would such censorship stop? In an attempt to prevent teen suicide, would an after-school version of Shakespeare's* Hamlet *be changed so that the soliloquy read, "To be, or...whatever"?*

Essay Topic 2:

> *"Is government bureaucracy to blame for the increased cost of government?"*
>
> *If you were to compare the United States government to Shakespeare's* Hamlet, *the poor bureaucrats would represent the forgotten and insignificant Rosencrantz and Guildenstern, not the scheming pretenders to the throne.*

Essay Topic 3:

> *"Should the maximum amount of a medical malpractice lawsuit be capped in the interest of lowering the cost of health care?"*
>
> *Malpractice awards are getting out of hand. If Shakespeare's era was reportedly the most litigious age in history, surely ours must come a close second. If he were writing today, you have the feeling Hamlet might have said, "Alas, poor Yorick, he should have gotten a better malpractice lawyer."*

You get the idea. Because your essays may be read by the admissions officers at the schools to which you apply, you might think it would be better to cite a book by a well-regarded economist or business guru rather than that of a playwright or novelist. As long as your example feels like an organic addition to your essay, it won't matter too much who you cite. But you may find that these economic references are harder to work into your essay—and they will almost certainly go over the heads of the essay graders.

THE AWA

Few people are rejected by a business school based on their writing score, so don't bother feeling intimidated. Think of it this way: The essays represent an *opportunity* if your Verbal score is low, or if English is your second language. For the rest of you, the essays are as good a way as any to warm up (and wake up) before the sections that count.

After you finish your essays, take advantage of the optional five-minute break to clear your head, and get ready for the multiple-choice questions to come.

SUMMARY

1. The GMAT Writing Assessment section consists of two essays, each to be written in 30 minutes, using a basic word-processing program and the computer keyboard. The essays will be given scores that range from 0 to 6 in half-point increments.

2. Each essay will be evaluated by at least two readers. One will be an underpaid, overworked college teaching assistant; the other will be a computer.

3. To score high on the Writing Assessment:

    A. Write as many words as possible.

    B. Use a prebuilt template to organize your thoughts.

    C. Use structure words, and vary your sentence structure and length to give the appearance of depth to your writing.

    D. If possible, refer to a well-known work of literature or nonfiction.

4. For the Analysis of an Issue topic:

    Step 1: Read the topic.

    Step 2: Decide the general position you are going to take on the issue.

    Step 3: Brainstorm. Come up with a bunch of supporting ideas or examples and write them down. These supporting statements are supposed to help convince the reader that your main thesis is correct.

    Step 4: Look over your supporting ideas and throw out the weakest ones. There should be three to five left over.

    Step 5: Write the essay, using all the preconstruction and template tools you learned in this chapter.

    Step 6: Read over the essay and edit your work.

5. For the Analysis of an Argument topic:

Step 1: Read the topic and separate out the conclusion from the premises.

Step 2: Because they ask you to critique (i.e., weaken) the argument, concentrate on identifying its assumptions. Brainstorm as many different assumptions as you can think of and write them down.

Step 3: Look at the premises. Do they actually help to prove the conclusion?

Step 4: Choose a template that allows you to attack the assumptions and premises in an organized way.

Step 5: At the end of the essay, take a moment to illustrate how these same assumptions could be used to make the argument more compelling.

Step 6: Read over the essay and edit your work.

PART V

Answer Key to Drills

DRILL 1
(page 59)

1. 77
2. 79
3. 10
4. 16
5. choice B

DRILL 2
(page 60)

1. $80 + 40 = 120$
2. $55 \times 100 = 5{,}500$
3. $ab + ac - ad$
4. $c(ab + xy)$
5. $\dfrac{12y - 6y}{y} = \dfrac{y(6)}{y} = 6$, choice B

DRILL 3
(page 64)

1. $\dfrac{145}{24}$ or $6\dfrac{1}{24}$
2. $\dfrac{1}{5}$
3. $\dfrac{29}{3}$
4. 18
5. choice C

DRILL 4
(page 68)

1. 33.30
2. 266.175
3. 6.09
4. 800
5. choice C

DRILL 5 (Angles and Lengths)
(page 130)

1. $x = 110°$
2. $x = 50°$ $y = 130°$ $z = 130°$
3. $x = 60°$ $y = 120°$ $z = 120°$
4. $\dfrac{3}{4}$
5. choice D

DRILL 6 (Triangles)
(pages 135–136)

1. $x = 8$
2. $x = 60$
3. $x = 5$
4. x must be less than 11 and greater than 3
5. $3\sqrt{2}$
6. $2\sqrt{3}$
7. choice B

DRILL 7 (Circles)
(pages 137–138)

1. area $= 25\pi$, circumference $= 10\pi$
2. circumference $= 12\pi$
3. $60°$
4. choice B

DRILL 8 (AD/BCE)

(page 156)

1. BCE. From Statement (1) all we know is a value for y. There is no telling what the value of x will be.

2. BCE. From Statement (1) we know that $2y$ is an integer, but does that mean y must be an integer? Not necessarily. What if y were $\frac{1}{2}$?

3. AD. If we know from the question that there are 12 children in a room and Statement (1) tells us there are 3 girls, then we know there are 9 boys, and we can answer the question.

4. AD. Statement (1) gives us an equation that we *could* solve to get the value of x (not that we need to). If we can solve for x, then we can answer the question.

DRILL 9 (Data Sufficiency Parts and Wholes)

(pages 158–159)

1. Choice C. Statement (1) tells us only how many people paid a deposit. This is not sufficient to answer the question, and we are down to BCE. Statement (2) tells us only what percent of the people who paid deposits actually showed up. Again, by itself, this does not give us the number of people who attended, so we can eliminate B. But if we put the two statements together, we now know how many people paid deposits (70), and what percentage of those people actually attended (60%) which means we can figure out how many people attended.

2. Choice D. You might think you need both statements together, but in fact, either is sufficient by itself. Statement (1) tells us there are 7 ounces of pigment in a 12-ounce can. Because there are only two ingredients, this means the other ingredient must make up the rest, or 5 ounces. This is sufficient to figure out the ratio (7 : 5) and we are down to a fifty-fifty choice: A or D. Similarly, Statement (2) tells us there are 5 ounces of alcohol in a 12-ounce can. Because there are only two ingredients, this means the other ingredient must make up the rest, or 7 ounces. Again, this is sufficient to figure out the ratio, so the answer must be D.

3. Choice C. To answer this question, we need the total number of miles. Statement (1) does not give us any concrete figures—just a fraction, so it is not sufficient, and that narrows our options down to BCE. Statement (2) gives us a concrete number, but it is only for part of the distance, so we can eliminate B. However, if we combine the two statements, we learn that those 12 miles must make up the remaining $\frac{2}{5}$ of the entire trip. From this we can learn the entire distance of the trip by setting up the equation $\frac{2}{5} = \frac{12}{x}$. The correct answer is C.

DRILL 10
(Strange Powers of Powers)
(pages 160–161)

1. Choice C. Statement (1) might *seem* to be sufficient, but remember, if $x^2 = 4$, then x could be either 2 or –2. The question asks for the one and only value of x. Statement (1) is not sufficient. Statement (2) by itself is not sufficient either, because the question is asking for the one and only value of x. But together, the two statements are sufficient because Statement (1) gets us down to two possibilities, 2 and –2, and Statement (2) eliminates the positive number.

2. Choice B. If $x^2 = 4$, then x could be either 2 or –2, so Statement (1) is not sufficient. You might not think Statement (2) is sufficient by itself, because it only gives us a value for y, not for x. However, the question is asking for the value of x times y. If $y = 0$, then we know the value of xy. Zero times anything equals zero.

3. Choice E. If $x^2 = 4$, then x could be either 2 or –2, so Statement (1) is not sufficient. If $y^2 = 9$, then y could be either 3 or –3. The question is asking for the one and only value of x, so Statement (2) is not sufficient by itself either. You might think that putting the two statements together would help us arrive at an answer, but in fact, we don't know. If $x = 2$ and $y = 3$, then $xy = 6$, but what if either x or y was negative? Then xy could also equal –6.

DRILL 11 (Yes or No)
(page 168)

1. Choice A. To answer this yes-or-no question, plug values into the statements. The only condition of the question itself is that x is positive. The only positive numbers that will make Statement (1) true are positive fractions less than $\frac{1}{2}$. This means Statement (1) always answers this question "yes" and we are down to AD. Plugging positive numbers into Statement (2), we could have $\frac{1}{2}$, which gives us a "yes," or 2, which gives us a "no." Therefore, the answer must be choice A.

2. Choice B. When we plug normal numbers 3 and 2 into Statement (1) x is positive. But if we plug in –3 and –2, x is negative, so we are down to BCE. Now, when we plug normal numbers 3 and 2 into Statement (2), we get a "yes." But when we try to plug weird numbers into Statement (2), we realize that (y^2) must always be positive—which means that x must always be positive as well, giving us a definitive "yes."

3. Choice C. To answer this yes-or-no question, plug values into the statements. Let's begin with Statement (1) and let's begin with normal numbers. How about 2 and 3? We get a "yes." Now, let's try some weird numbers. How about 2 and $\frac{1}{2}$? This time, we get a "no," which means we're down to BCE. Let's try Statement (2). Plugging in normal numbers 2 and 3 again, we get a "yes." Plugging in weird numbers $3\frac{1}{2}$ and $1\frac{1}{2}$ we get a "no," and we're down to C or E. Now, to consider C we must pick numbers that make both statements work at the same time. The regular numbers give us a "yes." But when we try to plug weird numbers into the two statements, we realize it can't be done. Only integers will make both statements true at the same time. The answer is choice C.

DRILL 12 (Spotting Critical Reasoning Question Types)

(page 266)

1. Strengthen-the-argument question. To find the correct answer, look for the gap in the argument, and try to close it.

2. Inference question. To find the correct answer, use scope and POE to rule out any answer choice that goes too far.

3. Evaluate-the-argument question. To find the correct answer, look for the unspoken assumptions in the passage.

4. Assumption question. To find the correct answer, look for the gap in the argument.

5. Weaken-the-argument question. To find the correct answer, look for the gap in the argument and try to widen it.

6. Resolve/explain question. To find the correct answer, look for the answer choice that allows both of the facts from the passage to be true at the same time.

7. Identify-the-reasoning question. To find the correct answer, identify the conclusion and the premises, and see how they relate to each other.

8. Parallel-the-reasoning question. To find the correct answer, simplify the argument (if A, then B), and look for an answer choice that matches.

PART ◆ VI

The Princeton Review GMAT Warm-Up Test and Explanations

18

GMAT
Warm-Up Test

GMAT WARM-UP TEST

The purpose of this 60-minute test is to get a rough idea of your current scoring range on the GMAT, and rough percentiles on your Math and Verbal scores. Using these scores as a guide, you can then select from the bins of practice questions that follow. According to the test makers, the computer-adaptive GMAT hones in on your approximate scoring level after only a few questions. You then spend the rest of the test time answering questions from around that level of difficulty, chosen by the computer from bins of potential questions.

To get a much more accurate assessment of where you are right now, we recommend that you take one of The Princeton Review computer adaptive tests (available free online). See the Introduction to this book for details. We also highly recommend that you take an actual computer adaptive GMAT, downloadable for free from the GMAT website at www.mba.com.

Math Test
Time—30 Minutes
20 Questions

This test is composed of both problem solving questions and data sufficiency questions.

Problem Solving Directions: Solve each problem and choose the best of the answer choices provided.

Data Sufficiency Directions: Data sufficiency problems consist of a question and two statements, labeled (1) and (2), in which certain data are given. You have to decide whether the data given in the statements are <u>sufficient</u> for answering the question. Using the data given in the statements <u>plus</u> your knowledge of mathematics and everyday facts (such as the number of days in July or the meaning of *counterclockwise*), you are to select

(A) if statement (1) ALONE is sufficient, but statement (2) alone is not sufficient to answer the question asked;

(B) if statement (2) ALONE is sufficient, but statement (1) alone is not sufficient to answer the question asked;

AND (C) if BOTH statements (1) and (2) TOGETHER are sufficient to answer the question asked, but NEITHER statement alone is sufficient;

OR (D) if EACH statement ALONE is sufficient to answer the question asked;

NAND (E) if statements (1) and (2) TOGETHER are NOT sufficient to answer the question asked, and additional data specific to the problem are needed.

---

1. If $(16)(3)^2 = x(2^3)$, then $x =$

   (A) 81
   (B) 72
   (C) 18
   (D) 16
   (E)   8

2. By how many dollars was the price of a certain portable tape recorder reduced during a sale?

   (1) During the sale, the price of the tape recorder was reduced by 25%.
   (2) The price of the tape recorder after the reduction was $36.

   (A) Statement (1) ALONE is sufficient, but statement (2) alone is not sufficient.

   (B) Statement (2) ALONE is sufficient, but statement (1) alone is not sufficient.

   (C) BOTH statements TOGETHER are sufficient, but NEITHER statement alone is sufficient.

   (D) EACH statement ALONE is sufficient.

   (E) Statements (1) and (2) TOGETHER are NOT sufficient.

GO ON TO THE NEXT PAGE.

B 3. At a certain softball tournament, 65% of the players traveled more than 200 miles to participate. If 720 players took part in the softball tournament, what is the difference between the number of participants who traveled more than 200 miles and the number of participants who traveled 200 miles or less?

(A) 108
(B) 216
(C) 252
(D) 468
(E) 655

D 4. If $r - s = 240$, does $r = 320$?

(1) $r = 4s$
(2) $s = 80$

(A) Statement (1) ALONE is sufficient, but statement (2) alone is not sufficient.
(B) Statement (2) ALONE is sufficient, but statement (1) alone is not sufficient.
(C) BOTH statements TOGETHER are sufficient, but NEITHER statement alone is sufficient.
(D) EACH statement ALONE is sufficient.
(E) Statements (1) and (2) TOGETHER are NOT sufficient.

A 5. If a heavy-load trailer traveled 7 miles in 1 hour and 10 minutes, what was its speed in miles per hour?

(A) 6
(B) 6.5
(C) 8
(D) 8.5
(E) 10

A 6. Bob purchased 18 cans of soda, some of which contained diet soda. How many of the cans did not contain diet soda?

(1) Of the cans Bob purchased, the number containing diet soda is equal to the number not containing diet soda.
(2) Of the cans Bob purchased, the number containing diet soda is odd.

(A) Statement (1) ALONE is sufficient, but statement (2) alone is not sufficient.
(B) Statement (2) ALONE is sufficient, but statement (1) alone is not sufficient.
(C) BOTH statements TOGETHER are sufficient, but NEITHER statement alone is sufficient.
(D) EACH statement ALONE is sufficient.
(E) Statements (1) and (2) TOGETHER are NOT sufficient.

E 7. If y is an odd integer, which of the following must be an even integer?

(A) $y + 2$
(B) $y + 6$
(C) $2y - 1$
(D) $3y$
(E) $3y + 1$

D 8. At Perry High School, the ratio of students who participate in either the band program or the choral program to students who participate in neither program is 3 to 8. If 220 students attend Perry High School, how many of them do NOT participate in either program?

(A) 40
(B) 60
(C) 100
(D) 160
(E) 180

GO ON TO THE NEXT PAGE.

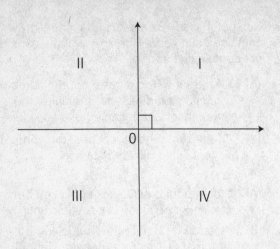

II   I

0

III   IV

C

E 9. If $wxyz \neq 0$, in what quadrant of the coordinate system above does point (x, y) lie?

(1) (x, z) lies in quadrant I. $xz > 0$
(2) (w, y) lies in quadrant III. $wy < 0$

(A)   Statement (1) ALONE is sufficient, but statement (2) alone is not sufficient.

(B)   Statement (2) ALONE is sufficient, but statement (1) alone is not sufficient.

(C)   BOTH statements TOGETHER are sufficient, but NEITHER statement alone is sufficient.

(D)   EACH statement ALONE is sufficient.

(E)   Statements (1) and (2) TOGETHER are NOT sufficient.

D 10. Laura borrowed $240, interest free, from her parents to pay for her college education. If she pays back $2\frac{1}{2}$ percent of this amount quarterly, and has already paid $42.00, for how many months has she been paying back her loan?

(A)   6
(B)   7
(C)   19
(D)   21
(E)   24

A 11. If x and y are positive integers, is x a factor of 12?

(1)   The product xy is a factor of 12.
(2) $y = 3$

(A)   Statement (1) ALONE is sufficient, but statement (2) alone is not sufficient.

(B)   Statement (2) ALONE is sufficient, but statement (1) alone is not sufficient.

(C)   BOTH statements TOGETHER are sufficient, but NEITHER statement alone is sufficient.

(D)   EACH statement ALONE is sufficient.

(E)   Statements (1) and (2) TOGETHER are NOT sufficient.

GO ON TO THE NEXT PAGE.

12. A zebra must get water from either a stream or pond. Which of the two sources of water is closer to the zebra's current position?

   (1)   Moving at a constant rate, it takes the zebra 2 hours to reach the stream from its current position.

   (2)   Moving at a constant rate, it takes the zebra 2 hours to reach the pond from the stream.

   (A)   Statement (1) ALONE is sufficient, but statement (2) alone is not sufficient.

   (B)   Statement (2) ALONE is sufficient, but statement (1) alone is not sufficient.

   (C)   BOTH statements TOGETHER are sufficient, but NEITHER statement alone is sufficient.

   (D)   EACH statement ALONE is sufficient.

   (E)   Statements (1) and (2) TOGETHER are NOT sufficient.

13. What is the value of $x^2 - y^2$?

   (1) $x - y = 0$
   (2) $x + y = 4$

   (A)   Statement (1) ALONE is sufficient, but statement (2) alone is not sufficient.

   (B)   Statement (2) ALONE is sufficient, but statement (1) alone is not sufficient.

   (C)   BOTH statements TOGETHER are sufficient, but NEITHER statement alone is sufficient.

   (D)   EACH statement ALONE is sufficient.

   (E)   Statements (1) and (2) TOGETHER are NOT sufficient.

14. If when a certain integer x is divided by 5 the remainder is 2, then each of the following could also be an integer EXCEPT

   (A) $\dfrac{x}{17}$

   (B) $\dfrac{x}{11}$

   (C) $\dfrac{x}{10}$

   (D) $\dfrac{x}{6}$

   (E) $\dfrac{x}{3}$

15. If a mixture of ground meat consists of 2 pounds of veal that costs x dollars per pound, and 5 pounds of beef that costs y dollars per pound, what is the cost, in dollars, per pound of the mixture?

   (A) $2x + 5y$

   (B) $\dfrac{2x + 5y}{xy}$

   (C) $5(2x + 5y)$

   (D) $x + y$

   (E) $\dfrac{2x + 5y}{7}$

GO ON TO THE NEXT PAGE.

A 16. Is $0 < y < 1$?

(1) $0 < \sqrt{y} < 1$

(2) $y^2 = \dfrac{1}{4}$

(A) Statement (1) ALONE is sufficient, but statement (2) alone is not sufficient.

(B) Statement (2) ALONE is sufficient, but statement (1) alone is not sufficient.

(C) BOTH statements TOGETHER are sufficient, but NEITHER statement alone is sufficient.

(D) EACH statement ALONE is sufficient.

(E) Statements (1) and (2) TOGETHER are NOT sufficient.

B 17. If a and b are positive integers, is the product ab odd?

(1) $b = 3$

(2) a and b are consecutive integers.

(A) Statement (1) ALONE is sufficient, but statement (2) alone is not sufficient.

(B) Statement (2) ALONE is sufficient, but statement (1) alone is not sufficient.

(C) BOTH statements TOGETHER are sufficient, but NEITHER statement alone is sufficient.

(D) EACH statement ALONE is sufficient.

(E) Statements (1) and (2) TOGETHER are NOT sufficient.

D 18. Last year, an appliance store sold an average (arithmetic mean) of 42 microwave ovens per month. In the first 10 months of this year, the store has sold an average (arithmetic mean) of only 20 microwaves per month. What was the average number of microwaves sold per month during the entire 22-month period?

(A) 21
(B) 30
(C) 31
(D) 32
(E) 44

D 19. A and B are the end points of the longest line that can be drawn in a circle with center X. If C is a point on the circle such that $AC = AX = 3$, what is the perimeter of triangle ABC?

(A) $\dfrac{9\sqrt{3}}{2}$

(B) 9

(C) $6 + 3\sqrt{3}$

(D) $9 + 3\sqrt{3}$

(E) $9\sqrt{3}$

GO ON TO THE NEXT PAGE.

| ADVANCED PURCHASE DISCOUNTS FOR AIRLINE TRAVEL ||
Days Prior to Departure	Percentage Discount
0–6 days	0%
7–13 days	10%
14–29 days	25%
30 days or more	40%

20. The table above shows the discount structure for advanced purchase of tickets at a particular airline. A passenger bought a ticket at this airline for $1,050. The ticket agent informed her that, had she purchased the ticket one day later, she would have paid $210 more. How many days before her departure did she purchase her ticket?

(A)   6 days
(B)   7 days
(C)   13 days
(D)   14 days
(E)   29 days

GO ON TO THE NEXT PAGE.

Verbal Test
Time—30 Minutes
20 Questions

This test is made up of sentence correction, critical reasoning, and reading comprehension questions.

Sentence Correction Directions: In sentence corrections, some part of the sentence or the entire sentence is underlined. Beneath each sentence you will find five ways of phrasing the underlined part. The first of these repeats the original; the other four are different. If you think the original is the best of these answer choices, choose answer (A); otherwise, choose the best version and select the corresponding letter.

Reading Comprehension Directions: After reading the passage, choose the best answer to each question. Answer all questions following a passage on the basis of what is <u>stated</u> or <u>implied</u> in that passage.

Critical Reasoning Directions: Select the best of the answer choices given.

---

21. Unseasonable weather in the months before a wine harvest can cool vineyards in the Bordeaux region enough <u>to affect the overall size of the grapes themselves, create</u> unwanted moisture that can cause mold in some grape varieties and deterioration in others.

    (A) to affect the overall size of the grapes themselves, create
    (B) to affect the overall size of the grapes themselves, and create
    (C) that the overall size of the grapes themselves are affected, create
    (D) that it affects the overall size of the grapes themselves, creates
    (E) that the size of the grapes are affected and creates

22. It is posited by some scientists that the near extinction of the sap-eating gray bat of northwestern America was caused by government-sponsored logging operations in the early 1920s that greatly reduced the species' habitat.

    Which of the following, if true, most strongly weakens the scientists' claims?

    (A) Logging operations in the 1920s are widely held responsible for the near extinction of other species that lived in the same area.
    (B) A boom in new home construction in the early 1920s led congress to open federal lands to logging operations.
    (C) A 5-year drought in the early 1920s severely reduced the output of sap in trees in northwestern America.
    (D) Numbers of sightings of sap-eating gray bats fell to their lowest numbers in 1926.
    (E) Sightings of sap-eating gray bats in Europe stayed roughly the same during the same period.

GO ON TO THE NEXT PAGE.

E **23.** Upset by the recent downturn in production numbers during the first half of the year, <u>the possibility of adding worker incentives was raised by the board of directors at its quarterly meeting</u>.

- (A) the possibility of adding worker incentives was raised by the board of directors at its quarterly meeting
- (B) the addition of worker incentives was raised as a possibility by the board of directors at its quarterly meeting
- (C) added worker incentives was raised by the board of directors at its quarterly meeting as a possibility
- (D) the board of directors raised at its quarterly meeting the possibility of worker incentives being added
- (E) the board of directors, at its quarterly meeting, raised the possibility of adding worker incentives

B
C **24.** *unlucky accident* Whenever a major airplane accident occurs, there is a dramatic increase in the number of airplane mishaps reported in the media, a phenomenon that may last for as long as a few months after the accident. Airline officials assert that the publicity given the gruesomeness of *horrible, disgusting* major airplane accidents focuses media attention on the airline industry, and the increase in the number of reported accidents is caused by an increase in the number of news sources covering airline accidents, not by an increase in the number of accidents.

Which of the following, if true, would seriously weaken the assertions of the airline officials?

- (A) The publicity surrounding airline accidents is largely limited to the country in which the crash occurred.
- (B) Airline accidents tend to occur far more often during certain peak travel months.
- (C) News organizations do not have any guidelines to help them decide how severe an accident must be for it to receive coverage.
- (D) Airplane accidents receive coverage by news sources only when the news sources find it advantageous to do so.
- (E) Studies by government regulators show that the number of airplane flight miles remains relatively constant from month to month.

GO ON TO THE NEXT PAGE.

Questions 25–28 are based on the following passage:

The function of strategic planning is to position a company for long-term growth and expansion in a variety of markets by analyzing
Line its strengths and weaknesses and examining
(5) current and potential opportunities. Based on this information, the company develops strategy for itself. That strategy then becomes the basis for supporting strategies for its various departments.

(10) This is where all too many strategic plans go *be lost* astray—at implementation. Recent business management surveys show that most CEOs who have a strategic plan are concerned with the potential breakdown in the implementation
(15) of the plan. Unlike 1980s corporations that blindly followed their 5-year plans, even when they were misguided, today's corporations tend to second-guess.

Outsiders can help facilitate the process,
(20) but in the final analysis, if the company doesn't make the plan, the company won't follow the plan. This was one of the problems with strategic planning in the 1980s. In that era, it was an abstract, top-down process involving
(25) only a few top corporate officers and hired guns. Number crunching experts came into a company and generated tome-like volumes *hard to* filled with a mixture of abstruse facts and grand *understand* theories which had little to do with the day-
(30) to-day realities of the company. Key middle managers were left out of planning sessions, resulting in lost opportunities and ruffled feelings.

However, more hands-on strategic planning
(35) can produce startling results. A recent survey queried more than a thousand small-to-medium sized businesses to compare companies with a strategic plan to companies without one. The survey found that companies with strategic
(40) plans had annual revenue growth of 6.2 percent as opposed to 3.8 percent for the other companies.

Perhaps most important a strategic plan helps companies anticipate—and survive—
(45) change. New technology and the mobility of capital mean that markets can shift faster than ever before. Some financial analysts wonder why they should bother planning two years ahead when market dynamics might be trans-
(50) formed by next quarter. The fact is that it's the very pace of change that makes planning so crucial. Now, more than ever, companies have to stay alert to the marketplace. In an environment of continual and rapid change, long-
(55) range planning expands options and organizational flexibility.

B 25. The primary purpose of the passage is to

(A) refute the idea that change is bad for a corporation's long-term health
(B) describe how long-term planning, despite some potential pitfalls, can help a corporation to grow
(C) compare and contrast two styles of corporate planning
(D) evaluate the strategic planning goals of corporate America today
(E) defend a methodology that has come under sharp attack

C 26. It can be inferred from the passage that, in general, strategic planning during the 1980s had all of the following shortcomings EXCEPT

(A) a reliance on outside consultants who did not necessarily understand the nuts and bolts of the business
(B) a dependence on theoretical models that did not always perfectly describe the workings of the company
(C) an inherent weakness in the company's own ability to implement the strategic plan
(D) an excess of information and data that made it difficult to get to key concepts
(E) the lack of a forum for middle managers to express their ideas

GO ON TO THE NEXT PAGE.

27. The author most likely mentions the results of the survey of 1,000 companies in order to

  (A) put forth an opposing view on strategic plans so that she can then refute it
  (B) illustrate that when strategic planning is "hands-on," it produces uninspiring results
  (C) give a concrete example of why strategic planning did not work during the 1980s
  (D) support her contention that strategic planning when done correctly can be very successful
  (E) give supporting data to prove that many companies have implemented strategic plans

28. The passage suggests which of the following about the "financial analysts" mentioned in lines 47–50?

  (A) They believe that strategic planning is the key to weathering the rapid changes of the marketplace.
  (B) They are working to understand and anticipate market developments that are two years ahead.
  (C) Their study of market dynamics has led them to question the reliability of short-term planning strategies.
  (D) They might not agree with the author that one way to survive rapidly changing conditions comes from long-range planning.
  (E) They consider the mobility of capital to be a necessary condition for the growth of new technology.

29. The Internal Revenue Service has directed that taxpayers who generate no self-employment income can no longer deduct home offices, home office expenses, <u>or nothing that was already</u> depreciated as a business expense the previous year.

  (A) or nothing that was already
  (B) or that was already
  (C) or anything that was already
  (D) and anything
  (E) and nothing that already was

30. Informed people generally assimilate information from several divergent sources before coming to an opinion. However, most popular news organizations view foreign affairs solely through the eyes of our State Department. In reporting the political crisis in foreign country B, news organizations must endeavor to find alternative sources of information.

Which of the following inferences can be drawn from the argument above?

  (A) To the degree that a news source gives an account of another country that mirrors that of our State Department, that reporting is suspect.
  (B) To protect their integrity, news media should avoid the influence of State Department releases in their coverage of foreign affairs.
  (C) Reporting that is not influenced by the State Department is usually more accurate than are other accounts.
  (D) The alternative sources of information mentioned in the passage might not share the same views as the State Department.
  (E) A report cannot be seen as influenced by the State Department if it accurately depicts the events in a foreign country.

GO ON TO THE NEXT PAGE.

31. When automatic teller machines were first installed in the 1980s, bank officials promised <u>they would be faster, more reliable, and less prone to make errors</u> than their human counterparts.

   (A) they would be faster, more reliable, and less prone to make errors
   (B) they would be faster, more reliable, and that they would be less prone for making errors
   (C) the machines would be faster, more reliable, and less prone to make errors
   (D) the machines were faster, more reliable, and errors would occur much less
   (E) faster, more reliable machines, and that errors would be less prone

32. With its plan to create a wildlife sanctuary out of previously unused landfill, Sweden is but one of a number of industrialized nations that <u>is accepting its responsibility to protect endangered species and promote</u> conservation.

   (A) is accepting its responsibility to protect endangered species and promote
   (B) is accepting its responsibility for protecting endangered species and promoting
   (C) are accepting its responsibility to protect endangered species and promoting
   (D) are accepting of their responsibility to protect endangered species and to promote
   (E) are accepting their responsibility to protect endangered species and promote

33. A decade after a logging operation in India began cutting down trees in a territory that serves as a sanctuary for Bengal tigers, the incidence of tigers attacking humans in nearby villages has increased by 300 percent. Because the logging operation has reduced the number of acres of woodland per tiger on average from 15 acres to approximately 12 acres, scientists have theorized that tigers must need a minimum number of acres of woodland in order to remain content.

Which of the following statements, if true, would most strengthen the scientists' hypothesis?

   (A) In other wildlife areas in India where the number of acres of woodland per tiger remains at least 15 acres, there has been no increase in the number of tiger attacks on humans.
   (B) Before the logging operation began, there were many fewer humans living in the area.
   (C) The largest number of acres per tiger before the logging operation began was 32 acres per tiger in one area of the sanctuary, whereas the smallest number of acres per tiger after the logging operation was 9 acres.
   (D) Other species of wild animals have begun competing with the Bengal tigers for the dwindling food supply.
   (E) The Bengal tiger has become completely extinct in other areas of Asia.

GO ON TO THE NEXT PAGE.

D 34. The machine press union and company management were not able to communicate effectively, and it was a major cause of the 1999 strike in Seattle.

(A) The machine press union and company management were not able to communicate effectively, and it

(B) Communications between the machine press union and company management were not effective, and it

(C) For the machine press union and company management, to be unable to communicate effectively

(D) The inability of the machine press union and company management to communicate effectively

(E) The machine press union, being unable to communicate effectively with company management,

E

X 35. A greater number of fresh vegetables are sold in City X than in City Y. Therefore, the people in City X have better nutritional habits than those in City Y.

Each of the following, if true, weakens the conclusion above EXCEPT:

(A) City X has more people living in it than City Y. *more people living in X → higher demand → more supply ≠ people eat healthy*

(B) Most of the people in City Y work in City X and buy their vegetables there.

(C) The people in City X buy many of their vegetables as decorations, not to eat.

(D) The per capita consumption of junk food in City X is three times that of City Y.

(E) The average price per pound of vegetables in City Y is lower than the average price per pound of vegetables in City X.

A 36. Heavy metals, toxic waste by-products that can cause tumors in fish, are generally found in the waters off industrial shorelines, but have been discovered in trace amounts even in the relatively pristine waters of the South Pacific.

(A) are generally found in the waters off industrial shorelines, but have been discovered in trace amounts even

(B) are generally to be found in the waters off industrial shorelines, and have even been discovered in trace amounts

(C) can, in general, be found in the waters off industrial shorelines, and have been discovered in trace amounts even

(D) had generally been found in the waters off industrial shorelines, but have even been discovered in trace amounts

(E) are found generally in the waters off industrial shorelines, but have been discovered in a trace amount even

GO ON TO THE NEXT PAGE.

Questions 37–40 are based on the following passage:

In Roman times, defeated enemies were generally put to death as criminals for having offended the emperor of Rome. In the Middle
Line Ages, however, the practice of ransoming, or
(5) returning prisoners in exchange for money, became common. Though some saw this custom as a step toward a more humane society, the primary reasons behind it were economic rather than humanitarian.
(10) In those times, rulers had only a limited ability to raise taxes. They could neither force their subjects to fight nor pay them to do so. The promise of material compensation in the form of goods and ransom was therefore the
(15) only way of inducing combatants to participate in a war. In the Middle Ages, the predominant incentive for the individual soldier was the expectation of spoils. Although collecting ransom clearly brought financial gain, keeping a
(20) prisoner and arranging for his exchange had its costs. Consequently, procedures were devised to reduce transaction costs.

One such device was a rule asserting that the prisoner had to assess his own value. This
(25) compelled the prisoner to establish a value without too much distortion; indicating too low a value would increase the captive's chances of being killed, while indicating too high a value would either ruin him financially or create a
(30) prohibitively expensive ransom that would also result in death.

37. The primary purpose of the passage is to

(A) discuss the economic basis of the medieval practice of exchanging prisoners for ransom
(B) examine the history of the treatment of prisoners of war
(C) emphasize the importance of a warrior's code of honor during the Middle Ages
(D) explore a way of reducing the costs of ransom
(E) demonstrate why warriors of the Middle Ages looked forward to battles

38. It can be inferred from the passage that a medieval soldier

(A) was less likely to kill captured members of opposing armies than was a soldier of the Roman Empire
(B) operated on a basically independent level and was motivated solely by economic incentives
(C) had few economic options and chose to fight because it was the only way to earn an adequate living
(D) was motivated to spare prisoners' lives by humanitarian rather than economic ideals
(E) had no respect for his captured enemies since captives were typically regarded as weak

GO ON TO THE NEXT PAGE.

39. Which of the following best describes the change in policy from executing prisoners in Roman times to ransoming prisoners in the Middle Ages?

   (A) The emperors of Rome demanded more respect than did medieval rulers, and thus Roman subjects went to greater lengths to defend their nation.

   (B) It was a reflection of the lesser degree of direct control medieval rulers had over their subjects.

   (C) It became a show of strength and honor for warriors of the Middle Ages to be able to capture and return their enemies.

   (D) Medieval soldiers were not as humanitarian as their ransoming practices might have indicated.

   (E) Medieval soldiers demonstrated more concern about economic policy than did their Roman counterparts.

40. The author uses the phrase "without too much distortion" (line 26) in order to

   (A) indicate that prisoners would fairly assess their worth

   (B) emphasize the important role medieval prisoners played in determining whether they should be ransomed

   (C) explain how prisoners often paid more than an appropriate ransom in order to increase their chances for survival

   (D) suggest that captors and captives often had understanding relationships

   (E) show that when in prison a soldier's view could become distorted

END OF WARM-UP TEST

19

GMAT Warm-Up Test Scoring Guide

GMAT WARM-UP TEST SCORING GUIDE

Detailed explanations to these answers can be found in the next chapter.

ANSWER KEY	
MATH	**VERBAL**
1. C	21. B
2. C	22. C
3. B	23. E
4. D	24. B
5. A	25. B
6. A	26. C
7. E	27. D
8. D	28. D
9. C	29. C
10. D	30. D
11. A	31. C
12. E	32. E
13. A	33. A
14. C	34. D
15. E	35. E
16. A	36. A
17. B	37. A
18. D	38. A
19. D	39. B
20. D	40. A

-2
18/20

-4
16/20

THE MATH SCORE

If you got 6 or fewer math questions correct: Your percentile rank is in the lower one-third of the testing group and you should begin by practicing the problems in Math Bin 1. Once you've mastered the material in Math Bin 1, you should move on to the questions in Math Bin 2 of our practice test.

If you got between 6 and 13 math questions correct: Your percentile rank is in the middle one-third of the testing group and you should begin by practicing the problems in Math Bin 2 of our practice test. Once you've mastered the material in Math Bin 2, you should move on to the questions in Math Bin 3.

If you got 14 or more math questions correct: Your percentile rank is in the top one-third of the testing group and you should begin by practicing the problems in Math Bins 3 and 4 of our practice test.

THE VERBAL SCORE

If you got 6 or fewer verbal questions correct: Your percentile rank is in the lower one-third of the testing group and you should begin by practicing the problems in Verbal Bin 1 of our practice test. Once you've mastered the material in Verbal Bin 1, you should move on to the questions in Verbal Bin 2.

If you got between 6 and 13 verbal questions correct: Your percentile rank is in the middle one-third of the testing group and you should begin by practicing the problems in Verbal Bin 2 of our practice test. Once you've mastered the material in Verbal Bin 2, you should move on to the questions in Verbal Bin 3 of our practice test.

If you got 14 or more verbal questions correct: Your percentile rank is in the top one-third of the testing group and you should begin by practicing the problems in Verbal Bin 3 of our practice test.

(If you want additional practice for either the Math or the Verbal section, you may find it helpful to do the problems in a bin with a lower number than the one suggested. So if your math diagnostic score indicates that you should do the questions in Math Bin 2, you might want to do the questions in Math Bin 1 as well.)

THE COMBINED SCORE

If you got 12 or fewer of the 40 total questions correct: Your combined score at the moment is less than 450.

If you got between 12 and 31 of the 40 total questions correct: Your combined score at the moment is between 450 and 550.

If you got 32 or more of the 40 total questions correct: Your combined score at the moment is more than 550.

20

GMAT Warm-Up Test: Answers and Explanations

Math Explanations

1. If $(16)(3)^2 = x(2^3)$, then $x =$

   (A) 81
   (B) 72
   (C) 18
   (D) 16
   (E)   8

1. C Rather than multiply out each side of the equation, let's simplify. We can rewrite 16 as 2^4. If we cancel 2^3 from each side of the equation, we are left with $2(3)^2 = x$. The correct answer is C, 18.

2. By how many dollars was the price of a certain portable tape recorder reduced during a sale?

   (1) During the sale, the price of the tape recorder was reduced by 25%.

   (2) The price of the tape recorder after the reduction was $36.

   (A) Statement (1) ALONE is sufficient, but statement (2) alone is not sufficient.

   (B) Statement (2) ALONE is sufficient, but statement (1) alone is not sufficient.

   (C) Both statements TOGETHER are sufficient, but NEITHER statement ALONE is sufficient.

   (D) EACH statement ALONE is sufficient.

   (E) Statements (1) and (2) TOGETHER are NOT sufficient.

2. C Statement (1) tells us the reduction as a percentage, but without a dollar figure we can't know the exact amount of the reduction. We're down to BCE.

Looking at Statement (2) we now know the dollar amount after the reduction, but without knowing either the original amount, or the percentage of the reduction, we don't know enough to answer the question. We're down to C or E.

However, when we put the two statements together, we have enough information to write an equation: $.75x = \$36$, where x is the original amount. Once we subtract the price after the reduction, we'll have answered the question. But remember, in Data Sufficiency, we don't need to answer it; we just need to know that we can. The best answer is choice C.

3. At a certain softball tournament, 65% of the players traveled more than 200 miles to participate. If 720 players took part in the softball tournament, what is the difference between the number of participants who traveled more than 200 miles and the number of participants who traveled 200 miles or less?

   (A) 108
   (B) 216
   (C) 252
   (D) 468
   (E) 655

3. B This is a percent problem, so let's start by finding the number of players who traveled more than 200 miles: 65% of 720 is 468. The number of players who traveled 200 miles or less, then, is $720 - 468 = 252$ (or, alternatively, 35% of 720 is 252). Although both 468 and 252 are answer choices, the question asks us for the difference between the two types of participants: $468 - 252 = 216$.

If you'd prefer, you can also deal with the difference of the percentages rather than that of the actual people: $65\% - 35\% = 30\%$ and 30% of 720 is 216. This approach might make it easier to ballpark with a reasonable degree of accuracy: since our difference is a little less than a third, our answer should be a little less than $720 \div 3$, or 240.

4. If $r - s = 240$, does $r = 320$?

   (1) $r = 4s$

   (2) $s = 80$

   (A) Statement (1) ALONE is sufficient, but statement (2) alone is not sufficient.

   (B) Statement (2) ALONE is sufficient, but statement (1) alone is not sufficient.

   (C) Both statements TOGETHER are sufficient, but NEITHER statement ALONE is sufficient.

   (D) EACH statement ALONE is sufficient.

   (E) Statements (1) and (2) TOGETHER are NOT sufficient.

4. **D** Joe Bloggs might be tempted by B on this yes-or-no problem, because Statement (2) certainly does answer the question. But look at Statement (1) by itself. If $r = 4s$, then we can substitute $4s$ for r in the first equation, making it $4s - s = 240$, or $3s = 240$, which means s equals 80, and r again must equal 320.

5. If a heavy-load trailer traveled 7 miles in 1 hour and 10 minutes, what was its speed in miles per hour?

   (A) 6
   (B) 6.5
   (C) 8
   (D) 8.5
   (E) 10

5. **A** Any problem with terms like "speed" or "miles per hour" can probably be solved with the formula: *distance = rate × time*. This problem asks for the speed, or rate, which means *distance* divided by *time*. 7 divided by $1\frac{1}{6}$ (or $\frac{7}{6}$) equals 6.

6. Bob purchased 18 cans of soda, some of which contained diet soda. How many of the cans did not contain diet soda?

    (1) Of the cans Bob purchased, the number containing diet soda is equal to the number not containing diet soda.

    (2) Of the cans Bob purchased, the number containing diet soda is odd.

    (A) Statement (1) ALONE is sufficient, but statement (2) alone is not sufficient.

    (B) Statement (2) ALONE is sufficient, but statement (1) alone is not sufficient.

    (C) Both statements TOGETHER are sufficient, but NEITHER statement ALONE is sufficient.

    (D) EACH statement ALONE is sufficient.

    (E) Statements (1) and (2) TOGETHER are NOT sufficient.

7. If y is an odd integer, which of the following must be an even integer?

    (A) $y + 2$
    (B) $y + 6$
    (C) $2y - 1$
    (D) $3y$
    (E) $3y + 1$

6. A The original question tells us the total number of cans. Statement (1) tells us there is an equal number of diet and non-diet cans. This answers the question (there are 9 of each, not that we really needed to know to get this data sufficiency question correct.) We are down to A or D.

Statement (2) may seem to *agree* with Statement (1) because we may have noticed that the number of diet cans supplied by the information in Statement (1) happens to be odd. However, there are lots of odd numbers. The correct answer is A.

7. E Variables in the answer choices means this is a Plug-In problem—a total gift as long as you use our techniques—but the word "must" means you may have to plug in *twice* to be sure you have the right answer. Whenever you Plug In, be sure to write down the number you are using so you won't forget it as you work. Because y must be an odd integer, let's use 3. Now, all we have to do is plug 3 into each of the answer choices. Any choice that does *not* yield an even integer can be crossed off immediately. If more than one of the choices yields an even integer, we will have to plug in a second number for y to see which choice *always* yields an even number. Using 3 as our value for y, we find that choices A, B, C, and D all yield odd numbers. Therefore, the correct answer is E.

8. At Perry High School, the ratio of students who participate in either the band program or the choral program to students who participate in neither program is 3 to 8. If 220 students attend Perry High School, how many of them do NOT participate in either program?

(A) 40
(B) 60
(C) 100
(D) 160
(E) 180

8. **D** This is a ratio problem, so we need to add the "parts" of our ratio to get the "whole" required to form a fraction. Since our parts are 3 and 8, our whole is 11; the fraction of the students that does not participate in the band or choral program is thus $\frac{8}{11}$. Now we can set up an equation: $\frac{8}{11} = \frac{x}{220}$. The correct answer is D, 160.

Be careful not to choose B, the number of students who do participate in one of the programs, or C, the difference between the number of students who participate and the number who don't. Judicious use of POE might have eliminated both answers, though, along with A: Since we know that more than half of the students do not participate in either program, we can eliminate any answer less than 110.

Math Explanations

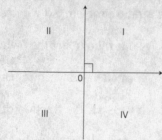

9. If $wxyz \neq 0$, in what quadrant of the coordinate system above does point (x, y) lie?

(1) (x, z) lies in quadrant I.

(2) (w, y) lies in quadrant III.

(A) Statement (1) ALONE is sufficient, but statement (2) alone is not sufficient.

(B) Statement (2) ALONE is sufficient, but statement (1) alone is not sufficient.

(C) Both statements TOGETHER are sufficient, but NEITHER statement ALONE is sufficient.

(D) EACH statement ALONE is sufficient.

(E) Statements (1) and (2) TOGETHER are NOT sufficient.

10. Laura borrowed $240, interest free, from her parents to pay for her college education. If she pays back $2\frac{1}{2}$ percent of this amount quarterly, and has already paid $42.00, for how many months has she been paying back her loan?

(A) 6
(B) 7
(C) 19
(D) 21
(E) 24

9. **C** To help understand this question, try Plugging In some values. Statement (1) tells us that point (x, z) lies in quadrant I, which essentially means that x and z must both be positive. For example, let's say (x, z) was $(3,4)$. We know x is positive, but does this tell us anything about y? Nope, so we are down to BCE.

Statement (2) tells us that point (w, y) lies in quadrant III, which essentially means that w and y must both be negative. For example, let's say (w, y) was $(-2,-5)$. In this case, we know y must be negative, but does this tell us anything about x? Nope, so we are down to answer choices C or E.

If we put the two statements together, we know x must be positive and we know y must be negative—for example, using the points we plugged in, (x, y) would be $(3, -5)$—which means point (x, y) must be in quadrant IV. The answer is C.

10. **D** Laura pays back 2.5 percent of the loan each quarter of the year. 2.5% of $240 is $6.00. If she has already paid $42.00, that means she has paid that $6.00 for seven quarters. How many months is that? Each quarter of the year is 3 months. The correct answer is D.

11. If *x* and *y* are positive integers, is *x* a factor of 12?

    (1) The product *xy* is a factor of 12.

    (2) *y* = 3

    (A) Statement (1) ALONE is sufficient, but statement (2) alone is not sufficient.

    (B) Statement (2) ALONE is sufficient, but statement (1) alone is not sufficient.

    (C) Both statements TOGETHER are sufficient, but NEITHER statement ALONE is sufficient.

    (D) EACH statement ALONE is sufficient.

    (E) Statements (1) and (2) TOGETHER are NOT sufficient.

12. A zebra must get water from either a stream or pond. Which of the two sources of water is closer to the zebra's current position?

    (1) Moving at a constant rate, it takes the zebra 2 hours to reach the stream from its current position.

    (2) Moving at a constant rate, it takes the zebra 2 hours to reach the pond from the stream.

    (A) Statement (1) ALONE is sufficient, but statement (2) alone is not sufficient.

    (B) Statement (2) ALONE is sufficient, but statement (1) alone is not sufficient.

    (C) BOTH statements TOGETHER are sufficient, but NEITHER statement alone is sufficient.

    (D) EACH statement ALONE is sufficient.

    (E) Statements (1) and (2) TOGETHER are NOT sufficient.

11. A To solve this yes-or-no question, plug values into the two statements. To be a factor of 12, the product of *xy* must be equal to 1, 2, 3, 4, 6, or 12. Let's make *x* equal 2 and *y* equal 3. Is *x* a factor of 12? Yes. In fact, as long as *xy* must be a factor of 12 and *x* and *y* are integers, *x* must ALWAYS be a factor of 12. We are down to AD.

Now, let's look at Statement (2). The fact that *y* = 3 does not help us know if *x* is a factor of 12. The answer is A. Joe Bloggs might have been tempted by C because it gives us a definitive value for *x*. But Statement (1) had already answered this yes-or-no question all by itself.

12. E Statement (1) only tells us the time it takes the zebra to reach the stream from its current position; since it gives us no information about the time required to reach the pond, Statement (1) is insufficient alone, and we're down to B, C, or E.

Similarly, since Statement (2) only tells us the time it takes the zebra to get from the pond to the stream—and doesn't mention the zebra's current position—Statement (2) is insufficient alone, and we're down to C or E.

Be careful when you combine the two statements: Although it may be tempting to simply add our travel time and calculate that it would take the zebra 4 hours to go from it's current position to the pond, this is only true if all 3 given locations were in a straight line, so that the pond would be directly on the other side of the stream. We, of course, can't assume that to be the case. For instance, if the zebra travels 2 hours due west from its current position to the stream, and then travels 2 hours due east from the stream to the pond, the zebra's current location would be *at* the pond! The correct answer to this question is E.

Math Explanations

13. What is the value of $x^2 - y^2$?

   (1) $x - y = 0$
   (2) $x + y = 4$

   (A) Statement (1) ALONE is sufficient, but statement (2) alone is not sufficient.
   (B) Statement (2) ALONE is sufficient, but statement (1) alone is not sufficient.
   (C) Both statements TOGETHER are sufficient, but NEITHER statement ALONE is sufficient.
   (D) EACH statement ALONE is sufficient.
   (E) Statements (1) and (2) TOGETHER are NOT sufficient.

13. **A** Joe Bloggs wants to pick either answer choice E (because he doesn't know how to factor $x^2 - y^2$) or answer C because he knows that $x^2 - y^2 = (x + y)(x - y)$ and he figures he will need both statements to give him the answer. But if $(x - y) = 0$, then what $(x + y)$ equals is irrelevant because zero times anything equals zero.

14. If when a certain integer x is divided by 5 the remainder is 2, then each of the following could also be an integer EXCEPT

   (A) $\dfrac{x}{17}$
   (B) $\dfrac{x}{11}$
   (C) $\dfrac{x}{10}$
   (D) $\dfrac{x}{6}$
   (E) $\dfrac{x}{3}$

14. **C** As always, when there are variables in the answer choices, the easiest thing to do is plug in. If you always get a remainder of 2 when you divide x by 5, then x has to be some multiple of 5 plus 2 more. In other words, x could be 7 or 12 or 17 or 22, etc. Now, we have to go through the answer choices Plugging In numbers for x that allow them to be integers as well. For example, in A, if we plugged in 17 for x, that would give us $\dfrac{17}{17}$, which is an integer. Cross off choice A. In choice B if we plugged in 22, we would get $\dfrac{22}{11}$ which is an integer. Cross off B. In D and E, Plugging In the number 12 would make both choices integers. Only choice C can never be an integer as long as x can be divided by 5 with a remainder of 2. The correct answer is C.

15. If a mixture of ground meat consists of 2 pounds of veal that costs x dollars per pound, and 5 pounds of beef that costs y dollars per pound, what is the cost, in dollars, per pound of the mixture?

   (A) $2x + 5y$

   (B) $\dfrac{2x + 5y}{xy}$

   (C) $5(2x + 5y)$

   (D) $x + y$

   (E) $\dfrac{2x + 5y}{7}$

15. **E** When you see variables among the answer choices, the best way to solve the problem is by Plugging In. Because the total number of pounds of meat will be 7, it makes sense to choose numbers that divide evenly by 7. Choosing $14 for x and $7 for y, we end up with $9 per pound for the mixture. Plugging our values for x and y into the answer choices, only one gives us $9: E.

16. Is $0 < y < 1$?

   (1) $0 < \sqrt{y} < 1$

   (2) $y^2 = \dfrac{1}{4}$

   (A) Statement (1) ALONE is sufficient, but statement (2) alone is not sufficient.

   (B) Statement (2) ALONE is sufficient, but statement (1) alone is not sufficient.

   (C) Both statements TOGETHER are sufficient, but NEITHER statement ALONE is sufficient.

   (D) EACH statement ALONE is sufficient.

   (E) Statements (1) and (2) TOGETHER are NOT sufficient.

16. **A** To solve this yes-or-no question, plug values into the two statements. Joe Bloggs liked Statement (2) because he forgot that y could equal $-\dfrac{1}{2}$. However only Statement (1) answered the question: On the GMAT, square roots are always positive. The correct answer is A.

17. If *a* and *b* are positive integers, is the product *ab* odd?

    (1) $b = 3$

    (2) *a* and *b* are consecutive integers.

    (A) Statement (1) ALONE is sufficient, but statement (2) alone is not sufficient.

    (B) Statement (2) ALONE is sufficient, but statement (1) alone is not sufficient.

    (C) Both statements TOGETHER are sufficient, but NEITHER statement ALONE is sufficient.

    (D) EACH statement ALONE is sufficient.

    (E) Statements (1) and (2) TOGETHER are NOT sufficient.

17. **B** To solve this yes-or-no question, try plugging values into the statements. Looking first at Statement (1) we know that $b = 3$. If we plug in 2 for *a*, we get a "no" answer to the question "is the product *ab* odd." If we plug in 5 for *a*, we get a "yes" answer, so we are down to BCE.

Now, Plugging In for Statement (2), we eventually realize that if *a* and *b* are consecutive integers, one of them must always be even, and the other odd. And the product of even times odd is always even. So Statement (2) answers this yes-or-no question with a resounding "No." Joe Bloggs was probably tempted by C.

18. Last year, an appliance store sold an average (arithmetic mean) of 42 microwave ovens per month. In the first 10 months of this year, the store has sold an average (arithmetic mean) of only 20 microwaves per month. What was the average number of microwaves sold per month during the entire 22-month period?

    (A) 21
    (B) 30
    (C) 31
    (D) 32
    (E) 44

18. **D** To find this average, you have to divide the total number of sales by the total number of months. The sales for the first year were 12 times 42 or 504. The sales for the first 10 months of this year were 10 times 20 or 200. So the average number of sales per month can be found by dividing the total number of sales, 704, by the total number of months, 22. The answer is 32. Note that A and E are completely out of the ballpark. Because there were more months when the sales averaged 42 than when they averaged 20, the correct answer is bound to be a *little* more than the average of the two averages, 31. Choice C, 31, is the Joe Bloggs answer; Joe loves to take an average of two averages.

19. A and B are the end points of the longest line that can be drawn in a circle with center X. If C is a point on the circle such that $AC = AX = 3$, what is the perimeter of triangle ABC?

(A) $\dfrac{9\sqrt{3}}{2}$

(B) 9

(C) $6 + 3\sqrt{3}$

(D) $9 + 3\sqrt{3}$

(E) $9\sqrt{3}$

19. **D** First, draw the picture. It should look something like this:

AB is the diameter—another way of saying "the longest line that can be drawn in"— of the circle. C is a point on the circle that's closer to A than it is to B. ABC is the triangle that connects the 3 points. AC and AX can be labeled 3—as can BX, since, like AX, it's a radius.

Hey! We've already got 2 of the 3 sides we need to find the perimeter! To find the 3rd, we'll need to recognize that triangle ABC, because it's inscribed in a semi-circle, is a right triangle. Now we can use the Pythagorean theorem—or, even better, recognize ABC as a 30–60–90 triangle—to determine that BC is $3\sqrt{3}$. Our perimeter is thus $6 + 3 + 3\sqrt{3}$, or $9 + 3\sqrt{3}$. The correct answer is D.

Be careful not to fall for any trap answers: A is the *area* of triangle ABC; B and C are the perimeters of the 2 smaller triangles.

ADVANCED PURCHASE DISCOUNTS FOR AIRLINE TRAVEL	
Days Prior to Departure	Percentage Discount
0–6 days	0%
7–13 days	10%
14–29 days	25%
30 days or more	40%

20. The table above shows the discount structure for advanced purchase of tickets at a particular airline. A passenger bought a ticket at this airline for $1,050. The ticket agent informed her that, had she purchased the ticket one day later, she would have paid $210 more. How many days before her departure did she purchase her ticket?

(A) 6 days
(B) 7 days
(C) 13 days
(D) 14 days
(E) 29 days

20. **D** If we add up what this passenger actually paid, $1,050, plus the $210 she saved, we get what the purchase price would have been the following day, or $1,260. Now, according to the table, if she had purchased her ticket 6 days before the flight, she would not have saved any money at all, so we can eliminate A. If she bought the ticket 7 days before, she would have saved 10%. Does 10% of $1,260 equal $210? Nope. She saved more than that. If she purchased her ticket 13 days before the flight, she would not have saved any more money than if she had bought it the next day (12 days before the flight) so we can eliminate choice C. At this point, you might want to guess between D and E. To see if she bought the ticket 14 days before the flight, the easiest thing to do is Plug In the Answers. Let's assume she bought the ticket 14 days in advance of the flight for $1,050, representing a $210 saving from what it would have cost the day after. That means the ticket would have cost $1,260 from day 13 through day 7, and $1,400 without the 10% discount (90% of $x = 1,260$). If D is correct, then 1,050 is 75% of 1,400. It is.

21. Unseasonable weather in the months before a wine harvest can cool vineyards in the Bordeaux region enough <u>to affect the overall size of the grapes themselves, create</u> unwanted moisture that can cause mold in some grape varieties and deterioration in others.

   (A) to affect the overall size of the grapes themselves, create
   (B) to affect the overall size of the grapes themselves, and create
   (C) that the overall size of the grapes themselves are affected, create
   (D) that it affects the overall size of the grapes themselves, creates
   (E) that the size of the grapes are affected and creates

21. **B** Go through your checklist of potential errors. Is there a misplaced modifier here? No. Is there a pronoun problem? No. Is there a parallel construction problem? Yes! At first it seems as if this sentence contains a list of three actions: to affect...create...and deteriorate—but wait! The third action is not an action, it's a noun: deterioration. However, since *deterioration* is not underlined, we can't fix this. Going back to the original sentence, it becomes clear that, in fact, there are only two main actions: to affect the overall size of the grapes and (to) create unwanted moisture. To correctly use this compound verb, the original sentence would need an "and" between the verbs. Only choice B gives you this option. Choices C, D, and E use the idiomatic expression "enough that" which is not necessarily wrong, but which would require the word "creating."

22. It is posited by some scientists that the near extinction of the sap-eating gray bat of north-western America was caused by government-sponsored logging operations in the early 1920s that greatly reduced the species' habitat.

Which of the following, if true, most strongly weakens the scientists' claims?

   (A) Logging operations in the 1920s are widely held responsible for the near extinction of other species that lived in the same area.
   (B) A boom in new home construction in the early 1920s led congress to open federal lands to logging operations.
   (C) A 5-year drought in the early 1920s severely reduced the output of sap in trees in northwestern America.
   (D) Numbers of sightings of sap-eating gray bats fell to their lowest numbers in 1926.
   (E) Sightings of sap-eating gray bats in Europe stayed roughly the same during the same period.

23. Upset by the recent downturn in production numbers during the first half of the year, <u>the possibility of adding worker incentives was raised by the board of directors at its quarterly meeting</u>.

   (A) the possibility of adding worker incentives was raised by the board of directors at its quarterly meeting
   (B) the addition of worker incentives was raised as a possibility by the board of directors at its quarterly meeting
   (C) added worker incentives was raised by the board of directors at its quarterly meeting as a possibility
   (D) the board of directors raised at its quarterly meeting the possibility of worker incentives being added
   (E) the board of directors, at its quarterly meeting, raised the possibility of adding worker incentives

22. C This is a causal argument. The scientists claim that the bat's near extinction was caused by logging. How do we weaken this argument? By presenting an alternate cause—another reason why the bat almost became extinct. Choices A and B actually strengthen the argument. Choice A says that other species were also threatened with extinction by logging, and choice B gives us a reason the government might have been tempted to agree to logging on federal lands. Choice D is outside the scope of the argument since "sightings" are irrelevant. Choice E also goes outside the scope of the argument by telling us about the bat population on another continent. But choice C gives us an alternate cause for the near extinction of these bats: the sap they depended on for nourishment was severely reduced at the time in question by a five-year drought.

23. E This is a misplaced modifier question. Who was "upset by the recent downturn"? It was the board of directors. This eliminates choices A, B, and C. Choice E correctly positions the prepositional phrase "at its quarterly meeting" and avoids the passive "being added" in D.

24. Whenever a major airplane accident occurs, there is a dramatic increase in the number of airplane mishaps reported in the media, a phenomenon that may last for as long as a few months after the accident. Airline officials assert that the publicity given the gruesomeness of major airplane accidents focuses media attention on the airline industry, and the increase in the number of reported accidents is caused by an increase in the number of news sources covering airline accidents, not by an increase in the number of accidents.

Which of the following, if true, would seriously weaken the assertions of the airline officials?

(A) The publicity surrounding airline accidents is largely limited to the country in which the crash occurred.

(B) Airline accidents tend to occur far more often during certain peak travel months.

(C) News organizations do not have any guidelines to help them decide how severe an accident must be for it to receive coverage.

(D) Airplane accidents receive coverage by news sources only when the news sources find it advantageous to do so.

(E) Studies by government regulators show that the number of airplane flight miles remains relatively constant from month to month.

24. **B** This is a statistical argument. The officials assert that there is in fact no increase in actual mishaps during the months after an accident, but an increase in the number of news sources *reporting* the mishaps—in other words, they argue that the statistics are not representative. To weaken this assertion, we would have to show that the statistics are in fact representative. B does this by implying that certain months are more likely to have more frequent accidents due to high volume of flights. A is outside the scope of the argument. C, D, and E would all *strengthen* the assertions of the officials.

The function of strategic planning is to position a company for long-term growth and expansion in a variety of markets by analyzing its strengths and weaknesses and examining current and potential opportunities. Based on this information, the company develops strategy for itself. That strategy then becomes the basis for supporting strategies for its various departments.

This is where all too many strategic plans go astray—at implementation. Recent business management surveys show that most CEOs who have a strategic plan are concerned with the potential breakdown in the implementation of the plan. Unlike 1980s corporations that blindly followed their 5-year plans, even when they were misguided, today's corporations tend to second-guess.

Outsiders can help facilitate the process, but in the final analysis, if the company doesn't make the plan, the company won't follow the plan. This was one of the problems with strategic planning in the 1980s. In that era, it was an abstract, top-down process involving only a few top corporate officers and hired guns. Number crunching experts came into a company and generated tome-like volumes filled with a mixture of abstruse facts and grand theories which had little to do with the day-to-day realities of the company. Key middle managers were left out of planning sessions, resulting in lost opportunities and ruffled feelings.

However, more hands-on strategic planning can produce startling results. A recent survey queried more than a thousand small-to-medium sized businesses to compare companies with a strategic plan to companies without one. The survey found that companies with strategic plans had annual revenue growth of 6.2 percent as opposed to 3.8 percent for the other companies.

Perhaps most important, a strategic plan helps companies anticipate—and survive—change. New technology and the mobility of capital mean that markets can shift faster than ever before. Some financial analysts wonder why they should bother planning two years ahead when market dynamics might be transformed by next quarter. The fact is that it's the very pace of change that makes planning so crucial. Now, more than ever, companies have to stay alert to the marketplace. In an environment of continual and rapid change, long-range planning expands options and organizational flexibility.

Verbal Explanations

25. The primary purpose of the passage is to

    (A) refute the idea that change is bad for a corporation's long-term health

    (B) describe how long-term planning, despite some potential pitfalls, can help a corporation to grow

    (C) compare and contrast two styles of corporate planning

    (D) evaluate the strategic planning goals of corporate America today

    (E) defend a methodology that has come under sharp attack

25. B Most reading comprehension passages ask some form of this question. Choice B best summarizes the main idea of the passage: that despite some potential problems, strategic planning can allow a company to expand and grow.

26. It can be inferred from the passage that, in general, strategic planning during the 1980s had all of the following shortcomings EXCEPT

    (A) a reliance on outside consultants who did not necessarily understand the nuts and bolts of the business

    (B) a dependence on theoretical models that did not always perfectly describe the workings of the company

    (C) an inherent weakness in the company's own ability to implement the strategic plan

    (D) an excess of information and data that made it difficult to get to key concepts

    (E) the lack of a forum for middle managers to express their ideas

26. C According to the passage, the difficulty in implementation of strategic plans is a more modern phenomenon, not related to the weaknesses of the 1980s.

27. The author most likely mentions the results of the survey of 1,000 companies in order to

    (A) put forth an opposing view on strategic plans so that she can then refute it

    (B) illustrate that when strategic planning is "hands-on," it produces uninspiring results

    (C) give a concrete example of why strategic planning did not work during the 1980s

    (D) support her contention that strategic planning when done correctly can be very successful

    (E) give supporting data to prove that many companies have implemented strategic plans

27. D Skim the passage quickly to find the survey, then read that portion carefully. According to the passage, the survey shows that companies with strategic plans outperformed companies without strategic plans.

28. The passage suggests which of the following about the "financial analysts" mentioned in lines 47–50?

(A) They believe that strategic planning is the key to weathering the rapid changes of the marketplace.

(B) They are working to understand and anticipate market developments that are two years ahead.

(C) Their study of market dynamics has led them to question the reliability of short-term planning strategies.

(D) They might not agree with the author that one way to survive rapidly changing conditions comes from long-range planning.

(E) They consider the mobility of capital to be a necessary condition for the growth of new technology.

28. **D** It's always a good idea to read a few lines above and below the cited lines, just to make sure you understand the context. The financial analysts mentioned in the passage seem to say that it is not worth trying to plan when the market is changing so rapidly. The author mentions their views in order to refute them.

29. The Internal Revenue Service has directed that taxpayers who generate no self-employment income can no longer deduct home offices, home office expenses, <u>or nothing that was already</u> depreciated as a business expense the previous year.

(A) or nothing that was already
(B) or that was already
(C) or anything that was already
(D) and anything
(E) and nothing that already was

29. **C** After running down your checklist of potential errors without encountering an ambiguous pronoun, a misplaced modifier, a tense problem or a subject-verb disagreement, you should begin thinking about the possibility of an idiomatic error. Try making your own sentence: "I no longer deduct...nothing on my taxes." Does that seem right? In fact, it is incorrect: a double negative.

Scanning the answer choices can give you a clue as well: You have a choice of "nothing" or "anything." Which is better? If you said "anything," you were absolutely correct. Choice D includes "anything" but begins with the conjunction "and." In a list of three things you can't do, use "or" instead of "and."

Verbal Explanations

30. Informed people generally assimilate information from several divergent sources before coming to an opinion. However, most popular news organizations view foreign affairs solely through the eyes of our State Department. In reporting the political crisis in foreign country B, news organizations must endeavor to find alternative sources of information.

Which of the following inferences can be drawn from the argument above?

(A) To the degree that a news source gives an account of another country that mirrors that of our State Department, that reporting is suspect.

(B) To protect their integrity, news media should avoid the influence of State Department releases in their coverage of foreign affairs.

(C) Reporting that is not influenced by the State Department is usually more accurate than are other accounts.

(D) The alternative sources of information mentioned in the passage might not share the same views as the State Department.

(E) A report cannot be seen as influenced by the State Department if it accurately depicts the events in a foreign country.

30. **D** To get an inference question correct, you almost never actually want to infer. Look for an answer that seems ludicrously obvious. Choice A implies that the State Department's views are always likely to diverge from other news sources, which is not only silly, but something the GMAT test writers would be unlikely to say. B implies that the State Department should never be used as a news source, which goes way too far. Choice C also goes much further than the passage itself. E is a bit bizarre, because sometimes the State Department is bound to be right. Choice D is the best answer because the argument makes it clear that the "alternative" sources of information would provide the "divergent" opinions mentioned in the first sentence.

31. When automatic teller machines were first installed in the 1980s, bank officials promised <u>they would be faster, more reliable, and less prone to make errors</u> than their human counterparts.

(A) they would be faster, more reliable, and less prone to make errors

(B) they would be faster, more reliable, and that they would be less prone for making errors

(C) the machines would be faster, more reliable, and less prone to make errors

(D) the machines were faster, more reliable, and errors would occur much less

(E) faster, more reliable machines, and that errors would be less prone

31. **C** Go through your checklist of potential errors. Is there a misplaced modifier here? No. Is there a pronoun problem? Well, wait a minute. There certainly is a pronoun here. Is it possible that the "they" could be ambiguous? As a matter of fact, "they" is obviously supposed to refer to the automatic teller machines, but it also could refer to the bank officials. Replacing "they" with "the machines" clarifies the sentence, which means we are down to C, D, or E, but C has a much more parallel construction.

32. With its plan to create a wildlife sanctuary out of previously unused landfill, Sweden is but one of a number of industrialized nations that <u>is accepting its responsibility to protect endangered species and promote</u> conservation.

    (A) is accepting its responsibility to protect endangered species and promote
    (B) is accepting its responsibility for protecting endangered species and promoting
    (C) are accepting its responsibility to protect endangered species and promoting
    (D) are accepting of their responsibility to protect endangered species and to promote
    (E) are accepting their responsibility to protect endangered species and promote

32. **E** This is a subject-verb question. The verb *is* in the underlined portion seems to agree with the subject of the sentence, *Sweden*, but in fact, the noun *is* must agree with *nations*, which is plural. We're down to C, D, or E. C keeps the singular pronoun *its* so we can eliminate that. Choice D contains the unidiomatic *accepting of*, making E the best answer.

33. A decade after a logging operation in India began cutting down trees in a territory that serves as a sanctuary for Bengal tigers, the incidence of tigers attacking humans in nearby villages has increased by 300 percent. Because the logging operation has reduced the number of acres of woodland per tiger on average from 15 acres to approximately 12 acres, scientists have theorized that tigers must need a minimum number of acres of woodland in order to remain content.

    Which of the following statements, if true, would most strengthen the scientists' hypothesis?

    (A) In other wildlife areas in India where the number of acres of woodland per tiger remains at least 15 acres, there has been no increase in the number of tiger attacks on humans.
    (B) Before the logging operation began, there were many fewer humans living in the area.
    (C) The largest number of acres per tiger before the logging operation began was 32 acres per tiger in one area of the sanctuary, whereas the smallest number of acres per tiger after the logging operation was 9 acres.
    (D) Other species of wild animals have begun competing with the Bengal tigers for the dwindling food supply.
    (E) The Bengal tiger has become completely extinct in other areas of Asia.

33. **A** In this causal argument, the decrease in the number of acres of woodland per tiger is said to cause the increasing number of tiger attacks on humans. To strengthen this argument, it would help if the Bengal tigers in areas with a normal number of acres of woodland per tiger have NOT increased their attacks on humans. That's what A tells us. B gives us an alternate cause for the increase in tiger attacks—in other words, it weakens the argument instead of strengthening it. Choice C adds details without really strengthening the argument. Choice D weakens the scientists' hypothesis by presenting a possible alternate cause for the tigers' attacks on humans. E emphasizes the seriousness of the problem without shedding light on its cause.

Verbal Explanations

34. The machine press union and company man-
    agement were not able to communicate ef-
    fectively, and it was a major cause of the 1999
    strike in Seattle.

    (A) The machine press union and company
        management were not able to commu-
        nicate effectively, and it
    (B) Communications between the machine
        press union and company manage-
        ment were not effective, and it
    (C) For the machine press union and com-
        pany management, to be unable to
        communicate effectively
    (D) The inability of the machine press union
        and company management to commu-
        nicate effectively
    (E) The machine press union, being unable
        to communicate effectively with com-
        pany management,

34. **D** The tip-off here is the pronoun *it*. To what does
    it refer? Not the union, or the management. Re-
    ally what *it* seems to refer to is the inability of
    the two sides to communicate. We can eliminate
    A and B. C seems to indicate that it was effective
    communication that led to the strike. E is both
    awkward and unidiomatic.

35. A greater number of fresh vegetables are sold
    in City X than in City Y. Therefore, the people in
    City X have better nutritional habits than those
    in City Y.

    Each of the following, if true, weakens the con-
    clusion above EXCEPT:

    (A) City X has more people living in it than
        City Y.
    (B) Most of the people in City Y work in City
        X and buy their vegetables there.
    (C) The people in City X buy many of their
        vegetables as decorations, not to eat.
    (D) The per capita consumption of junk food
        in City X is three times that of City Y.
    (E) The average price per pound of veg-
        etables in City Y is lower than the
        average price per pound of vegetables
        in City X.

35. **E** In this causal argument, more fresh vegetable
    sales in City X are said to mean that City X has
    better nutritional habits than City Y. Each of the
    answer choices pokes holes in that argument,
    except for E. It suggests that if vegetables are
    cheaper in City Y, and yet more vegetables are
    being sold in City X, then the argument that X
    has better nutritional habits might be right.

36. Heavy metals, toxic waste by-products that can cause tumors in fish, <u>are generally found in the waters off industrial shorelines, but have been discovered in trace amounts even</u> in the relatively pristine waters of the South Pacific.

   (A) are generally found in the waters off industrial shorelines, but have been discovered in trace amounts even
   (B) are generally to be found in the waters off industrial shorelines, and have even been discovered in trace amounts
   (C) can, in general, be found in the waters off industrial shorelines, and have been discovered in trace amounts even
   (D) had generally been found in the waters off industrial shorelines, but have even been discovered in trace amounts
   (E) are found generally in the waters off industrial shorelines, but have been discovered in a trace amount even

36. **A** In both B and C, the conjunction *and* wrongly gives the impression that the second half of the sentence is merely an added thought, instead of a new and dangerous development that goes beyond what *generally* happens. D needlessly changes the verb tense. E's *in a trace amount* does not agree with the plural *heavy metals*.

Verbal Explanations

In Roman times, defeated enemies were
generally put to death as criminals for having
offended the emperor of Rome. In the Middle
Ages, however, the practice of ransoming, or
returning prisoners in exchange for money, became common. Though some saw this custom
as a step toward a more humane society, the
primary reasons behind it were economic rather
than humanitarian.

In those times, rulers had only a limited
ability to raise taxes. They could neither force
their subjects to fight nor pay them to do so.
The promise of material compensation in the
form of goods and ransom was therefore the
only way of inducing combatants to participate
in a war. In the Middle Ages, the predominant
incentive for the individual soldier was the
expectation of spoils. Although collecting
ransom clearly brought financial gain, keeping a
prisoner and arranging for his exchange had its
costs. Consequently, procedures were devised
to reduce transaction costs.

One such device was a rule asserting that
the prisoner had to assess his own value. This
compelled the prisoner to establish a value
without too much distortion; indicating too low
a value would increase the captive's chances
of being killed, while indicating too high a value
would either ruin him financially or create a
prohibitively expensive ransom that would also
result in death.

Line (5), (10), (15), (20), (25), (30) denote line numbers in the passage.

37. The primary purpose of the passage is to

   (A) discuss the economic basis of the medi-
       eval practice of exchanging prisoners
       for ransom
   (B) examine the history of the treatment of
       prisoners of war
   (C) emphasize the importance of a warrior's
       code of honor during the Middle Ages
   (D) explore a way of reducing the costs of
       ransom
   (E) demonstrate why warriors of the Middle
       Ages looked forward to battles

37. **A** Choice A best summarizes the main idea of the
       first paragraph. While D reflects a part of the
       passage, it does not encompass the main idea
       of the passage.

38. It can be inferred from the passage that a medieval soldier

   (A) was less likely to kill captured members of opposing armies than was a soldier of the Roman Empire
   (B) operated on a basically independent level and was motivated solely by economic incentives
   (C) had few economic options and chose to fight because it was the only way to earn an adequate living
   (D) was motivated to spare prisoners' lives by humanitarian rather than economic ideals
   (E) had no respect for his captured enemies since captives were typically regarded as weak

38. **A**   The first paragraph gives us the information to answer this question. Note the trigger word *however* that underscores the difference between the Roman era and the Middle Ages.

39. Which of the following best describes the change in policy from executing prisoners in Roman times to ransoming prisoners in the Middle Ages?

   (A) The emperors of Rome demanded more respect than did medieval rulers, and thus Roman subjects went to greater lengths to defend their nation.
   (B) It was a reflection of the lesser degree of direct control medieval rulers had over their subjects.
   (C) It became a show of strength and honor for warriors of the Middle Ages to be able to capture and return their enemies.
   (D) Medieval soldiers were not as humanitarian as their ransoming practices might have indicated.
   (E) Medieval soldiers demonstrated more concern about economic policy than did their Roman counterparts.

39. **B**   The best answer can be found in the first line of the second paragraph. Ransom was one of the few ways a ruler could give his subjects what they wanted to get them to do something *he* wanted.

40. The author uses the phrase "without too much distortion" (line 26) in order to

    (A) indicate that prisoners would fairly assess their worth
    (B) emphasize the important role medieval prisoners played in determining whether they should be ransomed
    (C) explain how prisoners often paid more than an appropriate ransom in order to increase their chances for survival
    (D) suggest that captors and captives often had understanding relationships
    (E) show that when in prison a soldier's view could become distorted

40. **A** To get the best answer, we have to understand the meaning of the quoted words, but it also helps to read the rest of the paragraph. It talks about a value that was neither too low nor too high.

PART ◆ VII

The Princeton Review GMAT Practice Test and Explanations

21

GMAT Practice Test

Math Test
Bin One—Easier Questions
26 Questions

This test is composed of both problem solving questions and data sufficiency questions.

Problem Solving Directions: Solve each problem, and choose the best of the answer choices provided.

Data Sufficiency Directions: Data sufficiency problems consist of a question and two statements, labeled (1) and (2), in which certain data are given. You have to decide whether the data given in the statements are <u>sufficient</u> for answering the question. Using the data given in the statements <u>plus</u> your knowledge of mathematics and everyday facts (such as the number of days in July or the meaning of *counterclockwise*), you are to select

(A)   if statement (1) ALONE is sufficient, but statement (2) alone is not sufficient to answer the question asked;

(B)   if statement (2) ALONE is sufficient, but statement (1) alone is not sufficient to answer the question asked;

(C)   if BOTH statements (1) and (2) TOGETHER are sufficient to answer the question asked, but NEITHER statement alone is sufficient;

(D)   if EACH statement ALONE is sufficient to answer the question asked;

(E)   if statements (1) and (2) TOGETHER are NOT sufficient to answer the question asked, and additional data specific to the problem are needed.

---

1.   What percent of 112 is 14?

   (A)   .125%
   (B)   8%
   (C)   12.5%
   (D)   125%
   (E)   800%

2.   The number of flights leaving a certain airport doubles during every one-hour period between its 9 A.M. opening and noon; after noon, the number of flights leaving from the airport doubles during every two-hour period. If 4 flights left from the airport between 9 and 10 A.M., how many flights left the airport between 2 and 4 P.M.?

   (A)   32
   (B)   48
   (C)   64
   (D)   128
   (E)   256

GO ON TO THE NEXT PAGE.

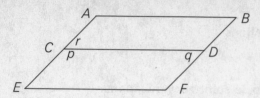

3. If both *ABDC* and *CDFE* are parallelograms, what is $q + r$?

   (1) $r = 70$

   (2) $p = 110$

   (A)   Statement (1) ALONE is sufficient, but statement (2) alone is not sufficient.
   (B)   Statement (2) ALONE is sufficient, but statement (1) alone is not sufficient.
   (C)   BOTH statements TOGETHER are sufficient, but NEITHER statement alone is sufficient.
   (D)   EACH statement ALONE is sufficient.
   (E)   Statements (1) and (2) TOGETHER are NOT sufficient.

4. Chris's convertible gets gas mileage that is 40% higher than that of Stan's SUV. If Harry's hatchback gets gas mileage that is 15% higher than that of Chris's convertible, then Harry's hatchback gets gas mileage that is what percent greater than that of Stan's SUV?

   (A)   25%
   (B)   46%
   (C)   55%
   (D)   61%
   (E)   66%

5. If *x* is equal to 1 more than the product of 3 and *z*, and *y* is equal to 1 less than the product of 2 and *z*, then 2*x* is how much greater than 3*y* when *z* is 4?

   (A)   1
   (B)   2
   (C)   3
   (D)   5
   (E)   6

6. In 2005, did Company A have more than twice the number of employees as did Company B?

   (1)   In 2005, Company A had 11,500 more employees than did Company B.

   (2)   In 2005, the 3,000 employees with advanced degrees at Company A made up 12.5% of that company's total number employees, and the 2,500 employees with advanced degrees at Company B made up 20% of that company's total number of employees.

   (A)   Statement (1) ALONE is sufficient, but statement (2) alone is not sufficient.
   (B)   Statement (2) ALONE is sufficient, but statement (1) alone is not sufficient.
   (C)   BOTH statements TOGETHER are sufficient, but NEITHER statement alone is sufficient.
   (D)   EACH statement ALONE is sufficient.
   (E)   Statements (1) and (2) TOGETHER are NOT sufficient.

GO ON TO THE NEXT PAGE.

7. Is x^3 equal to 125?

   (1) $x > 4$
   (2) $x < 6$

   (A) Statement (1) ALONE is sufficient, but statement (2) alone is not sufficient.
   (B) Statement (2) ALONE is sufficient, but statement (1) alone is not sufficient.
   (C) BOTH statements TOGETHER are sufficient, but NEITHER statement alone is sufficient.
   (D) EACH statement ALONE is sufficient.
   (E) Statements (1) and (2) TOGETHER are NOT sufficient.

8. Bob leaves point A and drives due west to point B. From point B, he drives due south to point C. How far is Bob from his original location?

   (1) Point A is 24 miles from point B.
   (2) Point B is 18 miles from point C.

   (A) Statement (1) ALONE is sufficient, but statement (2) alone is not sufficient.
   (B) Statement (2) ALONE is sufficient, but statement (1) alone is not sufficient.
   (C) BOTH statements TOGETHER are sufficient, but NEITHER statement alone is sufficient.
   (D) EACH statement ALONE is sufficient.
   (E) Statements (1) and (2) TOGETHER are NOT sufficient.

9. The formula $M = \sqrt{l^2 + w^2 + d^2}$ describes the relationship between M, the length of the longest line that can be drawn in a rectangular solid, and l, w, and d, the length, width, and depth of that rectangular solid. The longest line that can drawn in a rectangular solid with a length of 12, a width of 4, and a depth of 3 is how much longer than the longest line that can drawn in a rectangular solid with a length of 6, a width of 3, and a depth of 2?

   (A) 5
   (B) 6
   (C) 7
   (D) 9
   (E) 13

10. Is the average (arithmetic mean) of a, b, and c equal to 8?

   (1) Three times the sum of a, b, and c is equal to 72.
   (2) The sum of $2a$, $2b$, and $2c$ is equal to 48.

   (A) Statement (1) ALONE is sufficient, but statement (2) alone is not sufficient.
   (B) Statement (2) ALONE is sufficient, but statement (1) alone is not sufficient.
   (C) BOTH statements TOGETHER are sufficient, but NEITHER statement alone is sufficient.
   (D) EACH statement ALONE is sufficient.
   (E) Statements (1) and (2) TOGETHER are NOT sufficient.

GO ON TO THE NEXT PAGE.

11. $\sqrt{\sqrt{\left(1+\dfrac{17}{64}\right)}} =$

(A) $\dfrac{\sqrt{34}}{8}$

(B) $\dfrac{3\sqrt{2}}{4}$

(C) $\dfrac{9}{8}$

(D) $\dfrac{\sqrt{68}}{4}$

(E) $\dfrac{3\sqrt{2}}{2}$

12. A certain stadium is currently full to $\dfrac{13}{16}$ of its maximum seating capacity. What is the maximum seating capacity of the stadium?

(1) If 1,250 people were to enter the stadium, the stadium would be full to $\dfrac{15}{16}$ of its maximum seating capacity.

(2) If 2,500 people were to leave the stadium, the stadium would be full to $\dfrac{9}{16}$ of its maximum seating capacity.

(A) Statement (1) ALONE is sufficient, but statement (2) alone is not sufficient.
(B) Statement (2) ALONE is sufficient, but statement (1) alone is not sufficient.
(C) BOTH statements TOGETHER are sufficient, but NEITHER statement alone is sufficient.
(D) EACH statement ALONE is sufficient.
(E) Statements (1) and (2) TOGETHER are NOT sufficient.

GO ON TO THE NEXT PAGE.

13. Andre has already saved $\frac{3}{7}$ of the cost of a new car, and he has calculated that he will be able to save $\frac{2}{5}$ of the remaining amount before the end of the summer. If his calculations are correct, what fraction of the cost of the new car will he still need to save at the end of summer vacation?

   (A) $\frac{6}{35}$

   (B) $\frac{8}{35}$

   (C) $\frac{12}{35}$

   (D) $\frac{23}{35}$

   (E) $\frac{29}{35}$

$$\{1, 4, 6, y\}$$

14. If the average (arithmetic mean) of the set of numbers above is 6, then what is the median?

   (A)   5
   (B)   6
   (C)   7
   (D)   13
   (E)   24

15. A store sells a six-pack of soda for $2.40. If this represents a savings of 10 percent of the individual price of cans of soda, then what is the price of a single can of soda?

   (A) $ 0.35
   (B) $ 0.40
   (C) $ 0.44
   (D) $ 0.50
   (E) $ 0.55

16. If Beth spent $400 of her earnings last month on rent, how much did Beth earn last month?

   (1) Beth saved $\frac{1}{3}$ of her earnings last month and spent half of the remainder on rent.

   (2) Beth earned twice as much this month as last month.

   (A)   Statement (1) ALONE is sufficient, but statement (2) alone is not sufficient.
   (B)   Statement (2) ALONE is sufficient, but statement (1) alone is not sufficient.
   (C)   Both statements TOGETHER are sufficient, but NEITHER statement ALONE is sufficient.
   (D)   EACH statement ALONE is sufficient.
   (E)   Statements (1) and (2) TOGETHER are NOT sufficient.

17. If n is an integer, is n even?

   (1) $2n$ is an even integer.
   (2) $n - 1$ is an odd integer.

   (A)   Statement (1) ALONE is sufficient, but statement (2) alone is not sufficient.
   (B)   Statement (2) ALONE is sufficient, but statement (1) alone is not sufficient.
   (C)   Both statements TOGETHER are sufficient, but NEITHER statement ALONE is sufficient.
   (D)   EACH statement ALONE is sufficient.
   (E)   Statements (1) and (2) TOGETHER are NOT sufficient.

GO ON TO THE NEXT PAGE.

18. At apartment complex z, 30 percent of the residents are men over the age of 18, and 40 percent are women over the age of 18. If there are 24 children living in the complex, how many total residents live in apartment complex z?

(A) 32
(B) 80
(C) 94
(D) 112
(E) 124

19. Over the course of a soccer season, 30 percent of the players on a team scored goals. What is the ratio of players on the team who scored goals to those who did not?

(A) 3 to 10
(B) 1 to 3
(C) 3 to 7
(D) 1 to 1
(E) 3 to 1

20. At a restaurant, Luis left a tip for his waiter equal to 20 percent of his entire dinner check, including tax. What was the amount of the dinner check?

(1) The sum of the dinner check and the tip was $16.80.
(2) Luis's tip consisted of two bills and four coins.

(A) Statement (1) ALONE is sufficient, but statement (2) alone is not sufficient.
(B) Statement (2) ALONE is sufficient, but statement (1) alone is not sufficient.
(C) BOTH statements TOGETHER are sufficient, but NEITHER statement alone is sufficient.
(D) EACH statement ALONE is sufficient.
(E) Statements (1) and (2) TOGETHER are NOT sufficient.

21. Which sport utility vehicle has a higher list price, the Touristo or the Leisure?

(1) The list price of the Leisure is $\frac{5}{6}$ the list price of the Touristo.
(2) The list price of the Touristo is 1.2 times the list price of the Leisure.

(A) Statement (1) ALONE is sufficient, but statement (2) alone is not sufficient.
(B) Statement (2) ALONE is sufficient, but statement (1) alone is not sufficient.
(C) BOTH statements TOGETHER are sufficient, but NEITHER statement alone is sufficient.
(D) EACH statement ALONE is sufficient.
(E) Statements (1) and (2) TOGETHER are NOT sufficient.

GO ON TO THE NEXT PAGE.

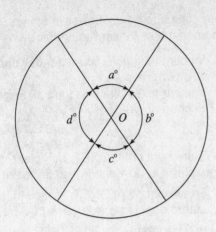

23. What is the value of integer w?

    (1) w is a multiple of 3.

    (2) $420 < w < 425$

    (A)   Statement (1) ALONE is sufficient, but statement (2) alone is not sufficient.

    (B)   Statement (2) ALONE is sufficient, but statement (1) alone is not sufficient.

    (C)   BOTH statements TOGETHER are sufficient, but NEITHER statement alone is sufficient.

    (D)   EACH statement ALONE is sufficient.

    (E)   Statements (1) and (2) TOGETHER are NOT sufficient.

22. In the circle above with center O, $3a = b$. What is the value of $b - a$?

    (A)   2
    (B)   30
    (C)   45
    (D)   90
    (E)   135

24. What is the quotient when .25% of 600 is divided by .25 of 600?

    (A)   10
    (B)   1
    (C)   .1
    (D)   .01
    (E)   .001

GO ON TO THE NEXT PAGE.

25. A certain town's economic development council has 21 members. If the number of females on the council is 3 less than 3 times the number of males on the council, then the town's economic development council has how many male members?

   (A)   5
   (B)   6
   (C)   7
   (D)   9
   (E)   15

26. Roger can chop down 4 trees in an hour. How long does it take Vincent to chop down 4 trees?

   (1)   Vincent spends 6 hours per day chopping down trees.
   (2)   Vincent takes twice as long as Roger to chop down trees.

   (A)   Statement (1) ALONE is sufficient, but statement (2) alone is not sufficient.
   (B)   Statement (2) ALONE is sufficient, but statement (1) alone is not sufficient.
   (C)   BOTH statements TOGETHER are sufficient, but NEITHER statement alone is sufficient.
   (D)   EACH statement ALONE is sufficient.
   (E)   Statements (1) and (2) TOGETHER are NOT sufficient.

GO ON TO THE NEXT PAGE.

Math Test
Bin Two—Medium Questions
27 Questions

This test is composed of both problem solving questions and data sufficiency questions.

Problem Solving Directions: Solve each problem, and choose the best of the answer choices provided.

Data Sufficiency Directions: Data sufficiency problems consist of a question and two statements, labeled (1) and (2), in which certain data are given. You have to decide whether the data given in the statements are <u>sufficient</u> for answering the question. Using the data given in the statements <u>plus</u> your knowledge of mathematics and everyday facts (such as the number of days in July or the meaning of *counterclockwise*), you are to select

(A) if statement (1) ALONE is sufficient, but statement (2) alone is not sufficient to answer the question asked;

(B) if statement (2) ALONE is sufficient, but statement (1) alone is not sufficient to answer the question asked;

(C) if BOTH statements (1) and (2) TOGETHER are sufficient to answer the question asked, but NEITHER statement alone is sufficient;

(D) if EACH statement ALONE is sufficient to answer the question asked;

(E) if statements (1) and (2) TOGETHER are NOT sufficient to answer the question asked, and additional data specific to the problem are needed.

---

1. If $x = \dfrac{\dfrac{5}{9} + \dfrac{15}{27} + \dfrac{45}{81}}{3}$, then $\sqrt{1-x} =$

    (A) $\dfrac{\sqrt{5}}{9}$

    (B) $\dfrac{5}{9}$

    (C) $\dfrac{2}{3}$

    (D) $\dfrac{\sqrt{5}}{3}$

    (E) $\dfrac{15}{9}$

2. For the past x laps around the track, Steven's average time per lap was 51 seconds. If a lap of 39 seconds would reduce his average time per lap to 49 seconds, what is the value of x?

    (A) 2
    (B) 5
    (C) 6
    (D) 10
    (E) 12

GO ON TO THE NEXT PAGE.

3. $200^2 - 2(200)(199) + 199^2 =$

   (A) −79,201
   (B)   −200
   (C)   1
   (D)   200
   (E) 79,999

4. If $x \neq -\dfrac{1}{2}$, then $\dfrac{6x^2 + 11x - 7}{2x - 1} =$

   (A) $3x + 7$
   (B) $3x - 7$
   (C) $3x + 1$
   (D) $x + 7$
   (E) $x - 7$

5. If Amy drove the distance from her home to the beach in less than 2 hours, was her average speed greater than 60 miles per hour?

   (1) The distance that Amy drove from her home to the beach was less than 125 miles.

   (2) The distance that Amy drove from her home to the beach was greater than 122 miles.

   (A) Statement (1) ALONE is sufficient, but statement (2) alone is not sufficient.
   (B) Statement (2) ALONE is sufficient, but statement (1) alone is not sufficient.
   (C) BOTH statements TOGETHER are sufficient, but NEITHER statement alone is sufficient.
   (D) EACH statement ALONE is sufficient.
   (E) Statements (1) and (2) TOGETHER are NOT sufficient.

6. If $x = m - 1$, which of the following is true when $m = \dfrac{1}{2}$?

   (A) $x^0 > x^2 > x^3 > x^1$
   (B) $x^0 > x^2 > x^1 > x^3$
   (C) $x^0 > x^1 > x^2 > x^3$
   (D) $x^2 > x^0 > x^3 > x^1$
   (E) $x^3 > x^2 > x^1 > x^0$

7. A comedian is playing two shows at a certain comedy club, and twice as many tickets have been issued for the evening show as for the afternoon show. Of the total number of tickets issued for both shows, what percentage has been sold?

   (1) A total of 450 tickets have been issued for both shows.

   (2) Exactly $\dfrac{3}{5}$ of the tickets issued for the afternoon show have been sold, and exactly $\dfrac{1}{5}$ of the tickets issued for the evening show have been sold.

   (A) Statement (1) ALONE is sufficient, but statement (2) alone is not sufficient.
   (B) Statement (2) ALONE is sufficient, but statement (1) alone is not sufficient.
   (C) BOTH statements TOGETHER are sufficient, but NEITHER statement alone is sufficient.
   (D) EACH statement ALONE is sufficient.
   (E) Statements (1) and (2) TOGETHER are NOT sufficient.

GO ON TO THE NEXT PAGE.

8. If $\dfrac{1}{y} = 2\dfrac{2}{3}$, then $\left(\dfrac{1}{y+1}\right)^2 =$

   (A) $\dfrac{9}{64}$

   (B) $\dfrac{3}{8}$

   (C) $\dfrac{64}{121}$

   (D) $\dfrac{121}{64}$

   (E) $\dfrac{64}{9}$

9. An operation $\sim$ is defined by the equation

   $a \sim b = \dfrac{a+b}{(ab)^2}$ for all numbers a and b such that

   $ab \neq 0$. If $c \neq 0$ and $a \sim c = 0$, then $c =$

   (A) $-a$

   (B) 0

   (C) $\sqrt{a}$

   (D) a

   (E) a^2

10. If x is a positive integer, is the greatest common factor of 150 and x a prime number?

    (1) x is a prime number.

    (2) $x < 4$

    (A) Statement (1) ALONE is sufficient, but statement (2) alone is not sufficient.
    (B) Statement (2) ALONE is sufficient, but statement (1) alone is not sufficient.
    (C) BOTH statements TOGETHER are sufficient, but NEITHER statement alone is sufficient.
    (D) EACH statement ALONE is sufficient.
    (E) Statements (1) and (2) TOGETHER are NOT sufficient.

$$X = \{9, 10, 11, 12\}$$
$$Y = \{2, 3, 4, 5\}$$

11. One number will be chosen randomly from each of the sets above. If x represents the chosen member of Set X and y represents the chosen member of Set Y, what is the probability that $\dfrac{x}{y}$ will be an integer?

    (A) $\dfrac{1}{16}$

    (B) $\dfrac{3}{8}$

    (C) $\dfrac{1}{2}$

    (D) $\dfrac{3}{4}$

    (E) $\dfrac{15}{16}$

GO ON TO THE NEXT PAGE.

12. If p and q are integers, is $\dfrac{p+q}{2}$ an integer?

(1) $p < 17$

(2) $p = q$

(A) Statement (1) ALONE is sufficient, but statement (2) alone is not sufficient.
(B) Statement (2) ALONE is sufficient, but statement (1) alone is not sufficient.
(C) BOTH statements TOGETHER are sufficient, but NEITHER statement alone is sufficient.
(D) EACH statement ALONE is sufficient.
(E) Statements (1) and (2) TOGETHER are NOT sufficient.

13. A perfectly spherical satellite with a radius of 4 feet is being packed for shipment to its launch site. If the inside dimensions of the rectangular crates available for shipment, when measured in feet, are consecutive even integers, then what is the volume of the smallest available crate that can be used? (Note: the volume of a sphere is given by the equation $V = \dfrac{4}{3}\pi r^3$.)

(A)   48
(B)   192
(C)   480
(D)   960
(E)   1,680

14. A certain family has 3 sons: Richard is 6 years older than David, and David is 8 years older than Scott. If in 8 years Richard will be twice as old as Scott, then how old was David 4 years ago?

(A)   8
(B)   10
(C)   12
(D)   14
(E)   16

15. What is the value of x?

(1) $x^2 - 5x + 4 = 0$

(2) x is not prime.

(A) Statement (1) ALONE is sufficient, but statement (2) alone is not sufficient.
(B) Statement (2) ALONE is sufficient, but statement (1) alone is not sufficient.
(C) BOTH statements TOGETHER are sufficient, but NEITHER statement alone is sufficient.
(D) EACH statement ALONE is sufficient.
(E) Statements (1) and (2) TOGETHER are NOT sufficient.

16. Sam and Jessica are invited to a dance. If there are 7 men and 7 women in total at the dance, and one woman and one man are chosen to lead the dance, what is the probability that Sam and Jessica will NOT be chosen to lead the dance?

(A) $\dfrac{1}{49}$

(B) $\dfrac{1}{7}$

(C) $\dfrac{6}{7}$

(D) $\dfrac{47}{49}$

(E) $\dfrac{48}{49}$

GO ON TO THE NEXT PAGE.

17. What is the surface area of rectangular solid y?

    (1) The dimensions of one face of rectangular solid y are 2 by 3.

    (2) The area of another face of rectangular solid y is 6.

    (A) Statement (1) ALONE is sufficient, but statement (2) alone is not sufficient.

    (B) Statement (2) ALONE is sufficient, but statement (1) alone is not sufficient.

    (C) Both statements TOGETHER are sufficient, but NEITHER statement ALONE is sufficient.

    (D) EACH statement ALONE is sufficient.

    (E) Statements (1) and (2) TOGETHER are NOT sufficient.

18. A six-sided die with faces numbered one through six is rolled three times. What is the probability that the face with the number 6 on it will NOT be facing upward on all three rolls?

    (A) $\dfrac{1}{216}$

    (B) $\dfrac{1}{6}$

    (C) $\dfrac{2}{3}$

    (D) $\dfrac{17}{18}$

    (E) $\dfrac{215}{216}$

19. What is the sum of x, y, and z?

    (1) $2x + y + 3z = 45$
    (2) $x + 2y = 30$

    (A) Statement (1) ALONE is sufficient, but statement (2) alone is not sufficient.

    (B) Statement (2) ALONE is sufficient, but statement (1) alone is not sufficient.

    (C) BOTH statements TOGETHER are sufficient, but NEITHER statement alone is sufficient.

    (D) EACH statement ALONE is sufficient.

    (E) Statements (1) and (2) TOGETHER are NOT sufficient.

20. A department store receives a shipment of 1,000 shirts, for which it pays $9,000. The store sells the shirts at a price 80 percent above cost for one month, after which it reduces the price of the shirts to 20 percent above cost. The store sells 75 percent of the shirts during the first month and 50 percent of the remaining shirts afterward. How much gross income did sales of the shirts generate?

    (A) $10,000
    (B) $10,800
    (C) $12,150
    (D) $13,500
    (E) $16,200

GO ON TO THE NEXT PAGE.

21. David has three credit cards: a Passport card, an EverywhereCard, and an American Local card. He owes balances on all three cards. Does he owe the greatest balance on the Everywhere-Card?

    (1) The sum of the balances on his Every-whereCard and American Local card is $1,350, which is three times the balance on his Passport card.

    (2) The balance on his EverywhereCard is $\frac{4}{3}$ of the balance on his Passport card and $\frac{4}{5}$ of the balance on his American Local card.

    (A) Statement (1) ALONE is sufficient, but statement (2) alone is not sufficient.
    (B) Statement (2) ALONE is sufficient, but statement (1) alone is not sufficient.
    (C) BOTH statements TOGETHER are sufficient, but NEITHER statement alone is sufficient.
    (D) EACH statement ALONE is sufficient.
    (E) Statements (1) and (2) TOGETHER are NOT sufficient.

22. Automobile A is traveling at two-thirds the speed that Automobile B is traveling. How fast is Automobile A traveling?

    (1) If both automobiles increased their speed by 10 miles per hour, Automobile A would be traveling at three-quarters the speed that Automobile B would be traveling.

    (2) If both automobiles decreased their speed by 10 miles per hour, Automobile A would be traveling at half the speed that Automobile B would be traveling.

    (A) Statement (1) ALONE is sufficient, but statement (2) alone is not sufficient.
    (B) Statement (2) ALONE is sufficient, but statement (1) alone is not sufficient.
    (C) BOTH statements TOGETHER are sufficient, but NEITHER statement alone is sufficient.
    (D) EACH statement ALONE is sufficient.
    (E) Statements (1) and (2) TOGETHER are NOT sufficient.

GO ON TO THE NEXT PAGE.

23. *a* and *b* are nonzero integers such that $0.35a = 0.2b$. What is the value of *b* in terms of *a*?

    (A)   0.07*a*
    (B)   0.57*a*
    (C)   0.7*a*
    (D)   1.75*a*
    (E)   17.5*a*

24. The Binary Ice Cream Shoppe sells two flavors, vanilla and chocolate. On Friday, the ratio of vanilla cones sold to chocolate cones sold was 2 to 3. If the store had sold 4 more vanilla cones, the ratio of vanilla cones sold to chocolate cones sold would have been 3 to 4. How many vanilla cones did the store sell on Friday?

    (A)   32
    (B)   35
    (C)   42
    (D)   48
    (E)   54

25. Is integer *a* a prime number?

    (1)   2*a* has exactly three factors.
    (2)   *a* is an even number.

    (A)   Statement (1) ALONE is sufficient, but statement (2) alone is not sufficient.
    (B)   Statement (2) ALONE is sufficient, but statement (1) alone is not sufficient.
    (C)   BOTH statements TOGETHER are sufficient, but NEITHER statement alone is sufficient.
    (D)   EACH statement ALONE is sufficient.
    (E)   Statements (1) and (2) TOGETHER are NOT sufficient.

GO ON TO THE NEXT PAGE.

26. Renee rides her bicycle 20 miles in m minutes. If she can ride x miles in 10 minutes, which of the following equals x?

   (A) $\dfrac{m}{200}$

   (B) $\dfrac{m}{20}$

   (C) $\dfrac{m}{2}$

   (D) $2m$

   (E) $\dfrac{200}{m}$

27. If s and w are integers, is $\dfrac{w}{5}$ an integer?

   (1) $4s + 2$ is divisible by 5.

   (2) $w + 3 = 4s$

   (A) Statement (1) ALONE is sufficient, but statement (2) alone is not sufficient.
   (B) Statement (2) ALONE is sufficient, but statement (1) alone is not sufficient.
   (C) BOTH statements TOGETHER are sufficient, but NEITHER statement alone is sufficient.
   (D) EACH statement ALONE is sufficient.
   (E) Statements (1) and (2) TOGETHER are NOT sufficient.

GO ON TO THE NEXT PAGE.

Math Test
Bin Three—Medium-Hard Questions
26 Questions

This test is composed of both problem solving questions and data sufficiency questions.

<u>Problem Solving Directions</u>: Solve each problem and choose the best of the answer choices provided.

<u>Data Sufficiency Directions</u>: Data Sufficiency problems consist of a question and two statements, labeled (1) and (2), in which certain data are given. You have to decide whether the data given in the statements are <u>sufficient</u> for answering the question. Using the data given in the statements <u>plus</u> your knowledge of mathematics and everyday facts (such as the number of days in July or the meaning of *counterclockwise*), you are to select

(A) if statement (1) ALONE is sufficient, but statement (2) alone is not sufficient to answer the question asked;

(B) if statement (2) ALONE is sufficient, but statement (1) alone is not sufficient to answer the question asked;

(C) if BOTH statements (1) and (2) TOGETHER are sufficient to answer the question asked, but NEITHER statement alone is sufficient;

(D) if EACH statement ALONE is sufficient to answer the question asked;

(E) if statements (1) and (2) TOGETHER are NOT sufficient to answer the question asked, and additional data specific to the problem are needed.

---

1. A discount electronics store normally sells all merchandise at a discount of 10 percent to 30 percent off the suggested retail price. If, during a special sale, an additional 20 percent were to be deducted from the discount price, what would be the lowest possible price of an item costing $260 before any discount?

(A) $130.00
(B) $145.60
(C) $163.80
(D) $182.00
(E) $210.00

2. During a special promotion, a certain filling station is offering a 10% discount on gas purchased <u>after the first 10 gallons</u>. If Kim purchased 20 gallons of gas, and Isabella purchased 25 gallons of gas, then Isabella's total per-gallon discount is what percent of Kim's total per-gallon discount?

(A) 80%
(B) 100%
(C) 116.7%
(D) 120%
(E) 140%

GO ON TO THE NEXT PAGE.

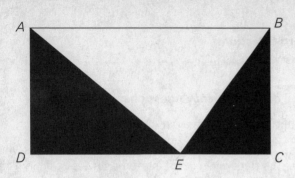

3. What is the area of the shaded region in the figure shown above?

    (1) The area of rectangle ABCD is 54.

    (2) DE = 2EC

    (A) Statement (1) ALONE is sufficient, but statement (2) alone is not sufficient.
    (B) Statement (2) ALONE is sufficient, but statement (1) alone is not sufficient.
    (C) BOTH statements TOGETHER are sufficient, but NEITHER statement alone is sufficient.
    (D) EACH statement ALONE is sufficient.
    (E) Statements (1) and (2) TOGETHER are NOT sufficient.

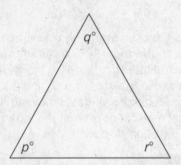

4. Is the triangle above equilateral?

    (1) $r = 180 - (p + r)$ ⟹ $q = r$

    (2) $p = 60$

    (A) Statement (1) ALONE is sufficient, but statement (2) alone is not sufficient.
    (B) Statement (2) ALONE is sufficient, but statement (1) alone is not sufficient.
    (C) BOTH statements TOGETHER are sufficient, but NEITHER statement alone is sufficient.
    (D) EACH statement ALONE is sufficient.
    (E) Statements (1) and (2) TOGETHER are NOT sufficient.

5. During a certain two-week period, 70% of the movies rented from a video store were comedies, and, of the remaining movies rented, there were 5 times as many dramas as action movies. If no other movies were rented during that two-week period, and there were A action movies rented, then how many comedies, in terms of A, were rented during that two-week period?

    (A) $\dfrac{A}{14}$

    (B) $\dfrac{5A}{7}$

    (C) $\dfrac{7A}{5}$

    (D) $14A$

    (E) $35A$

6. x, y, and z are consecutive positive integers such that $x < y < z$. If the units digit of x^2 is 6 and the units digit of y^2 is 9, what is the units digit of z^2?

    (A) 0
    (B) 1
    (C) 2
    (D) 4
    (E) 5

GO ON TO THE NEXT PAGE.

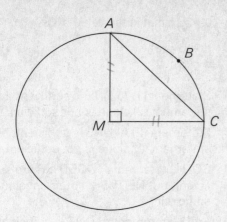

D

7. What is the area of the circle above with center *M*?

   (1) The length of *AC* is $8\sqrt{2}$.

   (2) The length of arc *ABC* is 4π .

   (A) Statement (1) ALONE is sufficient, but statement (2) alone is not sufficient.
   (B) Statement (2) ALONE is sufficient, but statement (1) alone is not sufficient.
   (C) BOTH statements TOGETHER are sufficient, but NEITHER statement alone is sufficient.
   (D) EACH statement ALONE is sufficient.
   (E) Statements (1) and (2) TOGETHER are NOT sufficient.

C
8. At a certain school, 60% of the senior class is female. If, among the members of the senior class, 70% of the females and 90% of the males are going on the senior trip, then what percent of the senior class is going on the senior trip?

   (A) 82%
   (B) 80%
   (C) 78%
   (D) 76%
   (E) 72%

A D
9. If *P* is a set of integers and 3 is in *P*, is every positive multiple of 3 in *P*?

   (1) For any integer in *P*, the sum of 3 and that integer is also in *P*. $\{0,3,6,9,...\}$
   (2) For any integer in *P*, that integer minus 3 is also in *P*. $\{...,-9,-6,-3,0\}$

   (A) Statement (1) ALONE is sufficient, but statement (2) alone is not sufficient.
   (B) Statement (2) ALONE is sufficient, but statement (1) alone is not sufficient.
   (C) BOTH statements TOGETHER are sufficient, but NEITHER statement alone is sufficient.
   (D) EACH statement ALONE is sufficient.
   (E) Statements (1) and (2) TOGETHER are NOT sufficient.

D
10. Sarah's seafood restaurant gets a delivery of fresh seafood every day, 7 days per week, and her delivery company charges her *d* dollars per delivery plus *c* cents per item delivered. If last week Sarah's seafood restaurant had an average of *x* items per day delivered, then which of the following is the total cost, in dollars, of last week's deliveries?

   (A) $\dfrac{7cdx}{100}$

   (B) $d + \dfrac{7cx}{100}$

   (C) $7d + \dfrac{xc}{100}$

   (D) $7d + \dfrac{7xc}{100}$

   (E) $7cdx$

GO ON TO THE NEXT PAGE.

11. The arithmetic mean of a data set is 46 and the standard deviation of the set is 4. Which of the following contains the interval two standard deviations from the mean of the set?

 (A) 38 to 46
 (B) 38 to 54
 (C) 42 to 50
 (D) 44 to 48
 (E) 46 to 50

12. If a and b are positive integers, is a a multiple of b?

 (1) Every prime factor of b is also a prime factor of a.

 (2) Every factor of b is also a factor of a.

 (A) Statement (1) ALONE is sufficient, but statement (2) alone is not sufficient.
 (B) Statement (2) ALONE is sufficient, but statement (1) alone is not sufficient.
 (C) BOTH statements TOGETHER are sufficient, but NEITHER statement alone is sufficient.
 (D) EACH statement ALONE is sufficient.
 (E) Statements (1) and (2) TOGETHER are NOT sufficient.

13. Set X contains 10 consecutive integers. If the sum of the 5 smallest members of Set X is 265, then what is the sum of the 5 largest members of Set X?

 (A) 290
 (B) 285
 (C) 280
 (D) 275
 (E) 270

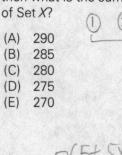

14. If $a - b = c$, what is the value of b?

 (1) $c + 6 = a$
 (2) $a = 6$

 (A) Statement (1) ALONE is sufficient, but statement (2) alone is not sufficient.
 (B) Statement (2) ALONE is sufficient, but statement (1) alone is not sufficient.
 (C) BOTH statements TOGETHER are sufficient, but NEITHER statement alone is sufficient.
 (D) EACH statement ALONE is sufficient.
 (E) Statements (1) and (2) TOGETHER are NOT sufficient.

$\{3, 5, 9, 13, y\}$

15. If the average (arithmetic mean) of the set of numbers above is equal to the median of the same set of numbers above, then what is the value of y?

 (A) 7
 (B) 8
 (C) 10
 (D) 15
 (E) 17

GO ON TO THE NEXT PAGE.

16. A foot race will be held on Saturday. How many different arrangements of medal winners are possible?

   (1) Medals will be given for 1st, 2nd, and 3rd place.

   (2) There are 10 runners in the race.

   (A) Statement (1) ALONE is sufficient, but statement (2) alone is not sufficient.

   (B) Statement (2) ALONE is sufficient, but statement (1) alone is not sufficient.

   (C) Both statements TOGETHER are sufficient, but NEITHER statement ALONE is sufficient.

   (D) EACH statement ALONE is sufficient.

   (E) Statements (1) and (2) TOGETHER are NOT sufficient.

$$\{x, y, z\}$$

17. If the first term in the data set above is 3, what is the third term?

   (1) The range of this data set is 0.

   (2) The standard deviation of this data set is 0.

   (A) Statement (1) ALONE is sufficient, but statement (2) alone is not sufficient.

   (B) Statement (2) ALONE is sufficient, but statement (1) alone is not sufficient.

   (C) Both statements TOGETHER are sufficient, but NEITHER statement ALONE is sufficient.

   (D) EACH statement ALONE is sufficient.

   (E) Statements (1) and (2) TOGETHER are NOT sufficient.

18. To fill a number of vacancies, an employer must hire 3 programmers from among 6 applicants, and 2 managers from among 4 applicants. What is the total number of ways in which she can make her selection?

   (A) 1,490
   (B) 132
   (C) 120
   (D) 60
   (E) 23

19. On Monday, a certain animal shelter housed 55 cats and dogs. By Friday, exactly $\frac{1}{5}$ of the cats and $\frac{1}{4}$ of the dogs had been adopted; no new cats or dogs were brought to the shelter during this period. What is the greatest possible number of pets that could have been adopted from the animal shelter between Monday and Friday?

   (A) 11
   (B) 12
   (C) 13
   (D) 14
   (E) 20

20. If x is an integer, then which of the following statements about $x^2 - x - 1$ is true?

   (A) It is always odd.
   (B) It is always even.
   (C) It is always positive.
   (D) It is even when x is even and odd when x is odd.
   (E) It is even when x is odd and odd when x is even.

GO ON TO THE NEXT PAGE.

21. During a five-day period, Monday through Friday, the average (arithmetic mean) high temperature was 86 degrees Fahrenheit. What was the high temperature on Friday?

    (1) The average high temperature for Monday through Thursday was 87 degrees Fahrenheit.

    (2) The high temperature on Friday reduced the average high temperature for the week by 1 degree Fahrenheit.

    (A) Statement (1) ALONE is sufficient, but statement (2) alone is not sufficient.

    (B) Statement (2) ALONE is sufficient, but statement (1) alone is not sufficient.

    (C) BOTH statements TOGETHER are sufficient, but NEITHER statement alone is sufficient.

    (D) EACH statement ALONE is sufficient.

    (E) Statements (1) and (2) TOGETHER are NOT sufficient.

22. What is the value of $x^2 - y^2$?

    (1) $x + y = 0$

    (2) $x - y = 2$

    (A) Statement (1) ALONE is sufficient, but statement (2) alone is not sufficient.

    (B) Statement (2) ALONE is sufficient, but statement (1) alone is not sufficient.

    (C) BOTH statements TOGETHER are sufficient, but NEITHER statement alone is sufficient.

    (D) EACH statement ALONE is sufficient.

    (E) Statements (1) and (2) TOGETHER are NOT sufficient.

GO ON TO THE NEXT PAGE.

23. If P is the perimeter of an equilateral triangle, which of the following represents the height of the triangle?

(A) $\dfrac{P}{3}$

(B) $\dfrac{P\sqrt{3}}{3}$

(C) $\dfrac{P}{4}$

(D) $\dfrac{P\sqrt{3}}{6}$

(E) $\dfrac{P}{6}$

24. If 75 percent of all Americans own an automobile, 15 percent of all Americans own a bicycle, and 20 percent of all Americans own neither an automobile nor a bicycle, what percent of Americans own *both* an automobile and a bicycle?

(A)   0 percent
(B)   1.33 percent
(C)   3.75 percent
(D)   5 percent
(E)   10 percent

GO ON TO THE NEXT PAGE.

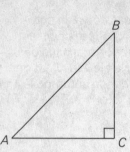

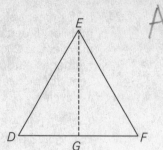

25. Triangle *ABC* is an isosceles right triangle; triangle *DEF* is an equilateral triangle with height *EG*. What is the ratio of the area of *ABC* to the area of *DEF*?

(1) The ratio of *BC* to *EG* is 1:1.

(2) The ratio of *AC* to *DF* is $\sqrt{3}$:2.

(A) Statement (1) ALONE is sufficient, but statement (2) alone is not sufficient.

(B) Statement (2) ALONE is sufficient, but statement (1) alone is not sufficient.

(C) BOTH statements TOGETHER are sufficient, but NEITHER statement alone is sufficient.

(D) EACH statement ALONE is sufficient.

(E) Statements (1) and (2) TOGETHER are NOT sufficient.

26. What is the value of integer *x*?

(1) $\sqrt[x]{64} = 4$

(2) $x^2 = 2x + 8$

(A) Statement (1) ALONE is sufficient, but statement (2) alone is not sufficient.

(B) Statement (2) ALONE is sufficient, but statement (1) alone is not sufficient.

(C) BOTH statements TOGETHER are sufficient, but NEITHER statement alone is sufficient.

(D) EACH statement ALONE is sufficient.

(E) Statements (1) and (2) TOGETHER are NOT sufficient.

Math Test
Bin Four—Hard Questions
26 Questions

This test is composed of both problem solving questions and data sufficiency questions.

Problem Solving Directions: Solve each problem and choose the best of the answer choices provided.

Data Sufficiency Directions: Data Sufficiency problems consist of a question and two statements, labeled (1) and (2), in which certain data are given. You have to decide whether the data given in the statements are <u>sufficient</u> for answering the question. Using the data given in the statements <u>plus</u> your knowledge of mathematics and everyday facts (such as the number of days in July or the meaning of *counterclockwise*), you are to select

(A) if statement (1) ALONE is sufficient, but statement (2) alone is not sufficient to answer the question asked;

(B) if statement (2) ALONE is sufficient, but statement (1) alone is not sufficient to answer the question asked;

(C) if BOTH statements (1) and (2) TOGETHER are sufficient to answer the question asked, but NEITHER statement alone is sufficient;

(D) if EACH statement ALONE is sufficient to answer the question asked;

(E) if statements (1) and (2) TOGETHER are NOT sufficient to answer the question asked, and additional data specific to the problem are needed.

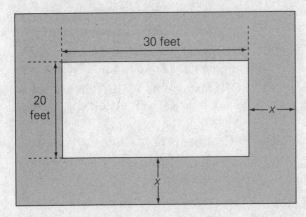

1. Martin planted a rectangular garden with dimensions 20 feet by 30 feet and then surrounded the garden with a rectangular brick walkway of uniform width (represented by the shaded area in the drawing above). If the area of the walkway equals the area of the garden, what is the width of the walkway?

(A) 1 foot
(B) 3 feet
(C) 5 feet
(D) 8 feet
(E) 10 feet

2. A fair 2-sided coin is flipped 6 times. What is the probability that tails will be the result at least twice, but not more than 5 times?

(A) $\dfrac{5}{8}$

(B) $\dfrac{3}{4}$

(C) $\dfrac{7}{8}$

(D) $\dfrac{57}{64}$

(E) $\dfrac{15}{16}$

GO ON TO THE NEXT PAGE.

3. The members of the newest recruiting class of a certain military organization are taking their physical conditioning test, and those who score in the bottom 16% will have to retest. If the scores are normally distributed, and have an arithmetic mean of 72, what is the score at or below which the recruits will have to retest?

(1)　There are 500 recruits in the class.

(2)　10 recruits scored 82 or higher.

(A)　Statement (1) ALONE is sufficient, but statement (2) alone is not sufficient.
(B)　Statement (2) ALONE is sufficient, but statement (1) alone is not sufficient.
(C)　BOTH statements TOGETHER are sufficient, but NEITHER statement alone is sufficient.
(D)　EACH statement ALONE is sufficient.
(E)　Statements (1) and (2) TOGETHER are NOT sufficient.

4. Jerome wrote each of the integers 1 through 20, inclusive, on a separate index card. He placed the cards in a box, then drew cards one at a time randomly from the box, without returning the cards he had already drawn to the box. In order to ensure that the sum of all the cards he drew was even, how many cards did Jerome have to draw?

(A)　19
(B)　12
(C)　11
(D)　10
(E)　3

5. The average (arithmetic mean) of integers r, s, t, u, and v is 100. Are exactly two of the integers greater than 100?

(1)　Three of the integers are less than 50.
(2)　None of the integers is equal to 100.

(A)　Statement (1) ALONE is sufficient, but statement (2) alone is not sufficient.
(B)　Statement (2) ALONE is sufficient, but statement (1) alone is not sufficient.
(C)　BOTH statements TOGETHER are sufficient, but NEITHER statement alone is sufficient.
(D)　EACH statement ALONE is sufficient.
(E)　Statements (1) and (2) TOGETHER are NOT sufficient.

6. Paul jogs at a constant rate for 80 minutes along the same route every day. How long is the route?

(1)　Yesterday, Paul began jogging at 5:00 P.M.
(2)　Yesterday, Paul had jogged 5 miles by 5:40 P.M. and 8 miles by 6:04 P.M.

(A)　Statement (1) ALONE is sufficient, but statement (2) alone is not sufficient.
(B)　Statement (2) ALONE is sufficient, but statement (1) alone is not sufficient.
(C)　BOTH statements TOGETHER are sufficient, but NEITHER statement alone is sufficient.
(D)　EACH statement ALONE is sufficient.
(E)　Statements (1) and (2) TOGETHER are NOT sufficient.

GO ON TO THE NEXT PAGE.

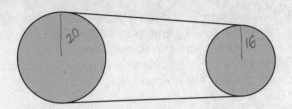

B 7. The diagram above shows two wheels that drive a conveyor belt. The larger wheel has a diameter of 40 centimeters; the smaller wheel has a diameter of 32 centimeters. In order for the conveyor belt to run smoothly, each wheel must rotate the exact same number of centimeters per minute. If the larger wheel makes r revolutions per minute, how many revolutions does the smaller wheel make per hour, in terms of r?

(A) $\dfrac{1{,}280\pi}{3}$

(B) $75r$

(C) $48r$

(D) $24r$

(E) $\dfrac{64\pi}{3}$

C 8. An automobile dealership sells only sedans and coupes. It sells each in only two colors: red and blue. Last year, the dealership sold 9,000 vehicles, half of which were red. How many coupes did the dealership sell last year?

(1) The dealership sold three times as many blue coupes as red sedans last year.

(2) The dealership sold half as many blue sedans as blue coupes last year.

(A) Statement (1) ALONE is sufficient, but statement (2) alone is not sufficient.

(B) Statement (2) ALONE is sufficient, but statement (1) alone is not sufficient.

(C) BOTH statements TOGETHER are sufficient, but NEITHER statement alone is sufficient.

(D) EACH statement ALONE is sufficient.

(E) Statements (1) and (2) TOGETHER are NOT sufficient.

GO ON TO THE NEXT PAGE.

9. At a college football game, $\frac{4}{5}$ of the seats in the lower deck of the stadium were sold. If $\frac{1}{4}$ of all the seating in the stadium is located in the lower deck, and if $\frac{2}{3}$ of all the seats in the stadium were sold, what fraction of the unsold seats in the stadium were in the lower deck?

(A) $\frac{3}{20}$

(B) $\frac{1}{6}$

(C) $\frac{1}{5}$

(D) $\frac{1}{3}$

(E) $\frac{7}{15}$

10. At Company R, the average (arithmetic mean) age of executive employees is 54 years old and the average age of non-executive employees is 34 years old. What is the average age of all the employees at Company R?

(1) There are 10 executive employees at Company R.

(2) The number of non-executive employees at Company R is four times the number of executive employees at Company R.

(A) Statement (1) ALONE is sufficient, but statement (2) alone is not sufficient.

(B) Statement (2) ALONE is sufficient, but statement (1) alone is not sufficient.

(C) BOTH statements TOGETHER are sufficient, but NEITHER statement alone is sufficient.

(D) EACH statement ALONE is sufficient.

(E) Statements (1) and (2) TOGETHER are NOT sufficient.

GO ON TO THE NEXT PAGE.

A 11. If a, b, c, d, and x are all nonzero integers, is the product $ax \times (bx)^2 \times (cx)^3 \times (dx)^4$ positive or negative?

>0

$ac^3x^4 >0$

(1) $a < c < x < 0$
(2) $b < d < x < 0$

(A) Statement (1) ALONE is sufficient, but statement (2) alone is not sufficient.
(B) Statement (2) ALONE is sufficient, but statement (1) alone is not sufficient.
(C) BOTH statements TOGETHER are sufficient, but NEITHER statement alone is sufficient.
(D) EACH statement ALONE is sufficient.
(E) Statements (1) and (2) TOGETHER are NOT sufficient.

D

12. A four-character password consists of one letter of the alphabet and three different digits between 0 and 9, inclusive. The letter must appear as the second or third character of the password. How many different passwords are possible?

(A) 5,040
(B) 18,720
(C) 26,000
(D) 37,440
(E) 52,000

13. If x is a positive integer, is x divisible by 48?

(1) x is divisible by 8.
(2) x is divisible by 6.

(A) Statement (1) ALONE is sufficient, but statement (2) alone is not sufficient.
(B) Statement (2) ALONE is sufficient, but statement (1) alone is not sufficient.
(C) BOTH statements TOGETHER are sufficient, but NEITHER statement alone is sufficient.
(D) EACH statement ALONE is sufficient.
(E) Statements (1) and (2) TOGETHER are NOT sufficient.

$$\begin{array}{r} FGF \\ \times\ G \\ \hline HGG \end{array}$$

A 14. In the multiplication problem above, F, G, and H represent unique odd digits. What is the value of the three-digit number FGF?

(A) 151
(B) 161
(C) 171
(D) 313
(E) 353

GO ON TO THE NEXT PAGE.

15. A group of 20 friends formed an investment club, with each member contributing an equal amount to the general fund. The club then invested the entire fund, which amounted to d dollars, in Stock X. The value of the stock subsequently increased 40 percent, at which point the stock was sold and the proceeds divided evenly among the members. In terms of d, how much money did each member of the club receive from the sale? (Assume that transaction fees and other associated costs were negligible.)

(A) $800d$

(B) $\dfrac{7d}{5}$

(C) $\dfrac{d}{20} + 40$

(D) $\dfrac{d}{2}$

(E) $\dfrac{7d}{100}$

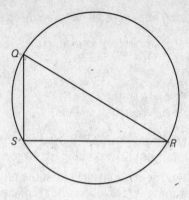

16. Triangle QSR is inscribed in a semi-circle. Is QSR a right triangle?

(1) QR is a diameter of the circle.
(2) Length QS equals 3 and length QR equals 5.

(A) Statement (1) ALONE is sufficient, but statement (2) alone is not sufficient.

(B) Statement (2) ALONE is sufficient, but statement (1) alone is not sufficient.

(C) BOTH statements TOGETHER are sufficient, but NEITHER statement alone is sufficient.

(D) EACH statement ALONE is sufficient.

(E) Statements (1) and (2) TOGETHER are NOT sufficient.

GO ON TO THE NEXT PAGE.

17. Jolene began building a picket fence by planting stakes in a row; the stakes were evenly spaced. After planting the first 10 stakes, Jolene measured the length of the row and found that the row was 27 feet long. She continued the row by planting another 10 stakes, then measured the length of the entire row. How many feet long was the row of stakes Jolene had planted?

C

(A) 37
(B) 54
(C) 57
(D) 60
(E) 81

18. Square G has sides of length 4 inches. Is the area of Square H exactly one half the area of Square G?

D

(1) The length of the diagonal of Square H equals the length of one side of Square G.
(2) The perimeter of Square H is twice the length of the diagonal of Square G.

(A) Statement (1) ALONE is sufficient, but statement (2) alone is not sufficient.

(B) Statement (2) ALONE is sufficient, but statement (1) alone is not sufficient.

(C) BOTH statements TOGETHER are sufficient, but NEITHER statement alone is sufficient.

(D) EACH statement ALONE is sufficient.

(E) Statements (1) and (2) TOGETHER are NOT sufficient.

19. In a particular state, 70 percent of the counties received some rain on Monday, and 65 percent of the counties received some rain on Tuesday. No rain fell either day in 25 percent of the counties in the state. What percent of the counties received some rain on Monday and Tuesday?

D

(A) 12.5%
(B) 40%
(C) 50%
(D) 60%
(E) 67.5%

GO ON TO THE NEXT PAGE.

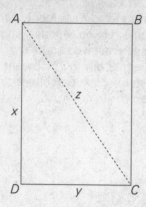

C

20. Figure *ABCD* is a rectangle with sides of length *x* centimeters and width *y* centimeters, and a diagonal of length *z* centimeters. What is the measure, in centimeters, of the perimeter of *ABCD*?

(1) $x - y = 7$

(2) $z = 13$

(A) Statement (1) ALONE is sufficient, but statement (2) alone is not sufficient.

(B) Statement (2) ALONE is sufficient, but statement (1) alone is not sufficient.

(C) BOTH statements TOGETHER are sufficient, but NEITHER statement alone is sufficient.

(D) EACH statement ALONE is sufficient.

(E) Statements (1) and (2) TOGETHER are NOT sufficient.

B 21. Together, Andrea and Brian weigh *p* pounds; Brian weighs 10 pounds more than Andrea. Brian and Andrea's dog, Cubby, weighs $\dfrac{p}{4}$ pounds more than Andrea. In terms of *p*, what is Cubby's weight in pounds?

(A) $\dfrac{p}{2} - 10$

(B) $\dfrac{3p}{4} - 5$

(C) $\dfrac{3p}{2} - 5$

(D) $\dfrac{5p}{4} - 10$

(E) $5p - 5$

A 22. A first-grade teacher uses ten flash cards, numbered 1 through 10, to teach her students to order numbers correctly. She has students choose four flash cards randomly, then arrange the cards in ascending order. One day, she removes the cards numbered "2" and "4" from the deck of flash cards. On that day, how many different correct arrangements of four randomly selected cards are possible?

(A)   70

(B)   210

(C)   336

(D)   840

(E) 1,680

GO ON TO THE NEXT PAGE.

E

23. If *a* and *b* are two-digit numbers that share the same digits, except in reverse order, then what is the sum of *a* and *b*?

same { (1) $a - b = 45$
      (2)   The difference between the two digits in each number is 5.

(A)   Statement (1) ALONE is sufficient, but statement (2) alone is not sufficient.

(B)   Statement (2) ALONE is sufficient, but statement (1) alone is not sufficient.

(C)   BOTH statements TOGETHER are sufficient, but NEITHER statement alone is sufficient.

(D)   EACH statement ALONE is sufficient.

(E)   Statements (1) and (2) TOGETHER are NOT sufficient.

D

24. A university awarded grants in the amount of either $7,000 or $10,000 to some incoming freshmen. The total amount of all such awards was $2,300,000. Did the university award more $7,000 grants than $10,000 grants to its incoming freshmen?

(1)   A total of 275 freshmen received grants in one of the two amounts.

(2)   The amount of money awarded in $10,000 grants was $200,000 more than the amount of money awarded in $7,000 grants.

(A)   Statement (1) ALONE is sufficient, but statement (2) alone is not sufficient.

(B)   Statement (2) ALONE is sufficient, but statement (1) alone is not sufficient.

(C)   BOTH statements TOGETHER are sufficient, but NEITHER statement alone is sufficient.

(D)   EACH statement ALONE is sufficient.

(E)   Statements (1) and (2) TOGETHER are NOT sufficient.

GO ON TO THE NEXT PAGE.

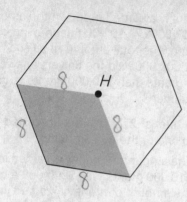

25. The figure above is a regular hexagon with center H. The shaded area is a parallelogram that shares three vertices with the hexagon; its fourth vertex is the center of the hexagon. If the length of one side of the hexagon is 8 centimeters, what is the area of the unshaded region?

(A) $16\sqrt{3}$ cm³

(B) 96 cm³

(C) $64\sqrt{3}$ cm³

(D) $96\sqrt{3}$ cm³

(E) 256 cm³

26. A fish tank contains a number of fish, including 5 Fantails. If two fish are selected from the tank at random, what is the probability that both will be Fantails?

(1) The probability that the first fish chosen will be a Fantail is $\frac{1}{2}$. 10 fish in total

(2) The probability that the second fish chosen will be a Fantail is $\frac{4}{9}$.

(A) Statement (1) ALONE is sufficient, but statement (2) alone is not sufficient.

(B) Statement (2) ALONE is sufficient, but statement (1) alone is not sufficient.

(C) BOTH statements TOGETHER are sufficient, but NEITHER statement alone is sufficient.

(D) EACH statement ALONE is sufficient.

(E) Statements (1) and (2) TOGETHER are NOT sufficient.

GO ON TO THE NEXT PAGE.

Verbal Test
Bin One—Easy Questions
25 Questions

This test is made up of sentence correction, critical reasoning, and reading comprehension questions.

Sentence Correction Directions: In sentence corrections, some part of the sentence or the entire sentence is underlined. Beneath each sentence you will find five ways of phrasing the underlined part. The first of these repeats the original; the other four are different. If you think the original is the best of these answer choices, choose answer A; otherwise, choose the best version and select the corresponding letter.

Reading Comprehension Directions: After reading the passage, choose the best answer to each question. Answer all questions following a passage on the basis of what is <u>stated</u> or <u>implied</u> in that passage.

Critical Reasoning Directions: Select the best of the answer choices given.

---

1. As its reputation for making acquisitions of important masterpieces has grown, the museum has increasingly turned down gifts of lesser-known paintings <u>they would in the past have accepted gratefully</u>.

   (A) they would in the past have accepted gratefully
   (B) they would have accepted gratefully in the past
   (C) it would in the past have accepted gratefully
   (D) it previously would have accepted gratefully in the past
   (E) that previously would have been accepted in the past

2. Over the past few decades, despite periodic attempts to reign in spending, currencies in South America <u>are devalued</u> by rampant inflation.

   (A) are devalued
   (B) are becoming more devalued
   (C) which have lost value
   (D) have become devalued
   (E) have since become devalued

3. A fashion designer's fall line for women utilizing new soft fabrics broke all sales records last year. To capitalize on her success, the designer plans to launch a line of clothing for men this year that makes use of the same new soft fabrics.

   The designer's plan assumes that

   (A) other designers are not planning to introduce new lines for men utilizing the same soft fabrics
   (B) men will be as interested in the new soft fabrics as women were the year before
   (C) the designer will have time to develop new lines for both men and women
   (D) the line for men will be considered innovative and daring because of its use of fabrics
   (E) women who bought the new line last year will continue to buy it this year

GO ON TO THE NEXT PAGE.

4. The standard lamp is becoming outmoded, and <u>so too is the incandescent light bulb, it is Edison's miraculous invention to use</u> so much more energy than the new low-wattage halogen bulbs.

(A) so too is the incandescent light bulb, it is Edison's miraculous invention to use

(B) so too is the incandescent light bulb, Edison's miraculous invention that uses

(C) so too the incandescent light bulb, Edison's miraculous invention using

(D) also the incandescent light bulb, it is Edison's miraculous invention that uses

(E) also the incandescent light bulb, which is Edison's miraculous invention to use

5. Over the last 20 years, <u>the growth of information technology has been more rapid than any other business field</u>, but has recently finally begun to lag behind as newly emerging fields seem more enticing to new graduates.

(A) the growth of information technology has been more rapid than any other business field

(B) the growth of information technology has been more rapid than any other fields of business

(C) information technology's growth has been more rapid than any other fields of business

(D) the growing of information technology has been more rapid than that of any other business field

(E) the growth of information technology has been more rapid than that of any other business field

6. According to mutual fund sales experts, a successful year for a stock fund should result not only in increased investor dollars flowing into the fund, but also in increased investor dollars flowing into other mutual stock funds offered by the same company. However, while last year the Grafton Mutual Company's "Growth Stock Fund" beat average market returns by a factor of two and recorded substantial new investment, the other stock funds offered by Grafton did not report any increase whatsoever.

Which of the following conclusions can properly be drawn from the statements above?

(A) When one of the mutual funds offered by a company beats average market returns, the other mutual funds offered by that company will beat average market returns.

(B) The mutual fund sales experts neglected to consider bond funds in formulating their theory.

(C) The performance of the Grafton "Growth Stock Fund" was a result of a wave of mergers and acquisitions that year.

(D) Investors currently dislike all stock mutual funds because of market volatility.

(E) The success of one mutual fund is not the only factor affecting whether investors will invest in other mutual funds run by the same company.

GO ON TO THE NEXT PAGE.

7. With <u>less than thirty thousand dollars in advance ticket sales and fewer</u> acceptances by guest-speakers than expected, the one-day symposium on art and religion was canceled for lack of interest.

   (A) less than thirty thousand dollars in advance ticket sales and fewer
   (B) fewer than thirty thousand dollars in advance ticket sales and less
   (C) fewer than thirty thousand dollars in advance ticket sales and fewer
   (D) lesser than thirty thousand dollars in advance ticket sales and fewer
   (E) less than thirty thousand dollars in advance ticket sales and as few

8. New technology now makes it feasible for computer call-in help desk services to route calls they receive to almost anywhere, theoretically allowing employees to work from home, without the need for a daily commute.

   The adoption of this policy would be most likely to increase productivity if employees did not

   _____.

   (A) commute from a distance of fewer than 10 miles
   (B) commute by car as opposed to by rail
   (C) live in areas with dependable phone service
   (D) need to consult frequently with each other to solve callers' problems
   (E) have more than one telephone line

9. The port cities of England in the 19th century saw a renaissance of ship construction, with some innovative designs breaking new ground, stretching the limits of ship-building theory, and <u>received</u> acclaim from around the world.

   (A) received
   (B) it received
   (C) receiving
   (D) would receive
   (E) it had received

10. According to a consumer research group survey, the majority of kitchen appliances purchased in the United States are purchased by men. This appears to belie the myth that women spend more time in the kitchen than men.

   The argument is flawed primarily because the author _____.

   (A) fails to differentiate between buying and using
   (B) does not provide information about the types of kitchen appliances surveyed
   (C) depends on the results of one survey
   (D) does not give exact statistics to back up his case
   (E) does not provide information on other appliances such as washers and dryers

11. <u>A contribution to a favorite charity being sent instead</u> of flowers when a colleague dies is becoming more the rule than the exception when it comes to funeral etiquette.

   (A) A contribution to a favorite charity being sent instead
   (B) A contribution being sent to a favorite charity as opposed
   (C) To send a contribution for a favorite charity instead
   (D) Sending a contribution to a favorite charity instead
   (E) Sending a contribution to a favorite charity as opposed

GO ON TO THE NEXT PAGE.

<u>Questions 12–15 are based on the following passage:</u>

As a business model, the world of publishing has always been a somewhat sleepy enclave, but now all that seems poised to change. Sev-
Line eral companies have moved aggressively into a
(5) new business endeavor whose genesis comes from the question: Who owns the great works of literature?

Text-on-demand is not a completely new idea, of course. In the 1990s, the Gutenberg
(10) project sought volunteers to type literary clas- sics that had expired copyrights into word processing files so that scholars would have searchable databases for their research. Most of the works of Shakespeare, Cervantes, Proust,
(15) and Moliere were to be found free online by as early as 1995.

However, now large-scale companies have moved into the market, with scanners and busi- ness plans, and are looking for bargain base-
(20) ment content. These companies are striking deals with libraries, and some publishers, to be able to provide their content, for a price, to individual buyers over the Internet.

At stake are the rights to an estimated store
(25) of 30 million books, most of which are now out of print. Many of these books are now also in the public domain, giving any company the right to sell them online. Still, a good portion of the books a general audience might actually
(30) want to buy is still under copyright. The urgent question: Who owns those copyrights? In the case of all too many books put out more than 20 years ago by now-defunct publishing com- panies, the answer is unclear—a situation the
(35) new text-on-demand companies are eager to exploit. An association of publishers has sued, claiming massive copyright infringement. The case is several years away from trial.

12. The primary purpose of the passage is to

(A) present the results of a statistical analy- sis and propose further study
(B) explain a recent development and explore its consequences
(C) identify the reasons for a trend and rec- ommend measures to address it
(D) outline several theories about a phenom- enon and advocate one of them
(E) describe the potential consequences of implementing a new policy and argue in favor of that policy

13. It can be inferred from the passage that the works of Shakespeare, Cervantes, and Moliere

(A) are some of the most popular works of literature
(B) are no longer copyrighted
(C) are among the works the association of publishers is suing text-on-demand companies
(D) do not currently exist as searchable data- bases
(E) were owned by now-defunct publishing companies

14. Which of the following is an example of a book that a text-on-demand company would not have to acquire the rights to?

(A) a book still under copyright
(B) a book more than 20 years old
(C) a book in the public domain
(D) a book a general audience might want to buy
(E) a book not already owned by publishers the company has a deal with

GO ON TO THE NEXT PAGE.

15. It can be inferred from the passage that text-on-demand companies are

    (A) using scanners to find books they want to acquire

    (B) creating business plans well before they have any actual business

    (C) buying content at premium prices

    (D) acquiring the rights to books for as little as possible

    (E) attempting to supplant the role of traditional publishers

16. Exit polls, conducted by an independent organization among voters at five polling locations during a recent election, suggested that the incumbent mayor—a Democrat—was going to lose the election by a wide margin. But, in fact, by the time the final results were tabulated, the incumbent had won the election by a narrow margin.

Which of the following, if true, would explain the apparent contradiction in the results of the exit polls?

    (A) The people chosen at random to be polled by the independent organization happened to be Democrats.

    (B) The exit poll locations chosen by the independent organization were in predominantly Republican districts.

    (C) The exit polls were conducted during the afternoon, when most of the districts' younger voters, who did not support the incumbent mayor, were at work.

    (D) The incumbent mayor ran on a platform that promised to lower taxes if elected.

    (E) An earlier poll, conducted the week before the election, had predicted that the incumbent mayor would win.

17. The spread of Avian flu from animals to humans has been well-documented, but less understood is the mechanism by which it is spread from one bird species to another. **In order to avoid a worldwide epidemic of Avian flu, scientists must make that study a first priority.** To solely tackle the human dimension of this possible pandemic is to miss half of the problem: its spread from one hemisphere to another.

The bolded phrase plays which of the following roles in the argument above?

    (A) The bolded phrase states a premise of the argument.

    (B) The bolded phrase contradicts the author's main point.

    (C) The bolded phrase makes a statement that the author is about to contradict.

    (D) The bolded phrase states the author's conclusion.

    (E) The bolded phrase states an assumption the author is making.

18. Successful business leaders not only anticipate potential problems and have contingency plans <u>ready, instead proceeding as if they are likely to occur at any time</u>.

    (A) ready, instead proceeding as if they are likely to occur at any time

    (B) ready, but also proceed as if such problems are likely to occur at any time

    (C) ready, but also proceeding as if the occurrence of them is at any time likely

    (D) ready; they instead proceed as if their occurrence is likely at any time

    (E) ready; such problems are likely to occur at any time, is how they proceed

GO ON TO THE NEXT PAGE.

19. An artist who sells her paintings for a fixed price decides that she must increase her income. Because she does not believe that customers will pay more for her paintings, she decides to cut costs by using cheaper paints and canvases. She expects that, by cutting costs, she will increase her profit margin per painting and thus increase her annual net income.

Which of the following, if true, most weakens the argument above?

(A) Other area artists charge more for their paintings than the artist charges for hers.
(B) The artist has failed to consider other options, such as renting cheaper studio space.
(C) The artist's plan will result in the production of inferior paintings which, in turn, will cause a reduction in sales.
(D) If the economy were to enter a period of inflation, the artist's projected increase in income could be wiped out by increases in the price of art supplies.
(E) The artist considered trying to complete paintings more quickly and thus increase production, but concluded that it would be impossible.

20. Although tapirs reared in captivity are generally docile and have even been kept as pets by South American villagers, it is nonetheless a volatile creature prone to unpredictable and dangerous temper tantrums.

(A) it is nonetheless a volatile creature
(B) it is nonetheless volatile creatures
(C) being nonetheless volatile creatures
(D) they are nonetheless a volatile creature
(E) they are nonetheless volatile creatures

21. According to a recent report, the original tires supplied with the Impressivo, a new sedan-class automobile, wore much more quickly than tires conventionally wear. The report suggested two possible causes: (1) defects in the tires, and (2) improper wheel alignment of the automobile.

Which of the following would best help the authors of the report determine which of the two causes identified was responsible for the extra wear?

(A) a study in which the rate of tire wear in the Impressivo is compared to the rate of tire wear in all automobiles in the same class
(B) a study in which a second set of tires, manufactured by a different company than the one that made the first set, is installed on all Impressivos and the rate of wear is measured
(C) a study in which the level of satisfaction of workers in the Impressivo manufacturing plant is measured and compared to that of workers at other automobile manufacturing plants
(D) a study that determines how often improper wheel alignment results in major problems for manufacturers of other automobiles in the Impressivo's class
(E) a study that determines the degree to which faulty driving techniques employed by Impressivo drivers contributed to tire wear

GO ON TO THE NEXT PAGE.

Questions 22–25 are based on the following passage:

Founded at the dawn of the modern industrial era, the nearly forgotten Women's Trade
Union League (WTUL) played an instrumental
Line role in advancing the cause of working women
(5) throughout the early part of the twentieth century. In the face of considerable adversity, the
WTUL made a contribution far greater than did
most historical footnotes.

The organization's successes did not come
(10) easily; conflict beset the WTUL in many forms.
During those early days of American unions,
organized labor was aggressively opposed by
both industry and government. The WTUL,
which represented a largely unskilled labor
(15) force, had little leverage against these powerful
opponents. Also, because of the skill level of
its workers as well as inherent societal gender bias, the WTUL had great difficulty finding
allies among other unions. Even the large and
(20) powerful American Federation of Labor (AFL),
which nominally took the WTUL under its wing,
kept it at a distance. Because the AFL's power
stemmed from its highly skilled labor force,
the organization saw little economic benefit in
(25) working with the WTUL. The affiliation provided
the AFL with political cover, allowing it to claim
support for women workers; in return, the
WTUL gained a potent but largely absent ally.

The WTUL also had to overcome internal
(30) discord. While the majority of the group's members were working women, a sizeable and powerful minority consisted of middle- and upper-
class social reformers whose goals extended
beyond labor reform. While workers argued that
(35) the WTUL should focus its efforts on collective
bargaining and working conditions, the reformers looked beyond the workplace, seeking
state and national legislation aimed at education reform and urban poverty relief as well as
(40) workplace issues.

Despite these obstacles, the WTUL accomplished a great deal. The organization
was instrumental in the passage of state laws
mandating an eight-hour workday, a minimum
(45) wage for women, and a ban on child labor. It
provided seed money to women who organized
workers in specific plants and industries, and
also established strike funds and soup kitchens
to support striking unionists. After the tragic
(50) Triangle Shirtwaist Company fire of 1911, the
WTUL launched a four-year investigation whose
conclusions formed the basis of much subsequent workplace safety legislation. The organization also offered a political base for all reform-
(55) minded women, and thus helped develop the
next generation of American leaders. Eleanor
Roosevelt was one of many prominent figures
to emerge from the WTUL.

The organization began a slow death in the
(60) late 1920s, when the Great Depression choked
off its funding. The organization limped through
the 1940s; the death knell eventually rang in
1950, at the onset of the McCarthy era. A turn-
of-the-century labor organization dedicated
65) to social reform, one that during its heyday
was regarded by many as "radical," stood little
chance of weathering that storm. This humble
ending, however, does nothing to diminish the
accomplishments of an organization that is yet
(70) to receive its historical due.

22. The primary purpose of this passage is to

(A) describe the barriers confronting women
   in the contemporary workplace
(B) compare and contrast the methods of
   two labor unions of the early industrial
   era
(C) critique the methods employed by an
   important labor union
(D) rebuke historians for failing to cover the
   women's labor movement adequately
(E) call readers' attention to an overlooked
   contributor to American history

GO ON TO THE NEXT PAGE.

23. Which of the following best characterizes the American Federation of Labor's view of the Women's Trade Union League, as it is presented in the passage?

(A) The WTUL was an important component of the AFL's multifront assault on industry and its treatment of workers.
(B) Because of Eleanor Roosevelt's affiliation with the organization, the WTUL was a vehicle through which the AFL could gain access to the White House.
(C) The WTUL was to be avoided because the radical element within it attracted unwanted government scrutiny.
(D) The WTUL offered the AFL some political capital but little that would assist it in labor negotiations.
(E) The WTUL was weakened by its hesitance in pursuing widespread social reform beyond the workplace.

24. Each of the following is cited in the passage as an accomplishment of the Women's Trade Union League EXCEPT

(A) It organized a highly skilled workforce to increase its bargaining power.
(B) It contributed to the development of a group of leaders in America.
(C) It provided essential support to striking women.
(D) It helped fund start-up unions for women.
(E) It contributed to the passage of important social and labor reform legislation.

25. The passage suggests which of the following about the "middle- and upper-class social reformers" mentioned in lines 32–33?

(A) They did not understand, nor were they sympathetic to, the plight of poor women workers.
(B) Their naive interest in Communism was ultimately detrimental to the Women's Trade Union League.
(C) It was because of their social and political power that the Women's Trade Union League was able to form an alliance with the American Federation of Labor.
(D) They represented only an insignificant fraction of the leadership of Women's Trade Union League.
(E) They sought to advance a broad political agenda of societal improvement.

GO ON TO THE NEXT PAGE.

Verbal Test
Bin Two—Medium Questions
27 Questions

This test is made up of sentence correction, critical reasoning, and reading comprehension questions.

<u>Sentence Correction Directions</u>: In sentence corrections, some part of the sentence or the entire sentence is underlined. Beneath each sentence you will find five ways of phrasing the underlined part. The first of these repeats the original; the other four are different. If you think the original is the best of these answer choices, choose answer A; otherwise, choose the best version and select the corresponding letter.

<u>Reading Comprehension Directions</u>: After reading the passage, choose the best answer to each question. Answer all questions following a passage on the basis of what is <u>stated</u> or <u>implied</u> in that passage.

<u>Critical Reasoning Directions</u>: Select the best of the answer choices given.

1. As its performance has risen on all the stock indexes, the bio-tech start-up has branched out into new markets to look for opportunities <u>they would previously have had to ignore</u>.

   (A) they would previously have had to ignore
   (B) they would have had to ignore previously
   (C) that previously they would have had to ignore
   (D) it previously would have had to ignore in past years
   (E) it would previously have had to ignore

2. Scientists wishing to understand the kinetic movements of ancient dinosaurs are today studying the movements of modern day birds, which many scientists believe are descended from dinosaurs. A flaw in this strategy is that birds, although once genetically linked to dinosaurs, have evolved so far that any comparison is effectively meaningless.

   Which of the following, if true, would most weaken the criticism made above of the scientists' strategy?

   (A) Birds and dinosaurs have a number of important features in common that exist in no other living species.
   (B) Birds are separated from dinosaurs by 65 million years of evolution.
   (C) Our theories of dinosaur movements have recently undergone a radical reappraisal.
   (D) The study of kinetic movement is a relatively new discipline.
   (E) Many bird experts do not study dinosaurs to draw inferences about birds.

GO ON TO THE NEXT PAGE.

3. A factory in China has two options to improve
    efficiency: adding robotic assembly lines, and
    subcontracting out certain small production
    goals that could be done more efficiently else-
    where. Adding robotic assembly lines will im-
    prove efficiency more than subcontracting some
    small production goals. Therefore, by adding
    robotic assembly lines, the factory will be doing
    the most that can be done to improve efficiency.

    Which of the following is an assumption on
    which the argument depends?

    (A) Adding robotic assembly lines will be
         more expensive than subcontracting
         some small production goals.
    (B) The factory has a choice of robotic as-
         sembly lines, some of which might be
         better suited to this factory than oth-
         ers.
    (C) The factory may or may not decide to
         choose either alternative
    (D) Efficiency cannot be improved more by
         using both methods together than by
         adding robotic assembly lines alone.
    (E) This particular factory is already the third
         most efficient factory in China.

4. Just as the early NASA space explorers attempt-
    ed on each flight to push the frontiers of our
    knowledge, so too are the new private consor-
    tium space explorers seeking to add to man's
    general understanding of the cosmos.

    (A) Just as the early NASA space explorers
         attempted on each flight to push the
         frontiers of our knowledge, so too
    (B) The early NASA space explorers
         attempted on each flight to push the
         frontiers of our knowledge, and in the
         same way
    (C) Like the case of the early NASA space ex-
         plorers who attempted on each flight
         to push the frontiers of our knowledge,
         so too
    (D) As in the early NASA space explorers'
         attempts on each flight to push the
         frontiers of our knowledge, so too
    (E) Similar to the early NASA space explorers
         attempted on each flight to push the
         frontiers of our knowledge, so too

5. A proposal for a new building fire safety code
    requires that fire-retardant insulation no longer
    be sprayed on steel girders in the factory, but be
    sprayed on once the girders have arrived at the
    building site. This will eliminate the dislodging
    of the insulation in transit, and reduce fatalities
    in catastrophic fires by an estimated 20%.

    Which of the following, if true, represents the
    strongest challenge to the new proposal?

    (A) The fire-retardant insulation will also be
         required to be one inch thicker than in
         the past.
    (B) Studies have shown that most dislodge-
         ment of insulation occurs after the
         girders arrive on site.
    (C) Catastrophic fires represent only 4% of
         the fires reported nationally.
    (D) The proposed safety code will add con-
         siderably to the cost of new construc-
         tion.
    (E) In most of Europe, spraying fire-retardant
         insulation onto steel girders at the
         building site has been required for the
         past ten years.

6. An attempt to ratify the Equal Rights Amend-
    ment, begun almost two decades ago, has been
    unsuccessful despite efforts by many important
    groups, including the National Organization for
    Women.

    (A) to ratify the Equal Rights Amendment,
         begun almost two decades ago,
    (B) begun almost two decades ago, for ratify-
         ing the Equal Rights Amendment
    (C) begun for ratifying the Equal Rights
         Amendment almost two decades ago
    (D) at ratifying the Equal Rights Amendment,
         begun almost two decades ago,
    (E) that has begun almost two decades ago
         to ratify the Equal Rights Amendment

GO ON TO THE NEXT PAGE.

7. A newly discovered disease is thought to be caused by a certain bacterium. However, recently released data note that the bacterium thrives in the presence of a certain virus, implying that it is actually the virus that causes the new disease.

Which of the following pieces of evidence would most support the data's implication?

(A) In the absence of the virus, the disease has been observed to follow infection by the bacterium.

(B) The virus has been shown to aid the growth of bacteria, a process which often leads to the onset of the disease.

(C) The virus alone has been observed in many cases of the disease.

(D) In cases where the disease does not develop, infection by the bacterium is usually preceded by infection by the virus.

(E) Onset of the disease usually follows infection by both the virus and the bacterium.

8. The company was not even publicly traded until 1968, when the owner and founder sold it to David P. Markham, a private investor, who took the company public and established a long and generous policy of stock options for valued employees.

(A) who took the company public and established a long and generous policy of stock options for

(B) who, taking the company public, established a long and generous policy of stock options to

(C) who, when he took the company public, established a long and generous policy of stock options to

(D) who had taken the company public, establishing a long and generous policy of stock options as

(E) taking the company public and establishing a long and generous policy of stock options for

9. Because of a quality control problem, a supplier of flu vaccines will not be able to ship any supplies of the vaccine for the upcoming flu season. This will create a shortage of flu vaccines and result in a loss of productivity as workers call in sick.

Which of the following, if true, most seriously weakens the argument above?

(A) The quality control problem of the supplier is not as severe as some experts had initially predicted.

(B) Other suppliers of flu vaccine have not been affected by the quality control problem.

(C) Last year there was also a shortage of flu vaccine available.

(D) The price of flu vaccines is expected to fall in the next ten years.

(E) The flu season is expected to last longer than usual this year.

GO ON TO THE NEXT PAGE.

10. Never before had the navy defeated <u>so many foes at once as it had in</u> the battle of Trafalgar in 1805.

    (A)   so many foes at once as it had in
    (B)   at once as many foes as
    (C)   at once as many foes that there were in
    (D)   as many foes at once as it did in
    (E)   so many foes at once as that it defeated in

11. The changes that may be part of a general global warming trend include an increase in the frequency and severity of hurricanes, a gradual rise in sea level, <u>depleting the ozone layer, and raising the temperature of the earth</u>.

    (A)   depleting the ozone layer, and raising the temperature of the earth
    (B)   depleting the ozone layer, and a rise in the earth's temperature
    (C)   a depletion of the ozone layer, and raising the earth's temperature
    (D)   a depletion of the ozone layer, and a raise of the temperature of the earth
    (E)   a depletion of the ozone layer, and a rise in the temperature of the earth

GO ON TO THE NEXT PAGE.

<u>Questions 12–16</u> are based on the following passage:

It has long been a tenet of business theory that the best decisions are made after careful review and consideration. Only after weighing

Line all the options and studying projections, say
(5) most professors of business, can a practical decision be made.

Now, that model is being questioned by some business thinkers in the light of the theories of Malcolm Gladwell, who states that
(10) human beings often make better decisions in the blink of an eye.

It is, at first glance, a theory so counter-intuitive as to seem almost ludicrous. Behind any decision, Gladwell posits, there is a behind-
(15) the-scenes subconscious process in which the brain analyzes; ranks in order of importance; compares and contrasts vast amounts of information; and dismisses extraneous factors, seemingly almost instantaneously, often arriv-
(20) ing at a conclusion in less than two seconds. Citing a multitude of studies and examples from life, Gladwell shows how that split-second decision is often better informed than a drawn-out examination.

(25) Evanston and Cramer were the first to apply this theory to the business world. Evanston videotaped the job interviews of 400 applicants at different firms. He then played only 10 seconds of each videotape to independent human re-
(30) sources specialists. The specialists were able to pick out the applicants who were hired with an accuracy of over 90%.

Cramer took the experiment even further, using only five seconds of videotape, without
(35) sound. To his astonishment, the rate of accuracy with which the HR specialists were able to predict the successful applicants fell only to 82%.

Critics argue that these results illustrate a
(40) problem with stereotyping that impedes human resources specialists from hiring the best candidates even when they have the time to get below the surface: going for the candidate who "looks the part." Gladwell argues that, on
(45) the contrary, the human mind is able to make complicated decisions quickly, and that intuition often trumps an extended decision-making process.

12. The primary purpose of the passage is to

(A) discuss reasons an accepted business theory is being reexamined
(B) present evidence that resolves a contradiction in business theory
(C) describe a tenet of business practices and how that tenet can be tested in today's economic environment
(D) argue that a counter-intuitive new business idea is, in the final analysis, incorrect
(E) present evidence that invalidates a new business model

13. According to the passage, all of the following are examples of the subconscious processes by which the brain makes a decision EXCEPT

(A) analysis of information
(B) ranking of information
(C) comparison and contrast of information
(D) rejecting information that is not pertinent
(E) consulting a multitude of studies and examples

14. The author's attitude toward the long-held view that decisions should be made carefully over time expressed in lines 1–6 can best be described as

(A) dismissive and scornful
(B) respectful but questioning
(C) admiring and deferential
(D) uncertain but optimistic
(E) condescending and impatient

15. The author most likely mentions the results of Cramer's extension of Evanston's experiment in order to _____ .

(A) show that Cramer's hypothesis was correct while Evanston's hypothesis turned out to be incorrect
(B) show that Evanston's hypothesis was correct, while Cramer's hypothesis turned out to be incorrect
(C) demonstrate that while both experiments were scientifically rigorous, neither ended up being scientifically valid
(D) illustrate that the principle of subconscious decisions continues to work even when less information is available
(E) demonstrate that Cramer's experiment was 8% more accurate than Evanston's, even though his subjects had less information to work with

GO ON TO THE NEXT PAGE.

16. It can be inferred that the critics referred to in line 38 believed the excellent results of the two experiments had less to do with the innate decision-making of the subjects than with

   (A)   the excellent decision-making of Evanston and Cramer
   (B)   the expertise of Malcolm Gladwell, who originated the theory
   (C)   not choosing candidates who "looked the part"
   (D)   the use of videotape as a method of choosing candidates
   (E)   their unconscious use of visual stereotypes in making their selections

17. The women's volleyball team at a local college finished fifth in its division, prompting the college to fire the team's general manager. The manager responded by suing the college, saying that the team's performance put it among the top teams in the country.

   Which of the following statements, if true, would support the claim of the team's manager, and resolve the apparent contradiction?

   (A)   The team won all of its "away" games during the season in question.
   (B)   Attendance at the volleyball team's games was up 35% from the year before.
   (C)   Of the starting team, three team members were unable to play for at least half the season because of injuries.
   (D)   There are 80 teams in this particular volleyball team's division.
   (E)   The team lost more games this year than it did the year before.

18. Country A recently broke off diplomatic relations with Country B when it was reported that Country B had been running a covert intelligence operation within the borders of Country A. While a spokesperson for Country B admitted the charge, the spokesperson said that it was common knowledge that all countries do this, and that Country A was no exception.

   Which of the following inferences can be drawn from the argument above?

   (A)   Country B should apologize and dismantle its intelligence operation in Country A.
   (B)   The spokesperson for Country B claims that Country A engages in intelligence gathering, too.
   (C)   Because all countries engage in this practice, Country A's outrage was disingenuous.
   (D)   Relations between Country A and Country B will be strained for some time.
   (E)   Country B would be just as outraged if it was reported that Country A was running a covert intelligence operation with Country B's borders.

19. Because cellular telephones emit signals that can interfere with cockpit-to-control-tower transmissions, airplane passengers' use of these instruments <u>at all times that the airplane is in motion, even while on the ground, are</u> prohibited.

   (A)   at all times that the airplane is in motion, even while on the ground, are
   (B)   at all times during which the airplane, even while on the ground, is in motion, are
   (C)   during airplane motion, even when it is on the ground, are
   (D)   during times of the airplane being in motion, even on the ground, is
   (E)   when the airplane is in motion, even while on the ground, is

GO ON TO THE NEXT PAGE.

20. In contrast to classical guitars, whose owners prefer the dulcet, rounded tones produced
by nylon strings, <u>folk guitar owners prefer the
bright and brassy sound</u> that only bronze or
steel can create.

(A) folk guitar owners prefer the bright and
brassy sound
(B) folk guitar owners prefer to get a sound
that is bright and brassy
(C) with a folk guitar the owner gets the preferably bright and brassy sound
(D) folk guitars produce a bright and brassy
sound, which their owners prefer,
(E) folk guitars produce a preferred bright
and brassy sound for their owners

<u>Questions 21–22</u> are based on the following
passage:

A system-wide county school anti-smoking
education program was instituted last year. The
program was clearly a success. Last year, the
incidence of students smoking on school premises decreased by over 70 percent.

21. Which of the following assumptions underlies
the argument in the passage?

(A) Cigarettes are detrimental to one's
health; once people understand this,
they will quit smoking.
(B) The doubling of the price of a pack of
cigarettes last year was not the only
cause of the students' altered smoking
habits.
(C) The teachers chosen to lead the anti-
smoking education program were the
most effective teachers in the school
system.
(D) The number of cigarettes smoked each
day by those students who continued
to smoke last year did not greatly
increase.
(E) School policy enforcers were less vigilant
in seeking out smokers last year than
they were in previous years.

22. Which of the following, if true, would most seriously weaken the argument in the passage?

(A) The author of this statement is a school
system official hoping to generate
good publicity for the anti-smoking
program.
(B) Most students who smoke stopped
smoking on school premises last year
continued to smoke when away from
school.
(C) Last year, another policy change made it
much easier for students to leave and
return to school grounds during the
school day.
(D) The school system spent more on anti-
smoking education programs last year
than it did in all previous years.
(E) The amount of time students spent in
anti-smoking education programs last
year resulted in a reduction of in-class
hours devoted to academic subjects.

23. Mild exercise throughout pregnancy <u>may reduce
the discomfort associated with pregnancy and
result in</u> a speedier, easier birth, according to a
recent study.

(A) may reduce the discomfort associated
with pregnancy and result in
(B) may reduce the discomfort associated
with pregnancy, with the result
(C) may cause a reduction in the discomfort
associated with pregnancy and as a
result
(D) might lead to a reduction in the discomfort associated with pregnancy and as
a result
(E) might reduce the discomfort associated
with pregnancy and resulting in

GO ON TO THE NEXT PAGE.

Questions 24–27 are based on the following passage:

What is it that keeps the developing world in an apparent state of perpetual poverty? Poor education, lack of basic medical care, and the

Line absence of democratic structures all certainly
(5) contribute to these nations' plight. However, according to Peruvian economist Hernando de Soto, the overriding cause is the overwhelming prevalence of black market activity, well outside the formal economy, in these countries. The
(10) losses incurred from this condition are twofold. First, they deny the government tax revenues which could be used to improve education, medical treatment, and government efficiency. More important, however, they deny earners
(15) the chance to accumulate assets recognized by law and thus prevent them from leveraging those assets to borrow. Reforming these nations' legal systems in order to confer owner- ship through titling, De Soto argues, would help
(20) the poor there access the assets their work should be generating. These assets could then be used to buy homes and construct business- es, thus building a more stable and prosperous economy. De Soto estimates the value of these
(25) assets, which he terms "dead capital," at nearly $10 trillion worldwide.

De Soto is not the first to locate the devel- oping world's problems in the domain of prop- erty rights. Others have tried property rights
(30) reform and failed. According to de Soto, this is because his predecessors attempted to model their plans on existing, successful property rights systems. In other words, they tried to transplant American and British property law
(35) to an inhospitable host. De Soto argues that, within many of the extralegal markets of the developing world, mutually agreed upon rules for distributing assets and recognizing property rights already exist. Rather than force these
(40) markets to adjust to a new, foreign system of property titling, reformers should focus on codifying the existing systems wherever it is practical to do so. This would facilitate a quicker, more natural transition to an economy
(45) that builds wealth rather than squanders it.

24. The author's primary goal in the passage is to

(A) compare several failed attempts to ad- dress a problem
(B) respond to criticism of a new theory
(C) identify the problems inherent in a new economic theory
(D) describe a novel approach to an old prob- lem
(E) compare different property rights sys- tems in the industrial world

25. According to the passage, de Soto believes that the quickest way to address poverty in the developing world is to

(A) increase funding for education
(B) build the infrastructure to support lending
(C) ensure medical care for all citizens
(D) aggressively root out corruption in gov- ernment
(E) increase tax rates on all citizens in devel- oping countries

26. The author's assertion that "reformers should focus on codifying the existing systems wherever it is practical to do so" (lines 41–43) suggests that

(A) in some instances, current systems are inadequate to meet the needs of a market economy
(B) these systems are already written down and need only be enacted as law
(C) where it is impractical to codify exist- ing systems, countries should adopt American property law
(D) the existing systems are superior to those currently in use in modern indus- trialized countries
(E) improving education and medical care in these countries should take priority over reforming property laws

27. The term "dead capital" (line 25) refers to

(A) loans that are never repaid
(B) failed investments in new businesses
(C) cities ruined by over-industrialization
(D) the proceeds of extralegal commerce
(E) property passed from generation to gen- eration

GO ON TO THE NEXT PAGE.

Verbal Test
Bin Three—Hard Questions
26 Questions

This test is made up of sentence correction, critical reasoning, and reading comprehension questions.

Sentence Correction Directions: In sentence corrections, some part of the sentence or the entire sentence is underlined. Beneath each sentence you will find five ways of phrasing the underlined part. The first of these repeats the original; the other four are different. If you think the original is the best of these answer choices, choose answer A; otherwise, choose the best version and select the corresponding letter.

Reading Comprehension Directions: After reading the passage, choose the best answer to each question. Answer all questions following a passage on the basis of what is <u>stated</u> or <u>implied</u> in that passage.

Critical Reasoning Directions: Select the best of the answer choices given.

---

1. Unlike <u>Franklin D. Roosevelt's bootstrap program that helped</u> to restart economic growth in the 1930s through public works, Ronald Reagan proposed a program of trickle-down economics to restart the economy.

    (A) Franklin D. Roosevelt's bootstrap program that helped
    (B) Franklin D. Roosevelt and his bootstrap program which helped
    (C) Franklin D. Roosevelt, whose bootstrap program helped
    (D) The bootstrap program of Franklin D. Roosevelt that has helped
    (E) Franklin D. Roosevelt and his bootstrap program helping

2. In the 1970s it became evident <u>that writing about someone else's research was much easier for social scientists who wanted to make a quick name for themselves</u> than it was to do their own research.

    (A) that writing about someone else's research was much easier for social scientists who wanted to make a quick name for themselves
    (B) that for social scientists who wanted to make a quick name for themselves, it was much easier to write about someone else's research
    (C) that for social scientists wanting to make a quick name for themselves, writing about someone else's research was much easier
    (D) for social scientists who wanted to make a quick name for themselves that writing about someone else's research was much easier
    (E) for social scientists who wanted to make a quick name for themselves, writing about someone else's research was much easier

GO ON TO THE NEXT PAGE.

Questions 3–4 are based on the following:

To improve the town's overcrowded school system, the town council has proposed an ambitious education plan to reduce classroom size and make capital improvements—a plan they intend to pay for with an increase in property taxes for homes valued over $500,000. Although the school system desperately needs improving, the town council's plan should be defeated because the majority of the people who would end up paying for the improvements receive no benefit from them.

3. Which of the following, if true, most strengthens the argument above?

   (A) The town's school system is currently ranked among the worst in the state

   (B) Other towns nearby that have made similar capital improvements did not find that the improvements translated to a better quality of education.

   (C) The town will need to spend additional money on architect's plans for the capital improvements.

   (D) An examination of the tax rolls shows that most homeowners in this category no longer have school-age children.

   (E) Some homeowners will delay home improvement projects in order to keep the value of their homes below $500,000.

4. Which of the following, if true, provides the town council with the strongest counter to the objection that its plan is unfair?

   (A) Even with the proposed increase, property taxes in the town are well below the national average.

   (B) Paying for the school system improvements using existing town funds will result in shortfalls that will force the town into arrears.

   (C) The teachers in the town's school system receive some of the lowest salary packages in the immediate area, which is a major cause of attrition.

   (D) Smaller class sizes and capital improvements in a school system tend to increase property values in the surrounding community.

   (E) A feasibility study has shown that the cost of the improvements will likely be 20% higher than projected.

5. The rules of engagement under which a border patrol station can decide to use deadly force <u>includes responding to an invasionary incursion and the return of</u> hostile fire.

   (A) includes responding to an invasionary incursion and the return of

   (B) includes responding to an invasionary incursion and returning

   (C) include responding to an invasionary incursion and the return of

   (D) include a response to an invasionary incursion and the return of

   (E) include a response to an invasionary incursion and returning

GO ON TO THE NEXT PAGE.

6. Although the word "phonetician" is popularly associated with Henry Higgins's task of improving the diction of Eliza Doolittle in *My Fair Lady*, in linguistics, <u>it is someone who studies</u> the formation of language.

   (A) it is someone who studies
   (B) it is a person studying
   (C) it refers to someone who studies
   (D) they are people who study
   (E) it is in reference to people who study

7. Experts studying patterns of shark attacks on humans have noted that attacks tend to diminish when the water temperature drops below 65 degrees Fahrenheit. Until recently, researchers believed this was because sharks prefer warmer water, and thus are present in fewer numbers in colder water. However, new research shows that sharks are present in equal numbers in cold and warm water.

   Which of the following, if true, best explains the apparent paradox?

   (A) In general, humans prefer warm water.
   (B) Sharks' keen sense of smell is enhanced in cold water.
   (C) In the Pacific, shark attacks tend to occur more frequently in the daytime.
   (D) Of the more than 200 types of sharks present in the ocean, only three attack humans.
   (E) The average temperature of the earth's oceans is 55 degrees.

8. As a result of surging economic indicators, most analysts upgraded the company's stock to a strong "buy," ignoring the advice of the head of a watchdog organization <u>who warned that the company's product would prove not only dangerous but</u> ineffective in the long run.

   (A) who warned that the company's product would prove not only dangerous but
   (B) warning that the company's product would prove not only dangerous and also
   (C) warning that the company's product would prove itself to be both dangerous and
   (D) who warned that the company's product would prove to be both dangerous and
   (E) who was warning that the company's product would prove not only dangerous but

GO ON TO THE NEXT PAGE.

9. Scientists today accept that the increased severity of hurricanes in the last 10 years has been a result of warmer water in the Caribbean, which "feeds" the storms as they pass over it by a mechanism not yet completely understood. Thus, these severe hurricanes are yet more evidence of global warming.

Which of the following, if true, would most strengthen the argument above?

(A) Accurate statistics on the warming of the earth do not go back more than 100 years.

(B) Scientists have not discovered a new undersea current, fueled by an undersea volcano, which could have funneled warmer water into the Caribbean.

(C) The arctic ice caps have been losing three feet of circumference each year for the past five years.

(D) A new modeling computer program projects that the severity of hurricanes will increase over the next 10 years.

(E) Some scientists believe they will soon prove that the mechanism by which a storm picks up energy from warm water is based on convection.

10. A new influx of unprecedented private investment should create a bright new future for manned space exploration, making the possibility of commercial space tourism much more viable than 10 years ago.

(A) making the possibility of commercial space tourism much more viable than 10 years ago

(B) and make the possibility of commercial space tourism much more viable than 10 years ago

(C) making the possibility of commercial space tourism much more viable than it was 10 years ago

(D) and make the possibility of commercial space tourism much more viable than it was 10 years in the past

(E) making the possibility of commercial space tourism much more viable than 10 years in the past

GO ON TO THE NEXT PAGE.

<u>Questions 11–15</u> are based on the following passage:

As the American workforce gets grayer, age discrimination will likely become a more prominent issue in the courts. It is, of course, illegal
Line to discriminate against an employee because
(5) of his or her age—and yet it is not illegal to dismiss a worker because he has a high salary and expensive health care.

This apparent contradiction is at the heart of a raft of cases now making their way through
(10) the courts. The outcome of these cases will have broad implications for the workplace in the coming years. By 2010, the Bureau of Labor Statistics has projected that more than half of all workers will be over 40—many of whom, by
(15) dint of seniority and promotions, will be earning higher than median salaries, eligible for more stock options, and carrying higher health care costs as a result of a larger number of dependents and the increased cost of health care for
(20) older workers.

Is it any wonder that a bottom-line oriented business might want to shed these workers, whose productivity is likely to plummet in the next few years, even as they become more
(25) expensive employees?

Still, the legal challenges of implementing this policy are daunting. Businesses have the right to rate workers on their productivity and to rank them against their peers. But they are not
(30) allowed to prejudge individuals based on their sex, race or age. Each worker must be treated on his or her own merits, rather than by how they fit into a larger profile of the group they belong to.
(35) For companies looking to lay off these workers, the cost of making a mistake are high; while only one in three age discrimination suits are won by the plaintive, the awards tend to be steep—and the political fall-out harsh.

11. The primary purpose of the passage is to

(A) advocate on behalf of the older American worker who could soon face dismissal
(B) describe the origin of two theories of labor law and their effects on the workplace
(C) present an overview of the legal ramifications of a practice some call discriminatory
(D) describe the process by which America's workforce is getting older
(E) describe the methods by which a company could reduce its bottom line

12. Which of the following best describes the organization of the second paragraph of the passage?

(A) An assertion is made and then briefly contradicted.
(B) A contradiction is stated and then quickly resolved.
(C) A new theory is described and then qualified.
(D) An apparent inconsistency is stated and its consequences outlined.
(E) A conventional model is described and an alternative is introduced.

13. Which of the following, if true, would most effectively weaken the author's assertion that a "bottom-line oriented business" might want to fire older workers?

(A) A new study shows that, on average, younger workers earn less and have lower associated medical costs than older workers.
(B) Older workers have a higher rate of absenteeism than younger workers.
(C) A new study shows that older workers are in fact more productive and have led medical expenses compared to younger workers.
(D) A forecasted downturn in the economy will erode profits in may American businesses.
(E) A new bill scheduled to become law will make it easier for employers to employ illegal aliens.

GO ON TO THE NEXT PAGE.

14. It can be inferred from the passage that

   (A) what is good for American companies is not necessarily good for older Americans

   (B) American companies are prohibited by law from practices that discriminate based on gender, color of skin, or age

   (C) large monetary judgments from age discrimination suits might prove more expensive than paying older employees' salaries

   (D) by the year 2020, the percentage of older employees will be even higher than in the year 2010

   (E) some older employees may well be more productive than some younger employees

15. The author mentions all of the following as driving up the cost to employers for employing workers over the age of 40 EXCEPT

   (A) the cost of out-placement services
   (B) a larger number of dependents
   (C) increased cost of health care
   (D) higher median salaries
   (E) the cost of employee stock options

16. A pharmaceutical company claims that its new drug promotes learning in children. To back up its claims, the company points to a study of 300 children who were given the drug, along with a control group of 300 children who were given a placebo. The 300 children who were given the drug reported that they were able to retain new information much more easily.

   Which of the following statements, if true, would most tend to weaken the claims of the pharmaceutical company?

   (A) The 300 children in the control group also reported that they were able to retain new information much more easily.

   (B) The drug has also been shown to prevent common skin rashes.

   (C) The drug has been proven to have severe side-effects.

   (D) The children in the study were not given any other medications during the study.

   (E) The children who were given the drug did better on cognitive measurement tests after the drug therapy than before.

17. In order to understand the dangers of the current real-estate bubble in Country Y, one has only to look to the real-estate bubble of the last decade in Country Z. In that country, incautious investors used the inflated value of their real estate as collateral in risky margin loans. When the real-estate market collapsed, many investors went bankrupt, creating a major recession. Country Y is in real danger of a similar recession if more-stringent laws restricting margin loans are not enacted promptly.

   The answer to which of the following questions would be most useful in evaluating the significance of the author's claims?

   (A) Was the real estate in Country Z located principally in rural areas or was it located in more urban communities?

   (B) Could the bankruptcies in Country Z have been prevented by a private bailout plan by the nation's banks?

   (C) Does Country Y currently have any laws on its books regarding margin loans?

   (D) Are there business ties and connections between Country Y and Country Z?

   (E) Were there other factors in the case of Country Y that would make the comparison with Country Z less meaningful?

18. Rules governing participation in a new extreme sports fantasy camp require that applicants should be physically fit enough to endure the demanding activities in which they will be engaging.

   (A) that applicants should be physically fit enough to endure the demanding

   (B) that applicants be physically fit enough to endure the demanding

   (C) applicants should have enough physical fitness to allow enduring the demands of

   (D) applicants are physically fit enough as to endure the demands of

   (E) physical fitness in applicants, enough for endurance of demanding

GO ON TO THE NEXT PAGE.

19. During the summer of 2002, the Outer Banks <u>suffered a massive toad infestation, discouraging</u> many vacationers from visiting the area.

(A) suffered a massive toad infestation, discouraging

(B) suffered from a massive toad infestation and discouraged

(C) suffered a massive infestation of toads, which discouraged

(D) was suffering a massive infestation of toads and discouraging

(E) had suffered from a massive toad infestation and this discouraged

20. A prolonged period of low mortgage rates resulted in a period of the most robust home sales ever. At the same time, the average sale price of resale homes actually dropped, when adjusted for inflation.

Which of the following, if true, would explain the apparent contradiction between the robust home sales and the drop in the average sale price of resale homes?

(A) The inflation rate during this period exceeded the increase in the average salary, thus preventing many buyers from securing mortgages.

(B) Resale homes represent the best value on the real estate market.

(C) Without the adjustment for inflation, the price of resale homes actually increased by a very slight amount.

(D) The decrease in mortgage rates was accompanied by a widening of the types of mortgages from which borrowers could choose.

(E) The increase in home sales was due entirely to an increase in the sale of new homes.

21. Luis is taller than Rei. Kiko is taller than Marcus. Therefore, Kiko is taller than Rei.

The conclusion drawn above is not supported by the argument; however, the addition of one additional piece of information would make the conclusion logically sound. All of the following could be that additional piece of information EXCEPT:

(A) Kiko is taller than Luis.
(B) Luis is taller than Marcus.
(C) Luis and Marcus are the same height.
(D) Marcus and Rei are the same height.
(E) Marcus is taller than Rei.

22. It has been estimated that <u>an increase in average regional temperature of even 0.5 degrees Fahrenheit could cost the southern United States more than than $10 billion in lost agricultural income annually</u>.

(A) an increase in average regional temperature of even 0.5 degrees Fahrenheit could cost the southern United States more than $10 billion in lost agricultural income annually

(B) every year $10 billion in agricultural income could be the cost to the southern United States as a result of an increase in the average temperature of the region of even 0.5 degrees Fahrenheit

(C) the cost to the southern United States could be more than $10 billion in income from agriculture that results from a regional increase in average temperature of even 0.5 degrees Fahrenheit annually

(D) annual income losses in agriculture of more than $10 billion could be the cost from increasing average temperatures in the southern United States of even 0.5 degrees Fahrenheit

(E) annual income losses to the southern United States from the increase in average regional temperature of even 0.5 percent costing more than $10 billion in agricultural income each year

GO ON TO THE NEXT PAGE.

23. Within the Green Party, an internal debate is raging <u>among those who believe in compromising with mainstream politicians in order to achieve some goals with those who believe the party must not abandon any of its principles</u>.

(A) among those who believe in compromising with mainstream politicians in order to achieve some goals with those who believe the party must not abandon any of its principles

(B) among those who believe that achieving some goals requires compromise with mainstream politicians and those believing that none of the party's principles must be abandoned

(C) between those believing in compromising with mainstream politicians in order to achieve some goals with those who believe the party must not abandon any of its principles

(D) between those who believe in compromising with mainstream politicians in order to achieve some goals and those who believe the party must not abandon any of its principles

(E) between those believing that achieving some goals means compromising with mainstream politicians and those who believe that the principles of the party must not be abandoned

24. In comparison to the drivers who live in Mountainview, a greater proportion of the drivers who live in Oak Valley exceed the speed limit regularly. This explains why there are more accidents each year in Oak Valley than in Mountainview.

All of the following statements, if true, weaken the conclusion drawn above EXCEPT:

(A) Oak Valley has a greater proportion of blind intersections and sharp turns than has Mountainview.

(B) There is a greater number of drivers in Oak Valley than in Mountainview.

(C) Drivers in Mountainview must travel to Oak Valley to shop and work.

(D) Per capita, there are fewer police officers monitoring traffic in Oak Valley than there are in Mountainview.

(E) The roads are icier for a greater portion of the year in Oak Valley than in Mountainview.

GO ON TO THE NEXT PAGE.

25. A study showed that only ten percent of American dog owners enroll their dogs in formal obedience training classes. More than twenty percent of these dog owners, the study also showed, participate in dog shows. Thus, it is obvious that people who train their dogs are more likely to participate in dog shows than are people who do not train their dogs.

The conclusion above is correct provided which of the following statements is also true?

(A) It is impossible for a dog to compete in a dog show if the dog has not completed at least one formal obedience training class.

(B) The proportion of dog owners who enroll their dogs in formal obedience training classes is representative of the proportion who train their dogs outside such classes.

(C) Dog owners who participate in dog shows only train their dogs by enrolling them in formal obedience training lessons.

(D) Participation in dog shows is a reliable indicator of how much attention a dog owner pays to his dog.

(E) Only purebred dogs can participate in dog shows, so many owners who enroll their dogs in formal obedience training classes are excluded from this activity.

26. A bullet train travels in excess of 150 miles per hour. Therefore, if a train travels slower than 150 miles per hour, it is not a bullet train.

Which of the following most closely parallels the reasoning used in the argument above?

(A) An orange ripens only on the vine. If it ripens on the vine, then it is not an orange.

(B) Newspapers are often read by more than one person. Therefore magazines are also likely to be read by more than one person.

(C) An earthquake of 5.0 or above on the Richter scale causes massive damage. If there is not massive damage, then the earthquake did not attain a 5.0 or above.

(D) A supersonic plane travels at speeds in excess of Mach 1. If it is not supersonic, then it will travel at speeds below Mach 1.

(E) Fluoride generally prevents cavities. If there are no cavities, then there was no fluoride used.

END OF EXAMINATION

ANSWER KEY

MATH				VERBAL		
Bin 1	**Bin 2**	**Bin 3**	**Bin 4**	**Bin 1**	**Bin 2**	**Bin 3**
1. C	1. C	1. B	1. C	1. C	1. E	1. C
2. C	2. B	2. D	2. C	2. D	2. A	2. B
3. D	3. C	3. A	3. C	3. B	3. D	3. D
4. D	4. A	4. C	4. B	4. B	4. A	4. D
5. D	5. B	5. D	5. E	5. E	5. B	5. D
6. B	6. A	6. D	6. B	6. E	6. A	6. C
7. E	7. B	7. D	7. B	7. A	7. C	7. A
8. C	8. C	8. C	8. C	8. D	8. A	8. D
9. B	9. A	9. A	9. A	9. C	9. B	9. B
10. D	10. C	10. D	10. B	10. A	10. D	10. C
11. B	11. B	11. B	11. A	11. D	11. E	11. C
12. D	12. B	12. B	12. D	12. B	12. A	12. D
13. C	13. D	13. A	13. E	13. B	13. E	13. C
14. A	14. B	14. A	14. A	14. C	14. B	14. B
15. C	15. E	15. D	15. E	15. D	15. D	15. A
16. A	16. E	16. C	16. A	16. B	16. E	16. A
17. B	17. E	17. D	17. C	17. D	17. D	17. E
18. B	18. E	18. C	18. D	18. B	18. B	18. B
19. C	19. C	19. C	19. D	19. C	19. E	19. C
20. A	20. D	20. A	20. C	20. E	20. D	20. E
21. D	21. B	21. D	21. B	21. B	21. B	21. B
22. D	22. D	22. A	22. A	22. E	22. C	22. A
23. C	23. D	23. D	23. E	23. D	23. A	23. D
24. D	24. A	24. E	24. D	24. A	24. D	24. D
25. B	25. A	25. D	25. C	25. E	25. B	25. B
26. B	26. E	26. A	26. D		26. A	26. C
	27. C				27. D	

-4   -4
22/26   22/26

22

GMAT Practice Test:
Answers and Explanations

MATH BIN 1

QUESTIONS	EXPLANATIONS

1. What percent of 112 is 14?

   (A)   .125%
   (B)   8%
   (C)   12.5%
   (D)   125%
   (E)   800%

1. C Since this is a percent problem, you can solve it by thinking in terms of $\frac{part}{whole}$. In this case, $\frac{part}{whole} = \frac{14}{112} = \frac{x}{100}$; cross-multiply to get $112x = 1{,}400$, so $x = \frac{1{,}400}{112}$, and $x = 12.5$.

Like most percent questions on the GMAT, you can also find the answer using POE. 14 is a little bigger than $\frac{1}{10}$, or 10%, of 112—11.2 would be exactly 10%—so the answer can only be C.

2. The number of flights leaving a certain airport doubles during every one-hour period between its 9 A.M. opening and noon; after noon, the number of flights leaving from the airport doubles during every two-hour period. If 4 flights left from the airport between 9 and 10 A.M., how many flights left the airport between 2 and 4 P.M.?

   (A)   32
   (B)   48
   (C)   64
   (D)   128
   (E)   256

2. C Rather than try to rely on high school-style exponential growth formulas, let's just count this one out. If 4 flights left the airport between 9 and 10 A.M., then 8 left between 10 and 11 A.M., and 16 left between 11 A.M. and noon. Starting at noon, the flights begin to double every *two* hours, so 32 left between noon and 2 P.M., and 64 left between 2 P.M. and 4 P.M. The correct answer is C. If you chose E, you may have forgotten to account for the afternoon change in the rate of increase—and the test writers, of course, made sure that your answer was there waiting for you.

MATH BIN 1

QUESTIONS	EXPLANATIONS

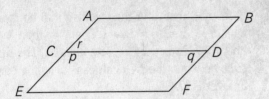

3. If both *ABDC* and *CDFE* are parallelograms, what is $q + r$?

   (1) $r = 70$

   (2) $p = 110$

   (A) Statement (1) ALONE is sufficient, but statement (2) alone is not sufficient.

   (B) Statement (2) ALONE is sufficient, but statement (1) alone is not sufficient.

   (C) BOTH statements TOGETHER are sufficient, but NEITHER statement alone is sufficient.

   (D) EACH statement ALONE is sufficient.

   (E) Statements (1) and (2) TOGETHER are NOT sufficient.

3. **D** Since we have parallelograms, we really only have two angles, big ones and small ones, and we know that a big angle plus a small one equals 180. Statement (1) tells us the value of r; q, like r, is a small angle, so $q + r = 70 + 70$, or 140. We're down to A and D.

Statement (2) gives us the value of a big angle, which we can subtract from 180 to get the value of a small angle. We now have the same information we had in Statement (1), and our answer is D.

4. Chris's convertible gets gas mileage that is 40% higher than that of Stan's SUV. If Harry's hatchback gets gas mileage that is 15% higher than that of Chris's convertible, then Harry's hatchback gets gas mileage that is what percent greater than that of Stan's SUV?

   (A) 25%
   (B) 46%
   (C) 55%
   (D) 61%
   (E) 66%

4. **D** This is a "cosmic" Plugging In problem. Since it's a percent problem, too, and the question asks us to find a percentage greater than the mileage of Stan's SUV, let's make Stan's mileage 100. Chris's mileage is therefore 140; 15% of 140 is 21, so Harry's mileage is 161. 161 is 61% greater than 100, and the correct answer is D.

Answer choices A and C are both traps, since they're simple addition and subtraction, respectively, of the numbers in the problem. If you got B, you probably increased Chris's mileage by 15% of 40, rather than 15% of 140.

MATH BIN 1

QUESTIONS	EXPLANATIONS

5. If x is equal to 1 more than the product of 3 and z, and y is equal to 1 less than the product of 2 and z, then $2x$ is how much greater than $3y$ when z is 4?

(A) 1
(B) 2
(C) 3
(D) 5
(E) 6

6. In 2005, did Company A have more than twice the number of employees as did Company B?

(1) In 2005, Company A had 11,500 more employees than did Company B.

(2) In 2005, the 3,000 employees with advanced degrees at Company A made up 12.5% of that company's total number employees, and the 2,500 employees with advanced degrees at Company B made up 20% of that company's total number of employees.

(A) Statement (1) ALONE is sufficient, but statement (2) alone is not sufficient.
(B) Statement (2) ALONE is sufficient, but statement (1) alone is not sufficient.
(C) BOTH statements TOGETHER are sufficient, but NEITHER statement alone is sufficient.
(D) EACH statement ALONE is sufficient.
(E) Statements (1) and (2) TOGETHER are NOT sufficient.

5. **D** Start by translating the two original equations: $x = 3z + 1$ and $y = 2z - 1$. If z is 4, then $x = 13$ and $y = 7$. $2x$ is thus 26, and $3y$ is 21. The difference between the two values is 5, so the correct answer is D.

If you chose A, you may have mistakenly added when the problem asked for a product. If you got E, you may have solved for $x - y$ when the problem asked for $2x - 3y$. And if you got C, you may have done both.

6. **B** Statement (1) tells us the difference between the numbers of employees at the two companies. Without the actual number of employees at either company, though, this information isn't sufficient to answer this yes-or-no question, so we're down to B, C, or E.

Statement (2), on the other hand, gives us the part-to-whole relationship we need to solve for the actual number of employees at each of the companies. We therefore know we can answer the question with a definitive "yes" or "no"—it doesn't matter which one is actually correct—so the answer is B.

(If you really want to crunch the numbers, that 12.5% at Company A is the same as $\frac{1}{8}$, and Company A had 24,000 employees; that 20% at Company B is the same as $\frac{1}{5}$, and Company B had 12,500 employees. The answer to the original question is "no"; Company A did not have more than twice the number of employees as did Company B.)

MATH BIN 1

QUESTIONS	EXPLANATIONS

7. Is x^3 equal to 125?

   (1) $x > 4$

   (2) $x < 6$

   (A) Statement (1) ALONE is sufficient, but statement (2) alone is not sufficient.

   (B) Statement (2) ALONE is sufficient, but statement (1) alone is not sufficient.

   (C) BOTH statements TOGETHER are sufficient, but NEITHER statement alone is sufficient.

   (D) EACH statement ALONE is sufficient.

   (E) Statements (1) and (2) TOGETHER are NOT sufficient.

7. E The question "Is x^3 equal to 125?" can be rewritten as "Is $x = 5$?" This is a yes-or-no question, and the best way to tackle it is to Plug In twice. In Statement (1), we can plug in 5, in which case the answer to the question "Is x^3 equal to 125?" is "yes." Or, we can plug in 6, in which case the answer is "no." Thus, because we get two different answers depending on the numbers we plug in, Statement (1) is not sufficient. We're down to B, C, or E.

In Statement (2), we can plug in 5, in which case the answer is "yes," or 4, in which case the answer is "no." Eliminate B.

To see if the answer is C, we must choose a number that satisfies the conditions of both Statements (1) and (2) at the same time. We can plug in 5, in which case the answer is "yes." You might have been tempted to choose C at this point because no other integer will satisfy the two equations at the same time, but does this problem limit us to picking integers? Nope. What about 4.5? Or 5.2? In either of these cases, the answer would be "no." Because we get two different answers depending on what numbers we plug in, the combination of Statements (1) and (2) is not sufficient either, and the correct answer is E.

QUESTIONS	EXPLANATIONS

8. Bob leaves point A and drives due west to point B. From point B, he drives due south to point C. How far is Bob from his original location?

(1) Point A is 24 miles from point B.

(2) Point B is 18 miles from point C.

(A) Statement (1) ALONE is sufficient, but statement (2) alone is not sufficient.
(B) Statement (2) ALONE is sufficient, but statement (1) alone is not sufficient.
(C) BOTH statements TOGETHER are sufficient, but NEITHER statement alone is sufficient.
(D) EACH statement ALONE is sufficient.
(E) Statements (1) and (2) TOGETHER are NOT sufficient.

8. **C** When a geometry problem comes without a diagram, always start by drawing one of your own. In this case, your diagram should look like this:

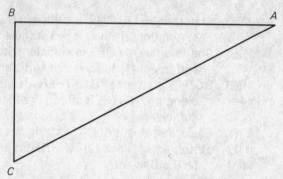

Statement (1) tells us the length of one side of our triangle, the distance from A to B. Since we know we have a right triangle (because Bob drove due west and due south), any two sides would be enough to find the remaining side. And *if* we knew that we had a "special" right triangle, one side might be enough. Neither of these cases applies, though, so we're down to B, C, or E.

Statement (2) gives us, again, a single side. Remember, though, that we can no longer consider the information from Statement (1), so this statement alone is also insufficient. We're down to C or E.

When we put the 2 statements together, we know we *could* solve for the remaining side using the Pythagorean theorem—although, since this is a Data Sufficiency question, there's no reason we would. The correct answer is C. Incidentally, if we did want to solve for the third side, we could save a lot of unnecessary calculation by recognizing this as a multiple of the old GMAT favorite, the 3-4-5 triangle. The two shorter sides of the triangle are multiplied by 6, so the remaining side must be 30.

MATH BIN 1

QUESTIONS	EXPLANATIONS

9. The formula $M = \sqrt{l^2 + w^2 + d^2}$ describes the relationship between M, the length of the longest line that can be drawn in a rectangular solid, and l, w, and d, the length, width, and depth of that rectangular solid. The longest line that can drawn in a rectangular solid with a length of 12, a width of 4, and a depth of 3 is how much longer than the longest line that can drawn in a rectangular solid with a length of 6, a width of 3, and a depth of 2?

   (A)   5
   (B)   6
   (C)   7
   (D)   9
   (E) 13

9. **B** Although the relationship provided in the problem is based on geometry, this isn't really a geometry problem for us: We can simply plug the given numbers into the given formula. Starting with the larger figure, $\sqrt{12^2 + 4^2 + 3^2} = \sqrt{144 + 16 + 9} = \sqrt{169} = 13$. For the smaller figure, $\sqrt{6^2 + 3^2 + 2^2} = \sqrt{36 + 9 + 4} = \sqrt{49} = 7$. Both 13 and 7 are, of course, answer choices, but the problem asked us for the *difference* between the two values, so the correct answer is 6, choice B.

QUESTIONS	EXPLANATIONS

10. Is the average (arithmetic mean) of a, b, and c equal to 8?

   (1) Three times the sum of a, b, and c is equal to 72.

   (2) The sum of $2a$, $2b$, and $2c$ is equal to 48.

   (A) Statement (1) ALONE is sufficient, but statement (2) alone is not sufficient.
   (B) Statement (2) ALONE is sufficient, but statement (1) alone is not sufficient.
   (C) BOTH statements TOGETHER are sufficient, but NEITHER statement alone is sufficient.
   (D) EACH statement ALONE is sufficient.
   (E) Statements (1) and (2) TOGETHER are NOT sufficient.

10. **D**   This is a yes-or-no question, and we need to recognize that it's not asking about the individual values of a, b, and c—it's asking only about the average of those values. Of course, we could easily find the average if we knew the individual values. But, we can also find the average if we know the sum of the values, since the average of any group of values is their sum divided by the number of values in the group. Therefore, the question is asking us whether $\frac{a + b + c}{3} = 8$. To simplify this equation, multiply both sides by 3 to get $a + b + c = 24$. If the sum is 24, then the average is 8.

Statement (1) tells us that $3(a + b + c) = 72$. We can divide both sides by 3 to find out that the sum is, indeed, 24; the average is 8; and the answer to the question is "yes." Since this is a Data Sufficiency problem, though, we can stop as soon as we know that we can find the sum of a, b, and c, and we're down to A and D.

Statement (2) tells us that $2a + 2b + 2c = 48$. If we factor a 2 out of the left side of the equation, we get $2(a + b + c) = 48$, and once again see that we can find the sum. The correct answer is D.

MATH BIN 1

QUESTIONS	EXPLANATIONS

QUESTIONS

11. $\sqrt{\sqrt{\left(1+\dfrac{17}{64}\right)}} =$

(A) $\dfrac{\sqrt{34}}{8}$

(B) $\dfrac{3\sqrt{2}}{4}$

(C) $\dfrac{9}{8}$

(D) $\dfrac{\sqrt{68}}{4}$

(E) $\dfrac{3\sqrt{2}}{2}$

EXPLANATIONS

11. **B** Since we should always calculate things inside the parentheses first—don't forget PEMDAS!—start by adding 1 and $\dfrac{17}{64}$ to get $\dfrac{81}{64}$. Those are both perfect squares, so the inner root sign will be easy to handle: $\sqrt{\dfrac{81}{64}} = \dfrac{\sqrt{81}}{\sqrt{64}} = \dfrac{9}{8}$. Don't grab answer choice C, though—we still need to work the outer sign: $\sqrt{\dfrac{9}{8}} = \dfrac{\sqrt{9}}{\sqrt{8}} = \dfrac{3}{2\sqrt{2}}$. Like in high school, we can't leave a radical on the bottom of a fraction, so we'll need to multiply our answer by $\dfrac{\sqrt{2}}{\sqrt{2}}$ to get our final answer of B, $\dfrac{3\sqrt{2}}{4}$.

If you're comfortable estimating fractions and roots, you can apply POE to this question. $1 + \dfrac{17}{64}$ is a little bigger than 1; the square root of something a little bigger than 1 is also something a little bigger than 1; and the square root of that number is, again, something a little bigger than 1. Only B and C are a little bigger than 1.

12. A certain stadium is currently full to $\frac{13}{16}$ of its maximum seating capacity. What is the maximum seating capacity of the stadium?

(1) If 1,250 people were to enter the stadium, the stadium would be full to $\frac{15}{16}$ of its maximum seating capacity.

(2) If 2,500 people were to leave the stadium, the stadium would be full to $\frac{9}{16}$ of its maximum seating capacity.

(A) Statement (1) ALONE is sufficient, but statement (2) alone is not sufficient.
(B) Statement (2) ALONE is sufficient, but statement (1) alone is not sufficient.
(C) BOTH statements TOGETHER are sufficient, but NEITHER statement alone is sufficient.
(D) EACH statement ALONE is sufficient.
(E) Statements (1) and (2) TOGETHER are NOT sufficient.

12. **D** This is a fraction problem, so the key is to convert fractions to actual numbers. Statement (1) tells us that 1,250 people will take the stadium from $\frac{13}{16}$ full to $\frac{15}{16}$ full; that's a difference of $\frac{2}{16}$, or $\frac{1}{8}$, so we know that 1,250 represents $\frac{1}{8}$ of the total seating capacity of the stadium. The stadium must, therefore, hold 8 × 1,250, or 10,000 people, and we're down to A or D.

Statement (2) allows us to find a similar equivalence: a change of 2,500 represents the difference between $\frac{9}{16}$ and $\frac{13}{16}$—that is, $\frac{4}{16}$, or $\frac{1}{4}$—of the stadium's total seating capacity. So we know we can find the total seating capacity (4 × 2,500, or 10,000 people) with Statement (2) as well, making D the correct answer.

MATH BIN 1

QUESTIONS	EXPLANATIONS

13. Andre has already saved $\frac{3}{7}$ of the cost of a new car, and he has calculated that he will be able to save $\frac{2}{5}$ of the remaining amount before the end of the summer. If his calculations are correct, what fraction of the cost of the new car will he still need to save at the end of summer vacation?

(A) $\frac{6}{35}$

(B) $\frac{8}{35}$

(C) $\frac{12}{35}$

(D) $\frac{23}{35}$

(E) $\frac{29}{35}$

$\{1, 4, 6, y\}$

14. If the average (arithmetic mean) of the set of numbers above is 6, then what is the median?

(A) 5
(B) 6
(C) 7
(D) 13
(E) 24

13. C Since there are fractions in the answer choices, and they're fractions of an unspecified amount, the quickest way to solve this problem is to Plug In. Let's make the price of Andre's dream car $35—the denominators of the fractions in the problem are 7 and 5 (both factors of 35) and, moreover, 35 is in the denominator of *all* of the answer choices.

If the car costs $35, and Andre has already saved $\frac{3}{7}$ of that, or $15, he currently has $20 left to save. If his (and your) calculations are correct, before the end of the summer he'll be able to save $\frac{2}{5}$ of that remaining $20, or $8. That will give him a total of $23 saved toward his car, leaving him $12 to go. Expressed as a fraction of the cost of the car, that's $\frac{12}{35}$, and the correct answer is C.

As always, watch those trap answers. Choice D is the fraction of the cost that Andre will have saved by the end of the summer. Choice A is what you'd get if you calculated Andre's summer earnings as two-fifths of the total cost of the car instead of two-fifths of what Andre has left to save. Choice E is what you'd get if you made both mistakes.

14. A The average of all four numbers is 6, so the numbers must add up to 6 times 4, or 24. That means y must equal 13. And if y equals 13, the median must be 5—that is, the average of the two middle numbers in the list. If you thought about it, the median and the mean are usually not too far away from each other, so choices D and E were much too large.

MATH BIN 1

15. A store sells a six-pack of soda for $2.40. If this represents a savings of 10 percent of the individual price of cans of soda, then what is the price of a single can of soda?

(A) $ 0.35
(B) $ 0.40
(C) $ 0.44
(D) $ 0.50
(E) $ 0.55

15. C If a six-pack sells for $2.40, then each can costs 40 cents when they're purchased together. Choice B is 40 cents, but we know the price of an individual can must be higher, so we can cross off choices A and B. 10% of 40 is 4, so the price of a single can is 44 cents, and the correct answer is choice C.

16. If Beth spent $400 of her earnings last month on rent, how much did Beth earn last month?

(1) Beth saved $\frac{1}{3}$ of her earnings last month and spent half of the remainder on rent.

(2) Beth earned twice as much this month as last month.

(A) Statement (1) ALONE is sufficient, but statement (2) alone is not sufficient.

(B) Statement (2) ALONE is sufficient, but statement (1) alone is not sufficient.

(C) BOTH statements TOGETHER are sufficient, but NEITHER statement ALONE is sufficient.

(D) EACH statement ALONE is sufficient.

(E) Statements (1) and (2) TOGETHER are NOT sufficient.

16. A Covering up Statement (2) and looking only at Statement (1), we see that Beth saved one-third of her earnings and spent half of the two-thirds that remained on rent. Half of two-thirds is one-third. So we can set up the equation:

$$\frac{1}{3} = \frac{400}{x}$$

And x equals $1,200. Note that we didn't actually need to find out how much Beth earned. We just needed to know that we *could* find out. We're down to A or D.

Now, looking at Statement (2) we see that it tells us how Beth did THIS month. But do we care? Nope. The question asks us about LAST month. The correct answer is choice A.

MATH BIN 1

QUESTIONS	EXPLANATIONS

17. If *n* is an integer, is *n* even?

    (1)   2*n* is an even integer.

    (2)   *n* − 1 is an odd integer.

    (A)   Statement (1) ALONE is sufficient, but statement (2) alone is not sufficient.

    (B)   Statement (2) ALONE is sufficient, but statement (1) alone is not sufficient.

    (C)   BOTH statements TOGETHER are sufficient, but NEITHER statement ALONE is sufficient.

    (D)   EACH statement ALONE is sufficient.

    (E)   Statements (1) and (2) TOGETHER are NOT sufficient.

17. B To answer this yes-or-no question, it helps to plug in values that make the statements true. Starting with Statement (1), let's plug in 4 for *n*, which makes the statement "2*n* is an even integer" true, and gives us a "yes" to our overall question. Now, let's plug in 3 for *n*, which still makes the statement true, but gives us a "no" to our overall question. Because the answer is sometimes yes and sometimes no, we're down to BCE.

Looking at Statement (2) only, let's plug in values that make the statement true. If *n* = 2, the statement is true, and the answer to our overall question is a tentative "yes." Now, if we can find even one case where we can plug a number into this statement that makes the statement true but answers the question "no," then we'll be down to CE. But as you try different numbers, you'll realize that in order to make Statement (2) true, *n* has to be even. So the answer to this question is B.

18. At apartment complex *z*, 30 percent of the residents are men over the age of 18, and 40 percent are women over the age of 18. If there are 24 children living in the complex, how many total residents live in apartment complex *z*?

    (A)   32
    (B)   80
    (C)   94
    (D)   112
    (E)   124

18. B Altogether, the percentages of men and women adds up to 70%, so that means 30% of the residents at this complex are children. Just set up an equation:

$$\frac{30}{100} = \frac{24}{x}$$

Solving for *x*, the total number of residents is 80. The answer is B.

You could also plug the answers back into the problem. Choice C seems difficult, so why not start with choice B, which has an easy number to work with? 30% of 80 = 24. 40% of 80 = 32. So there are a total of 24 + 32 = 56 adults. If choice B is correct, there should be 24 kids. And guess what? That's just what the problem says.

MATH BIN 1

QUESTIONS	EXPLANATIONS

19. Over the course of a soccer season, 30 percent of the players on a team scored goals. What is the ratio of players on the team who scored goals to those who did not?

   (A) 3 to 10
   (B) 1 to 3
   (C) 3 to 7
   (D) 1 to 1
   (E) 3 to 1

19. **C** If 30% of the players on the soccer team scored goals during the season, then 70% did not score goals. The ratio of those who scored to those who did not is 30 to 70, which reduces to 3 to 7.

Some will find that Plugging In is the easiest way to solve this problem. Plug in 10 for the number of players on the team (choose this number because it is easy to work with in a percentage problem). 30% of the 10 players—that is to say, 3 players—scored goals. The other 7, it then follows, did not score goals. The ratio of those who scored to those who did not is 3 to 7. The correct answer is C.

20. At a restaurant, Luis left a tip for his waiter equal to 20 percent of his entire dinner check, including tax. What was the amount of the dinner check?

   (1)   The sum of the dinner check and the tip was $16.80.
   (2)   Luis's tip consisted of two bills and four coins.

   (A) Statement (1) ALONE is sufficient, but statement (2) alone is not sufficient.

   (B) Statement (2) ALONE is sufficient, but statement (1) alone is not sufficient.

   (C) BOTH statements TOGETHER are sufficient, but NEITHER statement alone is sufficient.

   (D) EACH statement ALONE is sufficient.

   (E) Statements (1) and (2) TOGETHER are NOT sufficient.

20. **A** Because Luis tipped the waiter 20%, we know that the sum of the check and tip equals 1.2 times the amount of the check. Thus, we can write the equation

$$1.2x = 16.80$$

and solve for x to determine both the amount of the check and the amount of Luis's tip. The answer must be A or D.

Statement (2) is insufficient because it does not identify either the bills or the coins. The correct answer is A.

MATH BIN 1

QUESTIONS	EXPLANATIONS

21. Which sport utility vehicle has a higher list price, the Touristo or the Leisure?

(1) The list price of the Leisure is $\frac{5}{6}$ the list price of the Touristo.

(2) The list price of the Touristo is 1.2 times the list price of the Leisure.

(A) Statement (1) ALONE is sufficient, but statement (2) alone is not sufficient.

(B) Statement (2) ALONE is sufficient, but statement (1) alone is not sufficient.

(C) BOTH statements TOGETHER are sufficient, but NEITHER statement alone is sufficient.

(D) EACH statement ALONE is sufficient.

(E) Statements (1) and (2) TOGETHER are NOT sufficient.

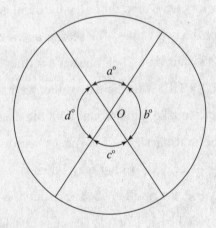

22. In the circle above with center O, $3a = b$. What is the value of $b - a$?

(A)　2
(B)　30
(C)　45
(D)　90
(E)　135

21. D According to Statement (1), the list price of the Leisure is $\frac{5}{6}$ the list price of the Touristo. The list price of the Touristo is therefore greater than the list price of the Leisure. Statement (1) is sufficient; the answer must be A or D. Statement (2) tells you that the list price of the Touristo is 1.2 times the list price of the Leisure. So Statement (2) also tells you that the list price of the Touristo is greater than the list price of the Leisure. The correct answer is D.

If you chose C, you were probably confused about the meaning of each answer choice. Review the AD-BCE method of eliminating answers in the Data Sufficiency section of this book.

22. D If you look carefully at the drawing, you should notice that a and b are supplementary angles; that is, together they make up a line. The sum of these angles, therefore, is 180°. Or, to put this in math-speak:

$$a + b = 180$$

Now, return to the equation in the question stem, $3a = b$. We can use this information to rewrite the equation $a + b = 180$ as

$$a + 3a = 180$$
$$4a = 180$$
$$a = 45$$

Because $a + b = 180$, and $a = 45$, b must equal 135, which is answer choice E. Wait, though, you're not done yet: The question asks for the solution $b - a$. Because $b - a = 135 - 45$, the answer to this question is 90. The correct answer is D.

QUESTIONS	EXPLANATIONS

23. What is the value of integer w?

   (1) w is a multiple of 3.
   (2) $420 < w < 425$

   (A) Statement (1) ALONE is sufficient, but statement (2) alone is not sufficient.

   (B) Statement (2) ALONE is sufficient, but statement (1) alone is not sufficient.

   (C) BOTH statements TOGETHER are sufficient, but NEITHER statement alone is sufficient.

   (D) EACH statement ALONE is sufficient.

   (E) Statements (1) and (2) TOGETHER are NOT sufficient.

23. C Because there are an infinite number of multiples of 3, it is clear that Statement (1) is not sufficient to answer the question. The answer must be B, C, or E. Statement (2) narrows the range of possible answers to 421, 422, 423, or 424. However, because it does not narrow the answer to a single solution, it is not sufficient. Eliminate B.

When you put the two statements together, you know that w is a multiple of 3 that is either 421, 422, 423, or 424. Because only one of these values, 423, is a multiple of 3, the two statements together are sufficient. (A quick way to test whether an integer is divisible by 3 is to add its digits; if the sum of the digits is divisible by 3, then the number is divisible by 3.) The correct answer is C.

24. What is the quotient when .25% of 600 is divided by .25 of 600?

   (A)   10.0
   (B)   1.0
   (C)   .1
   (D)   .01
   (E)   .001

24. D Before we worry about the division, let's solve for the two values. The second one is easier, so let's start there: "of" means multiply, so $.25 \times 600 = 150$. With the first value, we have to be sure to take into account both the decimal *and* the percent sign: .25% can be represented as $\frac{.25}{100}$, or .0025. Either way, when you multiply by 600, the result is 1.5. The quotient is thus 1.5 divided by 150, or .01. The answer is D.

If you're really comfortable with manipulating fractions, you can save yourself a lot of math. The whole question translates into $\dfrac{\frac{.25}{100} \times 600}{.25 \times 600}$, which easily cancels down to $\dfrac{1}{100}$, or .01.

MATH BIN 1

25. A certain town's economic development council has 21 members. If the number of females on the council is 3 less than 3 times the number of males on the council, then the town's economic development council has how many male members?

   (A) 5
   (B) 6
   (C) 7
   (D) 9
   (E) 15

25. B Although you could solve this by writing a pair of algebraic equations ($f + m = 21$ and $f = 3m - 3$), it's simpler to Plug In the Answers. Start with answer choice C, 7 men. The number of women would be 3 less than 3 times that number, or $21 - 3 = 18$ women. That's a total of 25 council members altogether, and we're looking for 21. Now that we know that C is too big, we can eliminate answer choices C, D, and E.

If we try answer choice B, 6 men, then we have $18 - 3 = 15$ women. This gives us our desired total of 21 council members, so the correct answer is B. If you got E, by the way, you solved for the number of *female* members on the board.

26. Roger can chop down 4 trees in an hour. How long does it take Vincent to chop down 4 trees?

   (1) Vincent spends 6 hours per day chopping down trees.
   (2) Vincent takes twice as long as Roger to chop down trees.

   (A) Statement (1) ALONE is sufficient, but statement (2) alone is not sufficient.
   (B) Statement (2) ALONE is sufficient, but statement (1) alone is not sufficient.
   (C) BOTH statements TOGETHER are sufficient, but NEITHER statement alone is sufficient.
   (D) EACH statement ALONE is sufficient.
   (E) Statements (1) and (2) TOGETHER are NOT sufficient.

26. B Statement (1) tells you how many hours Vincent spends chopping down trees in a day, but it provides no data to help you determine how long it takes him to chop down 4 trees. This statement is clearly insufficient to answer the question. The answer must be B, C, or E.

Statement (2) tells you that Vincent takes twice as long as Roger to chop down trees. Because the question stem tells you that Roger chops down 4 trees per hour, you can deduce that Vincent chops down 4 trees every 2 hours. Thus, Statement (2) is sufficient to answer the question. The correct answer is B.

MATH BIN 2

1. If $x = \dfrac{\dfrac{5}{9} + \dfrac{15}{27} + \dfrac{45}{81}}{3}$, then $\sqrt{1-x} =$

    (A) $\dfrac{\sqrt{5}}{9}$

    (B) $\dfrac{5}{9}$

    (C) $\dfrac{2}{3}$

    (D) $\dfrac{\sqrt{5}}{3}$

    (E) $\dfrac{15}{9}$

1. **C** You could start by converting all the fractions to their least common denominator of 81—an understandable temptation. However, in this case, it's quicker and simpler to reduce the fractions instead. They all reduce to $\dfrac{5}{9}$, so $x = \dfrac{\dfrac{5}{9} + \dfrac{5}{9} + \dfrac{5}{9}}{3}$, or $\dfrac{3\left(\dfrac{5}{9}\right)}{3}$ ...or $\dfrac{5}{9}$. Now that we know the value of x, we can solve for $\sqrt{(1-x)}$:

    $\sqrt{\left(1 - \dfrac{5}{9}\right)} = \sqrt{\dfrac{4}{9}} = \dfrac{\sqrt{4}}{\sqrt{9}} = \dfrac{2}{3}$. The correct answer is C. Answer choice B, of course, is x itself, and answer choice D is $\sqrt{x}$.

2. For the past x laps around the track, Steven's average time per lap was 51 seconds. If a lap of 39 seconds would reduce his average time per lap to 49 seconds, what is the value of x?

    (A) 2
    (B) 5
    (C) 6
    (D) 10
    (E) 12

2. **B** This is a multi-step average problem involving an unknown quantity—in short, a perfect place to Plug In the Answers! Start with answer choice C: If Steven has already driven 6 laps, then we know that he has driven for a total of 6 × 51, or 306, seconds. One more lap in 39 seconds would give him a total of 7 laps in 345 seconds, and our average works out to be a little greater than 49 seconds ($49\dfrac{2}{7}$, to be exact). Close, but not quite. We need fewer laps to bring down Steven's average speed, so answer choice B is the next logical choice. Five laps in 51 seconds means Steven has driven 5 × 51, or 255, seconds so far, and the additional 39-second lap gives us a total of 6 laps driven in 294 seconds. The average is now $\dfrac{294}{6} = 49$ seconds, and B is the correct answer.

MATH BIN 2

QUESTIONS	EXPLANATIONS

3. $200^2 - 2(200)(199) + 199^2 =$

   (A) −79,201
   (B) −200
   (C) 1
   (D) 200
   (E) 79,999

3. C Although you could solve this problem with lots of tedious multiplication, it's much faster to recognize the quadratic equation hidden in the numbers: $x^2 - 2xy + y^2 = (x - y)(x - y)$. That means we can rewrite the equation as $(200 - 199)(200 - 199)$, or $(1)(1)$. The correct answer is C.

Since the answer choices vary so widely, you might have been able to apply POE to the most extreme answer choices, A and E. The product of 200 and 199, which we have to double, is not too different from either 200^2 or 199^2. Thus, the negative value in the equation is roughly equal to the sum of the two positive values in the equation. If you did the math, by the way, and *got* one of those answers, you must have reversed an addition or subtraction sign.

4. If $x \neq -\dfrac{1}{2}$, then $\dfrac{6x^2 + 11x - 7}{2x - 1} =$

   (A) $3x + 7$
   (B) $3x - 7$
   (C) $3x + 1$
   (D) $x + 7$
   (E) $x - 7$

4. A Since this problem has variables in the answer choices, the simplest way to solve it is to Plug In. If $x = 2$, the equation becomes $\dfrac{6(2)^2 + 11(2) - 7}{2(2) - 1} = \dfrac{24 + 22 - 7}{4 - 1} = \dfrac{39}{3} = 13$. Now plug 2 in for x in the answer choices—only answer choice A gives us 13, so it must be the correct answer.

And if you *are* feeling algebraic on this problem, there's yet another approach that's simpler than trying to factor the top of the fraction: Plug In the Answers. Try multiplying your answer choices by the expression on the bottom of the fraction and see which one yields the expression on the top. Only answer choice A does, so it must, again, be the correct answer.

MATH BIN 2

5. If Amy drove the distance from her home to the beach in less than 2 hours, was her average speed greater than 60 miles per hour?

  (1) The distance that Amy drove from her home to the beach was less than 125 miles.
  (2) The distance that Amy drove from her home to the beach was greater than 122 miles.

  (A) Statement (1) ALONE is sufficient, but statement (2) alone is not sufficient.
  (B) Statement (2) ALONE is sufficient, but statement (1) alone is not sufficient.
  (C) BOTH statements TOGETHER are sufficient, but NEITHER statement alone is sufficient.
  (D) EACH statement ALONE is sufficient.
  (E) Statements (1) and (2) TOGETHER are NOT sufficient.

5. **B** This rate problem is also a yes-or-no question, so we don't need to know Amy's exact speed, just if her average speed was greater than 60 miles per hour. The simplest way to find out whether Statement (1) is sufficient is to try different possible times and distances. If her total driving time was, for instance, 1 hour, a distance of 61 miles would yield an answer of "yes." Meanwhile, a distance of 59 miles would yield an answer of "no." That means we're down to B, C, or E.

Regardless of what times and distances you plug in for Statement (2), on the other hand, you will always get an answer of "yes." Even if Amy were to have driven the *full* 2 hours and gone *only* 122 miles, she would be driving at a rate of 61 miles per hour; since she actually drove a greater distance in less time, her rate must really be greater than 61. Since Statement (2) always gives us the same answer, it must be sufficient, and our answer is B.

6. If $x = m - 1$, which of the following is true when $m = \dfrac{1}{2}$?

  (A) $x^0 > x^2 > x^3 > x^1$
  (B) $x^0 > x^2 > x^1 > x^3$
  (C) $x^0 > x^1 > x^2 > x^3$
  (D) $x^2 > x^0 > x^3 > x^1$
  (E) $x^3 > x^2 > x^1 > x^0$

6. **A** Once you've solved for x, which equals $-\dfrac{1}{2}$, this question is just a matter of putting the four values in order. Even better, you already know two of them: $x = -\dfrac{1}{2}$ and $x^0 = 1$. With the other two values, be especially careful about the negative sign: $x^2 = \dfrac{1}{4}$ and $x^3 = -\dfrac{1}{8}$. The correct order, then, is $x^0 > x^2 > x^3 > x^1$, and the answer is A.

MATH BIN 2

QUESTIONS	EXPLANATIONS

QUESTIONS

7. A comedian is playing two shows at a certain comedy club, and twice as many tickets have been issued for the evening show as for the afternoon show. Of the total number of tickets issued for both shows, what percentage has been sold?

   (1)   A total of 450 tickets have been issued for both shows.

   (2)   Exactly $\frac{3}{5}$ of the tickets issued for the afternoon show have been sold, and exactly $\frac{1}{5}$ of the tickets issued for the evening show have been sold.

   (A)   Statement (1) ALONE is sufficient, but statement (2) alone is not sufficient.

   (B)   Statement (2) ALONE is sufficient, but statement (1) alone is not sufficient.

   (C)   BOTH statements TOGETHER are sufficient, but NEITHER statement alone is sufficient.

   (D)   EACH statement ALONE is sufficient.

   (E)   Statements (1) and (2) TOGETHER are NOT sufficient.

8. If $\frac{1}{y} = 2\frac{2}{3}$, then $\left(\frac{1}{y+1}\right)^2 =$

   (A) $\frac{9}{64}$

   (B) $\frac{3}{8}$

   (C) $\frac{64}{121}$

   (D) $\frac{121}{64}$

   (E) $\frac{64}{9}$

EXPLANATIONS

7. **B** The information in Statement (1), along with that in the question itself, is enough for us to find the number of tickets issued for each show. Without any information about the number of those tickets that were sold, though, we can't answer the question, and we're down to B, C, or E.

Statement (2), along with the information in the question, is sufficient—even without the information in Statement (1). If we have the fraction of each type of ticket that was sold, and the ratio of one type of ticket to the other, we can figure out the overall percentage of tickets sold. The correct answer is B.

Want to prove it? Try Plugging In. In Statement (2), the denominator of both of our fractions is 5, so let's say that 25 tickets have been issued for the afternoon show and 50 have been issued for the evening show. That means 15 tickets have been sold for the afternoon show and 10 have been sold for the evening show, for a total of 25 tickets sold out of a total of 75 tickets issued. The answer is $\frac{1}{3}$, as it will always be if we meet the requirements of Statement (2) and the question itself.

8. **C** First, solve for y. Since $2\frac{2}{3} = \frac{8}{3}$, $\frac{1}{y} = \frac{8}{3}$ and thus $y = \frac{3}{8}$. Now plug the value of y into the equation: $\left(\dfrac{1}{\frac{3}{8}+1}\right)^2 = \left(\dfrac{1}{\left(\frac{11}{8}\right)}\right)^2 = \dfrac{1^2}{\left(\frac{11}{8}\right)^2} = \dfrac{1}{\frac{121}{64}} = \dfrac{64}{121}$. The correct answer is C.

Answer choice B, of course, is y itself. If you chose D, you forgot to flip over your final fraction. If you chose A, you forgot to add 1 when you put y in the equation. And if you chose E, you did both.

MATH BIN 2

QUESTIONS	EXPLANATIONS

9. An operation ~ is defined by the equation

$a \sim b = \dfrac{a+b}{(ab)^2}$ for all numbers a and b such that

$ab \neq 0$. If $c \neq 0$ and $a \sim c = 0$, then $c =$

(A) $-a$

(B) 0

(C) $\sqrt{a}$

(D) a

(E) a^2

9. **A** Answering a function problem on the GMAT is simply a matter of following the directions provided as the definition for the function. In this case, the operation signified by two numbers with the ~ between them is defined as the sum of the numbers on either side of the ~ sign divided by the square of the product of the two numbers. If $a \sim c = 0$, then $\dfrac{a+c}{(ac)^2} = 0$; since the numerator must be zero in order for the fraction itself to equal zero, we know that $a + c = 0$. Subtract a from both sides, and $c = -a$. Our answer is A.

10. If x is a positive integer, is the greatest common factor of 150 and x a prime number?

   (1) x is a prime number.

   (2) $x < 4$

   (A) Statement (1) ALONE is sufficient, but statement (2) alone is not sufficient.

   (B) Statement (2) ALONE is sufficient, but statement (1) alone is not sufficient.

   (C) BOTH statements TOGETHER are sufficient, but NEITHER statement alone is sufficient.

   (D) EACH statement ALONE is sufficient.

   (E) Statements (1) and (2) TOGETHER are NOT sufficient.

10. **C** The easiest way to determine whether Statement (1) by itself is sufficient is to plug in different values for x. If $x = 2$, the greatest common factor is 2, and the answer to this yes-or-no question is "yes." If $x = 7$, on the other hand, the greatest common factor is 1—and since 1 is not prime, the answer is "no." We're down to B, C, or E.

Statement (2) by itself is also not sufficient. If x is equal to 1, 2, or 3, then the greatest common factor of x and 150 is x itself. But since 2 and 3 are prime, and 1 is not, we're down to C and E.

When we put the statements together, the only possible values for x are 2 and 3. With either one, the greatest common factor is equal to x itself and is, therefore, prime. The correct answer is C.

MATH BIN 2

QUESTIONS	EXPLANATIONS

$$X = \{9, 10, 11, 12\}$$
$$Y = \{2, 3, 4, 5\}$$

11. One number will be chosen randomly from each of the sets above. If x represents the chosen member of Set X and y represents the chosen member of Set Y, what is the probability that $\dfrac{x}{y}$ will be an integer?

(A) $\dfrac{1}{16}$

(B) $\dfrac{3}{8}$

(C) $\dfrac{1}{2}$

(D) $\dfrac{3}{4}$

(E) $\dfrac{15}{16}$

11. **B** As with all probability problems, we'll have to find a fraction that has the total number of possibilities in the denominator and the number of those possibilities that meet a certain requirement in the numerator. The denominator is the easy part: Since there are 4 members of each set, there are $4 \times 4 = 16$ total possibilities for $\dfrac{x}{y}$. Now we just have to figure out how many of those possibilities meet the requirement.

The requirement, in this case, is that $\dfrac{x}{y}$ is an integer—in other words, that x is divisible by y—and we can count out all of the combinations that meet that requirement quickly and easily. The first member of Set X, 9, is only divisible by one member of Set Y, 3, so that's one. Then, working through Set X: 10 is divisible by both 2 and 5, so there's another two; 11 is prime, and so not divisible by any members of Set Y; and 12 gives us another three, because it's divisible by 2, 3, and 4. Thus, 6 of our total of 16 possibilities meet our requirement, and our probability is $\dfrac{6}{16}$, or $\dfrac{3}{8}$. The answer is B.

MATH BIN 2

QUESTIONS	EXPLANATIONS

12. If p and q are integers, is $\dfrac{p+q}{2}$ an integer?

(1) $p < 17$

(2) $p = q$

(A) Statement (1) ALONE is sufficient, but statement (2) alone is not sufficient.

(B) Statement (2) ALONE is sufficient, but statement (1) alone is not sufficient.

(C) BOTH statements TOGETHER are sufficient, but NEITHER statement alone is sufficient.

(D) EACH statement ALONE is sufficient.

(E) Statements (1) and (2) TOGETHER are NOT sufficient.

12. B Since Statement (1) doesn't tell us anything about the value of q, and very little about the value of p, it is, by itself, insufficient to answer this yes-or-no question. Statement (2), though, while it gives us no new specifics about the values of p or q, gives us enough information to know the answer to the question. Algebraically, if $p = q$, then $\dfrac{p+q}{2} = \dfrac{p+p}{2} = \dfrac{2p}{2} = p$ since we know from the question that p is an integer, the answer to the question is "yes," and our answer is B. Of course, we can easily show the sufficiency of Statement (2) by plugging in values for p and q: as long as the values are equal integers, our answer is always "yes."

13. A perfectly spherical satellite with a radius of 4 feet is being packed for shipment to its launch site. If the inside dimensions of the rectangular crates available for shipment, when measured in feet, are consecutive even integers, then what is the volume of the smallest available crate that can be used? (note: The volume of a sphere is given by the equation $V = \dfrac{4}{3}\pi r^3$.)

(A)   48
(B)   192
(C)   480
(D)   960
(E)   1680

13. D Although this may seem like a volume question, it's really about being able to fit the diameter of the satellite inside the crate—we can entirely disregard the given formula for the volume of a sphere. Let's start with what we know: Since the radius of the sphere is 4, the diameter is 8. So every dimension in our crate must be at least 8, so the smallest available crate will measure $8 \times 10 \times 12$. The volume of that crate is 960, and the correct answer is D.

In fact, if we try to use the volume formula we can easily go astray. Using a rough value of 3 for π, we can approximate the value of the sphere to be a little bigger than 250 (replacing π with 3 in the formula gives a value of 256, and the exact value is a little larger than 268). We might be tempted, therefore, to select answer choice C, but we can't: The only set of three consecutive integers that would yield a volume of 480 would be $6 \times 8 \times 10$, and we can't put a spherical object with a diameter of 8 feet into a crate that's only 6 feet across in one direction.

MATH BIN 2

QUESTIONS	EXPLANATIONS

14. A certain family has 3 sons: Richard is 6 years older than David, and David is 8 years older than Scott. If in 8 years Richard will be twice as old as Scott, then how old was David 4 years ago?

- (A) 8
- (B) 10
- (C) 12
- (D) 14
- (E) 16

14. B This problem could be an algebraic nightmare, so let's Plug In the Answers. We'll start with answer choice C, 12. If David was 12 years old 4 years ago, he's 16 now, and that means Richard is 22 and Scott is 8. In 8 years, then, Richard will be 30 and Scott will be 16; since Richard won't be twice as old as Scott at that point, this can't be the answer.

Run answer choice B, 10, through the same process. If David was 10 years old 4 years ago, he's 14 now, so Richard is 20 and Scott is 6. In 8 years, then, Richard will be 28 and Scott will be 14; since Richard will then be twice as old as Scott, our answer is B.

15. What is the value of x?

- (1) $x^2 - 5x + 4 = 0$
- (2) x is not prime.

- (A) Statement (1) ALONE is sufficient, but statement (2) alone is not sufficient.
- (B) Statement (2) ALONE is sufficient, but statement (1) alone is not sufficient.
- (C) BOTH statements TOGETHER are sufficient, but NEITHER statement alone is sufficient.
- (D) EACH statement ALONE is sufficient.
- (E) Statements (1) and (2) TOGETHER are NOT sufficient.

15. E Statement (1) is a quadratic equation, so let's factor it and see what our options are for x: $x^2 - 5x + 4 = 0$ factors into $(x - 4)(x - 1) = 0$, so x could be 4 or 1. Since we can't get a single value for x, Statement (1) alone is insufficient, and we're down to B, C, or E.

Statement (2) alone leaves us with the vast majority of all numbers in existence—*definitely* not sufficient, so we're down to C or E.

When we combine the statements, they're still not sufficient. Be careful not to fall for one of the classic GMAT traps: 1 is *not* prime. Since, of course, neither is 4, we're left with both values, and the correct answer is E.

16. Sam and Jessica are invited to a dance. If there are 7 men and 7 women in total at the dance, and one woman and one man are chosen to lead the dance, what is the probability that Sam and Jessica will NOT be chosen to lead the dance?

- (A) $\dfrac{1}{49}$
- (B) $\dfrac{1}{7}$
- (C) $\dfrac{6}{7}$
- (D) $\dfrac{47}{49}$
- (E) $\dfrac{48}{49}$

16. E The probability that Sam will be chosen is $\dfrac{1}{7}$. The probability that Jessica will be chosen is also $\dfrac{1}{7}$. The probability that they will both be chosen is $\dfrac{1}{7}$ times $\dfrac{1}{7}$ or $\dfrac{1}{49}$. This happens to be choice A, but we aren't done yet. The question asks for the probability that they will NOT both be chosen. The probability that an event does NOT happen can be expressed as 1 minus the probability that the event DOES happen. So 1 minus $\dfrac{1}{49}$ equals $\dfrac{48}{49}$, or choice E.

MATH BIN 2

17. What is the surface area of rectangular solid y?

   (1) The dimensions of one face of rectangular solid y are 2 by 3.

   (2) The area of another face of rectangular solid y is 6.

   (A) Statement (1) ALONE is sufficient, but statement (2) alone is not sufficient.

   (B) Statement (2) ALONE is sufficient, but statement (1) alone is not sufficient.

   (C) Both statements TOGETHER are sufficient, but NEITHER statement ALONE is sufficient.

   (D) EACH statement ALONE is sufficient.

   (E) Statements (1) and (2) TOGETHER are NOT sufficient.

17. E Whenever you see a geometry problem without a diagram, it's a good idea to make one. Statement (1) only tells us two of the three dimensions we need to find the surface area. We're down to BCE.

Statement (2) tells us the area of another face of the rectangular solid. If this were a square, Statement (2) would be sufficient by itself, but it's not, so we're down to C and E.

Putting the two statements together, you might be tempted to pick C because we know the area of two different faces of the rectangular solid.

But what if the two faces are facing each other? We still don't know the third dimension of the rectangular solid, and the answer must be E.

18. A six-sided die with faces numbered 1 through 6 is rolled three times. What is the probability that the face with the number 6 on it will NOT face upward on all three rolls?

   (A) $\dfrac{1}{216}$

   (B) $\dfrac{1}{6}$

   (C) $\dfrac{2}{3}$

   (D) $\dfrac{17}{18}$

   (E) $\dfrac{215}{216}$

18. E The probability that the first roll will yield the number 6 is $\dfrac{1}{6}$. The probability that the second roll will yield the number 6 is also $\dfrac{1}{6}$. The probability that the third roll will yield the number 6? You guessed it: $\dfrac{1}{6}$. To find the probability of the series of these three events happening, you multiply the probabilities of each of the individual events: $\dfrac{1}{6} \times \dfrac{1}{6} \times \dfrac{1}{6} = \dfrac{1}{216}$. That's choice A, but we aren't done yet. $\dfrac{1}{216}$ is the probability that the number 6 WILL face up on all three rolls. The probability that an event does NOT happen can be expressed as 1 minus the probability that the event DOES happen. So 1 minus $\dfrac{1}{216}$ equals $\dfrac{215}{216}$. The correct answer is choice E.

MATH BIN 2

QUESTIONS	EXPLANATIONS

19. What is the sum of x, y, and z?

   (1) $2x + y + 3z = 45$
   (2) $x + 2y = 30$

   (A) Statement (1) ALONE is sufficient, but statement (2) alone is not sufficient.

   (B) Statement (2) ALONE is sufficient, but statement (1) alone is not sufficient.

   (C) BOTH statements TOGETHER are sufficient, but NEITHER statement alone is sufficient.

   (D) EACH statement ALONE is sufficient.

   (E) Statements (1) and (2) TOGETHER are NOT sufficient.

19. C   Gut instinct may lead to you select E on this one; after all, Statement (1) provides a three-variable equation, which everyone knows is unsolvable. Statement (2) only refers to two of the three variables mentioned in the question stem, so clearly it cannot be sufficient. At first glance, it may be hard to imagine how the two statements together could be any more helpful than each is on its own.

Statement (1) is, in fact, insufficient on its own, for the reason stated above. Eliminate A and D. Statement (2) is also insufficient, again for the reason stated above. Eliminate B. The answer must be C or E.

Why is C the correct answer? If you add the two equations provided by (1) and (2), you get $3x + 3y + 3z = 75$. Factor a 3 out of both sides of the equation and you end up with $x + y + z = 25$. Thus, the two statements together *are* sufficient to answer the question "What is the sum of x, y, and z?" The correct answer is C.

20. A department store receives a shipment of 1,000 shirts, for which it pays $9,000. The store sells the shirts at a price 80 percent above cost for one month, after which it reduces the price of the shirts to 20 percent above cost. The store sells 75 percent of the shirts during the first month and 50 percent of the remaining shirts afterward. How much gross income did sales of the shirts generate?

   (A) $10,000
   (B) $10,800
   (C) $12,150
   (D) $13,500
   (E) $16,200

20. D   To answer this question, break the problem down into small, manageable steps. The first job at hand is to determine the selling price of the shirt, both during the first month they were on sale and then after. Because the store bought 1,000 shirts for $9,000, the cost of each shirt was $9.00. The store sold the shirts at an 80% markup during the first month. $1.8 \times \$9.00 = \$16.20$, so during the first month the shirts sold for $16.20 each. After the first month, the selling price was 20% above cost. $1.20 \times \$9.00 = \$10.80$, so that was the selling price after the first month.

The store sold 75% of the shirts during the first month. 75% of 1,000 is 750; the store sold 750 shirts at $16.20 each. $750 \times \$16.20 = \$12,150$. Note that this partial answer is answer choice C. Test takers who only half-finish their work will choose this incorrect answer. The store then sold 50% of its remaining stock at $10.80 per shirt. The remaining stock is 250 shirts $(1,000 - 750)$, half of which is 125. The store, then, sold 125 shirts at $10.80 each. $125 \times \$10.80 = \$1,350$. The store's gross income from the sale of these shirts, then, was $12,120 + $1,350 = $13,500. The correct answer is D.

21. David has three credit cards: a Passport card, an EverywhereCard, and an American Local card. He owes balances on all three cards. Does he owe the greatest balance on the Everywhere-Card?

(1) The sum of the balances on his Every-whereCard and American Local card is $1,350, which is three times the balance on his Passport card.

(2) The balance on his EverywhereCard is $\frac{4}{3}$ of the balance on his Passport card and $\frac{4}{5}$ of the balance on his American Local card.

(A) Statement (1) ALONE is sufficient, but statement (2) alone is not sufficient.

(B) Statement (2) ALONE is sufficient, but statement (1) alone is not sufficient.

(C) BOTH statements TOGETHER are sufficient, but NEITHER statement alone is sufficient.

(D) EACH statement ALONE is sufficient.

(E) Statements (1) and (2) TOGETHER are NOT sufficient.

21. **B** Statement (1) provides information only about the sum of the balances on David's Everywhere-Card and his American Local card. Therefore, the statement is insufficient to determine whether the balance on David's EverywhereCard is his highest balance, because it does not provide any information that allows you to compare the balance on the EverywhereCard to the balances on the other two cards. Eliminate A and D.

Statement (2) tells you that the balance on David's EverywhereCard is greater than the balance on his Passport card and less than the balance on his American Local card. Thus, it provides enough information to answer the question "Does David owe the greatest balance on the EverywhereCard?" The correct answer is B.

There are a couple of places where you can go wrong on this question. The first involves the fact that Statement (2) answers the question this way: "No, he does not owe the greatest balance on the EverywhereCard." Some test takers get confused and use a "No" answer to eliminate a statement. Remember, it doesn't matter how you answer a yes-or-no question, just so long as you can answer it conclusively.

Some test takers might realize that Statements (1) and (2) together provide enough information to calculate the exact balance on each credit card, and thus may choose C. But because Statement (2) is sufficient on its own, C cannot be the correct answer to this question.

MATH BIN 2

QUESTIONS	EXPLANATIONS

22. Automobile A is traveling at two-thirds the speed that Automobile B is traveling. How fast is Automobile A traveling?

(1) If both automobiles increased their speed by 10 miles per hour, Automobile A would be traveling at three-quarters the speed that Automobile B would be traveling.

(2) If both automobiles decreased their speed by 10 miles per hour, Automobile A would be traveling at half the speed that Automobile B would be traveling.

(A) Statement (1) ALONE is sufficient, but statement (2) alone is not sufficient.

(B) Statement (2) ALONE is sufficient, but statement (1) alone is not sufficient.

(C) BOTH statements TOGETHER are sufficient, but NEITHER statement alone is sufficient.

(D) EACH statement ALONE is sufficient.

(E) Statements (1) and (2) TOGETHER are NOT sufficient.

22. D To solve this problem, we need to write some equations. Let's call Automobile A's current speed A and Automobile B's current speed B. The question stem tells us that $A = \frac{2}{3}B$. Statement (1) tells us that $A + 10 = \frac{3}{4}(B + 10)$. Thus, between the question stem and Statement (1), we have two non-identical equations, which means we can solve for our two variables. (Best of all, because this is a data sufficiency question, just knowing this is enough; we don't have to actually solve it!) Rule out B, C, and E.

Statement (2) tells us that $A - 10 = \frac{1}{2}(B - 10)$. Once again, we have two non-identical equations and two variables. Statement (2) is sufficient, and the correct answer is D.

23. a and b are nonzero integers such that $0.35a = 0.2b$. What is the value of b in terms of a?

(A) $0.07a$
(B) $0.57a$
(C) $0.7a$
(D) $1.75a$
(E) $17.5a$

23. D What makes this problem tricky is the presence of decimals, so the best thing to do is to get rid of them right off the bat. Multiply both sides of the equation by 100 to produce the equation $35a = 20b$. (If you don't multiply both sides carefully, you could end up with answer E.) Now, you can Plug In, or simply solve for b by dividing both sides by 20 to get $b = \frac{35}{20}a$. Convert the fraction to a decimal by dividing 35 by 20 to yield $b = 1.75a$. The correct answer is D.

MATH BIN 2

QUESTIONS	EXPLANATIONS

24. The Binary Ice Cream Shoppe sells two flavors, vanilla and chocolate. On Friday, the ratio of vanilla cones sold to chocolate cones sold was 2 to 3. If the store had sold 4 more vanilla cones, the ratio of vanilla cones sold to chocolate cones sold would have been 3 to 4. How many vanilla cones did the store sell on Friday?

    (A)   32
    (B)   35
    (C)   42
    (D)   48
    (E)   54

24. **A** You could solve this problem algebraically, but do you really want to? Plugging In the Answers is so much easier! Let's start with answer C, because it's the middle value among the answer choices. If this is the correct answer, then the Binary Ice Cream Shoppe sold 42 vanilla cones on Friday. Because vanilla cones sold at a 2-to-3 ratio to chocolate cones, this would mean that the shop sold 63 chocolate cones $\left(\frac{2}{3} = \frac{42}{63}\right)$. If this is the correct answer, then the ratio of (42 + 4) to 63 would be 3 to 4. It is not, so this answer must be incorrect.

You must decide next whether the correct answer is more or less than 42. If you have good math instincts, you'll know it's less because of the result that answer C yielded. If you aren't sure, just pick a direction and go; you'll find the correct answer soon enough either way. Note that the answer cannot be B because B is an odd number. Because it is not divisible by 2, it cannot be the number of vanilla cones sold. A is the correct answer. 32 to 48 is a 2-to-3 ratio; add 4 more vanilla cones to get a ratio of 36 to 48, which reduces to 3 to 4.

MATH BIN 2

25. Is integer *a* a prime number?

    (1) 2*a* has exactly three factors.

    (2) *a* is an even number.

    (A) Statement (1) ALONE is sufficient, but statement (2) alone is not sufficient.

    (B) Statement (2) ALONE is sufficient, but statement (1) alone is not sufficient.

    (C) BOTH statements TOGETHER are sufficient, but NEITHER statement alone is sufficient.

    (D) EACH statement ALONE is sufficient.

    (E) Statements (1) and (2) TOGETHER are NOT sufficient.

25. **A** In order to answer this yes-or-no question correctly, you must remember that 2 is a prime number. If you forget that, you are lost. Statement (1) tells us that 2*a* has exactly 3 factors. Let's plug in some numbers. If you choose 3 for *a*, then 2*a* = 6. What are the factors of 6? 1, 6, 2, and 3. In other words, there are 4 factors. Is there any number we can plug in for *a* that gives us only 3 factors for the number 2*a*? As a matter of fact, there is only one: 2. Only 2 times 2, or 4, has exactly three factors: 1, 2, and 4. This tells us that *a* must be 2; any other multiple of 2 would have at least 4 factors (itself, 1, 2, and the product of itself and 2.) So if *a* can only be 2, can we definitely answer this yes-or-no question? Yes, 2 is a prime number.

Statement (2) is tempting for several reasons. If you forgot that 2 is prime, you would incorrectly conclude that this statement alone is sufficient to answer the question "No." If you figured out that *a* = 2 from Statement (1), you may be tempted to choose this because it confirms the information given in Statement (1). However, because it is not sufficient to answer the question on its own, you must resist temptation. The correct answer is A.

MATH BIN 2

26. Renee rides her bicycle 20 miles in m minutes. If she can ride x miles in 10 minutes, which of the following equals x?

(A) $\dfrac{m}{200}$

(B) $\dfrac{m}{20}$

(C) $\dfrac{m}{2}$

(D) $2m$

(E) $\dfrac{200}{m}$

26. **E** Solve this problem by plugging in values. Set m equal to a value that will transform the question into an easy arithmetic problem. For example, $m = 40$ is a good, easy value. It tells us that Renee can ride 1 mile every 2 minutes. How many miles, then, can she ride in 10 minutes? She can ride 5 miles in 10 minutes.

Now, plug in 40 for m in each of the answer choices. The correct answer will calculate to 5, the value of x when $m = 40$. Because E is the only answer that equals 5, E is the correct answer.

MATH BIN 2

QUESTIONS	EXPLANATIONS

27. If s and w are integers, is $\dfrac{w}{5}$ an integer?

   (1) $4s + 2$ is divisible by 5.

   (2) $w + 3 = 4s$

   (A) Statement (1) ALONE is sufficient, but statement (2) alone is not sufficient.

   (B) Statement (2) ALONE is sufficient, but statement (1) alone is not sufficient.

   (C) BOTH statements TOGETHER are sufficient, but NEITHER statement alone is sufficient.

   (D) EACH statement ALONE is sufficient.

   (E) Statements (1) and (2) TOGETHER are NOT sufficient.

27. **C** You can solve this yes-or-no problem by plugging in values to test the answer choices. However, before you start doing that, you can eliminate several answer choices.

Statement (1) by itself clearly is not sufficient to answer the question, because it tells us nothing about w. Eliminate A and D. Is Statement (2) sufficient? Let's plug in values. w could equal 5, because $5 + 3 = 4s$ can be solved in a way that satisfies the rules of this question (i.e., that s and w are integers). Thus, Statement (2) might be sufficient to tell us that $\dfrac{w}{5}$ is an integer. Wait a minute, though: w could also equal 13, because $13 + 3 = 4s$ is also solvable. Because $\dfrac{13}{5}$ is not an integer, Statement (2) is not sufficient. Sometimes it answers "yes," other times it answers "no." Eliminate B.

What about when we put the two statements together? Here, a little algebra illustrates the correct answer very elegantly. Statement (2) tells us that $4s = w + 3$; use this information to rewrite Statement (1) as $w + 3 + 2$ is divisible by 5. Thus, $w + 5$ is divisible by 5. Any number that is divisible by 5 when you add 5 to it is divisible by 5 on its own; if you don't believe it, plug some values in for w and prove it to yourself. The correct answer is C.

MATH BIN 3

1. A discount electronics store normally sells all merchandise at a discount of 10 percent to 30 percent off the suggested retail price. If, during a special sale, an additional 20 percent were to be deducted from the discount price, what would be the lowest possible price of an item costing $260 before any discount?

    (A) $130.00
    (B) $145.60
    (C) $163.80
    (D) $182.00
    (E) $210.00

1. **B** We don't need to worry about that range for the initial discount: Since we want the *lowest* possible price, we want the *greatest* possible discount. Thirty percent of 260 is 78, so the price after the initial discount is $260 – $78, or $182. The additional 20% discount amounts to $36.40—remember, the 20% discount is 20% of the already-discounted price. $182 – $36.40 = $145.60, and the correct answer is B.

2. During a special promotion, a certain filling station is offering a 10% discount on gas purchased after the first 10 gallons. If Kim purchased 20 gallons of gas, and Isabella purchased 25 gallons of gas, then Isabella's total per-gallon discount is what percent of Kim's total per-gallon discount?

    (A)   80%
    (B) 100%
    (C) 116.7%
    (D) 120%
    (E) 140%

2. **D** This problem never specifies the cost of a gallon of gas, so let's Plug In $1. Kim, then, paid $1 per gallon for the first 10 gallons and $.90 per gallon on the next 10; that's a total of 20 gallons for $19, an overall average of $.95 per gallon, and a total per-gallon discount of 5 cents. Isabella paid $1 per gallon for the first 10 gallons and $.90 per gallon on the next 15; that's a total of 25 gallons for $23.50, an overall average of $.94 per gallon, and a total per-gallon discount of 6 cents. The question asks us to relate Kim and Isabella's total per-gallon discounts, so 5 and 6 cents, respectively. Six is 120% of 5, and the correct answer is D. You might have applied POE to answer choices A and B: Since Isabella bought more gas at the discounted rate than did Kim, Isabella's discount is greater than, and therefore more than 100% of, Kim's.

MATH BIN 3

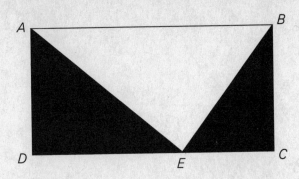

3. What is the area of the shaded region in the figure shown above?

(1)   The area of rectangle *ABCD* is 54.

(2)   *DE* = 2*EC*

(A)   Statement (1) ALONE is sufficient, but statement (2) alone is not sufficient.
(B)   Statement (2) ALONE is sufficient, but statement (1) alone is not sufficient.
(C)   BOTH statements TOGETHER are sufficient, but NEITHER statement alone is sufficient.
(D)   EACH statement ALONE is sufficient.
(E)   Statements (1) and (2) TOGETHER are NOT sufficient.

3. **A**   Statement (1) is sufficient, by itself, to answer the question. Although we can't determine, from Statement (1), the individual areas of the two triangular shaded regions, when combined they equal 27 (half of the total area of rectangle *ABCD*). The easiest way to see this is to draw a vertical line through point *E*, cutting the rectangle into two smaller ones. Now we have two rectangles that are divided by diagonals, and diagonals, by definition, cut rectangles in half. If half of the two smaller rectangles are shaded, then so is half of the larger rectangle. We're down to A and D.

Statement (2) gives us the relationship between the two smaller shaded regions, but it doesn't alone allow us to determine anything about their individual areas. Statement (2) is insufficient, and the correct answer is A.

MATH BIN 3

QUESTIONS	EXPLANATIONS

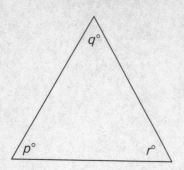

4. Is the triangle above equilateral?

(1) $r = 180 - (p + r)$

(2) $p = 60$

(A) Statement (1) ALONE is sufficient, but statement (2) alone is not sufficient.
(B) Statement (2) ALONE is sufficient, but statement (1) alone is not sufficient.
(C) BOTH statements TOGETHER are sufficient, but NEITHER statement alone is sufficient.
(D) EACH statement ALONE is sufficient.
(E) Statements (1) and (2) TOGETHER are NOT sufficient.

4. **C** Statement (1) is, by itself, insufficient to answer the question, although it does provide the very useful information that $r = q$. If you're comfortable working with triangles, you may have immediately read "180 minus the sum of p and r" as being equal to q. If not, you can discover this using algebra, though the route is a bit more arduous. Add $(p + r)$ to both sides to yield $r + p + r = 180$; but since $p + q + r$ also equals 180, you can combine the equations to get $r + p + r = p + q + r$. Subtract a p and a q from each side, and you're left with $r = q$. Nonetheless, this is still insufficient to answer the question. If r and q are both 60, the answer is "yes"; if they're both 45—remember, you can't trust the diagrams in Data Sufficiency—the answer is "no." We're down to B, C, or E.

Statement (2), by itself, is also insufficient to answer the question; the only thing it tells us about q and r is their sum, which equals 120. Eliminate B.

When we combine our statements, though, we can determine whether the triangle is equilateral. If r and q are equal and their sum is 120, then they, like p, must equal 60. If all three angles equal 60, the triangle must be equilateral, and the correct answer is C.

MATH BIN 3

QUESTIONS	EXPLANATIONS

5. During a certain two-week period, 70% of the movies rented from a video store were comedies, and, of the remaining movies rented, there were 5 times as many dramas as action movies. If no other movies were rented during that two-week period, and there were A action movies rented, then how many comedies, in terms of A, were rented during that two-week period?

(A) $\dfrac{A}{14}$

(B) $\dfrac{5A}{7}$

(C) $\dfrac{7A}{5}$

(D) $14A$

(E) $35A$

5. D Since the problem never specifies how many videos were rented during the two-week period, this is a good opportunity to Plug In. Rather than plugging in a value for A and trying to determine the total number of videos rented—possible but problematic—let's plug in an easy number, such as 100, for the total, and calculate the rest of the numbers from there.

If a total of 100 videos were rented in the two-week period, then 70 were comedies. Of the remaining 30, there were 5 times as many dramas as action movies, so that means 25 dramas and 5 action movies. We now know both our value for A, 5, and our target answer, 70. Only answer choice D yields 70 when 5 is plugged in for A, so D is the correct answer.

6. x, y, and z are consecutive positive integers such that $x < y < z$. If the units digit of x^2 is 6 and the units digit of y^2 is 9, what is the units digit of z^2?

(A) 0
(B) 1
(C) 2
(D) 4
(E) 5

6. D Because the units digit of x^2 is 6, the units digit of x must be either 4 or 6. Because x, y, and z are consecutive positive integers, the units digit of y must be 5 if the units digit of x is 4. However, the units digit of y *can't* be 5 because the problem tells us that the units digit of y^2 is 9; if the units digit of y were 5, then the units digit of y^2 would also be 5. Therefore, the units digit of x is 6, the units digit of y is 7, and the units digit of z is 8. The units digit of z^2, then, must be 4.

If that seems confusing, why not just Plug In? The units digit of x^2 is 6. Let's say $x^2 = 36$, so $x = 6$. The units digit of y^2 is 9, so let's say $y^2 = 49$ and $y = 7$. If x, y, and z are consecutive positive integers, that makes $z = 8$, and the units digit of $z^2 = 4$.

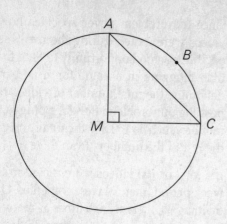

7. What is the area of the circle above with center *M*?

(1) The length of *AC* is $8\sqrt{2}$.
(2) The length of arc *ABC* is 4π .

(A) Statement (1) ALONE is sufficient, but statement (2) alone is not sufficient.
(B) Statement (2) ALONE is sufficient, but statement (1) alone is not sufficient.
(C) BOTH statements TOGETHER are sufficient, but NEITHER statement alone is sufficient.
(D) EACH statement ALONE is sufficient.
(E) Statements (1) and (2) TOGETHER are NOT sufficient.

7. **D** Statement (1) alone is sufficient to answer the question. Ordinarily, having one side of a right triangle isn't enough to solve for all three sides. However, since two of the sides of our triangle are also radii of our circle, this is no ordinary right triangle: It's an isosceles right triangle, also known as a 45–45–90 triangle. As such, knowing that the long side of the triangle is $8\sqrt{2}$ is enough to tell us that the short sides are both 8. Once we know the radius, we can solve for the area—64π, if you were wondering—and we're down to A or D.

Statement (2) alone is also sufficient to answer the question. Arc *ABC*, since it's subtended (or "cut out") by a 90° angle, must represent $\frac{90}{360}$, or $\frac{1}{4}$, of the entire circumference. That gives us an entire circumference of 16π; from the circumference, we can find the radius, 8, and from there the area. The correct answer is D.

MATH BIN 3

QUESTIONS	EXPLANATIONS

8. At a certain school, 60% of the senior class is female. If, among the members of the senior class, 70% of the females and 90% of the males are going on the senior trip, then what percent of the senior class is going on the senior trip?

(A) 82%
(B) 80%
(C) 78%
(D) 76%
(E) 72%

8. C Yet another question about an unspecified amount—in this case, the total number of students in the senior class—which means another opportunity to Plug In. Since the answers are percentages, let's plug in 100 for the total number of seniors. That means we have 60 females, of whom 70%, or 42, are going on the senior trip; they'll be joined by 90% of the 40 males, which gives us 36 males on the trip. That's a total of $42 + 36 = 78$ students who are going on the trip. Seventy-eight out of our senior class of 100 is, of course, 78%, so the correct answer is C.

9. If P is a set of integers and 3 is in P, is every positive multiple of 3 in P?

(1) For any integer in P, the sum of 3 and that integer is also in P. {0,3,6,9,...}

(2) For any integer in P, that integer minus 3 is also in P. {...,-9,-6,-3,0}

(A) Statement (1) ALONE is sufficient, but statement (2) alone is not sufficient.

(B) Statement (2) ALONE is sufficient, but statement (1) alone is not sufficient.

(C) BOTH statements TOGETHER are sufficient, but NEITHER statement alone is sufficient.

(D) EACH statement ALONE is sufficient.

(E) Statements (1) and (2) TOGETHER are NOT sufficient.

(B) Statement (2) ALONE is sufficient, but statement (1) alone is not sufficient.

(C) BOTH statements TOGETHER are suf

9. A To find the answer to this yes-or-no question, try Plugging In to the two statements, starting with the one number that you know is in the set: 3. Statement (1) gives us all the positive multiples of 3. Statement (2) gives us all the negative multiples of 3, plus 0. The correct answer is A. Joe might have picked D.

MATH BIN 3

10. Sarah's seafood restaurant gets a delivery of fresh seafood every day, 7 days per week, and her delivery company charges her d dollars per delivery plus c cents per item delivered. If last week Sarah's seafood restaurant had an average of x items per day delivered, then which of the following is the total cost, in dollars, of last week's deliveries?

(A) $\dfrac{7cdx}{100}$

(B) $d + \dfrac{7cx}{100}$

(C) $7d + \dfrac{xc}{100}$

(D) $7d + \dfrac{7xc}{100}$

(E) $7cdx$

10. **D** Since the answer choices are full of variables, this is a good place to Plug In. Let's make $d = 10$, $c = 200$ (a particularly helpful number, because it allows us to work the problem in whole dollar amounts), and $x = 5$. If Sarah had an average of 5 items per day delivered, then she had a total of 35 items delivered for the week. Multiplied by the 200 cents (or $2) charge per item, that's a total of $70 in per-item charges. When we add that amount to the $70 total for the per-delivery charges—7 deliveries at $10 per delivery—we get a total of $140 for the week. Our target answer, then, is 140; only D gives us 140 when we plug our values into our answer choices, and, therefore, D is the correct answer.

If you got C, by the way, check your calculations for your target answer. You likely calculated the per-item charges as though x were the total, rather than the daily average, of the items delivered.

MATH BIN 3

QUESTIONS	EXPLANATIONS

11. The arithmetic mean of a data set is 46 and the standard deviation of the set is 4. Which of the following contains the interval two standard deviations from the mean of the set?

- (A) 38 to 46
- (B) 38 to 54
- (C) 42 to 50
- (D) 44 to 48
- (E) 46 to 50

11. **B** Standard deviation is the measure of how greatly the individual elements in a data set vary from the arithmetic mean of the set. As a general rule, the more widely dispersed the data in a set, the greater the standard deviation.

You don't need to know how to calculate standard deviation on the GMAT. You do need to know that standard deviation is measured from the arithmetic mean of a data set. If a data set has an arithmetic mean of 10 and a standard deviation of 2, then 8 and 12 are the values that are exactly one standard deviation from the arithmetic mean of the set.

In this problem, the standard deviation is 4, and the question asks for an interval that covers two standard deviations from the arithmetic mean of 46. It's key here to remember that "two standard deviations" means two *in each direction*—that is, both above *and* below the mean. Thus, we need an interval that covers 2 × 4, or 8, from the mean in each direction: 46 − 8 = 38, so the bottom end of the interval is 38, and 46 + 8 = 54, so the top end of the interval is 54. The correct answer is B.

If you chose A, by the way, you only accounted for the two standard deviations below the mean. If you chose E, you only accounted for the two standard deviations above the mean. And if you chose C, you forgot to take two in each direction.

MATH BIN 3

12. If *a* and *b* are positive integers, is *a* a multiple of *b*?

> (1) Every prime factor of *b* is also a prime factor of *a*.

> (2) Every factor of *b* is also a factor of *a*.

> (A) Statement (1) ALONE is sufficient, but statement (2) alone is not sufficient.

> (B) Statement (2) ALONE is sufficient, but statement (1) alone is not sufficient.

> (C) BOTH statements TOGETHER are sufficient, but NEITHER statement alone is sufficient.

> (D) EACH statement ALONE is sufficient.

> (E) Statements (1) and (2) TOGETHER are NOT sufficient.

12. **B** To solve this yes-or-no problem, your best bet is to plug in values that meet the requirements given in the statements to determine whether Plugging In always yields the same answer to our question.

For Statement (1), for example, we could plug in 4 for both *a* and *b*—that's one easy way to make sure that every prime factor of *b* is also a prime factor of *a*—and since every number is a multiple of itself, our answer is "yes." However, if we leave *b* = 4 but make *a* = 2, we can still meet the requirement of Statement (1)—4 has only one prime factor, 2, which is also a prime factor of 2—but now our answer is "no." Since Statement (1) yields different answers, it's insufficient, and we're down to B, C, or E.

Similar attempts in Statement (2), however, will always yield the answer "yes." We could, of course, again plug in 4 for both variables, and we have our first "yes." If we leave *b* = 4, though, we can't make *a* = 2, since 4 isn't a factor of 2; *a* will have to be 4 (which we've already used), 4, 12, 16, or some other number that has 1, 2, and 4 as factors. Whichever one we pick, though, our answer is "yes"; Statement (2) is therefore sufficient, and the answer to the problem is B.

QUESTIONS	EXPLANATIONS

13. Set X contains 10 consecutive integers. If the sum of the 5 smallest members of Set X is 265, then what is the sum of the 5 largest members of Set X?

(A) 290
(B) 285
(C) 280
(D) 275
(E) 270

13. **A** We *could* solve this problem algebraically, although it's a bit of a chore. If we assign x to represent the smallest integer in the set, then $x + (x + 1) + (x + 2) + (x + 3) + (x + 4) = 265$, so $5x + 10 = 265$, $5x = 255$, and $x = 51$. The five smaller consecutive integers are thus 51 through 55; we can now add our five larger consecutive integers, which must be 56 through 60. Our total is 290, and the correct answer is A.

A much simpler way to solve the problem, though, is to recognize that the difference between the sums of *any* two adjacent sets of five consecutive integers will be the same; we can, therefore, find this difference using much easier numbers, and then add this difference to the total given in the problem. The sum of the integers from 1 to 5 is 15, and the sum of the integers from 6 to 10 is 40; our difference, thus, is 25, and $265 + 25 = 290$.

MATH BIN 3

14. If $a - b = c$, what is the value of b?

(1) $c + 6 = a$
(2) $a = 6$

(A) Statement (1) ALONE is sufficient, but statement (2) alone is not sufficient.

(B) Statement (2) ALONE is sufficient, but statement (1) alone is not sufficient.

(C) BOTH statements TOGETHER are sufficient, but NEITHER statement alone is sufficient.

(D) EACH statement ALONE is sufficient.

(E) Statements (1) and (2) TOGETHER are NOT sufficient.

14. **A** Consider Statement (1) on its own. It tells you that $c + 6 = a$; this information allows you to rewrite the equation in the question stem $(a - b = c)$, substituting $c + 6$ for a to come up with the equation $c + 6 - b = c$. Simplify the equation by combining like terms. You will see that the c's cancel out, leaving you with the equation $b = 6$. Statement (1) is sufficient, and the answer must be A or D. Statement (2) provides information about only one of the three variables in the original equation, so it cannot be sufficient on its own. The correct answer must be A.

MATH BIN 3

QUESTIONS	EXPLANATIONS

QUESTIONS

$$\{3, 5, 9, 13, y\}$$

15. If the average (arithmetic mean) of the set of numbers above is equal to the median of the same set of numbers above, then what is the value of y?

(A) 7
(B) 8
(C) 10
(D) 15
(E) 17

16. A foot race will be held on Saturday. How many different arrangements of medal winners are possible?

(1) Medals will be given for 1st, 2nd, and 3rd place.

(2) There are 10 runners in the race.

(A) Statement (1) ALONE is sufficient, but statement (2) alone is not sufficient.

(B) Statement (2) ALONE is sufficient, but statement (1) alone is not sufficient.

(C) Both statements TOGETHER are sufficient, but NEITHER statement ALONE is sufficient.

(D) EACH statement ALONE is sufficient.

(E) Statements (1) and (2) TOGETHER are NOT sufficient.

EXPLANATIONS

15. **D** You could no doubt set up some kind of an equation here, but it's much easier to Plug In the Answers. Let's assume for a minute that the correct answer was choice C, 10. So now, just substitute 10 for y in the problem. The average of the numbers $\{3, 5, 9, 13, 10\}$ is 8, but the median of those numbers is 9. Eliminate it. Can you tell which way to go, up or down? If you're not sure, just pick a direction and try. Let's assume for a minute that the correct answer was choice D, 15. The average of the numbers $\{3, 5, 9, 13, 15\}$ is 9, and the median of those numbers is—Bingo!—also 9. We're done. The correct answer is choice D.

16. **C** This is a permutation problem. Looking at Statement (1), it might seem enough to know that medals will be awarded for 1st, 2nd, and 3rd place. Unwary test takers might assume that there are $3 \times 2 \times 1$ possible arrangements of medal winners. But until we know the number of runners, we don't know enough. We're down to BCE.

Statement (2) tells us the number of runners. An unwary test taker might either assume all runners get medals (in which case the answer would be 10! permutations) or subconsciously assume that we already know there are 3 possible medals and pick B, but we don't know this without Statement (1). We're down to C or E.

Putting the two statements together, we can now find out how many different arrangements of medal winners there are: 10 times 9 times 8. The correct answer is C.

MATH BIN 3

$\{x, y, z\}$

17. If the first term in the data set above is 3, what is the third term?

    (1) The range of this data set is 0.

    (2) The standard deviation of this data set is 0.

    (A) Statement (1) ALONE is sufficient, but statement (2) alone is not sufficient.

    (B) Statement (2) ALONE is sufficient, but statement (1) alone is not sufficient.

    (C) Both statements TOGETHER are sufficient, but NEITHER statement ALONE is sufficient.

    (D) EACH statement ALONE is sufficient.

    (E) Statements (1) and (2) TOGETHER are NOT sufficient.

17. D The range of any data set is equal to the largest item in the set minus the smallest. Statement (1) gives us a value for the range. If that value were anything other than 0, we would not be able to solve the problem based only on this statement. After all, if the range was, say, 7, how could we know which of the three terms (x, y, or z) was the biggest and which was the smallest? However, because Statement (1) tells us that the range is 0, we actually know more than you might think about these three numbers. Because the problem tells us that x must equal 3, let's plug in values for y and z, just to see what happens. For example, if y and z both equal 5, will the range still equal 0? Nope. It would have to be the largest number (5) minus the smallest (2). When you start plugging in numbers, you realize that the only way for the range of these three numbers to be 0 is if each of the numbers is exactly the same. And because we know x equals 3, that means both y and z must equal 3 as well. We're down to AD.

Statement (2) tells us that all the values in the data set correspond exactly to the arithmetic mean—which tells us that x, y, and z are all equal to 3. The correct answer is choice D.

18. To fill a number of vacancies, an employer must hire 3 programmers from among 6 applicants, and 2 managers from among 4 applicants. What is the total number of ways in which she can make her selection?

    (A) 1,490
    (B)   132
    (C)   120
    (D)   60
    (E)   23

18. C In this combination problem, the employer's choice of a programmer can be written as

$$\frac{6!}{3!3!} \qquad \frac{6 \times 5 \times 4}{3 \times 2 \times 1} \text{ or } 20$$

The employer's choice of a manager can be written as

$$\frac{4!}{2!2!} \qquad \frac{4 \times 3}{2 \times 1} \text{ or } 6$$

To find the total number of ways she could make her selection, multiply the respective number of possibilities. 6 times 20 = 120. The correct answer is choice C.

MATH BIN 3

QUESTIONS	EXPLANATIONS

19. On Monday, a certain animal shelter housed 55 cats and dogs. By Friday, exactly $\frac{1}{5}$ of the cats and $\frac{1}{4}$ of the dogs had been adopted; no new cats or dogs were brought to the shelter during this period. What is the greatest possible number of pets that could have been adopted from the animal shelter between Monday and Friday?

   (A)   11
   (B)   12
   (C)   13
   (D)   14
   (E)   20

19. C The question asks you for the hypothetical greatest number of animals that could have been adopted from the shelter within the parameters of the problem. Because a greater proportion of dogs than cats was adopted, you should seek a scenario that maximizes the number of dogs adopted. You must also satisfy the other conditions of the problem, however; the number of cats, for example, must be a multiple of 5, because that is the only way that $\frac{1}{5}$ of the cats can be adopted (assuming, of course, that the shelter requires people to adopt an entire cat, not just a fractional part of one).

Because we want to maximize the number of dogs in the shelter, let's start assuming the minimum possible number of cats, 5. This would leave 50 dogs in the shelter. This solution, unfortunately, is impossible; because 50 is not evenly divisible by 4, there cannot be 50 dogs in the shelter. Could there be 10 cats at the shelter? No, because this would leave 45 dogs, again making it impossible for exactly $\frac{1}{4}$ of the dogs to be adopted. 15 cats is the magic number, as it means there are 40 dogs. $\left(\frac{1}{5} \times 15\right) + \left(\frac{1}{4} \times 40\right) = 3 + 10 = 13$ animals. The correct answer is C.

MATH BIN 3

20. If x is an integer, then which of the following statements about $x^2 - x - 1$ is true?

    (A) It is always odd.
    (B) It is always even.
    (C) It is always positive.
    (D) It is even when x is even and odd when x is odd.
    (E) It is even when x is odd and odd when x is even.

20. **A** Because x is an integer, x must be either even or odd. If x is even, then $x^2 - x$ must also be even, and therefore $x^2 - x - 1$ is always odd. If x is odd, then $x^2 - x$ must be even, and again $x^2 - x - 1$ is always odd.

You can also solve this problem by Plugging In. After plugging in several values for x and calculating $x^2 - x - 1$, you will discover that the result is always odd.

21. During a five-day period, Monday through Friday, the average (arithmetic mean) high temperature was 86 degrees Fahrenheit. What was the high temperature on Friday?

    (1) The average high temperature for Monday through Thursday was 87 degrees Fahrenheit.
    (2) The high temperature on Friday reduced the average high temperature for the week by 1 degree Fahrenheit.

    (A) Statement (1) ALONE is sufficient, but statement (2) alone is not sufficient.
    (B) Statement (2) ALONE is sufficient, but statement (1) alone is not sufficient.
    (C) BOTH statements TOGETHER are sufficient, but NEITHER statement alone is sufficient.
    (D) EACH statement ALONE is sufficient.
    (E) Statements (1) and (2) TOGETHER are NOT sufficient.

21. **D** The question stem tells us that the average high temperature for the five-day period was 86°; therefore, the sum of the high temperatures for those days was $5 \times 86 = 430°$. Statement (1) tells us that the average high temperature for the first four days was 87°; therefore, the sum of the high temperatures for those days was $4 \times 87 = 348°$. $430 - 348 = 82°$, the high temperature on Friday. Statement (1) is sufficient; the answer must be A or D.

Statement (2) tells us that Friday's temperature reduced the average high for the five-day period by 1 degree. This means that the average high for the first four days was 87°; thus, (2) is sufficient for the same reason that (1) is sufficient. The correct answer is D.

MATH BIN 3

22. What is the value of $x^2 - y^2$?

   (1) $x + y = 0$

   (2) $x - y = 2$

   (A)   Statement (1) ALONE is sufficient, but statement (2) alone is not sufficient.

   (B)   Statement (2) ALONE is sufficient, but statement (1) alone is not sufficient.

   (C)   BOTH statements TOGETHER are sufficient, but NEITHER statement alone is sufficient.

   (D)   EACH statement ALONE is sufficient.

   (E)   Statements (1) and (2) TOGETHER are NOT sufficient.

23. If P is the perimeter of an equilateral triangle, which of the following represents the height of the triangle?

   (A) $\dfrac{P}{3}$

   (B) $\dfrac{P\sqrt{3}}{3}$

   (C) $\dfrac{P}{4}$

   (D) $\dfrac{P\sqrt{3}}{6}$

   (E) $\dfrac{P}{6}$

22. **A**   Don't get caught making a careless assumption on this question. You may have immediately recognized that $x^2 - y^2$ factors to $(x + y)(x - y)$. Seeing that Statement (1) provides a value for $(x + y)$ and Statement (2) provides a value for $(x - y)$, you might have automatically assumed that the correct answer to this question is C. Look more closely, however; Statement (1) tells you that $(x + y) = 0$. Zero times any number equals zero; therefore, Statement (1) is sufficient to tell you that $(x + y)(x - y) = 0$. The correct answer is A.

23. **D**   This is an excellent Plugging In problem. Plug in a value that is easily divisible by 3 for P; let's use 18. That would make the length of each side of the equilateral triangle 6.

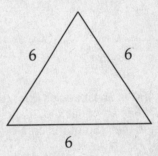

Draw a height for the triangle. Note that the height of an equilateral triangle divides the triangle into two 30–60–90 triangles.

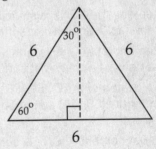

Now you can use the formula for the sides of a 30–60–90 triangle to determine that the height of the triangle is $3\sqrt{3}$ when $P = 18$. Finally, simply plug in 18 for P in every answer choice and eliminate those that do not yield a result of $3\sqrt{3}$. The correct answer is D.

MATH BIN 3

QUESTIONS	EXPLANATIONS

24. If 75 percent of all Americans own an automobile, 15 percent of all Americans own a bicycle, and 20 percent of all Americans own neither an automobile nor a bicycle, what percent of Americans own *both* an automobile and a bicycle?

    (A)   0 percent
    (B)   1.33 percent
    (C)   3.75 percent
    (D)   5 percent
    (E)   10 percent

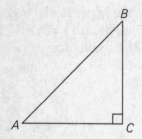 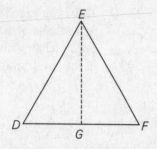

25. Triangle *ABC* is an isosceles right triangle; triangle *DEF* is an equilateral triangle with height *EG*. What is the ratio of the area of *ABC* to the area of *DEF*?

    (1)   The ratio of *BC* to *EG* is 1:1.

    (2)   The ratio of *AC* to *DF* is $\sqrt{3}$:2.

    (A)   Statement (1) ALONE is sufficient, but statement (2) alone is not sufficient.

    (B)   Statement (2) ALONE is sufficient, but statement (1) alone is not sufficient.

    (C)   BOTH statements TOGETHER are sufficient, but NEITHER statement alone is sufficient.

    (D)   EACH statement ALONE is sufficient.

    (E)   Statements (1) and (2) TOGETHER are NOT sufficient.

24. E These problems are a lot easier to solve than they appear to be at first glance. Remember, when you're done adding all these percentages, they have to add up to exactly 100. The numbers given us in the problem add up to 110. Why? Because some people are counted twice. Who are these people? Why, the folks who own bicycles AND automobiles, of course. They are the "extra" 10%. 65% of Americans own an automobile but no bicycle; 5% own only a bicycle; 10% own both; and 20% own neither. The correct answer is E.

25. D The formula for the area of a triangle, of course, is $\frac{base \times height}{2}$. Therefore, if we know the ratio of the bases and the heights of these triangles, it would be safe to assume that we know enough to calculate the ratios of their areas. This makes C a very tempting answer, because Statement (1) provides the ratio of the heights of the two triangles and Statement (2) provides the ratio of the bases of the two triangles. Well, now, if it were that easy, it wouldn't be in Bin 3, would it?

The reason that the answer to this question is D lies in the special nature of isosceles right triangles and equilateral triangles. Their sides are in a fixed proportion to one another, so when you have information about one side, you have of information about all sides and, consequently, the area of the triangles. For this reason, each statement is sufficient on its own.

To prove that to yourself, you can plug in values for the sides of the triangles. For example, in Statement (1), the ratio of *BC* to *EG* is 1 to 1. So, let's say *BC* and *EG* are both one meter long. Since *ABC* is isosceles, that means *AC* = 1, too, and the area of *ABC* is $\frac{1}{2}$. Since *DEF* is equilateral, that means *DG* and *GF* are each $\sqrt{3}$, and *DF* is $2\sqrt{3}$. Therefore, we can find the area of *DEF* ($\sqrt{3}$).

MATH BIN 3

QUESTIONS	EXPLANATIONS

26. What is the value of integer x?

    (1) $\sqrt[x]{64} = 4$

    (2) $x^2 = 2x + 8$

    (A) Statement (1) ALONE is sufficient, but statement (2) alone is not sufficient.

    (B) Statement (2) ALONE is sufficient, but statement (1) alone is not sufficient.

    (C) BOTH statements TOGETHER are sufficient, but NEITHER statement alone is sufficient.

    (D) EACH statement ALONE is sufficient.

    (E) Statements (1) and (2) TOGETHER are NOT sufficient.

26. **A** The only one solution to the equation in Statement (1) is $x = 3$. (If this is unclear, review radicals in the Arithmetic section of this book.) Therefore, the answer to this question must be A or D.

To determine whether (2) is sufficient, subtract $2x + 8$ from both sides of the equation to get

$$x^2 - 2x - 8 = 0$$

This equation can be factored to

$$(x - 4)(x + 2) = 0$$

Thus, the equation has two solutions: x can equal 4 or –2. Statement (2) is not sufficient. The correct answer is A.

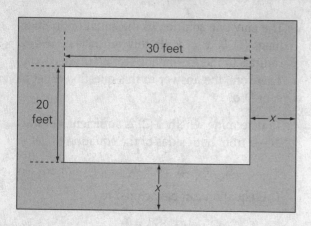

1. Martin planted a rectangular garden with dimensions 20 feet by 30 feet and then surrounded the garden with a rectangular brick walkway of uniform width (represented by the shaded area in the drawing above). If the area of the walkway equals the area of the garden, what is the width of the walkway?

   (A)   1 foot
   (B)   3 feet
   (C)   5 feet
   (D)   8 feet
   (E)   10 feet

1. **C**   To answer this question, first recognize that the area of the walkway can be calculated by subtracting the area of the smaller (white) rectangle from the larger rectangle in the figure. The difference between the areas of the two rectangles equals the area of the shaded region. This problem is ideal for Plugging In the Answers. Start with answer choice C; if it is incorrect, you may be able to tell whether it is too large or too small, and you will be able to eliminate not only C, but also two other answers.

   If C is correct, then the walkway is 5 feet wide. With a walkway of that width, the dimensions of the large rectangle in the figure are 30 feet (the width of the garden—20 feet—plus 5 feet on each side to account for the width of the walkway) by 40 feet (the length of the garden—30 feet—plus 5 feet on each side to account for the width of the walkway). The area of the large rectangle, then, is 40 × 30 = 1,200 square feet, and the area of the shaded region is 1,200 – (20 × 30) = 1,200 – 600 = 600 square feet.

   When the width of the walkway is 5 feet, the area of the walkway equals the area of the garden. That's the result we're looking for, so the correct answer is C.

MATH BIN 4

QUESTIONS	EXPLANATIONS

2. A fair 2-sided coin is flipped 6 times. What is the probability that tails will be the result at least twice, but not more than 5 times?

(A) $\dfrac{5}{8}$

(B) $\dfrac{3}{4}$

(C) $\dfrac{7}{8}$

(D) $\dfrac{57}{64}$

(E) $\dfrac{15}{16}$

2. **C** As is often the case with difficult probability questions, the bottom part of our fraction—the total number of possibilities—is a permutation problem in itself. In this case, we need to figure out how many different outcomes we can get if we flip a coin 6 times. Since we have 6 events with 2 possible outcomes each, our total number of different outcomes is $2 \times 2 \times 2 \times 2 \times 2 \times 2$, or 2^6, or 64. Now we just need to figure out how many of those possibilities meet the requirement.

For this problem, however, since there are so many different ways to meet the requirement, we'll be better off figuring out how many outcomes *don't* meet our requirement; we can then subtract this number from the total of 64. There are only three ways to *not* meet the requirement of 2 to 5 tails on 6 flips—we could get 0, 1, or 6 tails—and these can be quickly and easily counted out. There is only one way to get 6 tails, and, likewise, there is only one way to get 0 tails, which is another way of saying 6 heads. That's two. And there are only six different ways to get tails once: The single tails can come up in the first spot, the second spot, and so on. That's 8 out of our total of 64 possible outcomes that don't meet our requirement, so 56 do. The probability, therefore, is $\dfrac{56}{64}$, which reduces to $\dfrac{7}{8}$. The correct answer is C.

MATH BIN 4

3. The members of the newest recruiting class of a certain military organization are taking their physical conditioning test, and those who score in the bottom 16% will have to retest. If the scores are normally distributed, and have an arithmetic mean of 72, what is the score at or below which the recruits will have to retest?

(1) There are 500 recruits in the class.

(2) 10 recruits scored 82 or higher.

(A) Statement (1) ALONE is sufficient, but statement (2) alone is not sufficient.
(B) Statement (2) ALONE is sufficient, but statement (1) alone is not sufficient.
(C) BOTH statements TOGETHER are sufficient, but NEITHER statement alone is sufficient.
(D) EACH statement ALONE is sufficient.
(E) Statements (1) and (2) TOGETHER are NOT sufficient.

3. **C** Statement (1) is not alone sufficient to answer the question. It does let us determine *how many* recruits will have to retake the test, but we don't know anything about their scores. We're down to B, C, or E. Statement (2) alone is also insufficient—while those 10 recruits are certainly impressive, we don't know what part of the overall recruiting class they represent. We're down to C or E.

When we combine our statements, though, we do have enough information to answer the question. We can now calculate that those 10 top-scoring recruits make up the top 2% of the class as a whole—and since the scores are normally distributed, the top 2% represents the third standard deviation above the mean. If the mean is 72, and the third standard deviation above the mean begins at 82, then there are 2 standard deviations (the first and the second) between 72 and 82. The dividing line between them, then, must fall at the score halfway between 72 and 82, or 77. We now know the entire upper half of the curve: The first standard deviation runs from the mean of 72 to 77; the second standard deviation runs from 77 to 82; and the third standard deviation runs from 82 to 87. More important, we now know that one standard deviation equals 5 points, so that bottom 16%—also known as the second and third standard deviation below the mean—are those that score at or below 67. The correct answer is C.

MATH BIN 4

QUESTIONS	EXPLANATIONS

4. Jerome wrote each of the integers 1 through 20, inclusive, on a separate index card. He placed the cards in a box, then drew cards one at a time randomly from the box, without returning the cards he had already drawn to the box. In order to ensure that the sum of all the cards he drew was even, how many cards did Jerome have to draw?

(A) 19
(B) 12
(C) 11
(D) 10
(E) 3

4. **B** To determine how many cards Jerome must draw to achieve his desired goal, determine the worst-case scenario. How many cards could Jerome draw and still *not* have a pile of cards whose face values added up to an even number? His first card, obviously, would have to be an odd-numbered card. If he then drew an even-numbered card for his second card, the sum of the drawn cards would be odd. If he then drew *another* even-numbered card for his third card, the sum would still be odd. As long as Jerome kept drawing even-numbered cards, he would not have a pile of cards whose face values added up to an even number. In the worst-case scenario, then, Jerome would draw one odd-numbered card, then all ten even-numbered cards. At this point, he would have drawn 11 cards and still not have achieved his desired goal. The twelfth card, however, would *have* to be odd, which would make the sum of the 12 cards even. Therefore, Jerome must draw 12 cards to ensure that the sum of *all* the cards he draws is an even number.

MATH BIN 4

5. The average (arithmetic mean) of integers r, s, t, u, and v is 100. Are exactly two of the integers greater than 100?

(1) Three of the integers are less than 50.
(2) None of the integers is equal to 100.

(A) Statement (1) ALONE is sufficient, but statement (2) alone is not sufficient.

(B) Statement (2) ALONE is sufficient, but statement (1) alone is not sufficient.

(C) BOTH statements TOGETHER are sufficient, but NEITHER statement alone is sufficient.

(D) EACH statement ALONE is sufficient.

(E) Statements (1) and (2) TOGETHER are NOT sufficient.

5. **E** This is a yes-or-no question. Statement (1) tells us that three of the five integers are less than 50. This information by itself does not ensure that the other two integers *are* greater than 100. Both remaining values *could* be greater than 100; the solution set {10, 20, 30, 140, 300}, for example, satisfies this condition. However, the set {1, 2, 3, 4, 490} *also* satisfies the conditions of the problem, and it contains only one value greater than 100. Statement (1) is insufficient on its own; the correct answer must be B, C, or E. Statement (2) tells us only that none of the integers is equal to 100. By itself, this is clearly not sufficient to tell us that exactly two of the integers are greater than 100; eliminate answer B immediately. In fact, the statement provides no more useful information than that provided in Statement (1); both of the solutions provided above satisfy this statement as well. The purpose of this statement is to catch someone who might be tempted to choose C, thinking that Statement (1) would be sufficient if only it ensured that none of the remaining integers was equal to 100, and therefore *must* be greater than 100. That, of course, is an erroneous conclusion, as demonstrated by the counterexample provided in the previous paragraph. The correct answer is E.

MATH BIN 4

QUESTIONS	EXPLANATIONS

QUESTIONS

6. Paul jogs at a constant rate for 80 minutes along the same route every day. How long is the route?

(1) Yesterday, Paul began jogging at 5:00 P.M.

(2) Yesterday, Paul had jogged 5 miles by 5:40 P.M. and 8 miles by 6:04 P.M.

(A) Statement (1) ALONE is sufficient, but statement (2) alone is not sufficient.

(B) Statement (2) ALONE is sufficient, but statement (1) alone is not sufficient.

(C) BOTH statements TOGETHER are sufficient, but NEITHER statement alone is sufficient.

(D) EACH statement ALONE is sufficient.

(E) Statements (1) and (2) TOGETHER are NOT sufficient.

EXPLANATIONS

6. **B** Statement (1) clearly is not sufficient to answer the question "How long is the route along which Paul jogs?" because it tells us only Paul's starting time. The correct answer to this question must be B, C, or E. Statement (2) tells us that Paul had jogged 5 miles by 5:40 P.M. and 8 miles by 6:04 P.M. You might be tempted to answer C at this point; after all, you now know when Paul began jogging and how far he had jogged at various intervals, so you could easily figure out how far he had run by 6:20 P.M., the end of the 80-minute period beginning at 5:00 P.M. Resist the temptation; it is the voice of none other than Joe Bloggs himself telling you to choose C. Let's look more closely at Statement (2). It tells us that Paul covered 3 miles between 5:40 P.M. and 6:04 P.M. Thus, we know that Paul ran eight-minute miles during that 24-minute period. The question stem tells us that Paul jogs at a constant rate, and that he jogs for 80 minutes. Therefore, Statement (2), in combination with the question stem, provides all the information we need; Paul jogs eight-minute miles for 80 minutes, so the route along which he jogs is 10 miles long. The correct answer is B.

MATH BIN 4

QUESTIONS	EXPLANATIONS

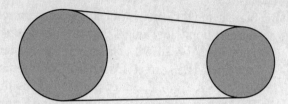

7. The diagram above shows two wheels that drive a conveyor belt. The larger wheel has a diameter of 40 centimeters; the smaller wheel has a diameter of 32 centimeters. In order for the conveyor belt to run smoothly, each wheel must rotate the exact same number of centimeters per minute. If the larger wheel makes r revolutions per minute, how many revolutions does the smaller wheel make per hour, in terms of r?

(A) $\dfrac{1{,}280\pi}{3}$

(B) $75r$

(C) $48r$

(D) $24r$

(E) $\dfrac{64\pi}{3}$

7. **B** Because the problem has variables in the answer choice, Plugging In is a great way to solve. Plug in an easy number, one that will make your calculations and answer checking simple. For the purposes of this explanation, let's set r equal to 2. With each rotation, each wheel rotates the length of its circumference. Thus, the wheel with diameter 40 centimeters rotates 40π centimeters with each rotation; the wheel with diameter 32 centimeters rotates 32π centimeters with each rotation. The larger wheel makes r revolutions per minute; because we've set r equal to 2, it makes 2 revolutions per minute and thus rotates 80π centimeters per minute. According to the problem, the smaller wheel must rotate the same distance; otherwise, the conveyor belt will not run smoothly. Therefore, the smaller wheel also rotates 80π centimeters per minute, meaning it rotates $60 \times 80\pi = 4{,}800\pi$ centimeters per hour. The smaller wheel covers 32π centimeters per rotation, so it must rotate $4{,}800\pi \div 32\pi = 150$ times per hour. Plug 2 in for r in each of the answer choices. Which yields an answer of 150? The correct answer is B, $75r$.

MATH BIN 4

8. An automobile dealership sells only sedans and coupes. It sells each in only two colors: red and blue. Last year, the dealership sold 9,000 vehicles, half of which were red. How many coupes did the dealership sell last year?

(1) The dealership sold three times as many blue coupes as red sedans last year.

(2) The dealership sold half as many blue sedans as blue coupes last year.

(A) Statement (1) ALONE is sufficient, but statement (2) alone is not sufficient.

(B) Statement (2) ALONE is sufficient, but statement (1) alone is not sufficient.

(C) BOTH statements TOGETHER are sufficient, but NEITHER statement alone is sufficient.

(D) EACH statement ALONE is sufficient.

(E) Statements (1) and (2) TOGETHER are NOT sufficient.

---

8. **C** Create a table to solve this proportions question. It should look something like this:

	Red	Blue	TOTAL
Coupes			
Sedans			
TOTAL	4,500	4,500	9,000

The question stem tells us how many cars were sold last year. Because it tells us that half the cars sold were red, it also tells us the number of red and blue cars sold last year.

Statement (1) tells us: "The dealership sold three times as many blue coupes as red sedans last year." Enter this information into the table in algebraic terms:

	Red	Blue	TOTAL
Coupes		3x	
Sedans	x		
TOTAL	4,500	4,500	9,000

Because two unknowns—red coupes and blue sedans—remain, Statement (1) does not provide enough information to solve the problem. The correct answer must be B, C, or E.

Use the same procedure to test Statement (2): "The dealership sold half as many blue sedans as blue coupes last year":

	Red	Blue	TOTAL
Coupes		2x	
Sedans		x	
TOTAL	4,500	4,500	9,000

Again, two unknowns remain. *This* time, though, we have all the information we need to write a solvable equation. We know that $2x + x = 4,500$. Therefore x equals 1,500. We now know the following:

	Red	Blue	TOTAL
Coupes		3,000	
Sedans		1,500	
TOTAL	4,500	4,500	9,000

Unfortunately, this still isn't enough information to answer the question "How many coupes did the dealership sell last year?" The answer must be C or E. Combine the information from the two statements. Statement (2) tells us that the dealership sold 3,000 blue coupes; combined with Statement (1), this tells us that the dealership sold 1,000 red sedans. We can now subtract 1,000 from 4,500 to determine that the dealership sold 3,500 red coupes. Therefore, it sold 6,500 coupes last year. The correct answer is C.

MATH BIN 4

QUESTIONS	EXPLANATIONS

9. At a college football game, $\frac{4}{5}$ of the seats in the lower deck of the stadium were sold. If $\frac{1}{4}$ of all the seating in the stadium is located in the lower deck, and if $\frac{2}{3}$ of all the seats in the stadium were sold, what fraction of the unsold seats in the stadium were in the lower deck?

(A) $\frac{3}{20}$

(B) $\frac{1}{6}$

(C) $\frac{1}{5}$

(D) $\frac{1}{3}$

(E) $\frac{7}{15}$

9. **A** Solve this one as a cosmic Plugging In. First, plug in a number of seats for the entire stadium. Choose a number that divides easily by 3, 4, and 5. For the purposes of this explanation, let's say the stadium seats 60,000 people. The problem states that $\frac{2}{3}$ of all the seating in the stadium was sold, meaning that 40,000 of the 60,000 seats were sold. It also states that $\frac{1}{4}$ of the seating is located in the lower deck. Because $\frac{1}{4}$ of 60,000 is 15,000, that means the stadium has 15,000 seats in the lower deck. Of those 15,000 seats, according to the problem, $\frac{4}{5}$, or 12,000, were sold. The question asks what fraction of the unsold seats in the stadium were in the lower deck. Because 40,000 seats were sold in the entire stadium, a total of 20,000 were unsold; of the 20,000 unsold seats, 15,000 − 12,000 = 3,000 were in the lower deck. The fraction $\frac{3,000}{20,000}$ reduces to $\frac{3}{20}$, so the correct answer is A.

MATH BIN 4

QUESTIONS	EXPLANATIONS

10. At Company R, the average (arithmetic mean) age of executive employees is 54 years old and the average age of non-executive employees is 34 years old. What is the average age of all the employees at Company R?

   (1) There are 10 executive employees at Company R.

   (2) The number of non-executive employees at Company R is four times the number of executive employees at Company R.

   (A) Statement (1) ALONE is sufficient, but statement (2) alone is not sufficient.

   (B) Statement (2) ALONE is sufficient, but statement (1) alone is not sufficient.

   (C) BOTH statements TOGETHER are sufficient, but NEITHER statement alone is sufficient.

   (D) EACH statement ALONE is sufficient.

   (E) Statements (1) and (2) TOGETHER are NOT sufficient.

10. **B** Statement (1) provides no information about the non-executive employees at Company R. Clearly it is not sufficient on its own; the correct answer must be B, C, or E. Statement (2) provides a ratio of executive employees to non-executive employees at Company R. Is this information by itself enough to determine the average age of all the employees? Yes, it is. Regardless of whether Company R has 2 executives and 8 non-executives or 200 executives and 800 non-executives, the resulting average for all employees will be the same, because the proportional contribution of each group to the average will remain fixed. The best way to prove this is simply to plug in some numbers and see for yourself. The average age of 1 executive and 4 non-executives is $\frac{54 + 4(34)}{5} = 38$. The average age of 30 executives and 120 non-executives is $\frac{30(54) + 120(34)}{150} = 38$. Thus, the correct answer is B. Joe Bloggs, by the way, picks C on this problem.

QUESTIONS	EXPLANATIONS

11. If a, b, c, d, and x are all nonzero integers, is the product $ax \times (bx)^2 \times (cx)^3 \times (dx)^4$ positive or negative?

   (1) $a < c < x < 0$

   (2) $b < d < x < 0$

   (A) Statement (1) ALONE is sufficient, but statement (2) alone is not sufficient.

   (B) Statement (2) ALONE is sufficient, but statement (1) alone is not sufficient.

   (C) BOTH statements TOGETHER are sufficient, but NEITHER statement alone is sufficient.

   (D) EACH statement ALONE is sufficient.

   (E) Statements (1) and (2) TOGETHER are NOT sufficient.

11. A   Joe Bloggs probably told you to pick answer choice C on this problem. You knew better than that, though, didn't you? Let's look at Statement (1). It tells us that a, c, and x are negative. Instinctively, we might conclude that this isn't enough information, because it tells us nothing about b or d. Look at the expression in the question stem again, though; b and d appear only in the expressions $(bx)^2$ and $(dx)^4$. Both of these expressions contain even exponents; we know, therefore, that these expressions *must* be positive regardless of the values b and d represent, because nonzero integers taken to an even power are always positive. From Statement (1) we know that ax is positive (a negative times a negative equals a positive) and, similarly, that $(cx)^3$ is positive. Statement (1) is sufficient, and the answer must be A or D. For reasons already explained, Statement (2) provides no valuable information. The correct answer is A.

MATH BIN 4

QUESTIONS	EXPLANATIONS

QUESTIONS

12. A four-character password consists of one letter of the alphabet and three different digits between 0 and 9, inclusive. The letter must appear as the second or third character of the password. How many different passwords are possible?

  (A)   5,040
  (B)   18,720
  (C)   26,000
  (D)   37,440
  (E)   52,000

13. If *x* is a positive integer, is *x* divisible by 48?

  (1)   *x* is divisible by 8.
  (2)   *x* is divisible by 6.

  (A)   Statement (1) ALONE is sufficient, but statement (2) alone is not sufficient.
  (B)   Statement (2) ALONE is sufficient, but statement (1) alone is not sufficient.
  (C)   BOTH statements TOGETHER are sufficient, but NEITHER statement alone is sufficient.
  (D)   EACH statement ALONE is sufficient.
  (E)   Statements (1) and (2) TOGETHER are NOT sufficient.

EXPLANATIONS

12. **D**   According to the problem, an acceptable password consists of either *DLDD* or *DDLD*, where *D* represents a digit and *L* represents a letter of the alphabet. Remember also that the digits must be different. First let's consider *DLDD*. The first character can be any of the ten digits, 0 through 9. The second character can be any of the 26 letters of the alphabet. There are only 9 possible digits for the third character, because the third character may not repeat the digit used for the first character. By the same reasoning, there are only 8 possible digits for the fourth character. Thus, there are $10 \times 26 \times 9 \times 8 = 18{,}720$ possible passwords that follow the *DLDD* pattern. Now consider *DDLD*. There will be an equal number of possible passwords that follow this pattern. The first character can be any of 10 digits; the second character can be any of the 9 remaining digits; the third character can be any of the 26 letters of the alphabet; and the fourth character can be any of the remaining 8 digits. $10 \times 9 \times 26 \times 8 = 18{,}720$. There are $18{,}720 + 18{,}720 = 37{,}440$ different passwords possible, and the correct answer is D.

13. **E**   This is a yes-or-no question, of course. If we plug in numbers for *x* in Statement (1), we will sometimes get a "yes" (by plugging in, for example, 48) and sometimes get a "no" (by plugging in, for example, 16) so we are down to BCE. The same is true with Statement (2). After all, some—but not all—numbers divisible by 6 are also divisible by 48, so Statement (2) also gives us both yes and no answers. The answer must be C or E. Which answer do you think Joe Bloggs would pick? C, probably, because 48 is the product of 6 and 8. He would probably carelessly conclude that any number divisible by both 6 and 8 must also be divisible by 48, thus answering the question with a "yes." Unfortunately, Joe doesn't think about 24, 72, and a whole host of other numbers that are divisible by 6 and 8 but *not* by 48. Even when we combine both statements, the answer to the question is sometimes yes and sometimes no. Therefore, the correct answer is E.

MATH BIN 4

QUESTIONS	EXPLANATIONS

$$
\begin{array}{r}
FGF \\
\times\ G \\
\hline
HGG
\end{array}
$$

14. In the multiplication problem above, *F*, *G*, and *H* represent unique odd digits. What is the value of the three-digit number *FGF*?

(A) 151
(B) 161
(C) 171
(D) 313
(E) 353

14. **A** At first it looks as though you'll have to substitute every odd digit for the three variables until you stumble onto the correct answer, but there's a trick to this problem that eliminates such guesswork. Look at the units column of the problem and you'll see that $F \times G$ yields a product with a units digit of *G*; therefore, it is quite possible that *F* is the identity element, 1. Actually, you can go even further: *F must* equal 1, because *G* cannot equal 1 (otherwise, the product of this multiplication problem would be *FGF*, not *HGG*). Plus, if both *F* and *G* were odd digits greater than 1, the product of this multiplication problem would be a four-digit number. Because the product is the three-digit number *HGG*, *F* must equal 1. Now we know that *F* equals 1. Look at the answer choices; you can now eliminate answer choices D and E, and you also know that *G* must equal 5 or 7 (*G* cannot equal 6 because the problem says *G* must be an odd digit). When *G* equals 7, the product is a four-digit number; therefore, *G* must equal 5, and the correct answer is A. But if all that seemed too complicated, you could have just plugged the answer choices into the problem, one at a time, to see which one works. The correct answer would still be A.

15. A group of 20 friends formed an investment club, with each member contributing an equal amount to the general fund. The club then invested the entire fund, which amounted to *d* dollars, in Stock X. The value of the stock subsequently increased 40 percent, at which point the stock was sold and the proceeds divided evenly among the members. In terms of *d*, how much money did each member of the club receive from the sale? (Assume that transaction fees and other associated costs were negligible.)

(A) 800*d*

(B) $\dfrac{7d}{5}$

(C) $\dfrac{d}{20} + 40$

(D) $\dfrac{d}{2}$

(E) $\dfrac{7d}{100}$

15. **E** The variables in the answer choices should tell you that this is a great problem for Plugging In. Choose a value easily divisible by 20 (the number of friends in the group) and one for which percentages are easy to calculate (because the value of the stock increases by a percentage). For the purpose of this explanation, let's set *d* equal to 100. The general fund of $100, then, was invested in Stock X, which subsequently increased in value by 40 percent; thus, its value increased to $140. At this point, the club sold the stock and divvied up the proceeds. Each member received $140 ÷ 20 = $7 in the process. Therefore, when *d* equals 100, the correct answer choice will yield a result of 7. Check each answer choice, Plugging In 100 for *d*. The correct answer is E.

QUESTIONS	EXPLANATIONS

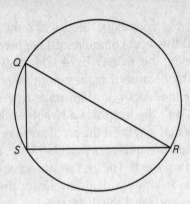

16. Triangle *QSR* is inscribed in a semi-circle. Is *QSR* a right triangle?

(1) *QR* is a diameter of the circle.
(2) Length *QS* equals 3 and length *QR* equals 5.

(A) Statement (1) ALONE is sufficient, but statement (2) alone is not sufficient.

(B) Statement (2) ALONE is sufficient, but statement (1) alone is not sufficient.

(C) BOTH statements TOGETHER are sufficient, but NEITHER statement alone is sufficient.

(D) EACH statement ALONE is sufficient.

(E) Statements (1) and (2) TOGETHER are NOT sufficient.

16. **A** This problem requires you to clear two hurdles. First, you must remember a rule about inscribed angles in semi-circles. Then, you must avoid succumbing to the power of suggestion. First, the rule about inscribed angles. Statement (1) tells us that *QR* is a diameter of the circle. The question stem tells us that triangle *QSR* is inscribed; thus ∠*QSR* is inscribed. A triangle inscribed in a semi-circle is always a right triangle. Therefore, ∠*QSR* measures 90°. Statement (1) is sufficient, and the correct answer must be A or D. Statement (2) can trick you if you don't forget all about Statement (1) first. It suggests that *QSR* is a right triangle, because the ratio of *QS* to *QR* recall the familiar 3-4-5 triangle that satisfies the Pythagorean theorem. However, Statement (2) does not preclude the possibility that *QR* is *not* a diameter and that therefore side *SR* does *not* measure 4. There is no way to determine from this information whether *QSR* is a right triangle. The correct answer is A.

MATH BIN 4

QUESTIONS	EXPLANATIONS

17. Jolene began building a picket fence by planting stakes in a row; the stakes were evenly spaced. After planting the first 10 stakes, Jolene measured the length of the row and found that the row was 27 feet long. She continued the row by planting another 10 stakes, then measured the length of the entire row. How many feet long was the row of stakes Jolene had planted?

(A) 37
(B) 54
(C) 57
(D) 60
(E) 81

17. **C** Your old friend Joe Bloggs should help you avoid the most common mistake here; namely, choosing the answer B, 54. This answer is appealing because it makes intuitive sense; after all, if the length of a ten-stake row is 27 feet, shouldn't the length of a twenty-stake row be twice that length? If the problem were that easy, though, this question wouldn't be in Bin 4. Get rid of answer B. The best way to solve this problem is to draw a diagram. Draw the first ten stakes and label the distance:

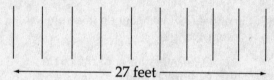

Notice that there are nine intervals between the ten stakes; each interval, then, measures exactly 3 feet ($27 \div 3 = 9$). Now look what happens when you add another ten stakes.

How many intervals are there among these 20 stakes? There are 19, each measuring exactly 3 feet. The length of the twenty-stake row, then, is $19 \times 3 = 57$ feet. The correct answer is C.

QUESTIONS	EXPLANATIONS

18. Square G has sides of length 4 inches. Is the area of Square H exactly one half the area of Square G?

   (1)   The length of the diagonal of Square H equals the length of one side of Square G.

   (2)   The perimeter of Square H is twice the length of the diagonal of Square G.

   (A)   Statement (1) ALONE is sufficient, but statement (2) alone is not sufficient.

   (B)   Statement (2) ALONE is sufficient, but statement (1) alone is not sufficient.

   (C)   BOTH statements TOGETHER are sufficient, but NEITHER statement alone is sufficient.

   (D)   EACH statement ALONE is sufficient.

   (E)   Statements (1) and (2) TOGETHER are NOT sufficient.

18. **D** Statement (1) tells us that the diagonal of Square H is 4 inches long. That is enough information to determine the length of a side of Square H, because the diagonal and two adjacent sides of a square form a 45-45-90 triangle, and the lengths of the sides of a 45-45-90 triangle are always in the proportion $1:1:\sqrt{2}$. One side of Square H has a length of $\frac{4}{\sqrt{2}} = \frac{4\sqrt{2}}{2} = 2\sqrt{2}$ inches. The area of Square H is 8 square inches, which is indeed half the area of Square G. The correct answer must be A or D. Statement (2) mentions the diagonal of Square G, which we know to be $4\sqrt{2}$ inches (the question stem tells us that the length of one side of Square G is 4 inches). Thus, the perimeter of Square H is $8\sqrt{2}$ inches, and the length of one side of Square H is $2\sqrt{2}$ inches. As in Statement (1), this information is sufficient to answer the question. The correct answer is D.

QUESTIONS	EXPLANATIONS

19. In a particular state, 70 percent of the counties received some rain on Monday, and 65 percent of the counties received some rain on Tuesday. No rain fell either day in 25 percent of the counties in the state. What percent of the counties received some rain on Monday and Tuesday?

(A) 12.5%

(B) 40%

(C) 50%

(D) 60%

(E) 67.5%

19. **D** You can solve this problem by drawing a Venn diagram. Because this is a problem that uses percentages without any hard numbers, you might find it easier to think of there being 100 counties. Start with all the information provided in the problem:

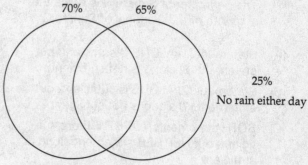

Because 25 percent of the counties did not receive rain on either day, 75 percent of the counties received rain on Monday, Tuesday, or both days. The sum of the number of counties that received rain on Monday and the number of counties that received rain on Tuesday is considerably greater than 75. Why? Because some counties are being counted twice. To figure out how many, subtract 75 from the sum of 70 and 65. $135 - 75 = 60$, so 60 percent of the counties received rain on both days. Write the number 60 in the space where the two circles interlock. You can fill in the rest of the missing values if you like, although you do not need to do so to answer this question.

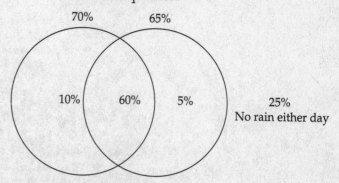

The correct answer is D.

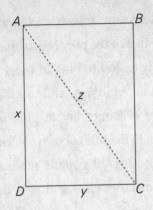

20. Figure *ABCD* is a rectangle with sides of length *x* centimeters and width *y* centimeters, and a diagonal of length *z* centimeters. What is the measure, in centimeters, of the perimeter of *ABCD*?

   (1) $x - y = 7$
   (2) $z = 13$

   (A) Statement (1) ALONE is sufficient, but statement (2) alone is not sufficient.

   (B) Statement (2) ALONE is sufficient, but statement (1) alone is not sufficient.

   (C) BOTH statements TOGETHER are sufficient, but NEITHER statement alone is sufficient.

   (D) EACH statement ALONE is sufficient.

   (E) Statements (1) and (2) TOGETHER are NOT sufficient.

20. **C** Statement (1) tells us that $x - y = z$. An infinite number of combinations satisfy this equation, yielding an infinite number of perimeters for *ABCD*. Clearly, Statement (1) is not sufficient, and the answer must be B, C, or E. Similarly, there are many different ways to draw a rectangle with diagonal 13. Not all of these rectangles have the same perimeter. Answer choice B is also out of the mix; the answer must be C or E. At first glance, the two statements together don't appear to offer much more help. However, by applying a bit of algebraic trickery and the Pythagorean theorem, we can wring more information from these two statements than is immediately apparent. Start by squaring Statement (1); this yields the equation $x^2 - 2xy + y^2 = 49$. The Pythagorean theorem tells us that $x^2 + y^2 = z^2$, so we can use Statement (2) to substitute 13^2, or 169, for $x^2 + y^2$. This yields the equation $169 - 2xy = 49$, which can be simplified to $xy = 60$. There's just one more step. We know that $x^2 + y^2 = 169$, and we know that $xy = 60$. Thus, we know that $x^2 - 2xy + y^2 = 289$. The square root of $x^2 - 2xy + y^2$ is $(x + y)$, so we also know that $x + y = 17$ (it cannot equal -17 because *x* and *y* are centimeter lengths). This equation, yielded by information from both statements, can be used in conjunction with Statement (1) to solve simultaneously for *x* and *y*, thus allowing you to calculate the perimeter of the rectangle. The correct answer is C. If you figured this one out on your own, have a cigar, or a bar of chocolate, or something to reward yourself. That was a mindbender!

QUESTIONS	EXPLANATIONS

21. Together, Andrea and Brian weigh p pounds; Brian weighs 10 pounds more than Andrea. Brian and Andrea's dog, Cubby, weighs $\dfrac{p}{4}$ pounds more than Andrea. In terms of p, what is Cubby's weight in pounds?

    (A) $\dfrac{p}{2} - 10$

    (B) $\dfrac{3p}{4} - 5$

    (C) $\dfrac{3p}{2} - 5$

    (D) $\dfrac{5p}{4} - 10$

    (E) $5p - 5$

21. **B** Variables in the answer choices mean it's time to Plug In. For the purposes of this problem, it's probably easiest to Plug In weights for Andrea and Brian, add them, and use the sum for the value of p. Remember to plug in values that conform to the rules of the problem; Brian must weigh exactly 10 pounds more than Andrea. Try to make p a value that is divisible by 4; that will make it easier to calculate Cubby's weight. For the purposes of this explanation, let's say Andrea weighs 45 pounds and Brian weighs 55 pounds. That makes p equal to 100, a nice, round number that is easily divisible by 4. Cubby weighs $\dfrac{p}{4}$ pounds more than Andrea, so he weighs 25 pounds more than Andrea, or 70 pounds. Plug 100 in for p in each of the answer choices and eliminate those that do not yield an answer of 70. The correct answer is B.

MATH BIN 4

QUESTIONS	EXPLANATIONS

22. A first-grade teacher uses ten flash cards, numbered 1 through 10, to teach her students to order numbers correctly. She has students choose four flash cards randomly, then arrange the cards in ascending order. One day, she removes the cards numbered "2" and "4" from the deck of flash cards. On that day, how many different correct arrangements of four randomly selected cards are possible?

(A)   70
(B)   210
(C)   336
(D)   840
(E)   1,680

22. **A** This question is easier than it first appears. At first glance, the restrictive rules—the cards must be arranged in order, some cards have been removed from the deck—seem to complicate the problem. In fact, they do not; because there is only one correct solution for each set of cards chosen, you need only figure out the number of possible combinations of the cards in order to determine the number of possible correct arrangements. The one-to-one correlation between combinations and correct solutions actually simplifies the problem. Because the teacher has removed two cards from the deck, only 8 cards remain. The values on the selected cards are immaterial, and are presented merely as a distracter; the answer to this question is the same regardless of the values written on the two cards she removes. Determine how many combinations are possible by applying the combinations formula: $C = \dfrac{n!}{r!(n-r)!}$ where n is the number of candidates from which to choose, and r is the number of items to be chosen. The number of candidates is 8 (10 cards, minus the two that have been removed); the number of items to be chosen is 4. Therefore, $C = \dfrac{8!}{4!(8-4)!} = \dfrac{8!}{4!(4!)} = \dfrac{8 \times 7 \times 6 \times 5}{4 \times 3 \times 2 \times 1} = 70$. The correct answer is A.

MATH BIN 4

QUESTIONS	EXPLANATIONS

23. If *a* and *b* are two-digit numbers that share the same digits, except in reverse order, then what is the sum of *a* and *b*?

(1) $a - b = 45$

(2) The difference between the two digits in each number is 5.

(A) Statement (1) ALONE is sufficient, but statement (2) alone is not sufficient.

(B) Statement (2) ALONE is sufficient, but statement (1) alone is not sufficient.

(C) BOTH statements TOGETHER are sufficient, but NEITHER statement alone is sufficient.

(D) EACH statement ALONE is sufficient.

(E) Statements (1) and (2) TOGETHER are NOT sufficient.

23. E As you consider each statement, you might be tempted to think, "How many numbers can possibly satisfy all the constraints of the question stem *and* this statement?" Or, you may figure that both statements together, in addition to the information in the question stem, *must* be sufficient to answer the question. That, of course, is just what the test writers *expect* you to think. It turns out that several values satisfy each of the statements: 61 and 16; 72 and 27; 83 and 38; and 94 and 49 all satisfy Statements (1) and (2). Thus, neither statement is sufficient on its own, nor are they sufficient together. The correct answer is E.

24. A university awarded grants in the amount of either $7,000 or $10,000 to some incoming freshmen. The total amount of all such awards was $2,300,000. Did the university award more $7,000 grants than $10,000 grants to its incoming freshmen?

(1) A total of 275 freshmen received grants in one of the two amounts.

(2) The amount of money awarded in $10,000 grants was $200,000 more than the amount of money awarded in $7,000 grants.

(A) Statement (1) ALONE is sufficient, but statement (2) alone is not sufficient.

(B) Statement (2) ALONE is sufficient, but statement (1) alone is not sufficient.

(C) BOTH statements TOGETHER are sufficient, but NEITHER statement alone is sufficient.

(D) EACH statement ALONE is sufficient.

(E) Statements (1) and (2) TOGETHER are NOT sufficient.

24. D This is a simultaneous equation problem dressed up as a word problem. If you recognized this wolf in sheep's clothing, you shouldn't have had too much trouble finding the correct answer. The question stem tells us that two types of grants were awarded; it also provides the sum of the grants. Let's call the group of freshmen who received $7,000 grants *x* and the group of freshmen who received $10,000 grants *y*. The question stem tells us that $7,000x + 10,000y = 2,300,000$. That's one equation; to solve simultaneous equations (which have two variables), we need two equations. Statement (1) provides a second equation. That equation is $x + y = 275$. You can solve simultaneously—although, of course, you don't have to because this is data sufficiency, not problem solving—to determine that $x = 150$ and $y = 125$. Statement (1) is sufficient; the answer must be A or D. Statement (2) also provides a second equation. That equation is $10,000y = 7,000x + 200,000$. Again, you can solve simultaneously to determine that $x = 150$ and $y = 125$. D is the correct answer to this question.

QUESTIONS	EXPLANATIONS

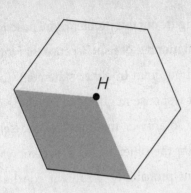

25. The figure above is a regular hexagon with center H. The shaded area is a parallelogram that shares three vertices with the hexagon; its fourth vertex is the center of the hexagon. If the length of one side of the hexagon is 8 centimeters, what is the area of the unshaded region?

(A) $16\sqrt{3}$ cm³

(B) 96 cm³

(C) $64\sqrt{3}$ cm³

(D) $96\sqrt{3}$ cm³

(E) 256 cm³

25. **C** When a problem includes a regular hexagon, you know a lot more than you might think. That's because you can divide a regular hexagon into 6 congruent equilateral triangles, all meeting at the center of the hexagon. Furthermore, if you know the length of one side of an equilateral triangle, you can determine its area simply by dividing the equilateral triangle into two 30-60-90 triangles and applying the 30-60-90 formula to determine the height of the equilateral triangle (the ratio of the sides of a 30-60-90 triangle is $1 : \sqrt{3} : 2$). The problem tells you that the length of one side of the hexagon is 8 centimeters. That means that the equilateral triangles that make up the hexagon have sides of 8 centimeters. Divide one into a 30-60-90 triangle and you'll get a triangle with sides $4 : 4\sqrt{3} : 8$; this tells you that the height of the equilateral triangle is $4\sqrt{3}$ and that its area is $\dfrac{8\left(4\sqrt{3}\right)}{2} = 16\sqrt{3}$ cm². The area of the unshaded region consists of four of the six equilateral triangles (the shaded region consists of the other two), so the area of the shaded region is $4 \times 16\sqrt{3} = 64\sqrt{3}$ cm². The correct answer is C.

26. A fish tank contains a number of fish, including 5 Fantails. If two fish are selected from the tank at random, what is the probability that both will be Fantails?

(1) The probability that the first fish chosen will be a Fantail is $\frac{1}{2}$.

(2) The probability that the second fish chosen will be a Fantail is $\frac{4}{9}$.

(A) Statement (1) ALONE is sufficient, but statement (2) alone is not sufficient.

(B) Statement (2) ALONE is sufficient, but statement (1) alone is not sufficient.

(C) BOTH statements TOGETHER are sufficient, but NEITHER statement alone is sufficient.

(D) EACH statement ALONE is sufficient.

(E) Statements (1) and (2) TOGETHER are NOT sufficient.

26. **D** To figure out this problem, you need to know the total number of fish. Because that total is never said out loud in either statement, Joe Bloggs's first response might be to conclude there is no way to answer the question and select choice E. On the other hand, if Joe knows just a *bit* about probability, he might conclude the answer was choice C, because the probability that both will be Fantails is equal to the probability that the first will be a Fantail times the probability that the second will be a Fantail. However, this question wouldn't be in Bin 4 if it were that easy. If you look at Statement (1) in combination with the question itself, you will realize that if there are 5 Fantails, and the probability that the first selection will be a Fantail is $\frac{1}{2}$, that means we actually know the total number of fish: $\frac{1}{2} = \frac{5}{x}$ or 10. You might think that the probability of the second fish being a Fantail would also be $\frac{1}{2}$, but in fact that's not the case: There are only 9 fish left in total when the second selection is made, and there are only 4 possible Fantails from which to chose. So the probability of them both being chosen is $\frac{1}{2}$ times $\frac{4}{9}$, or $\frac{2}{9}$. We are down to AD.

Now, looking at Statement (2), if the probability that the second fish will be a Fantail is $\frac{4}{9}$, that means that the probability of the first fish being a Fantail is $\frac{5}{10}$, which means we can answer the question based on Statement (2) alone as well. The correct answer is choice D.

QUESTIONS	EXPLANATIONS

1. As its reputation for making acquisitions of important masterpieces has grown, the museum has increasingly turned down gifts of lesser-known paintings <u>they would in the past have accepted gratefully</u>.

    (A) they would in the past have accepted gratefully

    (B) they would have accepted gratefully in the past

    (C) it would in the past have accepted gratefully

    (D) it previously would have accepted gratefully in the past

    (E) that previously would have been accepted in the past

1. **C** The pronoun *they* in this stem sentence doesn't agree with the noun it refers to: the museum. In everyday speech, of course, we often say "they" when we are referring to a large institution—but on the GMAT, the test writers won't let us get away with such imprecision. Choices A and B can both be eliminated because they use the plural pronoun. Choices D and E both fix the problem in different ways, but both add a redundancy: There is no need to have "previously" and "in the past" in the same sentence. The best answer is choice C.

2. Over the past few decades, despite periodic attempts to reign in spending, currencies in South America <u>are devalued</u> by rampant inflation.

    (A) are devalued

    (B) are becoming more devalued

    (C) which have lost value

    (D) have become devalued

    (E) have since become devalued

2. **D** This is a tense question. *Over the past few decades* implies a continued action over time—which needs the perfect tense. This eliminates choices A and B. Choice C creates a sentence fragment. E isn't bad, but the word *since* is a bit redundant because the sentence began with *over the past few decades*. D is best.

3. A fashion designer's fall line for women utilizing new soft fabrics broke all sales records last year. To capitalize on her success, the designer plans to launch a line of clothing for men this year that makes use of the same new soft fabrics.

    The designer's plan assumes that

    (A) other designers are not planning to introduce new lines for men utilizing the same soft fabrics

    (B) men will be as interested in the new soft fabrics as women were the year before

    (C) the designer will have time to develop new lines for both men and women

    (D) the line for men will be considered innovative and daring because of its use of fabrics

    (E) women who bought the new line last year will continue to buy it this year

3. **B** This is an analogy argument. The men's line is being introduced in the hope that men will like the new soft fabrics as much as women did the year before. The key word in the passage that might have alerted you to the analogy was the word *same*. The assumption on which this argument depends is that men and women will like the same new fabric. Choices A, C, D, and E are all outside the scope of the argument. The best answer is B.

4. The standard lamp is becoming outmoded, and <u>so too is the incandescent light bulb, it is Edison's miraculous invention to use</u> so much more energy than the new low-wattage halogen bulbs.

(A) so too is the incandescent light bulb, it is Edison's miraculous invention to use

(B) so too is the incandescent light bulb, Edison's miraculous invention that uses

(C) so too the incandescent light bulb, Edison's miraculous invention using

(D) also the incandescent light bulb, it is Edison's miraculous invention that uses

(E) also the incandescent light bulb, which is Edison's miraculous invention to use

4. **B** This is basically an idiom question, but your checklist may first uncover a pronoun issue. The pronoun *it* clearly refers back to *light bulb*, but in this case the pronoun isn't actually necessary: *Edison's miraculous invention* refers directly back to *light bulb* without the need of a pronoun. This eliminates choices A and D, both of which are actually run-on sentences. Next, you should turn your attention to the end of the underlined phrase. Do you have an invention *to use* energy (choices A and E), an invention *that uses* energy (choices B and D), or an invention *using* energy (choice C)? If you said *that uses*, then you are doing just fine. Since we've already eliminated choice D, the best answer is B.

5. Over the last 20 years, <u>the growth of information technology has been more rapid than any other business field</u>, but has recently finally begun to lag behind as newly emerging fields seem more enticing to new graduates.

(A) the growth of information technology has been more rapid than any other business field

(B) the growth of information technology has been more rapid than any other fields of business

(C) information technology's growth has been more rapid than any other fields of business

(D) the growing of information technology has been more rapid than that of any other business field

(E) the growth of information technology has been more rapid than that of any other business field

5. **E** The clue that tells you this is a potential parallel construction problem is the word *than*. This sentence is supposed to compare the *growth* of information technology to the *growth* in other fields. However, as written, the sentence is comparing the *growth* of information technology directly to other fields. Once you spot this, you should immediately start looking for the replacement phrase, *that of*. Only two answer choices contain it, D and E. However, Choice D uses the awkward and unidiomatic phrase *the growing of information technology*. The best answer is E.

6. According to mutual fund sales experts, a successful year for a stock fund should result not only in increased investor dollars flowing into the fund, but also in increased investor dollars flowing into other mutual stock funds offered by the same company. However, while last year the Grafton Mutual Company's "Growth Stock Fund" beat average market returns by a factor of two and recorded substantial new investment, the other stock funds offered by Grafton did not report any increase whatsoever.

Which of the following conclusions can properly be drawn from the statements above?

(A) When one of the mutual funds offered by a company beats average market returns, the other mutual funds offered by that company will beat average market returns.

(B) The mutual fund sales experts neglected to consider bond funds in formulating their theory.

(C) The performance of the Grafton "Growth Stock Fund" was a result of a wave of mergers and acquisitions that year.

(D) Investors currently dislike all stock mutual funds because of market volatility.

(E) The success of one mutual fund is not the only factor affecting whether investors will invest in other mutual funds run by the same company.

7. With <u>less than thirty thousand dollars in advance ticket sales and fewer</u> acceptances by guest-speakers than expected, the one-day symposium on art and religion was canceled for lack of interest.

(A) less than thirty thousand dollars in advance ticket sales and fewer

(B) fewer than thirty thousand dollars in advance ticket sales and less

(C) fewer than thirty thousand dollars in advance ticket sales and fewer

(D) lesser than thirty thousand dollars in advance ticket sales and fewer

(E) less than thirty thousand dollars in advance ticket sales and as few

6. **E** This is a causal argument. According to experts, the high returns of one mutual fund *cause* investors to invest in other mutual funds run by the same company. However, in the case of the Grafton "family" of mutual funds, that was not the case. What conclusion can we draw from this? The best answer is E, which asks us to consider that there might be alternate causes. Choices A, B, and C are outside the scope of the argument, while D is too extreme and illogical because the argument makes it clear that investors liked at least *one* stock mutual fund: Grafton's "Growth Stock Fund."

7. **A** This question is about quantity words, as you probably suspected just from looking at the answer choices. When it comes to money, you use *fewer* if you are referring to the number of actual bills you have, but *less* if you are referring to the total amount and don't know the actual number of bills. This would get you down to choices A and E. Acceptances, however, can be counted, so in the second half of the underlined portion of the underlined sentence, you would use *fewer*. If you were tempted by choice E, you didn't notice that it created a new idiomatic error: Would you say as few *than* or as few *as*? The best answer is choice A.

8. New technology now makes it feasible for computer call-in help desk services to route calls they receive to almost anywhere, theoretically allowing employees to work from home, without the need for a daily commute.

The adoption of this policy would be most likely to increase productivity if employees did not _____.

(A) commute from a distance of fewer than 10 miles
(B) commute by car as opposed to by rail
(C) live in areas with dependable phone service
(D) need to consult frequently with each other to solve callers' problems
(E) have more than one telephone line

8. **D** The tricky part of this inference question is dealing with the "did not." Choice A is outside the scope of the argument because eliminating such a short commute would presumably not have much effect on productivity. Choice B is also outside the scope since the *method* of the commute employees would no longer have to make is probably irrelevant. If employees did not live in areas of dependable phone service, that would likely *decrease* productivity, so that eliminates C. For similar reasons, if employees did not have more than one phone line, it might decrease productivity since they would presumably get some personal calls at their place of residence. Choice D is best, because if employees needed to consult each other to answer callers' questions, they would be at a distinct disadvantage if they were all in separate locations.

9. The port cities of England in the 19th century saw a renaissance of ship construction, with some innovative designs breaking new ground, stretching the limits of ship-building theory, and <u>received</u> acclaim from around the world.

(A) received
(B) it received
(C) receiving
(D) would receive
(E) it had received

9. **C** This is a parallel construction question, in which the second half of the sentence contains a list of three actions, which must all be expressed in the same way. The three actions are *breaking, stretching,* and...*received.* Hmm. Which of the three is wrong? Well, since only *received* is underlined, that might be a pretty good clue that we should change it to match the others. The best answer is choice C. None of the other choices is parallel to the other two verbs. Choices B and E also add the needless pronoun *it,* which has no clear referent.

10. According to a consumer research group survey, the majority of kitchen appliances purchased in the United States are purchased by men. This appears to belie the myth that women spend more time in the kitchen than men.

The argument is flawed primarily because the author _____.

(A) fails to differentiate between buying and using

(B) does not provide information about the types of kitchen appliances surveyed

(C) depends on the results of one survey

(D) does not give exact statistics to back up his case

(E) does not provide information on other appliances such as washers and dryers

10. **A** The faulty assumption of this argument is that the buyers of the kitchen appliances are also the users of the kitchen appliances. We do not know that this is true. While more men may buy kitchen appliances, they are not necessarily the ones who use them. Choice B is wrong because knowing the individual types of kitchen appliances would not enhance the argument. Although Choices C and D might seem tempting, the problem with this argument is not so much that the survey might not be representative, but rather that the author is using information about buying patterns to extrapolate how these appliances are later going to be used and by whom. Choice E is outside the scope of the argument. The best answer is A.

11. A contribution to a favorite charity being sent instead of flowers when a colleague dies is becoming more the rule than the exception when it comes to funeral etiquette.

(A) A contribution to a favorite charity being sent instead

(B) A contribution being sent to a favorite charity as opposed

(C) To send a contribution for a favorite charity instead

(D) Sending a contribution to a favorite charity instead

(E) Sending a contribution to a favorite charity as opposed

11. **D** The GMAT test writers have an aversion to the word *being*, which usually creates a passive voice. This eliminates choices A and B. Generally, when a sentence begins with the infinitive verb form (*To send*…), you would need a parallel infinitive verb form in the second half of the sentence, which is not the case in choice C (which also uses the incorrect idiomatic expression *contribution for*. Choice E might seem tempting except that the last two words—*as opposed*—don't go idiomatically with *of*. The best answer is D.

Questions 12–15 are based on the following passage:

As a business model, the world of publishing has always been a somewhat sleepy enclave, but now all that seems poised to change. Sev-
Line eral companies have moved aggressively into a
(5) new business endeavor whose genesis comes from the question: Who owns the great works of literature?

Text-on-demand is not a completely new idea, of course. In the 1990s, the Gutenberg
(10) project sought volunteers to type literary classics that had expired copyrights into word processing files so that scholars would have searchable databases for their research. Most of the works of Shakespeare, Cervantes, Proust
(15) and Moliere were to be found free online by as early as 1995.

However, now large-scale companies have moved into the market, with scanners and business plans, and are looking for bargain base-
(20) ment content. These companies are striking deals with libraries, and some publishers, to be able to provide their content, for a price, to individual buyers over the Internet.

At stake are the rights to an estimated store
(25) of 30 million books, most of which are now out of print. Many of these books are now also in the public domain, giving any company the right to sell them online. Still, a good portion of the books a general audience might actually
(30) want to buy is still under copyright. The urgent question: Who owns those copyrights? In the case of all too many books put out more than 20 years ago by now-defunct publishing companies, the answer is unclear—a situation the
(35) new text-on-demand companies are eager to exploit. An association of publishers has sued, claiming massive copyright infringement. The case is several years away from trial.

VERBAL BIN 1

QUESTIONS	EXPLANATIONS

12. The primary purpose of the passage is to

  (A) present the results of a statistical analysis and propose further study
  (B) explain a recent development and explore its consequences
  (C) identify the reasons for a trend and recommend measures to address it
  (D) outline several theories about a phenomenon and advocate one of them
  (E) describe the potential consequences of implementing a new policy and argue in favor of that policy

12. B Process of elimination is useful here. Does the author present a statistical analysis? No, so eliminate choice A. While the author might be said to identify the reasons for a trend, does she recommend measures to address it? No, so eliminate choice C. Does the author advocate anything whatsoever? No, so eliminate choice D. Does the author argue in favor of any policy? No, so eliminate choice E. The best answer is B.

13. It can be inferred from the passage that the works of Shakespeare, Cervantes, and Moliere

  (A) are some of the most popular works of literature
  (B) are no longer copyrighted
  (C) are among the works the association of publishers is suing text-on-demand companies
  (D) do not currently exist as searchable databases
  (E) were owned by now-defunct publishing companies

13. B This specific question has several good lead words: *Shakespeare, Cervantes,* and *Moliere,* and they all come from the end of the second paragraph. As always, read several lines above and below the lead words to make sure you understand what's going on. Remember, in Reading Comprehension, inference questions are not really about inferring. You are looking for an answer that restates something already said in the passage. While undoubtedly the works of these great authors are some of the most popular works of literature (choice A), how do we infer that from the passage? It was never stated. Choice C is outside the scope of this question: lawsuits are not discussed anywhere near the lead words. Choice D directly contradicts the passage. Choice E might be true but requires too big an inference for the GMAT. The best answer is B—a restatement right from the passage.

14. Which of the following is an example of a book that a text-on-demand company would not have to acquire the rights to?

  (A) a book still under copyright
  (B) a book more than 20 years old
  (C) a book in the public domain
  (D) a book a general audience might want to buy
  (E) a book not already owned by publishers the company has a deal with

14. C A text-on-demand company would not need to acquire a book if it was already free, which leads us to choice C. Choice B might have appeared tempting, but if you read the passage, you will note that books more than 20 years old are still usually under copyright, even if in some cases it is often difficult to determine who owns the copyright.

15. It can be inferred from the passage that text-on-demand companies are

(A) using scanners to find books they want to acquire
(B) creating business plans well before they have any actual business
(C) buying content at premium prices
(D) acquiring the rights to books for as little as possible
(E) attempting to supplant the role of traditional publishers

16. Exit polls, conducted by an independent organization among voters at five polling locations during a recent election, suggested that the incumbent mayor—a Democrat—was going to lose the election by a wide margin. But, in fact, by the time the final results were tabulated, the incumbent had won the election by a narrow margin.

Which of the following, if true, would explain the apparent contradiction in the results of the exit polls?

(A) The people chosen at random to be polled by the independent organization happened to be Democrats.
(B) The exit poll locations chosen by the independent organization were in predominantly Republican districts.
(C) The exit polls were conducted during the afternoon, when most of the districts' younger voters, who did not support the incumbent mayor, were at work.
(D) The incumbent mayor ran on a platform that promised to lower taxes if elected.
(E) An earlier poll, conducted the week before the election, had predicted that the incumbent mayor would win.

15. **D** In this inference question, the trick is not to infer too far. Perhaps it could be argued that these new companies might come to supplant the publishing industry, but it isn't said in the passage, so eliminate choice E. The same could be said for creating business plans before they have any business; it could well be true, but it isn't said. Eliminate choice B. Choice A is not said in the passage and is illogical. Choice C is the opposite of what was stated in the passage, while choice D is a nice restatement of the passage: "looking for bargain basement content."

16. **B** The key to this statistical argument is to understand that the sampling of the voters might not be representative of ALL the voters. Choice A says the voters chosen by the pollsters happened to be Democrats. But in that case, we would expect that the incumbent mayor, a Democrat, would have been predicted the winner of the election. Choice C says the exit poll was conducted at a time of day in which many people who disliked the mayor could not vote, implying that the actual election results for the incumbent would be worse, or at least no better. Choices D and E are outside the scope of the argument. The best answer is B, which gives a statistical reason for the skewed results: The exit polls were conducted in locations where the incumbent had little support—leaving open the possibility that his results would be stronger elsewhere.

QUESTIONS	EXPLANATIONS

17. The spread of Avian flu from animals to humans has been well-documented, but less understood is the mechanism by which it is spread from one bird species to another. **In order to avoid a world-wide epidemic of Avian flu, scientists must make that study a first priority.** To solely tackle the human dimension of this possible pandemic is to miss half of the problem: its spread from one hemisphere to another.

The bolded phrase plays which of the following roles in the argument above?

(A) The bolded phrase states a premise of the argument.
(B) The bolded phrase contradicts the author's main point.
(C) The bolded phrase makes a statement that the author is about to contradict.
(D) The bolded phrase states the author's conclusion.
(E) The bolded phrase states an assumption the author is making.

17. **D** Although there is no "therefore" or "hence" in front of it, the bolded phrase is the conclusion of the argument. The other phrases are premises of the argument. If you suspect a phrase may be the conclusion, it sometimes helps to imagine a "therefore" in front of it, to see if the sentence would make sense. If it does, chances are that's your conclusion. The best answer is D.

18. Successful business leaders not only anticipate potential problems and have contingency plans <u>ready, instead proceeding as if they are likely to occur at any time</u>.

(A) ready, instead proceeding as if they are likely to occur at any time
(B) ready, but also proceed as if such problems are likely to occur at any time
(C) ready, but also proceeding as if the occurrence of them is at any time likely
(D) ready; they instead proceed as if their occurrence is likely at any time
(E) ready; such problems are likely to occur at any time, is how they proceed

18. **B** The phrase *not only* must be followed by the phrase *but also* in order to complete the sentence properly. The answer must therefore be either B or C. Choice C lacks parallel structure in the words *anticipate* and *proceeding*. Correctly formulated, this sentence should read *business leaders not only anticipate...but also proceed...* The best answer is B.

19. An artist who sells her paintings for a fixed price decides that she must increase her income. Because she does not believe that customers will pay more for her paintings, she decides to cut costs by using cheaper paints and canvases. She expects that, by cutting costs, she will increase her profit margin per painting and thus increase her annual net income.

Which of the following, if true, most weakens the argument above?

(A) Other area artists charge more for their paintings than the artist charges for hers.
(B) The artist has failed to consider other options, such as renting cheaper studio space.
(C) The artist's plan will result in the production of inferior paintings which, in turn, will cause a reduction in sales.
(D) If the economy were to enter a period of inflation, the artist's projected increase in income could be wiped out by increases in the price of art supplies.
(E) The artist considered trying to complete paintings more quickly and thus increase production, but concluded that it would be impossible.

19. C To weaken an argument, look first at its conclusion. This argument concludes that the artist will *increase her profit margin...and thus increase her annual income* by using cheaper art supplies. Which answer choice undercuts this conclusion? Choice C does; if the artist's sales decrease, then her increased profit margin may not lead to an increase in annual income, because the decrease in sales may offset the increase in per-painting profit. The best answer is C.

20. Although tapirs reared in captivity are generally docile and have even been kept as pets by South American villagers, it is nonetheless a volatile creature prone to unpredictable and dangerous temper tantrums.

(A) it is nonetheless a volatile creature
(B) it is nonetheless volatile creatures
(C) being nonetheless volatile creatures
(D) they are nonetheless a volatile creature
(E) they are nonetheless volatile creatures

20. E This is a pronoun agreement question. The subject of the sentence is *tapirs*; therefore, the pronoun that refers to the subject must be plural. The answer, therefore, must be D or E. Choice D contains a new pronoun agreement error, because *they* is plural and *a volatile creature* is singular. The best answer is E.

21. According to a recent report, the original tires supplied with the Impressivo, a new sedan-class automobile, wore much more quickly than tires conventionally wear. The report suggested two possible causes: (1) defects in the tires, and (2) improper wheel alignment of the automobile.

Which of the following would best help the authors of the report determine which of the two causes identified was responsible for the extra wear?

(A) a study in which the rate of tire wear in the Impressivo is compared to the rate of tire wear in all automobiles in the same class

(B) a study in which a second set of tires, manufactured by a different company than the one that made the first set, is installed on all Impressivos and the rate of wear is measured

(C) a study in which the level of satisfaction of workers in the Impressivo manufacturing plant is measured and compared to that of workers at other automobile manufacturing plants

(D) a study that determines how often improper wheel alignment results in major problems for manufacturers of other automobiles in the Impressivo's class

(E) a study that determines the degree to which faulty driving techniques employed by Impressivo drivers contributed to tire wear

21. **B** Because the report identifies two possible causes of the tire wear, the best answer must identify a study that focuses on one of these possible causes. Studies focusing on car models other than the Impressivo (A and D), worker satisfaction C, or driver error E are all irrelevant to this study. The study described in B removes one of the two possible causes. If the newly installed tires made by another manufacturer also turn out to wear abnormally, then the authors will have good reason to suspect that faulty alignment caused the initial problem. If the new tires wear normally, then they will know that the original tires were faulty.

<u>Questions 22–25</u> are based on the following passage:

Founded at the dawn of the modern industrial era, the nearly forgotten Women's Trade Union League (WTUL) played an instrumental
Line role in advancing the cause of working women
(5) throughout the early part of the twentieth century. In the face of considerable adversity, the WTUL made a contribution far greater than did most historical footnotes.

The organization's successes did not come
(10) easily; conflict beset the WTUL in many forms. During those early days of American unions, organized labor was aggressively opposed by both industry and government. The WTUL, which represented a largely unskilled labor
(15) force, had little leverage against these powerful opponents. Also, because of the skill level of its workers as well as inherent societal gender bias, the WTUL had great difficulty finding allies among other unions. Even the large and
(20) powerful American Federation of Labor (AFL), which nominally took the WTUL under its wing, kept it at a distance. Because the AFL's power stemmed from its highly skilled labor force, the organization saw little economic benefit in
(25) working with the WTUL. The affiliation provided the AFL with political cover, allowing it to claim support for women workers; in return, the WTUL gained a potent but largely absent ally.

The WTUL also had to overcome internal
(30) discord. While the majority of the group's members were working women, a sizeable and powerful minority consisted of middle- and upper-class social reformers whose goals extended beyond labor reform. While workers argued that
(35) the WTUL should focus its efforts on collective bargaining and working conditions, the reformers looked beyond the workplace, seeking state and national legislation aimed at education reform and urban poverty relief as well as
(40) workplace issues.

Despite these obstacles, the WTUL accomplished a great deal. The organization was instrumental in the passage of state laws mandating an eight-hour workday, a minimum
(45) wage for women, and a ban on child labor. It provided seed money to women who organized workers in specific plants and industries, and

also established strike funds and soup kitchens
(50) to support striking unionists. After the tragic Triangle Shirtwaist Company fire of 1911, the WTUL launched a four-year investigation whose conclusions formed the basis of much subsequent workplace safety legislation. The organiz-
(55) ation also offered a political base for all reform-minded women, and thus helped develop the next generation of American leaders. Eleanor Roosevelt was one of many prominent figures to emerge from the WTUL.

(60) The organization began a slow death in the late 1920s, when the Great Depression choked off its funding. The organization limped through the 1940s; the death knell eventually rang in 1950, at the onset of the McCarthy era. A turn-
(65) of-the-century labor organization dedicated to social reform, one that during its heyday was regarded by many as "radical," stood little chance of weathering that storm. This humble ending, however, does nothing to diminish the
(70) accomplishments of an organization that is yet to receive its historical due.

QUESTIONS	EXPLANATIONS

22. The primary purpose of this passage is to

    (A) describe the barriers confronting women in the contemporary workplace

    (B) compare and contrast the methods of two labor unions of the early industrial era

    (C) critique the methods employed by an important labor union

    (D) rebuke historians for failing to cover the women's labor movement adequately

    (E) call readers' attention to an overlooked contributor to American history

22. E The author of the passage makes this point twice in the opening paragraph (*the nearly forgotten Women's Trade Union League...the WTUL made a contribution far greater than did most historical footnotes*) and again in the final sentence of the passage. The entire passage serves to focus readers' attention on "an overlooked contributor to American history," the WTUL.

Process of Elimination is helpful here: A is incorrect because the passage is about a defunct historical union, not contemporary working women; B is incorrect because the main focus of this passage is a single organization, the WTUL; C is incorrect because the WTUL's achievements, not its methods, are the focus of the passage; and D is incorrect because no such rebuke is ever stated. Remember also that the answer to a primary purpose question must apply to the entire passage, not just to one paragraph or section.

23. Which of the following best characterizes the American Federation of Labor's view of the Women's Trade Union League, as it is presented in the passage?

    (A) The WTUL was an important component of the AFL's multifront assault on industry and its treatment of workers.

    (B) Because of Eleanor Roosevelt's affiliation with the organization, the WTUL was a vehicle through which the AFL could gain access to the White House.

    (C) The WTUL was to be avoided because the radical element within it attracted unwanted government scrutiny.

    (D) The WTUL offered the AFL some political capital but little that would assist it in labor negotiations.

    (E) The WTUL was weakened by its hesitance in pursuing widespread social reform beyond the workplace.

23. D This answer is a good paraphrase of this excerpt from the second paragraph: *Because the AFL's power stemmed from its highly skilled labor force, the organization saw little economic benefit in working with the WTUL. The affiliation provided the AFL with political cover, allowing it to claim support for women workers...*

24. Each of the following is cited in the passage as an accomplishment of the Women's Trade Union League EXCEPT

    (A) It organized a highly skilled workforce to increase its bargaining power.

    (B) It contributed to the development of a group of leaders in America.

    (C) It provided essential support to striking women.

    (D) It helped fund start-up unions for women.

    (E) It contributed to the passage of important social and labor reform legislation.

24. A This answer choice describes the AFL, not the WTUL. The passage specifically states that the WTUL *represented a largely unskilled labor force [and so] had little leverage against [its] powerful opponents* (lines 14–16).

25. The passage suggests which of the following about the "middle- and upper-class social reformers" mentioned in lines 32–33?

    (A) They did not understand, nor were they sympathetic to, the plight of poor women workers.

    (B) Their naive interest in Communism was ultimately detrimental to the Women's Trade Union League.

    (C) It was because of their social and political power that the Women's Trade Union League was able to form an alliance with the American Federation of Labor.

    (D) They represented only an insignificant fraction of the leadership of Women's Trade Union League.

    (E) They sought to advance a broad political agenda of societal improvement.

25. E Process of Elimination is helpful on this question. Choice A defies common sense; if these reformers had not been sympathetic to the plight of poor women workers, they never would have joined an organization called the Women's Trade Union League. B and C can only be justified—poorly—by "reading between the lines," a definite no-no on reading comprehension. Because neither the reformers' interest in Communism nor their influence within the AFL is mentioned in paragraph three (the paragraph pertinent to this question), neither answer can be correct. D is contradicted by the passage, which states that the reformers constituted a *sizeable* minority within the WTUL. E is a good paraphrase of this excerpt from the passage: *…the reformers looked beyond the workplace, seeking state and national legislation aimed at education reform and urban poverty relief as well as workplace issues.*

VERBAL BIN 2

QUESTIONS	EXPLANATIONS

1. As its performance has risen on all the stock indexes, the bio-tech start-up has branched out into new markets to look for opportunities <u>they would previously have had to ignore</u>.

   (A) they would previously have had to ignore
   (B) they would have had to ignore previously
   (C) that previously they would have had to ignore
   (D) it previously would have had to ignore in past years
   (E) it would previously have had to ignore

1. **E** If you go through your mental checklist, you will probably spot the pronoun *they*. To whom does that pronoun refer? Even though there are a lot of plural nouns in the front half of the sentence, *they* must refer to the start-up company, which is singular. Never mind that many people in spoken English refer to a large company as *they*. On the GMAT, a singular noun needs a singular pronoun. That eliminates choices A, B, and C. To choose between D and E, look for a new error. That's what you'll find in choice D which uses both the words *previously* and *in the past*, creating a redundancy error. The best answer is E.

2. Scientists wishing to understand the kinetic movements of ancient dinosaurs are today studying the movements of modern day birds, which many scientists believe are descended from dinosaurs. A flaw in this strategy is that birds, although once genetically linked to dinosaurs, have evolved so far that any comparison is effectively meaningless.

   Which of the following, if true, would most weaken the criticism made above of the scientists' strategy?

   (A) Birds and dinosaurs have a number of important features in common that exist in no other living species.
   (B) Birds are separated from dinosaurs by 65 million years of evolution.
   (C) Our theories of dinosaur movements have recently undergone a radical reappraisal.
   (D) The study of kinetic movement is a relatively new discipline.
   (E) Many bird experts do not study dinosaurs to draw inferences about birds.

2. **A** In this passage, the author is questioning an analogical argument. To understand the kinetic movement of dinosaurs, says the argument, we should study the kinetic movement of birds, which are a lot like dinosaurs. The author is trying to weaken this analogy by saying that dinosaurs and birds are actually not very similar. Your job is to weaken the author's attempt to demonstrate that the argument is flawed. How do you do that? By showing that dinosaurs and birds *are* in fact alike. Choice B, if anything, actually strengthens the author's criticism of the analogy. Choices C and D are outside the scope of the argument. Choice E seems to strengthen the author's criticism of the analogy. It is also out of scope since the fact that some bird experts don't study dinosaurs doesn't mean that dinosaur experts shouldn't study birds. Choice A is best because it shows how birds and dinosaurs are alike.

3. A factory in China has two options to improve efficiency: adding robotic assembly lines, and subcontracting out certain small production goals that could be done more efficiently elsewhere. Adding robotic assembly lines will improve efficiency more than subcontracting some small production goals. Therefore, by adding robotic assembly lines, the factory will be doing the most that can be done to improve efficiency.

Which of the following is an assumption on which the argument depends?

(A) Adding robotic assembly lines will be more expensive than subcontracting some small production goals.

(B) The factory has a choice of robotic assembly lines, some of which might be better suited to this factory than others.

(C) The factory may or may not decide to choose either alternative

(D) Efficiency cannot be improved more by using both methods together than by adding robotic assembly lines alone.

(E) This particular factory is already the third most efficient factory in China.

3. **D** As always, if you don't immediately grasp the reasoning behind an argument, scope is key to eliminating wrong answers. For example, the expense of implementing these goals (choice A) was never mentioned and thus is outside the scope of the argument. The same goes for choice B: Choosing between different types of robotic assembly lines is not part of this argument. As for choice C, the argument does not depend on whether the two actions being considered are ever actually implemented—again it is outside the scope. And, come to think of it, so is choice E, which tells us that the factory is already quite efficient; the argument is about making it *more* efficient. By process of elimination, you have your answer. However, here's the logic: The conclusion of the argument is that choosing *one* of these two methods will result in the factory becoming the most efficient that it can be. What the argument is ignoring is the possibility that the factory could be even more efficient if it implemented *both* changes. The best answer is D.

VERBAL BIN 2

QUESTIONS	EXPLANATIONS

QUESTIONS

4. <u>Just as the early NASA space explorers attempted on each flight to push the frontiers of our knowledge, so too</u> are the new private consortium space explorers seeking to add to man's general understanding of the cosmos.

   (A)   Just as the early NASA space explorers attempted on each flight to push the frontiers of our knowledge, so too
   (B)   The early NASA space explorers attempted on each flight to push the frontiers of our knowledge, and in the same way
   (C)   Like the case of the early NASA space explorers who attempted on each flight to push the frontiers of our knowledge, so too
   (D)   As in the early NASA space explorers' attempts on each flight to push the frontiers of our knowledge, so too
   (E)   Similar to the early NASA space explorers attempted on each flight to push the frontiers of our knowledge, so too

5. A proposal for a new building fire safety code requires that fire-retardant insulation no longer be sprayed on steel girders in the factory, but be sprayed on once the girders have arrived at the building site. This will eliminate the dislodging of the insulation in transit, and reduce fatalities in catastrophic fires by an estimated 20%.

   Which of the following, if true, represents the strongest challenge to the new proposal?

   (A)   The fire-retardant insulation will also be required to be one inch thicker than in the past.
   (B)   Studies have shown that most dislodgement of insulation occurs after the girders arrive on site.
   (C)   Catastrophic fires represent only 4% of the fires reported nationally.
   (D)   The proposed safety code will add considerably to the cost of new construction.

EXPLANATIONS

4.   **A**   The idiom *just as...so too* is correct as written. Each of the other choices uses variations on unidiomatic expression instead. The best answer is A.

5.   **B**   The words *strongest challenge* in the question mean that you are trying weaken the argument. Choice A, if anything, appears to support the argument rather than weaken it, so you can eliminate it. Choices C and D do seem negative toward the argument, but both are outside the scope, as is choice E. Choice B is best because if the insulation comes loose *after* the girders arrive on site, then making an effort to prevent its dislodgement in transit to the building site will not have any effect, and will not necessarily reduce fatalities.

6. An effort <u>to control the crippling effects of poverty in Brazil's interior cities, begun almost thirty years ago,</u> has been partially successful, despite the setback of a major drought and the interruption of aid during an extended economic crisis.

(A) to control the crippling effects of poverty in Brazil's interior cities, begun almost thirty years ago,

(B) begun almost thirty years ago for controlling the crippling effects of poverty in Brazil's interior cities,

(C) begun for controlling the crippling effects of poverty in Brazil's interior cities almost thirty years ago,

(D) at controlling the crippling effects of poverty in Brazil's interior cities begun almost thirty years ago,

(E) that has begun almost thirty years ago to control the crippling effects of poverty in Brazil's interior cities,

6. A This is an idiom question. Do you attempt *to* do something, do you attempt *at* something, or do you attempt *for* something? The best answer is A.

7. A newly discovered disease is thought to be caused by a certain bacterium. However, recently released data note that the bacterium thrives in the presence of a certain virus, implying that it is actually the virus that causes the new disease.

Which of the following pieces of evidence would most support the data's implication?

(A) In the absence of the virus, the disease has been observed to follow infection by the bacterium.

(B) The virus has been shown to aid the growth of bacteria, a process which often leads to the onset of the disease.

(C) The virus alone has been observed in many cases of the disease.

(D) In cases where the disease does not develop, infection by the bacterium is usually preceded by infection by the virus.

(E) Onset of the disease usually follows infection by both the virus and the bacterium.

7. C The last line of this argument gives away its type: *...the virus that causes...* The cause of a certain disease was thought to be one thing, but now is believed to be something else. Recent evidence suggests that the cause is a virus (which also nourishes the bacterium once thought to be the cause of the disease). To support a causal argument, you take away possible alternate causes. Choice C does this by showing that while both virus and bacterium are often present at the same time, the virus has been found *without* the bacterium in many cases of the disease. Choice A directly contradicts this, suggesting that the bacterium is the sole cause. B and E suggest that the virus plays a supporting role to the bacterium. D is outside the scope of the argument. The best answer is C.

VERBAL BIN 2

QUESTIONS	EXPLANATIONS

8. The company was not even publicly traded until 1968, when the owner and founder sold it to David P. Markham, a private investor, <u>who took the company public and established a long and generous policy of stock options for</u> valued employees.

   (A) who took the company public and established a long and generous policy of stock options for
   (B) who, taking the company public, established a long and generous policy of stock options to
   (C) who, when he took the company public, established a long and generous policy of stock options to
   (D) who had taken the company public, establishing a long and generous policy of stock options as
   (E) taking the company public and establishing a long and generous policy of stock options for

8. **A** The second half of this sentence contains a correctly constructed parallel list. The private investor *took* and *established*, both verbs in the simple past. In choices B and D, the construction is less than parallel. In addition, several choices also use the unidiomatic *established... for* as opposed to *established...to*. In choice E, the construction is parallel, but it now seems to modify *the owner and founder* rather than *Markham*. The best answer is A.

9. Because of a quality control problem, a supplier of flu vaccines will not be able to ship any supplies of the vaccine for the upcoming flu season. This will create a shortage of flu vaccines and result in a loss of productivity as workers call in sick.

   Which of the following, if true, most seriously weakens the argument above?

   (A) The quality control problem of the supplier is not as severe as some experts had initially predicted.
   (B) Other suppliers of flu vaccine have not been affected by the quality control problem.
   (C) Last year there was also a shortage of flu vaccine available.
   (D) The price of flu vaccines is expected to fall in the next ten years.
   (E) The flu season is expected to last longer than usual this year.

9. **B** You might have been tempted by choice A, which seems to weaken the argument by saying the quality control problem of the supplier is not as severe as experts had predicted. However, the initial predictions of experts are outside the scope of the argument, because they don't change the fact that this supplier will not be supplying any vaccines, regardless of how minor the problems might be. Similarly, what happened last year (choice C) or what will happen in the next 10 years (choice D) is also outside the scope of the argument; we want to know what will happen *this* year. Choice E seems to strengthen the argument since a longer flu season will presumably result in more people getting sick. The best answer is B because if other suppliers have not been affected by quality control problems, then the overall shortage may be less severe.

QUESTIONS	EXPLANATIONS

10. Never before had the navy defeated <u>so many foes at once as it had in</u> the battle of Trafalgar in 1805.

  (A) so many foes at once as it had in
  (B) at once as many foes as
  (C) at once as many foes that there were in
  (D) as many foes at once as it did in
  (E) so many foes at once as that it defeated in

10. **D** This question is a swirling mixture of idiom and parallel comparison. The correct idiom in question: *as many…as*. When you say it out loud, does *so many…as* seem right? Of course, it's much easier to notice that it doesn't when the expression has already been pulled out of the problem for you. During the GMAT, you have to do your own pulling, but remember, you always have five sensational clues: the answer choices. Even if you initially have no idea what might or might not be wrong with this sentence, you can figure it out by scanning the answers; you'll see that you have a collection of *so many as*'s and *as many as*'s to choose from.

The other thing going on in this sentence, of course, is parallel comparison. Words such as *as* or *than* often mean a comparison is being made. The correct comparison would read: "Never before had a navy defeated as many foes at once as it *defeated*…," but as you know from reading our chapter on Sentence Correction, the test writers like to see if you know that you can replace the second verb with a replacement verb: *did*. The best answer is D.

11. The changes that may be part of a general global warming trend include an increase in the frequency and severity of hurricanes, a gradual rise in sea level, <u>depleting the ozone layer, and raising the temperature of the earth</u>.

  (A) depleting the ozone layer, and raising the temperature of the earth
  (B) depleting the ozone layer, and a rise in the earth's temperature
  (C) a depletion of the ozone layer, and raising the earth's temperature
  (D) a depletion of the ozone layer, and a raise of the temperature of the earth
  (E) a depletion of the ozone layer, and a rise in the temperature of the earth

11. **E** This sentence has what should be a parallel list of nouns, beginning with *an increase* and *a rise*, but then the last two items on the list are suddenly verb-like things: *depleting* and *raising*. Since it is the last two items that are underlined, these are the items that must change. Choices A, B, and C all have verb-like things in them. Choice D, with two noun-like things, seems tempting at first, but do you say *a raise of the temperature*? Nope, it's unidiomatic. Choice E is best.

Questions <u>12–16</u> are based on the following passage:

It has long been a tenet of business theory that the best decisions are made after careful review and consideration. Only after weighing
Line all the options and studying projections, say
(5) most professors of business, can a practical decision be made.

Now, that model is being questioned by some business thinkers in the light of the theories of Malcolm Gladwell, who states that
(10) human beings often make better decisions in the blink of an eye.

It is, at first glance, a theory so counter-intuitive as to seem almost ludicrous. Behind any decision, Gladwell posits, there is
(15) a behind-the-scenes subconscious process in which the brain analyzes; ranks in order of importance; compares and contrasts vast amounts of information; and dismisses extraneous factors, seemingly almost instantaneously,
(20) often arriving at a conclusion in less than two seconds. Citing a multitude of studies and examples from life, Gladwell shows how that split-second decision is often better informed than a drawn-out examination.

(25) Evanston and Cramer were the first to apply this theory to the business world. Evanston videotaped the job interviews of 400 applicants at different firms. He then played only 10 seconds of each videotape to independent human re-
(30) sources specialists. The specialists were able to pick out the applicants who were hired with an accuracy of over 90%.

Cramer took the experiment even further, using only five seconds of videotape, without
(35) sound. To his astonishment, the rate of accuracy with which the HR specialists were able to predict the successful applicants fell only to 82%.

Critics argue that these results illustrate a
(40) problem with stereotyping that impedes human resources specialists from hiring the best candidates even when they have the time to get below the surface: going for the candidate who "looks the part." Gladwell argues that, on
(45) the contrary, the human mind is able to make complicated decisions quickly, and that intuition often trumps an extended decision-making process.

12. The primary purpose of the passage is to

(A) discuss reasons an accepted business theory is being reexamined

(B) present evidence that resolves a contradiction in business theory

(C) describe a tenet of business practices and how that tenet can be tested in today's economic environment

(D) argue that a counter-intuitive new business idea is, in the final analysis, incorrect

(E) present evidence that invalidates a new business model

12. **A** In this passage, the accepted practice of making thoughtful business decisions based on careful review is being questioned in light of a new theory. Both choices D and E imply that the author has rejected this new model. Choice C uses a catchy word from the passage (*tenet*) and fails to indicate that there is a new idea that goes against that tenet. Choice B implies that the contradiction between the theory of making decisions based on careful review and the theory of making split-second decisions has in fact been resolved. The answer is A.

13. According to the passage, all of the following are examples of the subconscious processes by which the brain makes a decision EXCEPT

(A) analysis of information
(B) ranking of information
(C) comparison and contrast of information
(D) rejecting information that is not pertinent
(E) consulting a multitude of studies and examples

13. **E** Where do you find the key words *subconscious process*? In the second paragraph. Choices A, B, C, and D are all paraphrases of examples of the processes cited in that paragraph. Only choice (E) is not—in fact the multitude of studies and examples are cited in support of Gladwell's hypothesis. The answer is E.

14. The author's attitude toward the long-held view that decisions should be made carefully over time expressed in lines 1–6 can best be described as

(A) dismissive and scornful
(B) respectful but questioning
(C) admiring and deferential
(D) uncertain but optimistic
(E) condescending and impatient

14. **B** Both choices A and E are too extreme to be the correct answer on the GMAT. But clearly, the new theory being described is an attempt to go beyond the conventional wisdom. The best answer is choice B.

VERBAL BIN 2

QUESTIONS	EXPLANATIONS

15. The author most likely mentions the results of Cramer's extension of Evanston's experiment in order to _____.

   (A) show that Cramer's hypothesis was correct while Evanston's hypothesis turned out to be incorrect

   (B) show that Evanston's hypothesis was correct, while Cramer's hypothesis turned out to be incorrect

   (C) demonstrate that while both experiments were scientifically rigorous, neither ended up being scientifically valid

   (D) illustrate that the principle of subconscious decisions continues to work even when less information is available

   (E) demonstrate that Cramer's experiment was 8% more accurate than Evanston's, even though his subjects had less information to work with

15. D Cramer's experiment took Evanston's experiment even further, depriving the subjects of even more information as they tried to make a decision—and yet the subjects did nearly as well in choosing candidates. If you chose E, you got reversed: Cramer's experiment was 8% *less* accurate than Evanston's. The answer is D.

16. It can be inferred that the critics referred to in line 38 believed the excellent results of the two experiments had less to do with the innate decision-making of the subjects than with

   (A) the excellent decision-making of Evanston and Cramer

   (B) the expertise of Malcolm Gladwell, who originated the theory

   (C) not choosing candidates who "looked the part"

   (D) the use of videotape as a method of choosing candidates

   (E) their unconscious use of visual stereotypes in making their selections

16. E This inference question asks us to go only slightly further than the passage itself—to realize that what the critics objected to was a potential tendency of the subjects to choose candidates who *looked the part* without really looking at their actual qualifications. If you chose C, you missed the word *not* in the answer choice, which turns the meaning around completely. The answer is E.

|

17. The women's volleyball team at a local college finished fifth in its division, prompting the college to fire the team's general manager. The manager responded by suing the college, saying that the team's performance put it among the top teams in the country.

Which of the following statements, if true, would support the claim of the team's manager, and resolve the apparent contradiction?

(A) The team won all of its "away" games during the season in question.

(B) Attendance at the volleyball team's games was up 35% from the year before.

(C) Of the starting team, three team members were unable to play for at least half the season because of injuries.

(D) There are 80 teams in this particular volleyball team's division.

(E) The team lost more games this year than it did the year before.

18. Country A recently broke off diplomatic relations with Country B when it was reported that Country B had been running a covert intelligence operation within the borders of Country A. While a spokesperson for Country B admitted the charge, the spokesperson said that it was common knowledge that all countries do this, and that Country A was no exception.

Which of the following inferences can be drawn from the argument above?

(A) Country B should apologize and dismantle its intelligence operation in Country A.

(B) The spokesperson for Country B claims that Country A engages in intelligence gathering, too.

(C) Because all countries engage in this practice, Country A's outrage was disingenuous.

(D) Relations between Country A and Country B will be strained for some time.

(E) Country B would be just as outraged if it was reported that Country A was running a covert intelligence operation with Country B's borders.

17. **D** The manager was apparently fired because of his team's end-of-season statistics. If this made you wonder if the statistics were actually representative, your thinking was right on the money. To support the manager's claim we have to show that the team's fifth-place finish was actually better than it looked. Choices A, B, and C, while generally positive about the team (and by extension, perhaps, its manager) are outside the scope of the argument. Choice E actually puts the team's performance in a more negative light. On the other hand, Choice D puts the team's fifth-place finish in a very positive perspective: If the division was made up of 80 teams, finishing in fifth place is actually extremely good. The best answer is D.

18. **B** All of the answers to this inference question infer way too much to be the correct answer to a GMAT question—except for choice B, which simply restates a sentence from the argument itself. Choice A says an apology is needed, which is way beyond the scope of this argument. Choice C goes further than the argument to make a value judgment. Choice D looks into the future. And choice E takes a "what if" position and builds on it. The best answer is choice B.

VERBAL BIN 2

QUESTIONS	EXPLANATIONS

19. Because cellular telephones emit signals that can interfere with cockpit-to-control-tower transmissions, airplane passengers' use of these instruments <u>at all times that the airplane is in motion, even while on the ground, are</u> prohibited.

   (A) at all times that the airplane is in motion, even while on the ground, are
   (B) at all times during which the airplane, even while on the ground, is in motion, are
   (C) during airplane motion, even when it is on the ground, are
   (D) during times of the airplane being in motion, even on the ground, is
   (E) when the airplane is in motion, even while on the ground, is

20. In contrast to classical guitars, whose owners prefer the dulcet, rounded tones produced by nylon strings, <u>folk guitar owners prefer the bright and brassy sound</u> that only bronze or steel can create.

   (A) folk guitar owners prefer the bright and brassy sound
   (B) folk guitar owners prefer to get a sound that is bright and brassy
   (C) with a folk guitar the owner gets the preferably bright and brassy sound
   (D) folk guitars produce a bright and brassy sound, which their owners prefer,
   (E) folk guitars produce a preferred bright and brassy sound for their owners

19. **E** The subject of this sentence, *use*, is singular. Therefore, answers A, B, and C are incorrect; each states that *the passengers' use of these instruments...are prohibited*. Choice D is unidiomatic, and the phrase *even on the ground* is unnecessarily vague. Choice E is concise, clear, and employs the correct verb. The best answer is E.

20. **D** Choices A, B, and C include a parallel comparison error; A and B compare *classical guitars* and *folk guitar owners*, while C compares a plural (*classical guitars*) and a singular (*a folk guitar*) noun. Choice E incorrectly suggests that the *bright and brassy* sound is universally preferred rather than preferred specifically by folk guitar owners. Furthermore, the placement of *for their owners* is unnecessarily confusing, as it separates two elements of the sentence that should be closely connected (*bright and brassy sound ...that only bronze and steel can create*). Choice D corrects this error by setting the interceding phrase off with commas. The best answer is D.

VERBAL BIN 2

Questions 21–22 are based on the following passage:

A system-wide county school anti-smoking education program was instituted last year. The program was clearly a success. Last year, the incidence of students smoking on school premises decreased by over 70 percent.

21. Which of the following assumptions underlies the argument in the passage?

(A) Cigarettes are detrimental to one's health; once people understand this, they will quit smoking.

(B) The doubling of the price of a pack of cigarettes last year was not the only cause of the students' altered smoking habits.

(C) The teachers chosen to lead the anti-smoking education program were the most effective teachers in the school system.

(D) The number of cigarettes smoked each day by those students who continued to smoke last year did not greatly increase.

(E) School policy enforcers were less vigilant in seeking out smokers last year than they were in previous years.

21. B The argument presented is a causal argument. The significant underlying assumption of the argument, therefore, relates to the causal link between the anti-smoking education program and the reduction in smoking on school premises. The argument assumes that the program, and not some other set of circumstances, caused the reduction. It thus assumes that other possible causes—such as an increase in the price of cigarettes—were not substantial contributors to this result.

Process of Elimination is effective on this question, as it is on all critical reasoning questions. Because the argument hinges on one crucial piece of evidence—a decrease in the incidence of smoking on school premises—you can eliminate all answers that do not speak directly to that reduction. Thus you can eliminate A, C, and D. Choice E, if true, would weaken the argument and therefore cannot be correct. The best answer is B.

VERBAL BIN 2

QUESTIONS	EXPLANATIONS

22. Which of the following, if true, would most seriously weaken the argument in the passage?

(A) The author of this statement is a school system official hoping to generate good publicity for the anti-smoking program.

(B) Most students who smoke stopped smoking on school premises last year continued to smoke when away from school.

(C) Last year, another policy change made it much easier for students to leave and return to school grounds during the school day.

(D) The school system spent more on anti-smoking education programs last year than it did in all previous years.

(E) The amount of time students spent in anti-smoking education programs last year resulted in a reduction of in-class hours devoted to academic subjects.

23. Mild exercise throughout pregnancy <u>may reduce the discomfort associated with pregnancy and result in</u> a speedier, easier birth, according to a recent study.

(A) may reduce the discomfort associated with pregnancy and result in

(B) may reduce the discomfort associated with pregnancy, with the result

(C) may cause a reduction in the discomfort associated with pregnancy and as a result

(D) might lead to a reduction in the discomfort associated with pregnancy and as a result

(E) might reduce the discomfort associated with pregnancy and resulting in

---

22. **C** Once again, your focus should be on the evidence supporting the causal link between the anti-smoking education program and the reduction in smoking on school premises. What, other than the effectiveness of the program, would explain the reduced incidence of smoking on school premises? Choice C provides a possible alternate explanation: School policy made it easier for students to leave and return to campus. It is therefore possible, then, that the reduction in smoking on school premises was simply the result of students leaving school premises to smoke, then returning afterward.

Choice B, while tempting, does not provide an alternate cause for the observed result. None of the incorrect answers addresses the evidence supporting the conclusion of the passage; therefore, none of them truly weakens the argument. The best answer is C.

23. **A** The sentence, as written, maintains correct parallel construction between *reduce the discomfort ...and result in a speedier...*. Each of the incorrect answers violates the rule of parallel construction. The best answer is A.

VERBAL BIN 2

Questions 24–27 are based on the following passage:

What is it that keeps the developing world in an apparent state of perpetual poverty? Poor education, lack of basic medical care, and the absence of democratic structures all certainly contribute to these nations' plight. However, according to Peruvian economist Hernando de Soto, the overriding cause is the overwhelming prevalence of black market activity, well outside the formal economy, in these countries. The losses incurred from this condition are twofold. First, they deny the government tax revenues which could be used to improve education, medical treatment, and government efficiency. More important, however, they deny earners the chance to accumulate assets recognized by law and thus prevent them from leveraging those assets to borrow. Reforming these nations' legal systems in order to confer ownership through titling, de Soto argues, would help the poor there access the assets their work should be generating. These assets could then be used to buy homes and construct businesses, thus building a more stable and prosperous economy. De Soto estimates the value of these assets, which he terms "dead capital," at nearly $10 trillion worldwide.

De Soto is not the first to locate the developing world's problems in the domain of property rights. Others have tried property rights reform and failed. According to de Soto, this is because his predecessors attempted to model their plans on existing, successful property rights systems. In other words, they tried to transplant American and British property law to an inhospitable host. De Soto argues that, within many of the extralegal markets of the developing world, mutually agreed upon rules for distributing assets and recognizing property rights already exist. Rather than force these markets to adjust to a new, foreign system of property titling, reformers should focus on codifying the existing systems wherever it is practical to do so. This would facilitate a quicker, more natural transition to an economy that builds wealth rather than squanders it.

QUESTIONS	EXPLANATIONS

24. The author's primary goal in the passage is to

(A) compare several failed attempts to address a problem

(B) respond to criticism of a new theory

(C) identify the problems inherent in a new economic theory

(D) describe a novel approach to an old problem

(E) compare different property rights systems in the industrial world

24. D The passage describes an old problem—poverty in the developing world—and a new approach to it, that proposed by Peruvian economist Hernando de Soto. D is the best answer.

You can use Process of Elimination to get rid of all incorrect answers. Because the passage focuses on one approach and not several, its purpose cannot be to draw comparisons between two or more ideas; therefore, A and E are incorrect. The passage does not address criticism of de Soto's plan, so neither B nor C can be correct.

25. According to the passage, de Soto believes that the quickest way to address poverty in the developing world is to

(A) increase funding for education

(B) build the infrastructure to support lending

(C) ensure medical care for all citizens

(D) aggressively root out corruption in government

(E) increase tax rates on all citizens in developing countries

25. B This answer summarizes the following information from the first paragraph: *However, according to Peruvian economist Hernando de Soto, the overriding cause is the overwhelming prevalence of black market activity, well outside the formal economy, in these countries…Reforming these nations' legal systems in order to confer ownership through titling, De Soto argues, would help the poor there access the assets their work should be generating. These assets could then be used to buy homes and build businesses, thus building a more stable and prosperous economy.* The best answer is B.

QUESTIONS	EXPLANATIONS

26. The author's assertion that "reformers should focus on codifying the existing systems wherever it is practical to do so" (lines 41–43) suggests that

(A) in some instances, current systems are inadequate to meet the needs of a market economy

(B) these systems are already written down and need only be enacted as law

(C) where it is impractical to codify existing systems, countries should adopt American property law

(D) the existing systems are superior to those currently in use in modern industrialized countries

(E) improving education and medical care in these countries should take priority over reforming property laws

27. The term "dead capital" (line 25) refers to

(A) loans that are never repaid

(B) failed investments in new businesses

(C) cities ruined by over-industrialization

(D) the proceeds of extralegal commerce

(E) property passed from generation to generation

26. A The key phrase in the excerpted text is *wherever it is practical*, which suggests that in some cases it may be impractical to codify the existing systems. Because the purpose of codifying the existing systems is to allow developing nations to acquire market economies, it follows that where it is impractical to codify existing systems, the reason is that the systems do not meet the needs of a market economy. The best answer is A.

The incorrect answers are either unsupported by information in the passage (B, D) or directly contradicted by information in the passage (C, E).

27. D In lines 24–25, de Soto refers to *these assets* as *dead capital*. To answer this question, we have to find out more about *these assets*. Earlier in the paragraph, we learn that they are the result of black market activity. The answer is D.

VERBAL BIN 3

QUESTIONS	EXPLANATIONS

QUESTIONS

1. Unlike <u>Franklin D. Roosevelt's bootstrap program that helped</u> to restart economic growth in the 1930s through public works, Ronald Reagan proposed a program of trickle-down economics to restart the economy.

   (A) Franklin D. Roosevelt's bootstrap program that helped
   (B) Franklin D. Roosevelt and his bootstrap program which helped
   (C) Franklin D. Roosevelt, whose bootstrap program helped
   (D) The bootstrap program of Franklin D. Roosevelt that has helped
   (E) Franklin D. Roosevelt and his bootstrap program helping

2. In the 1970s it became evident <u>that writing about someone else's research was much easier for social scientists who wanted to make a quick name for themselves</u> than it was to do their own research.

   (A) that writing about someone else's research was much easier for social scientists who wanted to make a quick name for themselves
   (B) that for social scientists who wanted to make a quick name for themselves, it was much easier to write about someone else's research
   (C) that for social scientists wanting to make a quick name for themselves, writing about someone else's research was much easier
   (D) for social scientists who wanted to make a quick name for themselves that writing about someone else's research was much easier
   (E) for social scientists who wanted to make a quick name for themselves, writing about someone else's research was much easier

EXPLANATIONS

1. **C** What can we say? You're in Bin 3. Part of what normally makes misplaced modifiers easy to spot is that the test writers generally ask you to fix the second phrase; this time, you have to fix the first phrase. The modifying phrase *Unlike F.D.R's bootstrap program* is supposed to modify the noun *Ronald Reagan*, which, of course, is not possible. You can't directly compare a program to a person. We could fix the second half of the sentence (*unlike F.D.R.'s program…Reagan's program…*), but since the second half of the sentence isn't underlined, we'll have to fix the first half. Choices B and E still directly compare F.D.R.'s program to Ronald Reagan. So does choice D. Only choice C avoids the modifier error by directly comparing F.D.R. to Reagan.

2. **B** The problem in the stem sentence is that there are two actions that ought to be parallel but are not. *Writing* (about someone else's research) was easier than *to do* the research themselves. You could fix this two ways in the real world: *Writing* was easier than *doing*, or it was easier *to write* than *to do*. Each of the other answer choices mixes and matches these two ways incorrectly, except for choice B. Putting the phrase *for social scientists* first, as choices D and E do, would not necessarily be wrong if the verbs were parallel. Choices D and E also do not have the idiom *evident that*. The best answer is B.

QUESTIONS	EXPLANATIONS

<u>Questions 3–4</u> are based on the following:

To improve the town's overcrowded school system, the town council has proposed an ambitious education plan to reduce classroom size and make capital improvements—a plan they intend to pay for with an increase in property taxes for homes valued over $500,000. Although the school system desperately needs improving, the town council's plan should be defeated because the majority of the people who would end up paying for the improvements receive no benefit from them.

3. Which of the following, if true, most strengthens the argument above?

(A) The town's school system is currently ranked among the worst in the state

(B) Other towns nearby that have made similar capital improvements did not find that the improvements translated to a better quality of education.

(C) The town will need to spend additional money on architect's plans for the capital improvements.

(D) An examination of the tax rolls shows that most homeowners in this category no longer have school-age children.

(E) Some homeowners will delay home improvement projects in order to keep the value of their homes below $500,000.

3. **D** The author is arguing to nix the plan to improve the schools. We want to strengthen his argument, but before we do, there is usually at least one answer choice that actually weakens the argument. It is helpful to get rid of these first, since they are usually easier to spot. In this case, choice A gives a compelling reason to *improve* the school system; eliminate it. Now, the reason the author gives for defeating the plan is that the people who pay for it will not benefit. To strengthen this argument, we need to show why this would be true. Choice B is against the school improvements, but for a different reason: in other towns, similar improvements didn't increase the quality of education. While important in the real world, this is slightly outside the scope of this argument. Choice C provides another possible negative of the plan, but again it doesn't show why the people who pay for it will not benefit. Choice E implies that taxpayers will delay their own capital improvements to avoid paying for the schools' capital improvements, but again this doesn't strengthen the author's particular argument: that the plan should be defeated because the people who must pay for it do not benefit. The best answer is D, which explains how this could be true: Most of the people slotted to pay for the school improvements don't even have school-age children.

4. Which of the following, if true, provides the town council with the strongest counter to the objection that its plan is unfair?

(A) Even with the proposed increase, property taxes in the town are well below the national average.

(B) Paying for the school system improvements using existing town funds will result in shortfalls that will force the town into arrears.

(C) The teachers in the town's school system receive some of the lowest salary packages in the immediate area, which is a major cause of attrition.

(D) Smaller class sizes and capital improvements in a school system tend to increase property values in the surrounding community.

(E) A feasibility study has shown that the cost of the improvements will likely be 20% higher than projected.

4. D The author says the plan is unfair to the people who must pay for it. How do we counter that? By showing that they actually do receive a benefit. Before we weaken the author's argument, let's eliminate any answers that strengthen it. In this case, that means only choice E. Now, choice A points out that property taxes would still be quite low even after the increase, but that doesn't mean the increase is fair. Choice B tells us why an alternate way to finance the improvements won't work, but doesn't address the fairness of the way being discussed. Choice C tells us why the funds are urgently needed, but again doesn't show that the people who have to supply the funds actually would receive a benefit. But choice D finally gives us a reason the property tax increase might actually benefit those who pay for it: Good schools translates to higher property values.

5. The rules of engagement under which a border patrol station can decide to use deadly force <u>includes responding to an invasionary incursion and the return of</u> hostile fire.

(A) includes responding to an invasionary incursion and the return of

(B) includes responding to an invasionary incursion and returning

(C) include responding to an invasionary incursion and the return of

(D) include a response to an invasionary incursion and the return of

5. D As you know, GMAT test writers like to put as many words between the subject and the verb of a sentence as they can, in hopes that you will forget to check for agreement. The subject of this sentence was the plural *rules*. The verb: the singular *includes*. This eliminates choices A and B. Choices C and E are not parallel (neither is choice A), because they mix verb-like forms with noun-like forms. The best answer is D.

6. Although the word "phonetician" is popularly associated with Henry Higgins's task of improving the diction of Eliza Dolittle in *My Fair Lady*, in linguistics, <u>it is someone who studies</u> the formation of language.

   (A)   it is someone who studies
   (B)   it is a person studying
   (C)   it refers to someone who studies
   (D)   they are people who study
   (E)   it is in reference to people who study

6. C The question here is: to what does the pronoun *it* refer? You might think it refers to *phonetician*, (in which case you might have thought the sentence was fine the way it was), but in fact it refers to *the word*. Choices A, B, and D could give the impression that *the word* is a person or persons. Choice E is awkward, and, like choice D, needlessly uses the plural *people*. The best answer is C.

7. Experts studying patterns of shark attacks on humans have noted that attacks tend to diminish when the water temperature drops below 65 degrees Fahrenheit. Until recently, researchers believed this was because sharks prefer warmer water, and thus are present in fewer numbers in colder water. However, new research shows that sharks are present in equal numbers in cold and warm water.

   Which of the following, if true, best explains the apparent paradox?

   (A)   In general, humans prefer warm water.
   (B)   Sharks' keen sense of smell is enhanced in cold water.
   (C)   In the Pacific, shark attacks tend to occur more frequently in the daytime.
   (D)   Of the more than 200 types of sharks present in the ocean, only three attack humans.
   (E)   The average temperature of the earth's oceans is 55 degrees.

7. A We tend to try to explain shark attacks by thinking about the *shark's* behavior. But choice A points out that it takes two to tango. A shark attack requires A) one shark and B) one human to be attacked. One reason there might be fewer shark attacks on humans in cold water is that there are fewer humans swimming in cold water in the first place. If you were looking at choice B, and saying, "Hmm, if a sharks' olfactory powers were enhanced by cold water, then presumably he'd be better at attacking," or if you were thinking that if his olfactory powers were enhanced he would know enough *not* to attack a human—then either way, you were having to think way too hard for this to be inside the scope. Choice C is outside the scope, too, since it is dealing with only one ocean and does not address temperature at all. Choice D provides extraneous information, and choice E does not help to explain the apparent paradox. The best answer is A.

VERBAL BIN 3

QUESTIONS	EXPLANATIONS

8. As a result of surging economic indicators, most analysts upgraded the company's stock to a strong "buy," ignoring the advice of the head of a watchdog organization <u>who warned that the company's product would prove not only dangerous but</u> ineffective in the long run.

   (A) who warned that the company's product would prove not only dangerous but
   (B) warning that the company's product would prove not only dangerous and also
   (C) warning that the company's product would prove itself to be both dangerous and
   (D) who warned that the company's product would prove to be both dangerous and
   (E) who was warning that the company's product would prove not only dangerous but

8. **D** The sentence, as written, needs a *but also* to complement its *not only*. Choices A and E bite the dust. In choice B the same idiom comes into play, but this choice has bigger problems: Without the *who warned*, it is no longer clear who is doing the warning. Choice C can be eliminated for the same reason. The best answer is D.

9. Scientists today accept that the increased severity of hurricanes in the last 10 years has been a result of warmer water in the Caribbean, which "feeds" the storms as they pass over it by a mechanism not yet completely understood. Thus, these severe hurricanes are yet more evidence of global warming.

   Which of the following, if true, would most strengthen the argument above?

   (A) Accurate statistics on the warming of the earth do not go back more than 100 years.
   (B) Scientists have not discovered a new undersea current, fueled by an undersea volcano, which could have funneled warmer water into the Caribbean.
   (C) The arctic ice caps have been losing three feet of circumference each year for the past five years.
   (D) A new modeling computer program projects that the severity of hurricanes will increase over the next 10 years.
   (E) Some scientists believe they will soon prove that the mechanism by which a storm picks up energy from warm water is based on convection.

9. **B** To weaken a causal argument, propose an alternate cause. To strengthen a causal argument, *remove* an alternate cause. Choice A weakens the argument, so cross that off. Choices C and D both appear to strengthen the case for global warming in general, but do not make the important connection between the warming of the waters of the Caribbean and global warming in general. Choice E promises that the mechanism that creates more severe storms will soon be better understood, but that doesn't help to make the case that the warm water causing more severe hurricanes is related to global warming. The best answer is B. While choice B might seem unlikely, it strengthens this causal argument by removing a possible alternate cause. If there *were* an undersea volcano heating the Caribbean, then that might be what was causing the severe hurricanes, *not* global warming.

VERBAL BIN 3

10. A new influx of unprecedented private investment should create a bright new future for manned space exploration, <u>making the possibility of commercial space tourism much more viable than 10 years ago</u>.

(A) making the possibility of commercial space tourism much more viable than 10 years ago

(B) and make the possibility of commercial space tourism much more viable than 10 years ago

(C) making the possibility of commercial space tourism much more viable than it was 10 years ago

(D) and make the possibility of commercial space tourism much more viable than it was 10 years in the past

(E) making the possibility of commercial space tourism much more viable than 10 years in the past

10. **C** The key word here is *than*—and if you spotted it, you knew to look for a parallel comparison problem. Two actions are being compared in this sentence, so we need the words "it was" after *than* to make that clear. If you spotted this error, you could eliminate Choices A, B, and E. D might seem possible (and parallel in a different kind of way) until you get to the last words: *10 years in the past*. This is just not the same as *ago*. The best answer is C.

Questions 11–15 are based on the following passage:

As the American workforce gets grayer, age discrimination will likely become a more prominent issue in the courts. It is, of course, illegal
Line to discriminate against an employee because
(5) of his or her age—and yet it is not illegal to dismiss a worker because he has a high salary and expensive health care.

This apparent contradiction is at the heart of a raft of cases now making their way through
(10) the courts. The outcome of these cases will have broad implications for the workplace in the coming years. By 2010, the Bureau of Labor Statistics has projected that more than half of all workers will be over 40—many of whom, by
(15) dint of seniority and promotions, will be earning higher than median salaries, eligible for more stock options, and carrying higher health care costs as a result of a larger number of dependents and the increased cost of health care for
(20) older workers.

Is it any wonder that a bottom-line oriented business might want to shed these workers, whose productivity is likely to plummet in the next few years, even as they become more
(25) expensive employees?

Still, the legal challenges of implementing this policy are daunting. Businesses have the right to rate workers on their productivity and to rank them against their peers. But they are not
(30) allowed to prejudge individuals based on their sex, race or age. Each worker must be treated on his or her own merits, rather than by how they fit into a larger profile of the group they belong to.
(35) For companies looking to lay off these workers, the cost of making a mistake are high; while only one in three age discrimination suits are won by the plaintive, the awards tend to be steep—and the political fall-out harsh.

VERBAL BIN 3

QUESTIONS	EXPLANATIONS

11. The primary purpose of the passage is to

 (A) advocate on behalf of the older American worker who could soon face dismissal
 (B) describe the origin of two theories of labor law and their effects on the work- place
 (C) present an overview of the legal ramifica- tions of a practice some call discrimi- natory
 (D) describe the process by which America's workforce is getting older
 (E) describe the methods by which a com- pany could reduce its bottom line

11. **C** This passage presents an overview of the legal issues involved in age discrimination. Choices A and E are wrong because they imply that the passage takes sides on the matter. B is tempting, but the passage doesn't discuss the *origins* of the issues. Choice D implies that the passage is describing the aging process itself. The answer is C.

12. Which of the following best describes the orga- nization of the second paragraph of the pas- sage?

 (A) An assertion is made and then briefly contradicted.
 (B) A contradiction is stated and then quickly resolved.
 (C) A new theory is described and then quali- fied.
 (D) An apparent inconsistency is stated and its consequences outlined.
 (E) A conventional model is described and an alternative is introduced.

12. **D** The contradiction highlighted at the beginning of the second paragraph is not resolved or qual- ified; it is stated, and then its ramifications are outlined. The answer is D.

13. Which of the following, if true, would most ef- fectively weaken the author's assertion that a "bottom-line oriented business" might want to fire older workers?

 (A) A new study shows that, on average, younger workers earn less and have lower associated medical costs than older workers.
 (B) Older workers have a higher rate of ab- senteeism than younger workers.
 (C) A new study shows that older workers are in fact more productive and have led medical expenses compared to younger workers.
 (D) A forecasted downturn in the economy will erode profits in may American businesses.
 (E) A new bill scheduled to become law will make it easier for employers to employ illegal aliens.

13. **C** To weaken the assertion that it might be in the interest of employers to fire older people, it is necessary to show why employing older people would be GOOD for companies. C is the only answer that does so, suggesting that older em- ployees are actually more productive and have fewer health care costs.

QUESTIONS	EXPLANATIONS

14. It can be inferred from the passage that

(A) what is good for American companies is not necessarily good for older Americans

(B) American companies are prohibited by law from practices that discriminate based on gender, color of skin, or age

(C) large monetary judgments from age discrimination suits might prove more expensive than paying older employees' salaries

(D) by the year 2020, the percentage of older employees will be even higher than in the year 2010

(E) some older employees may well be more productive than some younger employees

15. The author mentions all of the following as driving up the cost to employers for employing workers over the age of 40 EXCEPT

(A) the cost of out-placement services
(B) a larger number of dependents
(C) increased cost of health care
(D) higher median salaries
(E) the cost of employee stock options

16. A pharmaceutical company claims that its new drug promotes learning in children. To back up its claims, the company points to a study of 300 children who were given the drug, along with a control group of 300 children who were given a placebo. The 300 children who were given the drug reported that they were able to retain new information much more easily.

Which of the following statements, if true, would most tend to weaken the claims of the pharmaceutical company?

(A) The 300 children in the control group also reported that they were able to retain new information much more easily.

(B) The drug has also been shown to prevent common skin rashes.

(C) The drug has been proven to have severe side-effects.

(D) The children in the study were not given any other medications during the study.

(E) The children who were given the drug did better on cognitive measurement tests after the drug therapy than before.

14. B The trick in any inference question is not to infer too far. Many of the possible answers here might well be inferred in a normal interchange, but on the GMAT, the best answer will generally seem almost laughably self-evident. In this case, that is B. Choices A and C are much too cynical to be correct answers on the GMAT, and choices D and E go well beyond the scope of the question.

15. A All of these costs were cited with one exception: the cost of out-placement services. The answer is A.

16. A The drug company says its drug caused enhanced learning ability. To weaken this causal argument, look for an alternate cause. Choices B, D, and E appear to strengthen the argument, so we can eliminate them. Choice C, while clearly a negative aspect of the drug, does not weaken the argument itself, which states simply that the drug enhances learning capability in children. Side effects are outside the scope of the argument. Choice A may not seem at first like an alternate cause, but if the control group (which did not receive the medicine) reported the exact same results as the children who did receive the drug, then clearly there is some other, as yet unnamed, alternate cause. The best answer is A.

QUESTIONS	EXPLANATIONS

17. In order to understand the dangers of the current real-estate bubble in Country Y, one has only to look to the real-estate bubble of the last decade in Country Z. In that country, incautious investors used the inflated value of their real estate as collateral in risky margin loans. When the real-estate market collapsed, many investors went bankrupt, creating a major recession. Country Y is in real danger of a similar recession if more-stringent laws restricting margin loans are not enacted promptly.

The answer to which of the following questions would be most useful in evaluating the significance of the author's claims?

(A) Was the real estate in Country Z located principally in rural areas or was it located in more urban communities?

(B) Could the bankruptcies in Country Z have been prevented by a private bailout plan by the nation's banks?

(C) Does Country Y currently have any laws on its books regarding margin loans?

(D) Are there business ties and connections between Country Y and Country Z?

(E) Were there other factors in the case of Country Y that would make the comparison with Country Z less meaningful?

17. **E** To evaluate the significance of the author's claims, we need to recognize what kind of argument it is: an analogy. The author is saying that the situation in Country Y is analogous to that of Country Z. To weaken an analogy, you merely have to question whether the two situations were really analogous. Choices A and B are outside the scope of the argument. Choice C is incorrect because the author's argument stated that *more-stringent laws* were needed, making it irrelevant whether Country Y had any laws about this in the first place. Choice D goes off on an interesting tangent by asking if there were business ties between the two countries, but it does not weaken the argument's analogy. Only choice E questions whether the two situations are in fact analogous. E is the best answer.

18. Rules governing participation in a new extreme sports fantasy camp require <u>that applicants should be physically fit enough to endure the demanding</u> activities in which they will be engaging.

(A) that applicants should be physically fit enough to endure the demanding

(B) that applicants be physically fit enough to endure the demanding

(C) applicants should have enough physical fitness to allow enduring the demands of

(D) applicants are physically fit enough as to endure the demands of

(E) physical fitness in applicants, enough for endurance of demanding

18. **B** This question tests two concepts. The first is idiomatic and concerns the word *require*. Because the word *require* indicates something that is compulsory (as opposed to optional), it cannot be followed by the word *should*; in other words, you can't require that something should happen, because then it's not really a requirement. This eliminates A and C.

The second concept is a little more arcane. Requirements, like hypothetical situations posited in the future, take the subjunctive mood. In the subjunctive, the proper way to phrase the idea expressed in this sentence is *the rules require that applicants be physically fit*. Tough and obscure, but that's why this question is in Bin 3. If you get this question wrong, suck it up and move on, confident in the knowledge that you can miss this one and still score a 790.

VERBAL BIN 3

QUESTIONS	EXPLANATIONS

19. During the summer of 2002, the Outer Banks <u>suffered a massive toad infestation, discouraging</u> many vacationers from visiting the area.

   (A) suffered a massive toad infestation, discouraging

   (B) suffered from a massive toad infestation and discouraged

   (C) suffered a massive infestation of toads, which discouraged

   (D) was suffering a massive infestation of toads and discouraging

   (E) had suffered from a massive toad infestation and this discouraged

19. C This question presents two ways to discuss the unfortunate toad incident on the Outer Banks. Was there a *massive toad infestation* or a *massive infestation of toads*? The second option is better, because the first leaves it unclear whether *massive* refers to the infestation or the toads themselves. Under the first option, it is theoretically possible that the Outer Banks was infested by a single 50-foot-tall toad. Thus, A, B, and E are all incorrect. Choice D incorrectly suggests that the Outer Banks, not the infestation of toads, discouraged vacationers.

20. A prolonged period of low mortgage rates resulted in a period of the most robust home sales ever. At the same time, the average sale price of resale homes actually dropped, when adjusted for inflation.

Which of the following, if true, would explain the apparent contradiction between the robust home sales and the drop in the average sale price of resale homes?

   (A) The inflation rate during this period exceeded the increase in the average salary, thus preventing many buyers from securing mortgages.

   (B) Resale homes represent the best value on the real estate market.

   (C) Without the adjustment for inflation, the price of resale homes actually increased by a very slight amount.

   (D) The decrease in mortgage rates was accompanied by a widening of the types of mortgages from which borrowers could choose.

   (E) The increase in home sales was due entirely to an increase in the sale of new homes.

20. E During a period of robust home sales, one would expect the prices of all homes to increase; that would be the natural effect of the law of supply and demand. The question tells us, however, that the real price of resale homes during this period actually decreased. Thus, it is reasonable to assume that the demand for resale homes decreased. How can we resolve this apparent contradiction? If all the increased demand for homes was in the new home market, then it would be possible that the overall increase in home sales would not result in an increase in resale home prices and may, in fact, even accompany a drop in those prices. The best answer is E.

21. Luis is taller than Rei. Kiko is taller than Marcus. Therefore, Kiko is taller than Rei.

The conclusion drawn above is not supported by the argument; however, the addition of one additional piece of information would make the conclusion logically sound. All of the following could be that additional piece of information EXCEPT:

(A) Kiko is taller than Luis.
(B) Luis is taller than Marcus.
(C) Luis and Marcus are the same height.
(D) Marcus and Rei are the same height.
(E) Marcus is taller than Rei.

21. **B** This question is best solved by drawing a diagram to represent the information in the question stem.

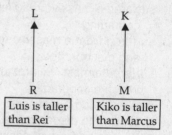

We are looking for information that will allow us to draw the diagram

According to the question stem, four of the answer choices are sufficient to accomplish this. Your job is to find the one that is NOT sufficient.

Choice A is sufficient; if Kiko is taller than Luis and Luis is taller than Rei, Kiko must be taller than Rei.

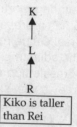

Choice B is NOT sufficient; if Luis is taller than Marcus, then it is conceivable that Luis is taller than Kiko. Consequently, it is also possible that Rei, who is shorter than Luis, is also taller than Kiko; however, Rei may also be shorter. The best answer is B.

Use the diagrams we have already created to demonstrate, on your own, that C, D, and E are sufficient to make the conclusion logically sound.

QUESTIONS	EXPLANATIONS

22. It has been estimated that <u>an increase in average regional temperature of even 0.5 degrees Fahrenheit could cost the southern United States more than $10 billion in lost agricultural income annually</u>.

   (A)   an increase in average regional temperature of even 0.5 degrees Fahrenheit could cost the southern United States more than $10 billion in lost agricultural income annually

   (B)   every year $10 billion in agricultural income could be the cost to the southern United States as a result of an increase in the average temperature of the region of even 0.5 degrees Fahrenheit

   (C)   the cost to the southern United States could be more than $10 billion in income from agriculture that results from a regional increase in average temperature of even 0.5 degrees Fahrenheit annually

   (D)   annual income losses in agriculture of more than $10 billion could be the cost from increasing average temperatures in the southern United States of even 0.5 degrees Fahrenheit

   (E)   annual income losses to the southern United States from the increase in average regional temperature of even 0.5 percent costing more than $10 billion in agricultural income each year

22. **A**   Well, you've got five choices here and none is particularly good. Only four, however, contain grammatical errors, so the best way to proceed on a question like this one is to eliminate as many answer choices as you can, take your best guess from among the remaining answers, and move on. Choice B is an endless string of prepositions; furthermore, the placement of the phrase *of the region* between *increase in the average temperature* and *of even 0.5 degrees Fahrenheit* is needlessly confusing. Choice C incorrectly suggests that it is agriculture, and not lost income, that results from the temperature increase. In D, *cost from* is unidiomatic; the correct phrasing is *cost of*. Choice E is redundant, as it refers to *annual losses* that occur *each year*. The best answer is A.

VERBAL BIN 3

QUESTIONS	EXPLANATIONS

23. Within the Green Party, an internal debate is raging <u>among those who believe in compromising with mainstream politicians in order to achieve some goals with those who believe the party must not abandon any of its principles</u>.

(A) among those who believe in compromising with mainstream politicians in order to achieve some goals with those who believe the party must not abandon any of its principles

(B) among those who believe that achieving some goals requires compromise with mainstream politicians and those believing that none of the party's principles must be abandoned

(C) between those believing in compromising with mainstream politicians in order to achieve some goals with those who believe the party must not abandon any of its principles

(D) between those who believe in compromising with mainstream politicians in order to achieve some goals and those who believe the party must not abandon any of its principles

(E) between those believing that achieving some goals means compromising with mainstream politicians and those who believe that the principles of the party must not be abandoned

23. **D** This is a tricky *between/among* question. The rule is that *between* is used to compare two items, *among* to compare three or more. Here we are talking about thousands of people, so you might think that *among* is the correct choice. However, because the sentence compares two groups of people, the correct answer is *between*. The argument is between the two groups, not among the thousands of people who make up those groups. Eliminate A and B.

We can eliminate C because it is unidiomatic: It draws a comparison between one group *with* another when it should draw a comparison between one group *and* another. Choice E can be eliminated because it lacks parallel structure: It compares *those **believing** that achieving some goals...* and *those who **believe** that the principles of the party must not be abandoned*. The best answer is D.

VERBAL BIN 3

24. In comparison to the drivers who live in Mountainview, a greater proportion of the drivers who live in Oak Valley exceed the speed limit regularly. This explains why there are more accidents each year in Oak Valley than in Mountainview.

All of the following statements, if true, weaken the conclusion drawn above EXCEPT:

(A) Oak Valley has a greater proportion of blind intersections and sharp turns than has Mountainview.

(B) There is a greater number of drivers in Oak Valley than in Mountainview.

(C) Drivers in Mountainview must travel to Oak Valley to shop and work.

(D) Per capita, there are fewer police officers monitoring traffic in Oak Valley than there are in Mountainview.

(E) The roads are icier for a greater proportion of the year in Oak Valley than in Mountainview.

24. **D** Answer D may explain why people are more likely to exceed the speed limit in Oak Valley than in Mountainview, but it has no necessary correlation to the number of accidents in the two towns; therefore, it does nothing to weaken the conclusion that the greater proportion of speeders in Oak Valley results in a greater number of accidents there.

Answers A and E provide an alternate explanation: Driving conditions are poor, which certainly could contribute to accidents. Choice B indicates that there is much more traffic in Oak Valley, which could well explain why there are more traffic accidents there. Choice C states that many Mountainview residents travel to Oak Valley regularly; it is possible, then, that they, not the drivers who live in Oak Valley, cause the accidents.

25. A study showed that only ten percent of American dog owners enroll their dogs in formal obedience training classes. More than 20 percent of these dog owners, the study also showed, participate in dog shows. Thus, it is obvious that people who train their dogs are more likely to participate in dog shows than are people who do not train their dogs.

The conclusion above is correct provided which of the following statements is also true?

(A) It is impossible for a dog to compete in a dog show if the dog has not completed at least one formal obedience training class.

(B) The proportion of dog owners who enroll their dogs in formal obedience training classes is representative of the proportion who train their dogs outside such classes.

(C) Dog owners who participate in dog shows only train their dogs by enrolling them in formal obedience training lessons.

(D) Participation in dog shows is a reliable indicator of how much attention a dog owner pays to his dog.

(E) Only purebred dogs can participate in dog shows, so many owners who enroll their dogs in formal obedience training classes are excluded from this activity.

25. **B** The statement draws a conclusion about *people who train their dogs* based on statistics relating only to people who take their dogs for formal obedience training classes. In order for the statement to be correct, then, these statistics must be valid for all people who train their dogs, not only those who train them in formal classes. Choice B plugs this hole in the argument, thus making the conclusion necessarily true.

QUESTIONS	EXPLANATIONS

26. A bullet train travels in excess of 150 miles per hour. Therefore, if a train travels slower than 150 miles per hour, it is not a bullet train.

Which of the following most closely parallels the reasoning used in the argument above?

(A) An orange ripens only on the vine. If it ripens on the vine, then it is not an orange.

(B) Newspapers are often read by more than one person. Therefore magazines are also likely to be read by more than one person.

(C) An earthquake of 5.0 or above on the Richter scale causes massive damage. If there is not massive damage, then the earthquake did not attain a 5.0 or above.

(D) A supersonic plane travels at speeds in excess of Mach 1. If it is not supersonic, then it will travel at speeds below Mach 1.

(E) Fluoride generally prevents cavities. If there are no cavities, then there was no fluoride used.

26. **C** To answer this parallel-the-reasoning question, you have to break down the original argument, and then find an answer choice that mimics it exactly. In this case, the argument says a bullet train travels in excess of 150 miles per hour (if A, then B). Therefore, if a train travels less than 150 miles per hour, then it is not a bullet train (if not B, then not A). Now all you have to do is find an answer choice that mimics that reasoning exactly. Choice A, broken down, reads, "if A, then B...so if B, then not A." This isn't it. Eliminate it. Choice B breaks down to "if A, then B...therefore C will also cause B." That's not it either. Choice C breaks down to "if A, then B...therefore if not B, then not A." This is the best answer.

Choice D might seem tempting because it also has to do with a fast means of transportation, but what counts here is the reasoning: if A, then B...if not A, then not B. This is close, but no cigar. Choice E is also appealing; you may even think it mimics the argument exactly. But there's a trick. The first half of the sentence reads, "Fluoride generally prevents cavities" (if A then B). Note that the B part is about the prevention—not the presence—of cavities. So the second half, "If there are no cavities, there was no fluoride," actually breaks down to "if B, then not A."

ABOUT THE AUTHOR

Geoff Martz attended Dartmouth College and Columbia University before joining The Princeton Review in 1985 as a teacher and writer. Martz headed the development team that designed The Princeton Review's GMAT course. He is the author or coauthor of *Cracking the ACT, Paying for College, Cracking the GED,* and *How to Survive Without Your Parents' Money.*

NOTES

NOTES

NOTES

NOTES

NOTES

NOTES

NOTES

NOTES

NOTES

Need More?

If you're looking to learn more about how to raise your GMAT score, you're in the right place. We have helped countless students get into their top-choice business schools.

One way to increase the number of acceptance letters you get is to raise your test scores. So if you're experiencing some trepidation, consider all your options.

We consistently improve prospective business school students' scores through our books, classroom courses, private tutoring, and online courses. To learn more about any of our courses and services, call 800-2Review or visit PrincetonReview.com for details.

Check out all the ways you can raise your GMAT score:
- GMAT Classroom Courses
- GMAT Online Courses
- GMAT Private Tutoring
- *Math Workout for the GMAT*
- *Verbal Workout for the GMAT*